Life Change, Life Events, and Illness

Life Change,
Life Events,
and Illness

Selected Papers

Edited by
Thomas H. Holmes and
Ella M. David

PRAEGER

New York
Westport, Connecticut
London

Library of Congress Cataloging-in-Publication Data

Life, change, life events, and illness : selected papers / edited by
   Thomas H. Holmes and Ella M. David.
      p. cm.
      Bibliography: p.
      Includes index.
      ISBN 0-275-92480-7 (alk. paper)
      1. Medicine, Psychosomatic. 2. Life change events. I. Holmes,
Thomas H. II. David, Ella M.
RC49.L475   1989
155.9'16—dc19   88-28610

Library of Congress Catalog Card Number: 88-28610
ISBN: 0-275-92480-7

First published in 1989

Praeger Publishers, One Madison Avenue, New York, NY 10010
A division of Greenwood Press, Inc.

Printed in the United States of America

∞

The paper used in this book complies with the Permanent
Paper Standard issued by the National Information Standards
Organization (Z39.48-1984).

10 9 8 7 6 5 4 3 2 1

Contents

PART III   CLINICAL APPLICATIONS: LIFE CHANGE STUDIES

Preface

This volume gathers together most of the published life change research that has come from the Holmes laboratory at the University of Washington from 1957 to 1981.

The first chapter introduces the readings by describing the historical context for our work. Chapter 1 shows where our new research questions came from, and it explains why we were ready to ask them at that time. Chapters 2 through 10 review the development, testing, and validation of three innovative research instruments: the Social Readjustment Rating Scale (SRRS), the Seriousness of Illness Rating Scale (SIRS), and the Schedule of Recent Experience (SRE). Chapters 11 through 16 reconstruct our initial applications of the new methodology, culminating in our formulation of a paradigm for the relationship of life change and illness susceptibility. Finally, Chapters 17 through 22 illustrate many of the realms into which our life change research has expanded.

For archival purposes, Chapters 2 through 22 are reprinted here in their original form. A credit note at the beginning of each chapter identifies its source and date of publication. We have restricted our editorial revisions to three areas: correcting errata; revising references that are no longer "in press," "in preparation," or "from unpublished data"; and establishing stylistic conformity among the chapters (by omitting abstracts, standardizing the style and format of references, renumbering tables and figures, and consolidating acknowledgments of funding sources and academic affiliations of authors). These limitations ensure that readers may confidently cite these readings as primary sources.

We designed this volume to serve as a reference book and as a resource for anyone interested in life change research. For readers new to the field, it provides ready access to the historical record of the Holmes psychosocial laboratory. These readings may hold a few surprises even for readers already familiar with our research. I suspect many readers will discover some studies that escaped earlier notice and will rediscover others that may have been lost sight of over the years.

In many respects this volume summarizes my professional career at the University of Washington. The task of putting the collection together has evoked pleasant memories of faculty, resident, and student colleagues with whom I have collaborated. And the task has also prompted some surprising recollections of how we got started in this line of research, what we thought we were doing at the time, and what it now appears we accomplished. It is gratifying, when these studies are brought together, to see the pattern of connections that emerges.

Acknowledgments

Completion of this volume was supported by the Thomas H. Holmes Endowment Fund of the Department of Psychiatry and Behavioral Sciences, University of Washington. Preparation of the original manuscript was supported in part by the Margaret H. O'Donnell Psychiatric Research Fund. We gratefully acknowledge the support of both.

The investigations collected in this volume were supported in part by the following:

National Heart and Lung Institute, PSCOR, Grant no. HL-14152 (Chapter 18)

O'Donnell Psychiatric Research Fund (Chapters 2, 3, 5, 8, 11–16, and 18–21)

Public Health Service General Research Support Grant no. 1-S01-FR-5432-04 (Chapter 3)

Public Health Service Graduate Training in Psychiatry Grant no. 5-T2-MH-5557 from NIMH (Chapters 3, 5, 10, 20, and 21)

Public Health Service Undergraduate Training in Human Behavior Grant no. 5-T2-MH-7871 from NIMH (Chapters 2, 3, 5–8, 10, 13–16 and 18–21)

Public Health Service Undergraduate Training in Psychiatry Grant no. 5-T2-MH-5939 from NIMH (Chapters 2, 6–8, 12–16, and 19–21)

Scottish Rite Committee for Research in Schizophrenia (Chapters 2, 6, 14, 19, and 21)

State of Washington Initiative 171 Funds for Research in Biology and Medicine (Chapter 12)

Stuht Psychiatric Research Fund (Chapters 6, 8, 13, 15, 20, and 21)

The editors thank Susan Martin and Bob Watkins for their great help in the production of this volume.

PART I

THE HISTORICAL CONTEXT

1

"It Was in This Setting . . ."

Thomas H. Holmes

My interest in psychosomatic medicine was catalyzed in Dr. Harold G. Wolff's laboratory at Cornell University Medical College and the New York Hospital. To this day, Wolff's book *Life Stress and Bodily Disease* (Baltimore, Williams and Wilkins, 1950) is known simply as "the bible" in my office. When I moved west to join the faculty at the University of Washington School of Medicine in 1949, I brought with me a way of thinking about health and disease that has served as the foundation for all my work as a physician, a scientist, and a teacher. And I soon discovered that I had also brought with me a certain way of talking about patients and their illnesses.

Not long after taking up my duties on the medical staff of Firland Sanatorium in Seattle, I noticed at staff meetings that my colleagues were adopting one of my customary phrases to summarize a case review: ". . . and it was in this setting that the tuberculosis had its onset." The little pause and smile with which they preceded the phrase showed their amused recognition and acceptance of an imported concept called the *life chart*.

In Wolff's program we had used the life chart to treat patients in the clinic and to study the psychophysiological mechanisms of disease in the laboratory. In Seattle the life chart was soon adopted to treat patients in the tuberculosis sanatorium and then adapted to serve as a model for research instruments used in illness prediction studies. It is only fitting that I introduce the readings collected in this volume by describing the setting out of which they grew.

Parts of this chapter were published as "Development and Application of a Quantitative Measure of Life Change Magnitude," in *Stress and Mental Disorder,* edited by James E. Barrett, Robert M. Rose, and Gerald L. Klerman (New York: Raven Press, 1979), pp. 37–53. Copyright 1979 by Raven Press Books, Ltd. Reprinted with permission.

STUDIES OF THE NATURAL HISTORY OF DISEASE

What we have done in my laboratory for almost 35 years is address ourselves to the assertion of Alexander Pope about 300 years ago that "The proper study of mankind is man." We are interested in the natural history of disease, and these are some of the questions that we ask: What are some of the distant and proximate antecedents or precipitants of the onset of disease? What is the nature of the reaction when disease does occur? What are some of the factors that influence or modify the course of disease? Why do people get one disease rather than another? Can one discern any generalizations that would enable us to predict disease and to use prediction of disease as a basis for possible preventive intervention?

We have done many kinds of experiments in our study of the natural history of disease, and in each experiment the technique or method used to generate data has depended on the question asked and the context of the problem encountered. The research described here begins—as Pope suggested—with "man" and takes advantage of the doctor–patient relationship to study sick people at the bedside or in the clinic.

From the patient in the diagnostic or treatment situation we move into the laboratory, where we will make observations while conducting experiments in which, for example, certain kinds of stimuli are held constant while the subject's mood and behavior are varied. We will then proceed to studies of the individual not as a patient or laboratory subject but as a member of the community, in order to see what can be learned about the relationship of life-style to the natural history of disease. After studying the patient as an individual in the clinic, the laboratory, and the community, we will consider the patient as a member of a population, applying some epidemiologic principles and techniques. Finally we will look at possibilities for prevention of disease.

The Life Chart

The starting point is the clinic and a device invented by Adolf Meyer [1]. Meyer was interested in the relationship of three open-ended disciplines— biology, psychology, and sociology—to the processes of health and disease in human beings. To schematize those relationships he created the life chart, a device that organizes medical data as a dynamic biography.

Information is provided by the patient and is arranged by year and the patient's corresponding age. The entries on the life chart describe life situations—experiences having to do with growth, development, maturation, and senescence—as well as the patient's emotional responses to those situations. Certain life experiences that we arbitrarily call "disease" are listed in a separate column. In this approach to patients and their problems, the word "disease" applies to change in health status and includes a broad spectrum of medical, surgical, and psychiatric disorders. The life chart thus allows us to take into account not only the occurrence of disease, but also the setting in which it occurs.

Nasal Disease and Associated Head Pain

The patient whose life chart (Figure 1.1) I shall introduce first is a woman born in Holland, married, and without children [2]. She has a long history of headaches, head colds, and sinus disease as well as other diseases. She is tense and frustrated. A review of her life shows the recurrence of episodes of bitter weeping, with feelings of helplessness associated with conflicts, doubts, and misgivings. It is in this setting that illness occurs. We now take patients such as this into the laboratory to see what we can learn about the relationship between the onset of the patient's illness and the setting in which it occurred.

Observations are made of blood flow, secretions, swelling, and obstruction to breathing in the nasal mucous membranes before, during, and after an interview; biopsies are also taken before the interview and during it (Figure 1.2). At the same time that these observations are being made, we begin the interview, asking questions about the subject's life situation: "How do you feel? What do you see as happening to you? What position does that put you in? What does it feel like inside?" And when we ask these questions, we get responses like this: "I feel helpless, unable to face the situation. I wish it would go away, leave me alone. I feel left out in the cold."

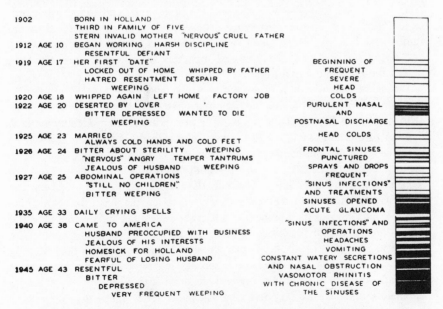

Figure 1.1   Life chart illustrating coincidence of situational threats and nasal disturbances in an insecure, dissatisfied, resentful woman. The black bars at the right indicate the occurrence, duration, and intensity of troublesome symptoms.

From T. H. Holmes, H. Goodell, S. Wolf, and H. G. Wolff, *The Nose* (1950), p. 79. Courtesy of Charles C Thomas, Publisher, Springfield, Illinois.

As the individual discusses feeling "left out in the cold," we observe hyperemia, hypersecretion, and swelling in the mucous membranes. Obstruction to breathing is reported. An increase in the secretion of eosinophils and polymorphonuclear leukocytes is documented. When we compare a biopsy taken when the mucous membranes are in a reasonably normal state to one taken at the height of the reaction during the interview, we see that discussion of things having to do with coping in real life situations produces edema of the nasal tissue and other pathologic tissue change. We have produced nasal disease in the laboratory by introducing a sensitive topic about a boss or a mother-in-law or financial difficulties or any number of other disturbing life situations.

We explore further this relationship between nasal hyperfunction and coping in life situations by again going into the laboratory, this time to ask a relevant question about adaptation to being left out in the cold. In these experiments human subjects are exposed to low ambient temperatures [3]. The results of measuring the temperature of the inspired air as it progresses toward the nasopharynx show that the nose is an effective air conditioning unit. Increased blood flow rapidly warms the inspired air so that, by the time it reaches the pharynx, the air is warmed from $-25°$ C to room temperature. Teleologically speaking, the observed nasal hyperfunction is nature's way of protecting the organism from frostbite of the lungs. We can say, then, that this pattern of hyperemia, hypersecretion, swelling, and obstruction to breathing is a biologically appropriate protective reaction when the organism is exposed to cold air or noxious chemical fumes—but that it is a biologically inappropriate reaction as an attempt to shut out, neutralize, and wash away an unsympathetic spouse or anyone else who makes one feel left out in the cold.

During the course of daily observations on one male subject [2], his mother-in-law comes to visit shortly after the birth of his first baby (Figure 1.3). During the following seven days the subject's nasal tissues exhibit progressive hyperemia, hypersecretion, and swelling. Chronic nasal disease is the consequence. Swelling is intense; the mucous membranes appear boggy, and they pit in response to probing. Discharge of nasal secretions is continuous. In addition, at the height of the situation with his mother-in-law, pain develops in the individual's head and face. Experiments on pain mechanisms of the nasal and paranasal tissues indicate that the sinus mucous membranes are relatively insensitive to pain. But the nasal tissues are exquisitely sensitive to pain, and stimulation evokes pain of high intensity. The sinus headache is really a nasal headache. Pain is generated by pathologic tissue change in the nasal tissue, and it is referred to the sinus area of the head, which is also supplied by two divisions of the fifth cranial nerve: the ophthalmic and the maxillary divisions. The pain over the face can be eliminated by anesthetizing the nasal mucous membranes.

In looking into the genesis of head pain associated with nasal disease, we began in the clinic where the subject identified and described his pain, and then moved into the laboratory where we stimulated the nasal tissue under carefully controlled conditions. We found that the individual's psychological state—his attitude toward the situation in which he finds himself—is demonstrably linked to the nature of the physiologic reaction generating illness.

Backache

Probably the most common source of pain in chronic intractable pain syndromes is skeletal muscle, and one of the most common pain syndromes seen in clinical medicine is the backache syndrome. We look now at mechanisms of skeletal muscle pain, and once again we start in the clinic with the life chart

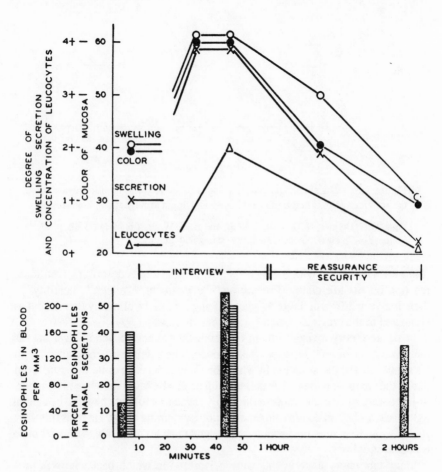

Figure 1.2 Eosinophil and neutrophil reaction in the nasal cavities, accompanying feelings of resentment, frustration, humiliation, and guilt. (Stippled bars represent number of eosinophils in circulating blood.)

From T. H. Holmes, H. Goodell, S. Wolf, and H. G.. Wolff, *The Nose* (1950), p. 111. Courtesy of Charles C Thomas, Publisher, Springfield, Illinois.

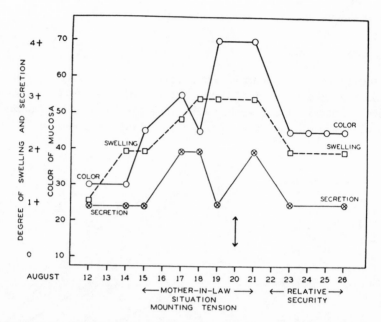

Figure 1.3   Nasal changes during periods of anxiety and conflict regarding the activities of an officious mother-in-law and threat to subject's independence.

From T. H. Holmes, H. Goodell, S. Wolf, and H. G. Wolff, *The Nose* (1950), p. 63. Courtesy of Charles C Thomas, Publisher, Springfield, Illinois.

(Figure 1.4) of a man with backache [4]. Notice the words describing emotional reaction on his life chart. "Frustration," "resentment," "anger," "hostility"—there is a very different flavor to what is being said in the clinic by this patient as compared to the previous patients with nasal disease.

In the laboratory we again attempt to define the patient's psychological state as the discussion of life situations takes place. The attitude of the patient with backache toward the situation in which he finds himself is quite different from that of the weeping patient. The patient with backache says that when his mother-in-law comes to visit, he wants to run away. He cannot tolerate her, and he cannot fight back; all he can do is avoid the situation by running away. He feels this very strongly, but he cannot take action; his skeletal muscles are ready to move, but he is held motionless.

Many laboratory experiments were performed in which backache was produced during discussions with the individual about salient life situations (Figure 1.5). As the interview begins we see the genesis of muscle tension as recorded by electromyogram and, after a short latency, the report of backache. When we change to neutral topics, the muscle tension subsides and the pain goes away. We then reintroduce the sensitive topic; muscle tension returns and so does the pain.

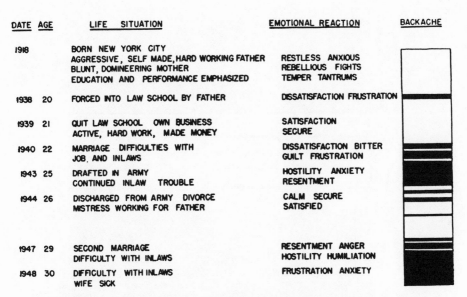

DATE	AGE	LIFE SITUATION	EMOTIONAL REACTION	BACKACHE
1918		BORN NEW YORK CITY AGGRESSIVE, SELF MADE, HARD WORKING FATHER BLUNT, DOMINEERING MOTHER EDUCATION AND PERFORMANCE EMPHASIZED	RESTLESS ANXIOUS REBELLIOUS FIGHTS TEMPER TANTRUMS	
1938	20	FORCED INTO LAW SCHOOL BY FATHER	DISSATISFACTION FRUSTRATION	
1939	21	QUIT LAW SCHOOL OWN BUSINESS ACTIVE, HARD WORK, MADE MONEY	SATISFACTION SECURE	
1940	22	MARRIAGE DIFFICULTIES WITH JOB AND INLAWS	DISSATISFACTION BITTER GUILT FRUSTRATION	
1943	25	DRAFTED IN ARMY CONTINUED INLAW TROUBLE	HOSTILITY ANXIETY RESENTMENT	
1944	26	DISCHARGED FROM ARMY DIVORCE MISTRESS WORKING FOR FATHER	CALM SECURE SATISFIED	
1947	29	SECOND MARRIAGE DIFFICULTY WITH INLAWS	RESENTMENT ANGER HOSTILITY HUMILIATION	
1948	30	DIFFICULTY WITH INLAWS WIFE SICK	FRUSTRATION ANXIETY	

Figure 1.4 Temporal correlation of life situations, emotional reactions, and exacerbations and remissions of the backache syndrome.

From T. H. Holmes and H. G. Wolff, "Life Situations, Emotions and Backache," *Psychosomatic Medicine* 14 (1952):18–33. Copyright 1952 by the American Psychosomatic Society, Inc. Reprinted by permission of Elsevier Science Publishing Co., Inc.

We are, in effect, demonstrating the nonbacterial equivalent of Koch's postulates, manipulating the experimental situation by directing the interview toward and away from sensitive topics.

Blood flow is another parameter in the genesis of backache. During the course of skeletal muscle tension or contraction, the circulation of the blood is decreased in proportion to the strength of the contractions [5]. In strong contractions pain develops rapidly and assumes high intensity, and the endurance of the sustained contraction is reduced. When the tense contracting muscles are relaxed, the blood flow is reestablished with a rapid surge in volume, and pain promptly disappears. The pain threshold is rapidly restored to normal, endurance comes back, and blood flow returns to normal.

In these skeletal muscle tension and blood flow experiments we see another biologically inappropriate pattern of responses evoked as an attempt to cope with a disturbing life situation. In this case the individual who wants to run away from the situation prepares for action: Muscles get tense, blood flow is reduced, and pain occurs. This is not unlike Sir Thomas Lewis's formulation regarding the genesis of pain in intermittent claudication and angina [6]. Lewis suggested that a metabolic factor P (pain factor) was produced during sustained anaerobic muscle

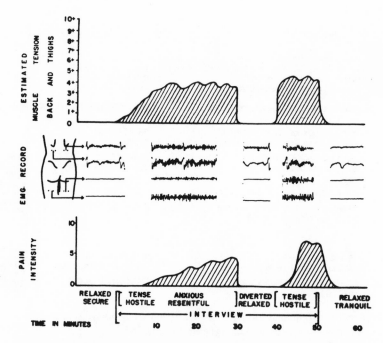

Figure 1.5   The genesis of low back pain accompanying interview provocative of conflict, anxiety, and generalized skeletal muscle hyperfunction.

From T. H. Holmes and H. G. Wolff, "Life Situations, Emotions and Backache," *Psychosomatic Medicine* 14 (1952):18–33. Copyright 1952 by the American Psychosomatic Society, Inc. Reprinted by permission of Elsevier Science Publishing Co., Inc.

contraction, accounting for the initiation of pain. The available evidence suggests that potassium is this pain factor [5].

Pain of Combined Mechanisms

We turn to one final example of our investigations into a clearer understanding of clinical pain syndromes [7]. Our subject is an individual who has two illnesses with widely varying but coexisting pathophysiologic processes. This patient is a 55-year-old man who has the backache syndrome with pain, tenderness, and muscle spasm as the cardinal features. He has had backache from time to time for many years, and now is in the hospital with intractable abdominal pain. In order to find out what is going on, we give the subject a small amount of intravenous sodium amytal to make him relax. Soon all the muscle tension, pain, and tenderness are essentially gone. At this time we discover a mass in the upper left quadrant of the abdomen. The patient is completely comfortable—he feels no pain—but when one lightly manipulates the mass, pain of high intensity returns.

The pain goes away when manipulation ceases. Clearly there are two different mechanisms of pain at work here.

The abdominal mass—a hypernephroma—initiates noxious afferent impulses, which travel into the spinal cord and elicit reflex muscle contractions. The mass also sends afferent impulses to the brain where the sensation of pain is registered. The subject reacts with anxiety and tension: He would like to run away from the situation, but cannot; and this reaction sends more motor impulses to the anterior horn cell, which stimulates the skeletal muscle to contract further. This sustained contraction gives rise to pain by the mechanisms defined in the previous experiments. The noxious afferent impulses from the sustained muscle contraction feed back into the central nervous system, and the result is chronic pain.

The sodium amytal allows us to distinguish the two mechanisms of pain operating here. It has no direct effect on pain, muscle, or cancer tissue, but it does relieve the subject's tension. When the subject relaxes, most of the efferent outflow from the central nervous system to the skeletal muscles is reduced. As the skeletal muscles relax, blood flow is reestablished and the pain from the muscle tension goes away. The subject still has the cancer; but to activate the pain-sensitive mechanisms associated with it, one must displace or exert traction on the cancer tissue. This manipulation then provides a demonstration of the other mechanisms of pain in this combined syndrome.

Dyspnea

Let us look at another way to focus studies of the natural history of disease. In this approach, a well-established chronic disease is held as a constant in our experiments. This illustration comes from studies done in collaboration with Dudley et al. [8] concerning people with diffuse obstructive pulmonary disease.

These subjects frequently experienced shortness of breath, or dyspnea. One of the first things observed about the subjects was that there was no predictable relationship between the respiratory physiologic variables and the occurrence of dyspnea (Table 1.1). Since this did not make sense, we took our subjects back into the laboratory to look at their psychological as well as their physiological state.

We found a pattern. Subjects were apt to feel short of breath on days when they felt "bad"; on the days when they felt "good," they did not complain of shortness of breath. We began to analyze more carefully the particular psychophysiological state of each subject on dyspneic days. We found that on some "bad" days they were feeling angry, anxious—or both—and action oriented. On the other days when they were dyspneic, they felt depressed, apathetic, withdrawn, and nonaction oriented. When we distinguish these moods and analyze them separately, we get a beautiful correlation between the respiratory variables and the mood and dyspnea (Table 1.2). The physiologic state associated with anger and anxiety—or action-oriented behavior—is hyperventilation (increased ventilation and decreased alveolar carbon dioxide). Under these circumstances our subjects

Table 1.1
Dyspneic Days Compared to Nondyspneic Days (16 Subjects)*

	RR	$\dot{V}$ (l/min)	$\dot{V}_A$ (l/min)	V_T (ml)	$F_{A_{CO_2}}$ (%)	$\dot{V}_{CO_2}$ (ml/min)
No dyspnea	18	9.5	6.4	528	5.3	339
Dyspnea†	21	10.1	6.6	481	5.5	363

* Data collected in part by R. W. Anderson ("Psychic Influences in Pulmonary Ventilation," University of Washington medical thesis, 1960) and by F. G. Gleeson ("The Relationship of Mood, Dyspnea and Pulmonary Function Studies in Respiratory Cripples," University of Washington medical thesis, 1958)

† p = N.S.

Mean number of dyspneic days = 3.7

Mean number of non-dyspneic days = 12.3

Note: RR = respiratory rate; $\dot{V}$ = minute ventilation; $\dot{V}_A$ = alveolar ventilation; V_T = tidal volume; $F_{A_{CO_2}}$ = fractional concentration of alveolar carbon dioxide; $\dot{V}_{CO_2}$ = carbon dioxide consumption.

Source: D. L. Dudley, C. J. Martin, and T. H. Holmes, "Dyspnea: Psychologic and Physiologic Observations," *Journal of Psychosomatic Research* 11 (1968):325–39. Copyright 1968 by Pergamon Press, Ltd. Reprinted with permission.

Table 1.2
Dyspneic Breathing Compared with Eupneic Breathing (7 subjects)

	RR	$\dot{V}$ (l/min)	$\dot{V}_A$ (l/min)	V_T (ml)	$F_{A_{CO_2}}$ (%)
Dyspnea with anger and anxiety (5 subjects)					
Control	20	7.1	5.2	355	4.9
Dyspnea	29*	10.5†	7.8*	362	4.6
Dyspnea with depression (4 subjects)					
Control	15	5.7	4.3	380	5.4
Dyspnea	13	4.4‡	3.2‡	338	5.6

* $p < 0.05$

† $p < 0.02$

‡ $p < 0.01$

Note: RR = respiratory rate; $\dot{V}$ = minute ventilation; $\dot{V}_A$ = alveolar ventilation; V_T = tidal volume; $F_{A_{CO_2}}$ = fractional concentration of alveolar carbon dioxide.

Source: D. L. Dudley, C. J. Martin, and T. H. Holmes, "Dyspnea: Psychologic and Physiologic Observations," *Journal of Psychosomatic Research* 11 (1968):325–39. Copyright 1968 by Pergamon Press, Ltd. Reprinted with permission.

complained of dyspnea. The observations of dyspnea with depression or other nonaction-oriented behaviors show just the opposite state. When subjects felt depressed, action was the farthest thing from their intent. The physiologic change associated with that attitude is hypoventilation (reduced ventilation and alveolar oxygen and increased alveolar carbon dioxide).

And that explains why our original comparison of respiratory variables failed to detect significant differences between dyspneic and nondyspneic days. When added together, the hyperventilation of dyspnea associated with anger and anxiety and the hypoventilation of dyspnea associated with depression cancel each other out. In order to understand better the natural history of a disease like emphysema, it is important to take into account not only the physiological but also the psychological dimensions of the illness. We need to ask about the patient's perception of the setting in which he or she is situated and what—if anything—that individual has decided to do about it.

Reaction to Noxious Agents: Hay Fever

Our subject in this experiment [9] has hay fever (but not very serious hay fever). Here we study the relationship of two noxious agents acting simultaneously on the host, and we observe the effects of the two. We will assume that the constitutional dimension of the hay fever is a constant.

The two noxious agents we observe at work here are pollen and the home situation (Figure 1.6). After making controlled observations of the nasal mucous membranes in both left and right nasal chambers when the subject is calm, secure, and relaxed, we introduce the subject into the pollen room. The response is mild hay fever. About 20 minutes later we introduce the second noxious agent, by interviewing the subject about a situation at home that has engendered much conflict. The subject feels tense, helpless, left out in the cold, and unable to do anything about his situation. The reaction of the nasal mucous membranes to this added insult is one of enhanced hyperfunction and hay fever symptoms.

After half an hour of discussing the sensitive domestic situation with the subject, we redirect the interview and give him reassurance, support, and understanding. The effects of our "psychotherapy"—of talking these things out, of reassurance and emotional support—become evident. Although the pollen is still present in the laboratory, the subject's acute reaction subsides.

Let us look at the neural mechanisms involved in the nasal hyperfunction just observed. In another experiment [9] with a hay fever subject (Figure 1.7), after making controlled observations of the nasal mucous membranes in both nasal chambers, we inject into the left stellate ganglion a solution of 2 percent procaine. The left stellate ganglion is part of the sympathetic nerve chain that gives rise to the sympathetic nerve supply to one side of the head; and the procaine blocks the flow of sympathetic impulses from the spinal cord up to the left side of the head, including the tissues of the left nasal chamber. This interference in the nerve supply to the head produces a Horner's syndrome: Along with the changes in the eye and face, the mucous membranes in the left nasal chamber get red, wet, and swollen. We now have a control side (the right nasal chamber, which still receives sympathetic nerve impulses) and an experimental side (the left nasal chamber which receives only parasympathetic nerve supply). The hyperfunction in the left nasal mucous membrane is now the result of parasympathetic impulses from the brain to the nose. This is the mechanism by which environmental stimuli such as a mother-in-law evoke nasal mucous membrane reactions.

When we add pollen to both the left and right nasal cavities, we observe two distinct reactions. In the left nasal chamber we see the effect of adding the antigen—pollen—to the neuromechanism of, say, mother-in-law: Adding the noxious agent pollen to the already hyperfunctioning mucous membranes produces a typical hay fever reaction to the left side of the nose. The insult of pollen also produces a reaction in the right nasal cavity, but it is transient and of low magnitude—not enough to produce symptoms. The dramatically intensified hyperfunction associated with two noxious agents like pollen and the life disturbing situation shows that they exert a summative or additive effect. We are dealing with very solid, readily demonstrable neuromechanisms. What the brain can control, the environmental situation—with its afferent input to the brain—can

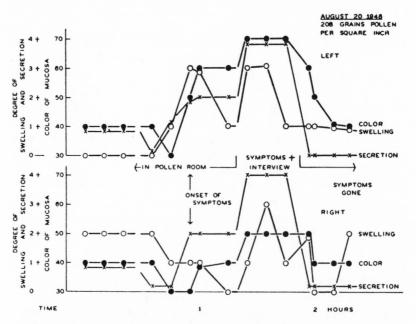

Figure 1.6   Summative effects of the nasal hyperfunction produced in a sensitive subject by introducing a conflict situation during exposure to pollen.

From T. H. Holmes, T. Treuting, and H. G. Wolff, "Life Situations, Emotions and Nasal Disease," *Psychosomatic Medicine* 13 (1951):71–82. Copyright 1951 by the American Psychosomatic Society, Inc. Reprinted by permission of Elsevier Publishing Co., Inc.

also control. Pollen alone was not sufficient to produce symptoms in our hay fever subject, but the combined assault of pollen and life situation was.

Resistance to Noxious Agents: Tuberculosis

These different reactions in the same subject with hay fever lead us to wonder about the influence of the life situation on resistance to attack by noxious agents. We begin asking questions in the laboratory and then move back to the clinic, where we will pursue this line of inquiry by studying patients' resistance to attack by a specific noxious stimulus: the pulmonary tuberculosis germ.

In experimental studies of skin inflammation, we introduce a constant amount of a noxious agent and vary mood and behavior [10]. The noxious agent in this

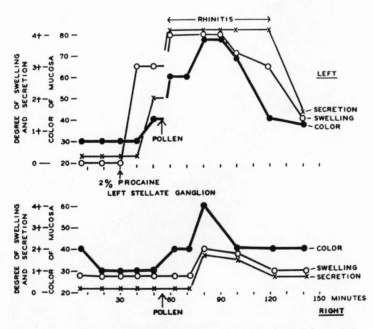

Figure 1.7 Hyperemia, hypersecretion, and swelling in the left nasal chamber following left stellate ganglion block with 2 percent procaine. Production of "hay fever rhinitis" following introduction of 2 mg pollen onto the acutely and intensely hyperfunctioning mucous membrane in the left nasal cavity. Note that hyperfunction in the right nasal cavity following introduction of pollen was delayed in its appearance and of low intensity.

From T. H. Holmes, H. Goodell, S. Wolf, and H. G. Wolff, *The Nose* (1950), p. 121. Courtesy of Charles C Thomas, Publisher, Springfield, Illinois.

instance is trypsin—a proteolytic enzyme that we inject intradermally. The results are mild tissue damage and a sterile inflammatory reaction. We measure the magnitude of the inflammatory reaction and correlate the intensity of this reaction with the mood and behavior of the individual on a given day. In a composite plotting of our observations (Figure 1.8), we distinguish the intensity of reactions associated with three distinct mood states. The inflammatory reaction is greatest on days when subjects feel calm and secure. When subjects are tense and preoccupied, they have a much more intense inflammatory reaction

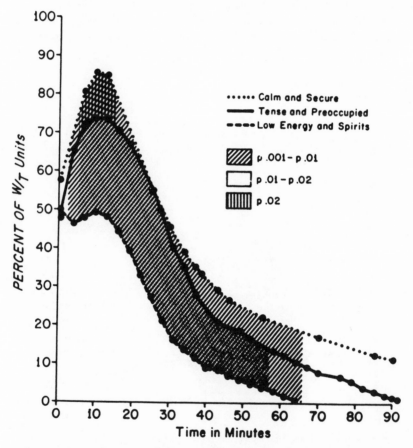

Figure 1.8   Composite plot of 28 observations in five subjects showing relation of naturally occurring stress to experimental skin inflammation.
    Note: "W/T Units" is a measure of whealing response.

From N. E. Ely, J. W. Verhey, and T. H. Holmes, "Experimental Studies of Skin Inflammation," *Psychosomatic Medicine* 25 (1963):264–84. Copyright 1963 by the American Psychosomatic Society, Inc. Reprinted by permission of Elsevier Science Publishing Co., Inc.

than when they are low in energy and spirits. We see here dramatic changes in resistance to attack by the same amount of noxious agent, depending on mood and behavior. Formulated in teleological perspective, the more acute inflammatory reaction observed in the calm-secure and in the tense-anxious is protective of the host. It walls off, localizes, and destroys the invading noxious agent. Nature preserves the whole by sacrificing the part. Systemic dissemination of the invading agent and its ominous consequences for the patient is much more apt to occur in the state of low energy and spirits, or depression.

Tuberculosis: The Patient in the Clinic

In the clinic we then apply our observations in the laboratory to a study of tuberculosis. Once again, we hold the noxious stimulus constant—here it is the pulmonary tuberculosis germ—while varying mood and behavior. We choose 17-ketosteroid excretion rate as our index of resistance to inflammation because it reflects adrenocortical function.

At the bedside we study a man with far-advanced, bilateral, acute, exudative pulmonary tuberculosis [11] and carefully follow his progress under treatment (Figure 1.9). When he entered the hospital he was depressed, withdrawn, and inactive, and felt overwhelmed. He had steroid excretion rates of 2 mg per 24 hours, which was about the level that one would expect in someone with Addison's disease (though he did not have this). The patient was given antibiotics immediately; but for the first three months of treatment he did not get better. Improvement did not occur until his mood and behavior changed from feelings of depression to a more optimistic and outgoing behavior, and until the ketosteroid level increased toward normal. At nine months, improvement stopped as he became depressed again; but within another several months, he was once again improved and was finally discharged. What we see here is a particular disease state (far-advanced tuberculosis) associated with a particular biological state of reduced resistance (reduced ketosteroid excretion levels) and a particular psychological state (depression and being overwhelmed). Improvement in this patient's disease state is associated with a changed biological state (ketosteroid level increased to normal) and a changed psychological state (from depression to optimism).

Studies conducted on the hospital course of 206 tuberculosis patients [11] revealed associations between the biological, psychological, and disease states. The 17-ketosteroid levels are associated with the state of the disease. In general, with minimal tuberculosis the *average* steroid excretion is relatively high. With moderate tuberculosis the average steroid level is a little lower; and with far-advanced tuberculosis, lower still. We also noticed that the *daily* steroid excretion levels within all three groups ranged from very low to very high.

When we correlated the progress of the disease, the level of the index of resistance to infection or inflammation, and the psychological state expressed in mood and behavior, some interesting relationships emerged [11]. Those patients with far-advanced, acute, exudative tuberculosis are depressed, overwhelmed, older men with considerably reduced steroid excretion. At the other end of the spectrum are those with minimal tuberculosis, and steroid levels above normal (corrected for age and sex). They are tense, anxious, conflict-ridden people and are predominantly younger women.

Tuberculosis: The Subject in the Community

Taking into account the relationship of the acid-fast bacillus and the mood and behavior associated with the disease state, we now consider the social situation

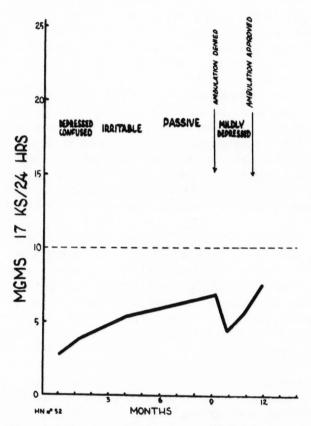

Figure 1.9   *Case 5* (H. N., a 52-year-old white male admitted to the hospital with far-advanced, bilateral, exudative, and cavitary tuberculosis). Changes in emotional state and 17-ketosteroid excretion during treatment.

Note: The dotted line at 10 mgms represents normal ketosteroid excretion level.

From E. R. Clarke, D. W. Zahn, and T. H. Holmes, "The Relationship of Stress, Adrenocortical Function, and Tuberculosis," *American Review of Tuberculosis* 69 (1954):362. Courtesy of the *American Review of Respiratory Disease.*

[12;13]. We introduce our subject into the community at large to study the relationship of life-style to the natural history of tuberculosis. The community we studied was the city of Seattle, and we used area of residence (determined by census tract) as our index of life-style. We divided the city into four areas: I, a skid road residential area (or city-center ghetto); II, a blue-collar residential area; III, a white-collar residential area; and IV, a better socioeconomic residential area. We then correlated tuberculosis morbidity rates with residential areas, our index of life-style [14].

Whites who live in area I (the city center) have a high morbidity rate, but it progressively decreases in areas II, III, and IV. For nonwhites, the morbidity is even higher than for whites in the city center, and is cut in half in the blue-collar (II) and white-collar (III) residential areas, but is one-third higher in area IV than in area I. There are also clear differences between nonwhite females and nonwhite males. The morbidity rate for the nonwhite females is exactly the same in area IV as in area I, while nonwhite males have almost twice the risk of getting tuberculosis when they live in area IV (the better socioeconomic residential area) than in area I (the city center).

What we are seeing for the whites in area I is the role of their marginal social status; and for the nonwhites in area IV, the culture conflict engendered by the close residential juxtaposition of a minority and a majority population. Such conflicts in life-style evoke depression, withdrawal, and feelings of being overwhelmed—thereby reducing resistance to infection or inflammation and making it possible for the germ, if present, to produce the tissue reaction of tuberculosis.

Prognosis: Factors That Influence the Course of Disease

An entirely different—but equally important—area of psychosomatic medicine is the study of factors that influence or modify the course of disease once it gets started. Here I draw on work done by Dr. Herbert S. Ripley, a pioneer in this field, to emphasize some of the techniques used in the management of patients under treatment in a medical clinic [15]. What follows is a representative list of therapeutic devices that doctors have at their disposal to manage patients with illnesses of all sorts—medical, surgical, and psychiatric. The treatment techniques are arranged in descending order of saliency and frequency:

Reassurance and emotional support

Free expression of conflicts and feelings

Advice regarding attitudes, habits, and activities

Explanation of psychophysiologic processes

Symptomatic drug therapy

Intravenous use of sodium amytal

Ruling out neoplastic and infectious disease

Dealing with other members of the family

Development of insight

Analysis of emotional support

Attempts to modify the situation

Dream analysis

Help from social service department

In successful doctor–patient relationships, the doctor's words and actions are free from moral judgment; they convey warmth, interest, and understanding to the patient.

Armed with the list above, we now ask, "What can we expect to gain from applying these doctor–patient relationship techniques in the care of sick people?" Let us go back to our study of tuberculosis patients for one answer. The patients at Firland Sanatorium were managed by physicians who used not only appropriate medication—including antibiotic drugs—but also techniques for an effective doctor–patient relationship.

In general, we found that those who recovered quickly were the patients whose mood, behavior, and biological resistance were changing toward normal (Table 1.3). Those whose disease stayed the same or became worse were patients who were anxious or depressed and whose steroid levels were correspondingly elevated or lowered. Those who died from the disease in our study were usually depressed, with reduced levels of 17-ketosteroids. When we compare the number who improved to the number who did not, we see that, by using skill in interpersonal relationships and by transmitting the special things that doctors transmit, the physician can effect a dramatic change in the natural history of disease: 80

Table 1.3
Course of Tuberculosis in Relation to 17-Ketosteroid Excretion

Course of Disease	Course of Ketosteroid Excretion			
	Stationary near normal	Changing toward normal	Stationary above or below	Widely fluctuating
Moderate or rapid improvement	8	36	6	5
Slight or slow improvement	1	9	20	2
Stationary	1	2	7	1
Worse		1	5	1
Dead		3	1	

Note: N = 109 patients at Firland Sanatorium, Seattle, Washington.

Source: E. R. Clarke, Jr., D. W. Zahn, and T. H. Holmes, "The Relationship of Stress, Adrenocortical Function, and Tuberculosis," *American Review of Tuberculosis* 69 (1954):351–69. Courtesy of the *American Review of Respiratory Disease.*

percent of patients are improved to a greater or lesser degree. This figure of 80 percent (± 10 percent) improvement seems to be the general result reported for the treatment outcome of most chronic diseases. This is an impressive achievement for modern medicine.

Let us take a different approach. Instead of asking what the doctor brings to the treatment situation, we could ask what the patient brings to the equation that may influence the course of disease. We did a prospective quantitative study of psychosocial assets in a representative sample of pulmonary tuberculosis patients [16]. We found that those who got better were people who had many psychosocial assets: strong family ties, steady employment, adequate income and job satisfaction, regular recreation (through clubs or hobbies, for example), frequent social participation, flexibility and reliability, realistic goals, and adequate or good performance. Those patients who did not get better were more likely to have no family, only transient employment, income from welfare, no job satisfaction, substandard residence, no outside interests, and no goals or responsibilities; and they were socially isolated and deviant.

When we combine the factors in our equation, the net result is that with good techniques, good drugs, and good patients—patients with many psychosocial assets—the treatment outcome is favorable.

Predicting Time of Illness Onset

At this point in our research we were ready to ask another kind of question. Given all these things that we know about the natural history of disease, is it possible to make predictions about the onset of illness? Can we discover why

Table 1.4
Social Taxis of a Typical Case (white male, age 36, single, third generation, unemployed, city-center resident, dormitory quarters, unskilled laborer)

Factor	Years Prior to Admission											
	12	11	10	9	8	7	6	5	4	3	2	1
Residential changes	2	1		1	3	3	5	10	7	10	12	15
Job changes	2	1	1		2	2	4	5	8	12	15	15
Financial worry					1	3	3	3	3	4	4	4
Disabling illness										1		
Jail terms												3
TOTAL	4	2	1	1	6	8	12	18	18	27	31	37

Source: T. H. Holmes, N. G. Hawkins, C. E. Bowerman, E. R. Clarke, Jr., and J. R. Joffe, "Psychosocial and Psychophysiological Studies of Tuberculosis," *Psychosomatic Medicine* 19 (1957):134–43. Copyright 1957 by the American Psychosomatic Society, Inc. Reprinted by permission of Elsevier Science Publishing Co., Inc.

people get sick when they do—not with *what* they get sick, but *when* they get sick? That question generated the 25 years of research collected in this volume.

When we began to ask our questions about predicting the onset of illness, our clinical model—the life chart—suggested the direction our inquiries should take. Let me return to the study of a patient with tuberculosis, this time to note the occurrence of job changes, residential changes, financial changes, health change, and jail term in the 12 years prior to admission to the hospital with tuberculosis (Table 1.4). As time of admission to the hospital is approached, there is a mounting frequency of these social events. In the two-year period prior to admission to the hospital, there occurs a life crisis—a veritable crescendo of life change events—that is the setting for the onset of tuberculosis.

In pursuing the problem of prediction, we systematically studied the social events or life events that require adjustment or change of coping style in the individual. We studied thousands of these situations to see what we could learn about the types of social events that require readjustment, their frequency of occurrence, the magnitude of change they require, and their relationship to the onset of disease. The readings in this book retrace the path that our investigations have taken.

LIFE CHANGE AND ILLNESS STUDIES

I have used examples from my own research to illustrate the advances in psychosomatic medicine that prepared the way for the life change research done in my laboratory from 1957 to 1981. But one does not work alone in these things. Over the years I have collaborated with many people, and I have benefited from the work of other colleagues. Behind and alongside the research described above lies the research of a brilliant group of physician-scientists with whom I worked at Cornell [17]. While I studied nasal function and disease, Stewart Wolf studied human gastric function and William Grace studied human colon function; together we produced a trilogy of books on the function of mucous membrane in human subjects. At the same time, Robert Marcusson pursued research on head pain; Ian Stevenson worked on cardiovascular disease; Herbert Ripley, on hypertension and kidney function; and David Graham, on skin disease and reactions. All of that research supported and expanded the body of evidence relating to protective reaction patterns and to the mechanisms involved in effecting tissue change and tissue damage and in reducing resistance to noxious agents.

At the same time, our understanding of the relationship of etiologic agents and bodily mechanisms in the occurrence of disease was deepened by studies of the human as a psychological being and by studies of the human being in community. Graham and Grace produced classic publications on the relationship of attitudes to specific disease states. And Lawrence Hinkle and Norman Plummer applied the life chart concept to large groups of subjects in order to study the distribution of illness in the general population. Their epidemiologic studies showed that illness is not randomly distributed, but rather that a small part of the population experiences a majority of the illness and that illnesses occur in clusters or chains separated by periods of relative health. From the work of Hinkle and Plummer we learned that neither the timing of illness nor susceptibility to illness is randomly distributed.

Adolph Meyer's life chart [1] opened the way for all the studies of Wolff et al. because it gave us a way to document the relationship of life situations, emotions, and disease. We kept life charts on patients and subjects over the course of weeks, months, and even years as we followed them in the clinic and the laboratory. We had the opportunity to observe the natural occurrence of life events and to study the psychophysiologic reactions that they evoked. My colleagues and students in Seattle carried on the practice of using life charts to work with patients and research subjects.

This wealth of empirical observation was behind us when we developed our research questionnaires: the Schedule of Recent Experience (SRE) around 1956 and—some eight years later—the Social Readjustment Rating Scale (SRRS). The choice of life event items for these instruments was neither arbitrary nor speculative: The events selected were those that time and again had appeared as salient events in the life charts of clinic patients, beginning in 1943 in New York and continuing on from 1949 in Seattle. In the earlier studies of mechanisms of disease, life situations figured primarily as topics that could evoke psychophysiological reactions. We brought life events to the foreground of study when we began asking questions about the time of illness onset.

The turning point in our work was when we adapted the life chart concept into a form suitable for research with groups, as well as single subjects. Once we had the Schedule of Recent Experience, our life change and life events research took off in several directions at once. As the publication dates show, we conducted a number of projects simultaneously; others followed in quick succession. For this collection of readings, however, we have arranged the chapters in a thematic—rather than strictly chronological—scheme. We present the Social Readjustment Rating Scale and related methodology papers first (Chapters 2–8), then backtrack to the development of the Schedule of Recent Experience (Chapters 9 and 10)—all by way of preparing for the chronological retracing of our clinical studies (Chapters 11–22).

It gives me great satisfaction to note that many of the people with whom I have collaborated on these papers were University of Washington medical students, graduate students, or medical residents at the time. I have long believed that student research is undervalued at our medical schools. Doing research enhances the student's training—and this is as true for the student who enters private practice as for the student who pursues a career in academic medicine. Equally important, students do excellent work. They can produce research that advances the state of our knowledge.

Education is at the heart of all the work that I do, and contributing to the prevention of illness is my ultimate goal. Some fifteen years ago I appeared on a national television show and explained much of the research that this book contains. During the hour-long program I spelled out the background of our research and the relationship between the magnitude of life change and illness onset and seriousness of illness. Many of the program viewers wrote in to ask for the Social Readjustment Rating Scale, so I wrote back and asked them if they would participate in an informal prospective study of prevention. Of the several thousand people who had written in, 225 randomly selected subjects were chosen to participate in the study; and we followed these people for the next year.

This was a study of the effects of primary intervention: Using an educational approach (the television program and our mailings), we told people what the experimental data were and what the probabilities are in the relationship of life change and onset of illness. The results indicate that 15 percent more people stayed well in the year following intervention than in the year preceding intervention. The number of people who got one illness stayed about the same, and those who got two or more illnesses showed a dramatic reduction of 20 percent in morbidity. In essence, using an hour of intervention, we had a saving in morbidity of somewhere between 15 and 20 percent.

When people write to me today and ask for information about life change and onset of illness, I often send along the following list of preventive measures, which we sent to participants in the preventive study:

1. Become familiar with the life events and the amount of change that they require.

2. Put the Social Readjustment Rating Scale where you and your family can see it easily several times a day.

3. With practice you can recognize when a life event happens.

4. Think about the meaning of the life event for you, and try to identify some of the feelings that you experience from it.

5. Think about the different ways you might best adjust to the event.

6. Take your time in arriving at decisions.

7. Anticipate life changes—and plan for them well in advance, if possible.

8. Pace yourself. This can be done even if you are in a hurry.

9. Look at the accomplishment of a task as part of daily living, and avoid looking at such an achievement as a "stopping point" or as a time for letting down.

10. *Remember*: The more change you experience, the more likely you are to get sick. Of those people with 300 or more life change units (LCU) for the past year, almost 80 percent get sick in the near future; with 150–299 LCU, about 50 percent get sick in the near future; and with less than 150 LCU, only about 30 percent get sick in the near future. So, the higher your Life Change Score, the harder you should work to stay well.

Let me close with a phrase that formulates what I have been saying about the natural history of disease: Disease is a by-product or epiphenomenon of our goals and of the techniques we use in achieving our aspirations. My message is direct. There are a lot of things that are worse than illness. One of them may be not taking a promotion, or not letting your mother-in-law come to visit. But at least recognize the risk that you are under and be willing to pay the price.

REFERENCES

1. Lief, A., ed. *The Commonsense Psychiatry of Dr. Adolf Meyer.* New York: McGraw-Hill, 1948.

2. Holmes, T. H., H. Goodell, S. Wolf, and H. G. Wolff. *The Nose: An Experimental Study of Reactions within the Nose in Human Subjects during Varying Life Experiences.* Springfield, Ill.: Charles C Thomas, 1950.

3. Webb, P. "Air Temperatures in Respiratory Tracts of Resting Subjects in Cold." *Journal of Applied Physiology* 4 (1951):378–82.

4. Holmes, T. H., and H. G. Wolff. "Life Situations, Emotions and Backache." *Psychosomatic Medicine* 14 (1952):18–33.

5. Dorpat, T. L., and T. H. Holmes. "Mechanisms of Skeletal Muscle Pain and Fatigue." *Archives of Neurology and Psychiatry* 74 (1955):628–40.

6. Lewis, T. *Pain.* New York: McMillan, 1942.

7. Holmes, T. H., and H. S. Ripley. "Experimental Studies on Anxiety Reactions." *American Journal of Psychiatry* 111 (1955):921–29.

8. Dudley, D. L., in collaboration with C. J. Martin, M. Masuda, H. S. Ripley, and T. H. Holmes. *The Psychophysiology of Respiration in Health and Disease.* New York: Appleton-Century-Croft, 1969.

9. Holmes, T. H., T. Treuting, and H. G. Wolff. "Life Situations, Emotions and Nasal Disease: Evidence on Summative Effects Exhibited in Patients with 'Hay Fever.'" *Psychosomatic Medicine* 13 (1951):71–82.

10. Ely, N. E., J. W. Verhey, and T. H. Holmes. "Experimental Studies of Skin Inflammation." *Psychosomatic Medicine* 25 (1963):264–84.

11. Clarke, E. R., D. W. Zahn, and T. H. Holmes. "The Relationship of Stress, Adrenocortical Function and Tuberculosis." *American Review of Tuberculosis* 69 (1954):351–69.

12. Holmes, T. H. "Multidiscipline Studies of Tuberculosis." In *Personality, Stress and Tuberculosis,* edited by P. J. Sparer, pp. 65–152. New York: International Universities Press, 1956.

13. Holmes, T. H. "Infectious Diseases and Human Ecology." *Journal of the Indian Medical Profession* 10 (1964):4825–29.

14. Holmes, T. H., N. G. Hawkins, C. E. Bowerman, E. R. Clarke, Jr., and J. R. Joffe. "Psychosocial and Psychophysiologic Studies of Tuberculosis." *Psychosomatic Medicine* 19 (1957):134–43.

15. Ripley, H. S., S. Wolf, and H. G. Wolff. "Treatment in a Psychosomatic Clinic." *Journal of the American Medical Association* 138 (1948):949–51.

16. Holmes, T. H., J. R. Joffe, J. W. Ketcham, and T. F. Sheehy. "Experimental Study of Prognosis." *Journal of Psychosomatic Research* 5 (1961):235–52.

17. Holmes, T. H. "Stress: The New Etiology." In *Health for the Whole Person,* edited by A. C. Hastings, J. Fadiman, and J. S. Gordon, pp. 345–62. Boulder: Westview Press, 1980.

PART II

METHODOLOGY: SCALING STUDIES

Introduction

Quantifying Social Experiences

The renown of the Social Readjustment Rating Scale is remarkable. People who have never seen the list of 43 life events and who would not recognize its name (much less the names of its inventors) still know about "that stress scale." And even 20 years after the Social Readjustment Rating Scale first appeared in print, new generations of readers rediscover it with undiminished excitement. This widespread fascination with the scale is most gratifying, but it is only fair to admit that no one in the Holmes laboratory foresaw such a response. We conceived of the Social Readjustment Rating Scale as simply a means to an end. Its development did not inaugurate our work in life events research (the development of the Schedule of Recent Experience did that), but—out of deference to its fame—we shall present it as the first of the 21 studies collected in this volume.

The Social Readjustment Rating Scale was the second methodological breakthrough in our work. We knew from studies (Chapters 11 and 12) of tuberculosis, cardiac disease, skin disease, hernia, and pregnancy that life events cluster significantly in the two-year period before the time of illness onset. But to make the Schedule of Recent Experience into a more powerful predictive tool, we needed a way to quantify the *nature* of life events as well as their frequency of occurrence. In 1962 the answer to our problem found us, arriving in the form of Dr. Eugene Gallanter. Gallanter gave a lecture to our faculty at the University of Washington in which he spoke on the new field of psychophysics—the study of the psychological perception of the quality, quantity, magnitude, and intensity of physical phenomena. Gallanter explained how he and S. S. Stevens had demonstrated the ability of subjects to make reliable subjective magnitude estimations of physical dimensions such as length of object, intensity of sound, brightness of light, number of objects, and so on. Dr. Richard Rahe and I saw the relevance to our problem immediately. Applied to the field of psychosocial phenomena, the subjective magnitude estimation technique could give us a method for quantifying life events.

Chapter 2 is the original scale study. The Social Readjustment Rating Questionnaire (SRRQ) reproduced in Table 2.1 is the final version of an instrument that was several years in the making. Dr. Rahe (who was then a resident in our department) and I tested different forms of the Social Readjustment Rating Questionnaire—experimenting with the number of items and their wording, and deciding which event to use as the modulus item. The earliest draft of the Social Readjustment Rating Questionnaire had 38 life event items and used retirement as the modulus event, given an arbitrary value of 500. The final form has 43 items. (We used Christmas on the Social Readjustment Rating Questionnaire as part of the test of our scaling technique, but Christmas has never been included among the 42 items in the Schedule of Recent Experience. We learned early on that everyone in the United States experiences Christmas every year, no matter what their religious beliefs.)

There have been no major revisions to the Social Readjustment Rating Scale since 1967. The Social Readjustment Rating Scale in use today has undergone only two slight modifications. Inflation made the dollar amounts obsolete in the items referring to mortgage or loan greater than $10,000 or less than $10,000. They now read "mortgage or loan for a major purchase" or "for a lesser purchase." However, there is one change that we would like to make in the scale. As originally published, the Social Readjustment Rating Scale uses abbreviated wording for the life event items (see Table 2.3). The full wording of the items is what subjects read when completing the Social Readjustment Rating Questionnaire (see Table 2.1) and the Schedule of Recent Experience. We regret the decision to save space on the Social Readjustment Rating Scale, because the complete wording is the accurate and more helpful form.

Chapters 3 and 4 provide the statistical support for our new scaling method. My longtime colleague, Dr. Minoru Masuda, suggested that the geometric mean might prove to be a better measure of central tendency in ratio scaling than the arithmetic mean that Dr. Rahe and I had used in the original scale paper. Chapter 3 shows that Dr. Masuda was right; our later scaling studies adopted the geometric mean. In Chapter 4 Dr. Libby Ruch (then a sociology graduate student) and I demonstrate two separate points. First, we compared the new ratio scaling method to the older method of paired comparisons. Subjective magnitude estimation is the simpler and faster method. Second, we replicated the first scale paper's demonstration of the consensus in rating life events between younger and older populations.

My colleagues and I have conducted a number of validation studies of the Social Readjustment Rating Scale, within the United States and also with cross-cultural samples. Unlike the psychophysicists, we could not compare some physical attribute to the experience rated by subjective magnitude estimations, but we could correlate the magnitudes assigned by discrete subsamples in the population.

Chapter 5 reproduces our first cross-cultural validation study, using Japanese and U.S. subjects. The consensus demonstrated in that study was supported in subsequent work of equal interest: a cross-cultural study of Western Europeans and Americans by David K. Harmon et al. (*Journal of Psychosomatic Research* 14 [1970]:391–400) and a cross-cultural study of Malaysians and Americans by Tai-Hwang Woon et al. (*Journal of Cross-Cultural Psychology* 2, no. 4 [December 1971]:373–86). In Chapter 6 we compare consensus and variation in the perception of life events within a culture by studying the scaling responses of three U.S. subcultures.

Essentially, we found in these studies that—worldwide—death of a spouse requires about twice as much change in adjustment as getting married, and ten times as much change and adjustment as getting a traffic ticket. Cultural variations do exist, and they often prove to be as fascinating as cross-cultural consensus; but we did not find a startling difference in scaling responses until the study of a Peruvian town hit by earthquake (Chapter 7). The impact of a natural catastrophe on perception of life events is dramatically revealed in the Social Readjustment Rating Questionnaire scores of the earthquake victims.

Later in the book—Part III, "Clinical Applications"—there are two chapters that provide additional data and comments on the Social Readjustment Rating Scale and the technique of subjective magnitude estimation. Chapter 19 provides an example of how we modified the Social Readjustment Rating Questionnaire for use with a specific subculture—in this case, college football players. Group-specific instruments, called the Athletic Schedule of Recent Experience and the Social and Athletic Readjustment Rating Scale, improved the prediction of injury and illness in that study. Chapter 21 summarizes more than a decade of scaling studies using the Social Readjustment Rating Questionnaire (and some using the Seriousness of Illness Rating Questionnaire) in different populations, including data from several unpublished student theses. Readers are directed to both of these chapters to complete the record of life event scaling studies conducted in the Holmes laboratory.

The Social Readjustment Rating Scale brings quantification to the social dimension; and, as such, it fits into the same category as wristwatches and calendars. The Social Readjustment Rating Scale is simply a device to quantify human experience. Its development has enabled us to apply the scientific method—which is measurement—to the texture of human lives. What we measure is the amount of change that certain events require of people: the readjustment necessary in their coping style and life-style. The Social Readjustment Rating Scale does not measure the event's desirability, its meaning, or the emotional associations that the event holds for any individual. Both "desirable" and "undesirable" events require readjustment. Our long experience interviewing patients with the life chart has clearly shown that individuals will interpret the same event different ways, and that the individual's emotional response will vary according to his or her past experiences and coping mechanisms. What all 43 events have in common is this: The individual's life-style is disrupted by the event, and he or she must adjust to the change brought about by it.

Once we had developed the Social Readjustment Rating Scale, we had a research orientation. "Life stress" can—and does—mean many things. The Social Readjustment Rating Scale defined the concept of "life change," and thereby defined exactly what we were studying. The combined Social Readjustment Rating Scale and the Schedule of Recent Experience methodology made possible the study of the relationship of life change magnitude to the time of illness onset.

3

Magnitude Estimations
of Social Readjustments

Minoru Masuda and Thomas H. Holmes

In previous studies [1–5] it had been established that a cluster of social events requiring change in ongoing life adjustment was significantly correlated with the time of illness onset. It had been adduced from these investigations that this clustering of social or life events achieved etiologic significance as a necessary but not sufficient cause of illness and accounted, in part, for the time of onset of disease.

In one of these reports [3] a method was defined for quantifying the amount of change in life adjustment required by 43 items of life events. The method, derived from psychophysics, consisted of a paper-and-pencil test, the Social Readjustment Rating Questionnaire (SRRQ), containing items to be scaled. One item was used as the module; it had been arbitrarily selected and assigned a numerical value. The subjects were asked to compare each of the items in turn with the module and determine numerically whether the item's required social readjustment was proportionally greater or lesser than that of the module. The arithmetic mean score derived for each item served as the number identifying the magnitude of change in adjustment required by the life event. In 16 comparisons of mean item scorings of groups different in age, sex, marital status, education, social class, generation American, religion, and race, the range of correlation coefficients (Pearson's r) was 0.820 to 0.975, the average r being 0.945. Spearman's rank order correlation coefficients were almost identical.

It is the purpose of this report to present the results of further statistical analysis of the data.

This chapter is reprinted with permission from Minoru Masuda and Thomas H. Holmes, "Magnitude Estimations of Social Readjustments," *Journal of Psychosomatic Research* 11 (1967):219–25. Copyright 1967 by Pergamon Press, Ltd.

METHODS

The Social Readjustment Rating Questionnaire was completed by 394 subjects. The details of the method and characteristics of this sample of convenience have been presented elsewhere [3]. Three measures of central tendency were derived for each item: the arithmetic mean; the geometric mean, which was computed as the mean log of the scores [6]; and the median, which was calculated using Edward's correction for ties in the same set [7].

RESULTS

The data compiled from the SRRQ are shown in Table 3.1. The following observations were made:

1. The arithmetic mean scores were consistently higher than the scores of the other two measures of central tendency.
2. Above the score of 120, the geometric mean was generally lower than the median; below this score, the median was consistently lower than the geometric mean.
3. The geometric means and the medians were closer in magnitude to each other than to the arithmetic mean.
4. There was a close parallel in the ranking order of all three measures of central tendencies. Kendall's coefficient of concordance (W) [8] for the rank ordering of the three kinds of central measures was 0.992. This parallel of rank ordering and item scoring of the geometric mean and the arithmetic mean is shown in Figure 3.1. The irregularities in the downward descent of the curve for arithmetic means indicate deviations from the geometric mean ordering.

The distribution of the arithmetic mean scores of three life events is shown in the upper part of Figure 3.2. These were item 40, vacation; item 2, troubles with boss; and item 4, death of spouse. The skewness of the frequency distribution is readily apparent. The lower part of Fig. 3.2 shows the distribution of the same items plotted on a logarithmic scale. A normalization of the score distributions is seen whether the range of scores is 500, 1,000, or 10,000. The geometric progression of scores indicates that the geometric mean is a more accurate measure of the central tendency than is the arithmetic mean.

The general principle that variability in scores is a function of the magnitude of scores (Ekman's Law) [9] is clearly demonstrated in Figure 3.3. The linear relationship between the standard errors of the geometric mean and the geometric mean score is manifest.

In Figure 3.4, the ratio of the geometric mean scores and the arithmetic mean scores of the same item is plotted as a function of the magnitude of the arithmetic mean item score. These ratios remain relatively constant through the greater part of the range, deviating only at the lower end.

Table 3.1
Item Scores and Rankings on the Geometric Mean, the Median,
and the Arithmetic Mean

Item*	Item scores					Item rankings		
	Geo- metric mean	(S.E.)	Median	Arith- metic mean	(S.E.)	Geo- metric mean	Median	Arith- metic mean
Death of a spouse	771	(24)	805	1020	(83)	1	1	1
Divorce	593	(19)	602	727	(53)	2	2	2
Marital separation	516	(17)	517	652	(49)	3	4	3
Marriage†	500		500	500		4	5	7
Death of a close family member	469	(16)	489	626	(52)	5	6	5
Jail detention	439	(21)	586	631	(49)	6	3	4
Major personal injury or illness	416	(13)	448	528	(44)	7	7	6
Fired from work	378	(14)	397	466	(19)	8	11	8
Marital reconciliation	366	(13)	404	451	(27)	9	9	10
Retirement from work	361	(14)	412	455	(27)	10	8	9
Gain of new family member	337	(11)	350	391	(28)	11	14.5	14
Change in health of family member	335	(11)	350	438	(37)	12	14.5	11
Sexual difficulties	316	(13)	399	392	(11)	13	10	13
Business readjustment	308	(12)	352	385	(15)	14.5	13	15
Change in financial state	308	(10)	306	377	(16)	14.5	16	16
Change to different work	287	(10)	304	363	(26)	16	17	18
Change in arguments with spouse	286	(9)	297	345	(12)	17	18.5	19
Pregnancy	284	(15)	358	403	(29)	18	12	12
Death of close friend	270	(11)	297	369	(26)	19	18.5	17
Change in work responsibility	243	(8)	246	288	(8)	20	21.5	22
Foreclosure of mortgage	231	(11)	288	304	(10)	21	20	21
Son or daughter leaving home	219	(9)	230	286	(12)	22	23	23.5
Trouble with in-laws	213	(10)	211	286	(10)	23	24	23.5
Mortgage/loan > $10,000	210	(10)	199	311	(28)	24	26	20
Wife start or end work	204	(8)	209	257	(10)	25	25	27

cont'd

Table 3.1, continued

Item*	Item scores					Item rankings		
	Geo-metric mean	(S.E.)	Median	Arith-metic mean	(S.E.)	Geo-metric mean	Median	Arith-metic mean
Outstanding personal achievement	192	(9)	195	277	(16)	26	30	25
Begin or end formal schooling	191	(9)	246	259	(9)	27	21.5	26
Change in living conditions	186	(8)	198	246	(8)	28	27.5	28
Trouble with boss	178	(7)	196	227	(8)	29	29	30
Revision of personal habits	149	(8)	119	239	(16)	30	32	29
Change in work conditions	148	(7)	188	202	(7)	31	31	31
Change in residence	140	(7)	109	201	(8)	32	33.5	32
Change in schools	135	(7)	198	196	(8)	33	27.5	33
Change in recreation	127	(5)	109	189	(26)	34	33.5	34
Change in social activities	125	(6)	105	177	(7)	35	35	36
Change in church activities	112	(7)	102	188	(9)	36	36	35
Mortgage/loan < $10,000	105	(6)	97	173	(9)	37.5	37	37
Change in sleeping habits	105	(5)	96	156	(7)	37.5	38	38
Change in family get-togethers	103	(6)	95	151	(7)	39	39	39
Change in eating habits	98	(5)	93	147	(6)	40	40	40
Vacation	74	(5)	60	130	(6)	41	41	41
Christmas	59	(4)	50	119	(7)	42	42	42
Minor violations of law	54	(4)	48	106	(6)	43	43	43

* According to rank on geometric mean
† Module

DISCUSSION

The analysis of the responses to the SRRQ indicated that the U.S. population was homogeneous both as to item scoring and rank ordering of items. This was true regardless of the measure of central tendency used. However, it was also apparent that these three measures showed some magnitude differences in item scoring. For the construction of an instrument that attempts to establish a valid scale of magnitude estimations of the significance of life events, it seems cogent to consider the relative merits of these three measures of central tendency.

The statistical difficulties and limitations that are inherent in the evaluation of the quantitative aspects of psychological events have been discussed by Stevens [10] and Siegel [8]. They are in agreement that the use of parametric methods in the analysis of nonparametric, noninterval data is undesirable. In the present study, the fact that a noninterval scale was being used and the finding of the skewed distribution of arithmetic mean scores indicated the need to consider the use of the median and the geometric mean.

The median makes no assumption about the distribution, discounts extreme scores, and has been used and recommended as an appropriate statistic when in doubt [9]. Its limitation lies in the fact that it is a less powerful statistical tool [11]

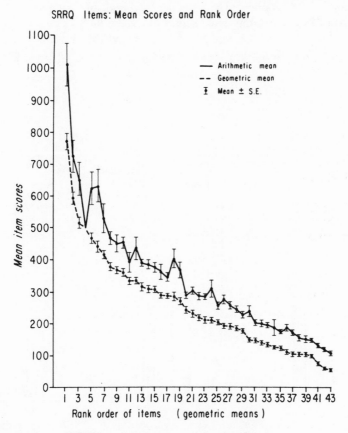

Figure 3.1   SRRQ items: mean scores and rank order.

because of the loss of information. In addition, the median is less amenable to statistical procedures [6].

The geometric mean also has the advantage of discounting the extreme score; but unlike the median, it takes into account the distribution of scores and hence does not lose its power. In addition, it is a more statistically useful tool. This study has indicated that the geometric mean was the statistic of choice as a measure of central tendency in view of the logarithmic distribution of the subjective magnitude estimation scores.

Stevens and Galanter [12] in a series of experiments explored the validity of Fechner's Law regarding the logarithmic nature of psychophysical evaluations. These experiments demonstrated that the subjective magnitude estimation was related to some power function of the physical stimulus. This process for quantifying human perception, developed in psychophysics, has recently been carried further to study opinions and attitudes. Sellin and Wolfgang [13] constructed a scale, using the geometric mean, of the seriousness of juvenile delinquent acts. The validity of their conclusions was based on the logarithmic relation between the category scales of seriousness and the magnitude of scale scores, the power function of money relating scale scores to money thefts, and the logarithmic relationships between the delinquency scores and the maximum penalties as provided by law. Rashevsky [14] analyzed the data from the Hollingshead and

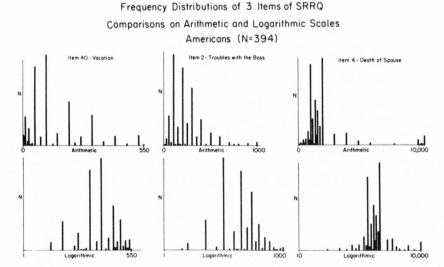

Frequency Distributions of 3 Items of SRRQ
Comparisons on Arithmetic and Logarithmic Scales
Americans (N=394)

Figure 3.2   Distribution of scores on three items of the SRRQ: comparisons on arithmetic and logarithmic scales.

Redlich study on social class and mental illness and found a logarithmic relationship between social position and aspiration. The recent comprehensive review by
Stevens [9] concluded that human judgment of a social consensus was effectively
quantifiable and recommended the use of the geometric mean as the best average
statistic.

The present study has also demonstrated an extension of Ekman's Law from
the field of metric stimuli psychophysics into the nonmetric field of psychosocial
phenomena. The fact that judgmental variability is proportional in a linear
fashion to the magnitude estimation can be regarded as an adjunct to the general
scientific law of relative variability. The extension of this law into the area
encompassed by this investigation adds further support to the validity of subjective magnitude estimations [9].

It is apparent from the rapidly mounting evidence that, in subjective magnitude
estimations of psychosocial events, one is dealing with a ratio scale. This gener-
alization states that individuals can and do make valid psychological magnitude
estimations which can be treated with parametric methods of statistical analyses.
This is supported by the fact that the correlation coefficients of item scoring
between different subgroups in the present study were found to be almost
identical whether calculated as parametric Pearson's r on mean item scoring or
nonparametric Spearman's rank order, r_s. Also, the arithmetic mean had been

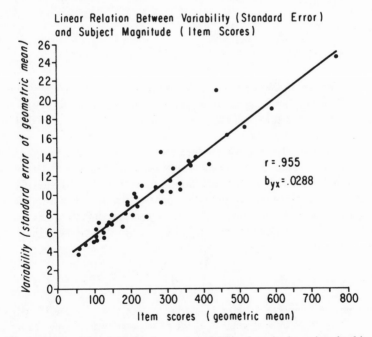

Figure 3.3   Linear relation between variability (standard error) and subjective magnitude (item scores).

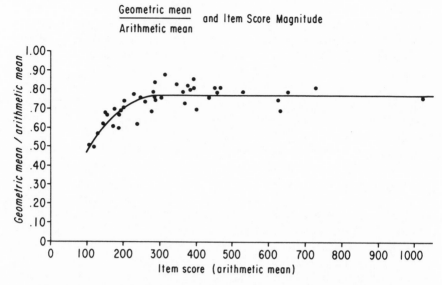

Figure 3.4   Relationship of ratio of the geometric to arithmetic means and the item score magnitude.

used with success in the previous studies associating onset of illness with life crises [4;5]. Furthermore, application of the geometric mean scores to disease onset data did not improve on the association of illness onset provided by the arithmetic mean scores.

The evidence for the pragmatic value of the arithmetic mean was obtained in spite of the demonstrated appropriateness of the geometric mean. The probable explanation for this is that, in either case, a ratio scale is generated. This was evidenced by the constancy of the ratio of these two measures throughout the major part of the scale, deviating only at the lower end. It is this preservation of ratio scaling that enhances the validity of subjective magnitude estimations of social readjustments.

SUMMARY

1. An American sample ($N = 394$) responded to the Social Readjustment Rating Questionnaire by rating the magnitude of 42 life events as compared to a given score of a modular item.

2. The rankings and the item scores of the arithmetic mean, the geometric mean, and the

median were in close parallel although the scores differed considerably in magnitude.

3. The skewed frequency distribution of raw magnitude scores was normalized by logarithmic plotting, indicating the propriety of the geometric mean as the measure of central tendency.

4. A linear relationship between the variability of item scores and the magnitude of item scores was demonstrated.

5. Preservation of the ratio between geometric-mean and arithmetic-mean scores was found.

REFERENCES

1. Hawkins, N.G., R. Davies, and T. H. Holmes. "Evidence of Psychosocial Factors in the Development of Pulmonary Tuberculosis." *American Review of Tuberculosis and Pulmonary Diseases* 75 (1957):768–80. Reprinted in this volume, Chapter 11.

2. Rahe, R. H., M. Meyer, M. Smith, G. Kjaer, and T. H. Holmes. "Social Stress and Illness Onset." *Journal of Psychosomatic Research* 8 (1964):35–44. Reprinted in this volume, Chapter 12.

3. Holmes, T.H., and R. H. Rahe. "The Social Readjustment Rating Scale." *Journal of Psychosomatic Research* 11 (1967):213–18. Reprinted in this volume, Chapter 2.

4. Rahe, R. H., and T. H. Holmes. "Life Crisis and Disease Onset. I. Qualitative and Quantitative Definition of the Life Crisis and Its Association with Health Change." First published as pt. 2 of R. H. Rahe, "Life Crisis and Health Change." In *Psychotropic Drug Response: Advances in Prediction,* edited by P. R. A. May and J. R. Wittenborn, pp. 92–125. Springfield, Ill.: Charles C Thomas, 1969. Reprinted in this volume, Chapter 13.

5. Rahe, R. H., and T. H. Holmes. "Life Crisis and Disease Onset. II. A Prospective Study of Life Crises and Health Changes." First published as pt. 3 of R. H. Rahe, "Life Crisis and Health Change." In *Psychotropic Drug Response: Advances in Prediction,* edited by P. R. A. May and J. R. Wittenborn, pp. 92–125. Springfield, Ill.: Charles C Thomas, 1969. Reprinted in this volume, Chapter 14.

6. Arkin, H., and R. R. Colton. *Statistical Methods.* 4th ed. New York: Barnes and Noble, 1959, p. 26.

7. Edwards, A. E. *Statistical Analysis.* New York: Rinehart, 1958, p. 44.

8. Siegel, S. *Nonparametric Statistics for the Behavioral Sciences.* New York: McGraw-Hill, 1956.

9. Stevens, S. S. "A Metric for the Social Consensus." *Science* 151 (1966):530–41.

10. Stevens, S. S. "Mathematics, Measurements and Psychophysics." In *Handbook of Experimental Psychology,* edited by S. S. Stevens, pp. 1–49. New York: John Wiley, 1951.

11. Walker, H. M., and J. Lev. *Statistical Inference.* New York: Henry Holt, 1953.

12. Stevens, S. S., and E. H. Galanter. "Ratio Scales and Category Scales for a Dozen Perceptual Continua." *Journal of Experimental Psychology* 54 (1957):377–411.

13. Sellin, T., and M. E. Wolfgang. *The Measurement of Delinquency.* New York: John Wiley, 1964.

14. Rashevsky, N. *Some Medical Aspects of Mathematical Biology.* Springfield, Ill.: Charles C Thomas, 1964.

4

Scaling of Life Change: Comparison of Direct and Indirect Methods

Libby O. Ruch and Thomas H. Holmes

Previous studies [1–7] have shown that a cluster of life events requiring change in the individual's accustomed way of life are significantly associated with the onset of disease. Holmes and Rahe [3] have developed a method for the quantification of the amount of change associated with these life events. Subjects were asked to judge the amount of social readjustment necessitated by 43 life events taken from medical case histories, reflecting changes in such areas as family structure, occupation, income, education, health, and peer relationships. One of the life event items was arbitrarily valued at 500, and the subjects rated the remaining items numerically in proportion to this value. The life events were then arranged in rank order of magnitude. A high agreement was found among subjects on the rating of the relative severity of the social readjustment necessitated by the life events. This finding was supported by follow-up studies with various national populations [8–12], which revealed an essential agreement with the U.S. sample despite some cultural differences.

The first purpose of the present study is to replicate the study of Holmes and Rahe [3], using a different sample to test further the degree of value consensus concerning the amount of change involved in the various life events [13]. A younger sample was selected to determine if age influenced how individuals perceive the magnitude of change associated with life events. It was assumed that, as late adolescents have usually not actually experienced many of these life changes, their evaluations of them may be different. Moreover, sociological literature [14–16] suggests that adolescents are not only different from adults in

This chapter is reprinted with permission from Libby O. Ruch and Thomas H. Holmes, "Scaling of Life Change: Comparison of Direct and Indirect Methods," *Journal of Psychosomatic Research* 15 (1971):221–27. Copyright 1971 by Pergamon Press, Ltd.

being relatively inexperienced but also that they participate in a distinct subculture with its own norms and values. In addition, the adolescent world has its particular challenges, anxieties, and opportunities. If the late adolescent group scales the life events differently from the adult group, then a pervasive value consensus can be questioned; if the items are scaled similarly by both samples, then weight is added to the conclusions drawn by Holmes and Rahe.

The second purpose of this study is the comparison of two scaling methods—magnitude estimation and paired comparisons—used to measure the perceived amount of change associated with the social phenomena [13]. The method of magnitude estimation used by Holmes and Rahe is a relatively new scaling device in the field of sociology and so was supplemented by Thurstone's method of paired comparisons [17], which has different theoretical assumptions and has been widely applied in sociological research. In paired comparisons, each stimulus is paired and compared with every other stimulus so that each stimulus functions as a standard. Thus, subjects are asked to decide whether marriage or divorce involves the greater amount of life change. With the magnitude estimation method, one stimulus is arbitrarily given a numerical value and the subjects rate the other events numerically in proportion to this value. For example, if the amount of life change associated with marriage is set at 500, the subject is asked to compare divorce with marriage and give divorce a proportional number. A previous experiment by Stevens [18] found that the direct (magnitude estimation) and indirect (paired comparisons) measurement devices generated different results when used to scale identical stimuli, and, furthermore, that the resultant scales were mathematically related regardless of the physical variable scaled: The Thurstonian paired comparisons scale was a logarithmic function of the Stevens magnitude estimation scale.

In summary, the purposes of this replication are (1) to compare the adolescent sample with the adult sample of Holmes and Rahe, and (2) to compare the scaling methods of magnitude estimation and paired comparisons.

METHODS AND PROCEDURES

The Subjects

Table 4.1 shows the distribution of the total adult and adolescent samples with respect to age, education, class, ethnicity, generation American, and religion. The sample of 394 adult individuals used by Holmes and Rahe [3] was a sample of convenience. The late adolescent sample of 211 used in this study was selected to test the hypothesis of a uniform value consensus and so differs from the Holmes and Rahe sample in respect to age: 52 percent of the adult sample were between 21 and 30 years old, and 48 percent were 30 years old or over. Although slightly more than half of the adult sample was under 30, the youngest were medical students in their middle twenties. The adolescent sample was composed of college students who were all under 30, with a mean age of 18 years.

While the age differences were of primary concern in this study, the adolescent group also differed from the adult group in respect to ethnicity and religion due to the greater proportion of Asian Americans in the adolescent sample. However, as the scaling of life events by adults in the United States and Japan [8] was not significantly affected by ethnicity and religion, it is assumed that these variables did not affect the results of this study.

The Scaling Methods

Magnitude Estimation

The Social Readjustment Rating Questionnaire (SRRQ) was administered to the late adolescent group. The instructions and items have been previously described [3]. Each respondent gave a number to each item (life event), expressing the amount of life change involved. The total sum for the item was calculated, and the mean number divided by 10 gave a scale score for that item, thus generating a scale of the life events in terms of the intensity and duration of social readjustment.

Paired Comparisons

With this method, each item was paired with every other one, one member of the pair was judged more severe than the other. The original 43 life events were reduced to 11 representative items to make the computation less unwieldly and were randomized to reduce rater fatigue. The 11 items made 55 pairs. Subjects were asked to compare and underline the member of each pair judged more serious for the average person. In computing the paired comparison scale scores, the Thurstone method of paired comparisons (Case V) was used [19]. First a frequency table was calculated showing the number of times each item was chosen as more serious over every other item, followed by a proportion matrix specifying in what proportion the item was selected. Then the proportions were translated into a normal deviate matrix, and the scale scores were derived from computing the difference between the means of the normal deviates.

RESULTS

Comparison of Adolescent and Adult Samples

Table 4.2 compares the item scale scores (arithmetic means) and their rankings for the adult and adolescent groups. The findings indicate a high agreement between the adult and adolescent samples concerning the amount of social readjustment involved in the 43 life events. The Spearman's rank order correlation coefficient (r_s) between the adult and adolescent groups is very high (0.97). The adolescent judges place about 25 percent of the 43 items in exactly the same position as the adults and 80 percent of the items within three places of their original position. The three items that are ranked most differently by the two

Table 4.1

Distribution of Adult and Adolescent Samples by Age, Education, Class, Ethnic Affiliation, Generation American, and Religion

		Adult	Adolescent
Age	Under 30	206	211
	30–60	137	0
	Over 60	51	0
Education	Below college level	182	0
	College level or more	212	211
Class	Middle class	323	158
	Lower class	71	57
Ethnic affiliation	Caucasian	363	50
	Oriental	12	136
	Negro	19	0
	Others	0	25
Generation American	First	19	19
	Second	69	112
	Third or more	306	70
Religion	Protestant	241	71
	Catholic	42	32
	Buddhist	12	30
	Jewish	19	1
	Others	33	20
	Agnostic, atheist, or none	47	55

samples are sexual difficulties, mortgages or loans of less than $10,000, and revision of personal habits. The adolescent sample regarded sexual difficulties and mortgages as involving more change than did the adult group whereas they gave less weight to the revision of personal habits.

Comparison of Magnitude Estimation and Paired Comparisons Methods

Table 4.3 allows comparison of the rank order of the items and the scale scores for the adolescent group generated by the two different scaling methods (magnitude estimation and paired comparisons) and also comparison of the rank order of the items and the scale scores for the adolescent and the adult groups by magnitude estimation. Comparison of the direct (magnitude estimation) and indirect (paired comparisons) scale scores shows that the two measures yield quite similar results in the adolescent group. The Spearman's rank order correlation coefficient (r_s) between the scale scores is positive and very high (0.93). By

Table 4.2
Ranking and Item Scale Scores of the Total Adult and Adolescent Sample on the SRRQ

Life Event	Adult Group		Adolescent Group	
	Rank of arithmetic mean value	Arithmetic mean value	Rank of arithmetic mean value	Arithmetic mean value
Death of spouse	1	100	1	69
Divorce	2	73	2	60
Marital separation	3	65	3	55
Jail term	4	63	8	50
Death of a close family member	5	63	4	54
Major personal injury or illness	6	53	6	50
Marriage	7	50	9	50
Fired from work	8	47	7	50
Marital reconciliation	9	45	10	47
Retirement	10	45	11	46
Major change in health of family member	11	44	16	44
Pregnancy	12	40	13	45
Sex difficulties	13	39	5	51
Gain of new family member	14	39	17	43
Business readjustment	15	39	15	44
Change in financial state	16	38	14	44
Death of a close friend	17	37	12	46
Change to a different line of work	18	36	21	38
Change in number of arguments with spouse	19	35	19	41
Mortgage over $10,000	20	31	18	41
Foreclosure of mortgage or loan	21	30	23	36

both scaling methods, death of spouse is considered to produce the most change and minor law violations the least. On the other hand, marriage is ranked lower than divorce and death of close family member with the magnitude estimation method, whereas it is the second highest ranked with the paired comparisons method. The next three items—change in financial state, pregnancy, and retirement—in the paired comparisons scale are ranked in reverse order on the magnitude estimation scale. Change in social activities is ranked higher than begin or end school in the paired comparisons scale whereas the reverse is true in the magnitude estimation scale. Thus the order of the paired comparisons varies from the rank order of the magnitude estimations in both the adult and adolescent groups, and the rank order of the magnitude estimations of the 11 life events is identical by both the adolescent and the adult groups.

Table 4.2, continued

Life Event	Adult Group		Adolescent Group	
	Rank of arithmetic mean value	Arithmetic mean value	Rank of arithmetic mean value	Arithmetic mean value
Change in responsibilities at work	22	29	20	38
Son or daughter leaving home	23	29	25	34
Trouble with in-laws	24	29	22	36
Outstanding personal achievement	25	28	28	31
Wife begins or stops work	26	26	27	32
Begin or end school	27	26	26	34
Change in living conditions	28	25	24	35
Revision of personal habits	29	24	35	26
Trouble with boss	30	23	33	26
Change in work hours or conditions	31	20	29	30
Change in residence	32	20	30	28
Change in schools	33	20	34	26
Change in recreation	34	19	36	26
Change in church activities	35	19	38	21
Change in social activities	36	18	32	28
Mortgage or loan less than $10,000	37	17	31	28
Change in sleeping habits	38	16	41	18
Change in number of family get-togethers	39	15	37	22
Change in eating habits	40	15	40	18
Vacation	41	13	39	19
Christmas	42	12	42	16
Minor violations of the law	43	11	43	12

DISCUSSION

There is a high agreement between the adult and the adolescent samples on the seriousness of life events. The rank order correlation between the adult and adolescent groups of 0.97 indicates a high consensus and supports the hypothesis of a general value agreement concerning the amount of change involved in the life events. Some of the life events are evaluated differently by the adolescents than by the adults, which suggests subcultural differences as well as a common value system. The three most variant items are revision of personal habits, taking on a mortgage of less than $10,000, and sexual difficulties. Evaluation of an event may depend in part on the value placed on its seriousness and also on the individual's amount of experience or familiarity with the event. Thus there are two pairs of dichotomies possible: An event can be ranked as high or low depending on the presence or absence of experience. It may be that the adolescent group tends to rank revision of personal habits lower than the adult group because they are accustomed to this type of change from their educational experience whereas they rank taking out a mortgage of less than $10,000 and sexual difficulties higher than the adult sample because the relative lack of experience in these areas produces an overestimation of the social readjustment required. Taking out a mortgage of more than $10,000 was also considered more serious by the adolescent than by the adult sample. On the other hand, it is also possible that adolescents would tend to rate sexual difficulties more highly as sexual identification is one of the crucial tasks of the adolescent years and so much interest and value are placed on sexual adjustment, regardless of the particular individual's experience.

In summary, comparison of the scale scores of the items for the two groups suggests a broad value consensus concerning the estimation of change required by these life events with some variation due to subcultural norms and values. These findings support the hypothesis of a general value agreement on the significance of life events.

Although Stevens' experiment [18] found that direct and indirect scaling

Table 4.3

Ranking and Scale Scores of the Total Adolescent Group Using Magnitude Estimation and Paired Comparisons Scaling Methods and Ranking and Scale Scores of the Total Adult Group Using the Magnitude Estimation Method

| | Adolescent | | | | Adult | |
| | Paired Comparison | | Magnitude Estimation | | Magnitude Estimation | |
Item	Rank order	Scale value	Rank order	Scale value	Rank order	Scale value
Death of spouse	1	2.1685	1	69	1	100
Marriage	2	1.7725	4	50	4	50
Divorce	3	1.5954	2	60	2	73
Death of close family member	4	1.4894	3	54	3	63
Change in financial state	5	1.1259	7	44	7	38
Pregnancy	6	1.0730	6	45	6	40
Retirement	7	1.9860	5	46	5	45
Trouble with in-laws	8	0.9075	8	36	8	29
Change in social activities	9	0.4789	10	28	10	36
Begin or end school	10	0.3397	9	34	9	26
Minor law violations	11	0.0000	11	12	11	11

methods yielded consistently different results, in this study the magnitude estimation and paired comparisons scaling methods yielded similar results in the adolescent group. The Spearman's rank order correlation coefficient (r_s) of 0.93 indicates a strong positive relationship between the results of the magnitude estimation and the paired comparisons methods. Galanter and Messick [20] found that the relationship between the magnitude estimation and the paired comparisons scales was nonlinear, and so they used an antilog transformation to change Thurstone's values to correct for nonlinearity. The paired comparisons and the magnitude estimations in this study correlate almost as highly $(r_s = 0.93)$ as do the magnitude estimations by the different groups $(r_s = 1.00$ for 11 items; and $r_s = 0.97$ for 43 items), and the relationship between the two scales is virtually linear when plotted (see Figure 4.1.). If the two methods had yielded very different results, one would question the possibility of scaling life events and the

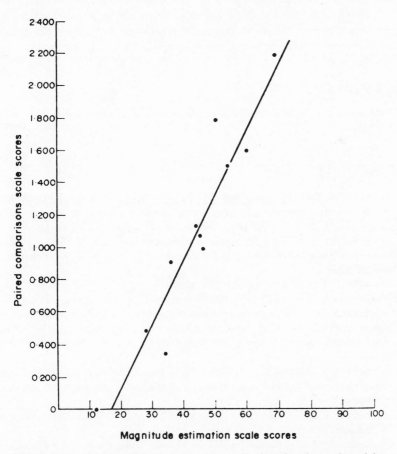

Figure 4.1   Linear relation between the magnitude estimation scale and the paired comparisons scale.

theoretical assumptions underlying the two methods. However, in this study this was not the case. The two methods scaled the life events so similarly that the relationship between the two scales appears linear. These results indicate that both the magnitude estimation and the paired comparisons methods are useful devices for scaling the social readjustment associated with life events. As the magnitude estimation method involves less statistical computation and can scale a relatively larger number of stimuli than the paired comparisons method, it is suggested that this direct scaling method developed in psychophysical research can be of considerable usefulness in sociological research.

SUMMARY

The data from an adolescent sample compared with an adult sample supported the hypothesis of a general value consensus about the seriousness of life events. The analysis also revealed that the direct (magnitude estimation) and indirect (paired comparisons) scaling methods, which are based on different assumptions, produced similar scales of live events when applied to the same sample.

ACKNOWLEDGMENT

The authors are indebted to Minoru Masuda, Ph.D., for his helpful advice and criticism.

REFERENCES

1. Hawkins, N. G., R. Davies, and T. H. Holmes. "Evidence of Psychosocial Factors in the Development of Pulmonary Tuberculosis." *American Review of Tuberculosis and Pulmonary Diseases* 75 (1957):768–80. Reprinted in this volume, Chapter 11.

2. Rahe, R. H., M. Meyer, M. Smith, G. Kjaer, and T. H. Holmes. "Social Stress and Illness Onset." *Journal of Psychosomatic Research* 8 (1964):35–44. Reprinted in this volume, Chapter 12.

3. Holmes, T. H., and R. H. Rahe. "The Social Readjustment Rating Scale." *Journal of Psychosomatic Research* 11 (1967):213–18. Reprinted in this volume, Chapter 2.

4. Rahe, R. H. "Life Crisis and Health Change." In *Psychotropic Drug Response: Advances in Prediction,* edited by P. R. A. May and J. R. Wittenborn, pp. 92–125. Springfield, Ill.: Charles C Thomas, 1969. Parts 2 and 3 reprinted in this volume, Chapters 13 and 14.

5. Holmes, T. S., and T. H. Holmes. "Short-term Intrusions into the Life Style Routine." *Journal of Psychosomatic Research* 14 (1970):121–32. Reprinted in this volume, Chapter 15.

6. Holmes, T. S. "Adaptive Behavior and Health Change." Medical thesis, University of Washington, 1970.

7. Wyler, A. R., M. Masuda, and T. H. Holmes. "Magnitude of Life Events and Seriousness of Illness." *Psychosomatic Medicine* 33 (1971):115–22. Reprinted in this volume, Chapter 16.

8. Masuda, M., and T. H. Holmes. "The Social Readjustment Rating Scale: A Cross-cultural Study of Japanese and Americans." *Journal of Psychosomatic Research* 11 (1967):227–37. Reprinted in this volume, Chapter 5.

9. Celdrán, H. H. "The Cross-cultural Consistency of Two Social Consensus Scales: The Seriousness of Illness Rating Scale and the Social Readjustment Rating Scale in Spain." Medical thesis, University of Washington, 1970.

10. Harmon, D. K., M. Masuda, and T. H. Holmes. "The Social Readjustment Rating Scale: A Cross-cultural Study of Western Europeans and Americans." *Journal of Psychosomatic Research* 14 (1970):391–400.

11. Komaroff, A. L., M. Masuda, and T. H. Holmes. "The Social Readjustment Rating Scale: A Comparative Study of Negro, Mexican, and White Americans." *Journal of Psychosomatic Research* 12 (1968):121–28. Reprinted in this volume, Chapter 6.

12. Rahe, R. H. "Multi-cultural Correlations of Life Change Scaling: America, Japan, Denmark and Sweden." *Journal of Psychosomatic Research* 13 (1969):191–95.

13. Ruch, L. O. "Scaling of Life Stress with Direct and Indirect Scaling Methods." Master's thesis, University of Hawaii, 1967.

14. Keniston, K. "Social Change and Youth in America." In *The Challenge of Youth,* edited by E. H. Erikson, pp. 161–87. New York: Doubleday, 1963.

15. E. H. Erikson, ed. *The Challenge of Youth.* New York: Doubleday, 1963.

16. Parsons, T. "Youth in the Context of American Society." In *The Challenge of Youth,* edited by E. H. Erikson, pp. 93–119. New York: Doubleday, 1963.

17. Torgerson, W. S. *Theory and Methods of Scaling.* New York: Wiley, 1958.

18. Stevens, S. S. "A Metric for the Social Consensus: Methods of Sensory Psychophysics Have Been Used to Gauge the Intensity of Opinions and Attitudes." *Science* 151 (1966):530–41.

19. Thurstone, L. L. *The Measurement of Values.* Chicago: University of Chicago Press, 1959.

20. Galanter, E., and S. Messick. "The Relation between Category and Magnitude Scales of Loudness." *Psychological Review* 68 (1961):363–72.

5

The Social Readjustment
Rating Scale: A Cross-Cultural
Study of Japanese and Americans

Minoru Masuda and Thomas H. Holmes

Beginning in this laboratory in 1949, a systematic study of the quality and quantity of life events empirically observed to cluster at the time of disease onset has been carried out in more than 5000 patients. This experience has generated 43 unique life event items that are either indicative of the life-style of the individual or of occurrences involving the individual. Evolving mostly from ordinary social and interpersonal transactions, these events pertain to major areas of dynamic significance in the social structure of the American way of life. These areas include family constellation, marriage, occupation, economics, residence, group and peer relationship, education, religion, recreation, and health. Some events are socially undesirable; others are socially desirable and are consonant with the American values of achievement, success, materialism, practicality, efficiency, future orientation, conformism, and self-reliance.

These life events have one theme in common: The occurrence of each usually evokes or is associated with some adaptive or coping behavior on the part of the involved individual. The emphasis is on change from the existing steady state, and not on psychological meaning, emotion, or social desirability.

In a recent report [1] a method was defined for quantifying the amount of change in life adjustment required by these 43 categories of life events. The method, derived from psychophysics, consisted of a self-administered instrument, the Social Readjustment Rating Questionnaire (SRRQ), containing the items to be scaled. One item was used as the module; it was arbitrarily selected and assigned a numerical value. The subjects were asked to compare each of the

This chapter is reprinted with permission from Minoru Masuda and Thomas H. Holmes, "The Social Readjustment Rating Scale: A Cross-cultural Study of Japanese and Americans," *Journal of Psychosomatic Research* 11 (1967):227–37. Copyright 1967 by Pergamon Press, Ltd.

items in turn with the module and its given magnitude and to assign it a numerical value proportionate to that of the module. The arithmetic mean score derived for each item was the magnitude of change in adjustment required by the life event.

As expected, because of cultural homogeneity, this method yielded high consensus on the magnitude and rank order of the life events among white, middle-class, third-generation, Protestant Americans. Because of obvious sociocultural differences from this middle class, it was anticipated that minority status subjects such as Asian Americans, blacks, lower social class members, and first-generation (foreign-born) Americans would scale the items with significant differences. It was, therefore, surprising to find that the correlation between blacks and whites was 0.82; between Asian Americans and whites, 0.94; and between first- and third-generation Americans, 0.92. The high degree of consensus indicated a universal agreement on the part of the subjects about the significance of the life events under study—transcending differences in age, sex, marital status, education, social class, generation American, religion, and race.

The findings suggested the desirability of extending the investigation further into the cross-cultural area. Since agreement was high despite the obvious cultural differences among populations within the U.S. sample, it seemed reasonable to expect consensus to exist between subjects from other contemporary societies and U.S. subjects. This report contains the data adduced from a comparative study of Japanese and U.S. middle-class subjects, using the recently developed social readjustment rating method.

METHODS AND PROCEDURES

The Social Readjustment Rating Questionnaire (SRRQ) was administered to the U.S. and Japanese samples. The instructions and order of items has been previously described [1]. For the Japanese study a translation from the original SRRQ was done by a Tokyo-born graduate student recently enrolled in the University of Washington. The translation was modified for idiomatic clarity by a native Japanese businessman currently based in the United States. It was found necessary to change only items 33 and 34. These items are concerned with mortgage or loans greater or less than $10,000. Rather than the exact yen equivalent of $10,000 (3,600,000 yen), the amount of 1,500,000–2,000,000 yen ($4,167–$5,555) was judged to be a more appropriate figure.

The Japanese Sample

The Japanese colleagues* who distributed the questionnaires in Hiroshima and Sendai were instructed to obtain a sample of approximately 100 subjects of equal

---

*Dr. Hiroshi Irisawa, professor, Department of Physiology, Hiroshima University, Hiroshima, Japan; and Dr. Toshiyuki Yamamoto, professor, Department of Anatomy, Tohoku University, Sendai, Japan.

Table 5.1
The Japanese Sample

Subgroup	No.	Age mean years and (range)	Education mean years and (range)	Religion*		Marital status†	
Hiroshima males	44	39 (25–58)	18 (11–24)	B C N	35 1 8	M S	36 8
Hiroshima females	11	34 (22–50)	14 (10–18)	B C N	9 1 1	M S	5 6
Subtotal	55						
Sendai males	28	40 (25–56)	16 (9–21)	B C N	17 2 9	M S	28 0
Sendai females	29	35 (23–44)	14 (10–18)	B C N	15 2 12	M S	28 1
Subtotal	57						

* B = Buddhist
  C = Christian
  N = No religious preference
† M = Married
  S = Single

sex distribution from their own circle of friends and associates. Table 5.1 summarizes the pertinent information on the Japanese samples. The Sendai sample was equally distributed as to sex, but the Hiroshima males outnumbered the females. There were no differences in mean age or education, and the religious backgrounds were alike except that there was a greater proportion of Sendai females who expressed no religious preference. In the Hiroshima sample 14 individuals were unmarried as compared to the single unmarried individual in the Sendai sample.

The selection of Hiroshima and Sendai was a fortuitous one based on the presence of colleagues at the respective universities. These two cities—one in the southwestern part of the main island of Honshu, and the other on the northeastern coast about 200 miles from Tokyo—are alike in many ways. Hiroshima by the 1960 population census [2] had 431,336 inhabitants while Sendai had 425,752 [3]. Both have national universities, both are on the sea, and both have a nationally famous scenic spot nearby.

However, the 1960 census tabulated certain interesting differences that may be pertinent. Hiroshima was a faster growing city than was Sendai, gaining 19.5 percent in population since 1955, while Sendai gained 11.8 percent. There was also a greater influx of population into Hiroshima from other prefectures and abroad. In 1959, 33,431 people moved into Hiroshima while only 21,074 moved into Sendai. Those going to Hiroshima moved to a city that had a population density of 5,103 people/km^2 as compared to Sendai's density of 1,796 people/km^2. The destruction of Hiroshima in 1945 meant a complete rebuilding and repopulation of the city.

Sendai appears to be a more stable city in terms of migration and residence changes. Sendai in 1930 was considered to be one of the three stable cities in Japan [4]. There is probably less industrialization and more family work establishments in Sendai as judged from labor force statistics.

The U.S. Sample

The U.S. sample obtained in Seattle, Washington, has previously been described [1] and included 394 individuals varying in socioeconomic status, education, religion, and race. This original U.S. sample was screened for subjects having the following characteristics:

1. Middle class
2. Adults 25–59 years of age
3. Education

   Male—college or more

   Female—college or less
4. Second or third generation American
5. Nonblack.

This selective matching, for comparison with the Japanese sample, resulted in a sample of 168 Americans: 101 males and 67 females.

RESULTS

In a previous study [5] on the U.S. sample, the frequency distribution of scores on individual items in the SRRQ had revealed a skewness that tended to be normalized when plotted semilogarithmically. This was also found to be true of the Japanese sample. A representative distribution is shown in Figure 5.1 (item 4, death of spouse). Inasmuch as this skewness indicated a geometric progression and the scores were not true interval scores, it was decided to use the geometric mean as the appropriate measure of the central tendency.

Because of such considerations it was decided to use nonparametric statistical methods [6]. The Kruskal-Wallis one-way analysis of variance determined whether there were any differences between four Japanese subgroups (Hiroshima males, Hiroshima females, Sendai males, and Sendai females) on each of the 42 items of the SRRQ. If a significant difference appeared, then a Mann-Whitney U-test was used to determine which of the groups were different. The comparative rank order of the scale items among the four groups was done using Kendall's coefficient of concordance, W. The geometric mean was computed as the anti-logarithm of the mean of the logs of the scores [7] and the median was calculated using Edwards's corrections for ties in the same set [8].

The relative rank ordering of the 43 items of the SRRQ by the four Japanese subgroups was found to be significantly concordant (Kendall's $W = 0.504$; $p = 0.001$). That is, members of the four groups ranked the items in a similar way. Table 5.2 lists the geometric mean, median, and the ranks of each of the 43 items for the total Japanese sample. The geometric mean was larger than the median with scores above 500 and smaller than the median with scores below 500. The

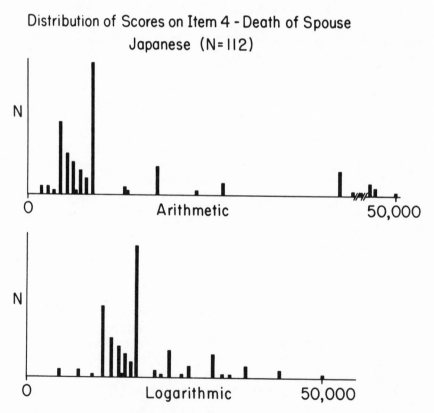

Figure 5.1   Comparison of distribution of scores on item 4 on arithmetic scale and logarithmic scale.

order of the ranking between these two measures of central tendency was almost identical.

Comparison of the Japanese Subgroups

The four Japanese subgroups were quite homogeneous in their response to the SRRQ. Of the 42 item scores that were compared between the four subgroups, there were only seven items that were scored significantly different between groups. The Sendai males were discrepant from all the other three groups in two items: (1) new member to the family, and (2) son or daughter leaving the family. The Sendai males and the Hiroshima males differed from the two female groups by showing greater regard for work adjustments. The Sendai males and females differed from the Hiroshima groups in regarding detention in jail with less concern. The Hiroshima males regarded a death of a friend as being less disrupting than did the Sendai males and females.

Comparison of Japanese and U.S. Samples

In view of the homogeneity of the Japanese sample as reflected in the concordance of the four subgroups in the rankings of the items and the similarity of the item scores, the groups were combined for comparison with the U.S. sample. The latter was also shown to be significantly concordant for the 168 individual rankers on the 42 item scores (Kendall's $W = 0.562$; $p < 0.001$).

Table 5.3 compares the item scores (geometric means) and their rankings for the Japanese and U.S. samples. The Japanese and the Americans ranked the items in a highly concordant manner (Kendall's $W = 0.518$; $p \leq 0.001$). Spearman's rank order correlation coefficient (r_s) between the mean rankings for the Japanese and U.S. sample was also highly significant (0.752).

The 42 item scores of the U.S. and Japanese samples were compared by the Mann-Whitney U-tests supplemented by Student's t-tests using log scores. Table 5.3 also identifies the 17 items scored significantly different by the two groups.

The Japanese regarded detention in jail and minor violations of the law as requiring more change than did the Americans. They showed a higher concern for a mortgage or loans greater or less than \$10,000 while the Americans showed a greater concern for a major change in financial state and retirement from work. The Americans gave greater weight to marital separation, marital reconciliation, and change in number of arguments with spouse, but the Japanese regarded death of a spouse as a grave concern although both samples ranked this item the highest.

DISCUSSION

The samples from Hiroshima and Sendai were almost identical in terms of the rank ordering of items on the SRRQ and in the magnitude of the item scores. This

Table 5.2
Central Tendencies of Item Scores of Total Japanese Sample

Item number* and name	Rank on geometric mean	Geometric mean	Rank on median	Median
4 Death of spouse	1	1079	1	962
3 Detention in jail	2	721	2	684
26 Divorce	3	637	3	522
6 Death of close family member	4	573	5	510
35 Major personal injury or illness	5	542	4	516
1 Marriage	6	500	6	500
22 Marital separation	7	459	7	484
25 Fired from work	8	373	8	422
14 Major change in health of family member	9	327	12	312
15 Sex difficulties	10	311	12	312
39 Retirement from work	11	289	12	312
36 Major business readjustment	12	284	14	304
13 Pregnancy	13.5	274	15	300
27 Change to different line of work	13.5	274	9	319
24 Marital reconciliation	15	272	10	318
10 Death of close friend	16	269	18	291
8 Mortgage loan foreclosure	17	252	16	294
21 Son or daughter leaving home	18	247	17	292
33 Mortgage loan of $10,000 or more	19	225	19	281
16 In-law troubles	20	221	20	262
18 Major change in financial state	21	210	21	222
29 Major change in responsibility at work	22	197	22	213

is a reflection of the narrowness of the selection, with similarities in socioeconomic and educational background. Both samples were drawn from a university population of professional and technical status. It is obvious that any conclusions that can be drawn are tentative in view of the relative restriction in the samplings from the Japanese and U.S. populations.

There was high concordance between the Japanese and the U.S. samples in the manner in which they established a relative order of magnitude to life events. This remarkable consensus about common life events was obtained in spite of the obvious cultural differences—one imbedded in the democratic Western ethic of internalized Christian moral values, and the other in a particularistic, hierarchical system emphasizing family-oriented, externally sanctioned rules of ethical conduct [9].

Anthropologists have long considered the fact of commonalities in the charac-

Table 5.2, continued

Item number* and name	Rank on geometric mean	Geometric mean	Rank on median	Median
19 New member to family	23	181	24	206
12 Outstanding personal achievement	24	166	23	212
30 Wife starting or ceasing work	25	165	25	205
38 Major change in living conditions	26	162	26	194
2 Troubles with boss	27	145	27	192
11 Minor violations of law	28	138	30	165
9 Revision of personal habits	29	135	28	180
34 Mortgage loan of less than $10,000	30	133	33	112
31 Major change in work hours or conditions	31	131	29	172
43 Begin or end formal schooling	32	126	31	152
28 Major change in arguments with spouse	33	118	34	111
42 Change to new school	34	108	32	128
5 Major change in sleeping habits	35	94	36	103
7 Major change in eating habits	36	93	35	104
20 Change in residence	37	91	37.5	101
32 Major change in recreation	38	85	37.5	101
37 Major change in social activities	39	72	39	99
17 Major change in family get-togethers	40	60	40	96
40 Vacation	41	56	41.5	92
23 Major change in church activities	42	46	41.5	92
41 Christmas	43	40	43	52

* Items listed in descending order of geometric mean

teristics of cultures. This universality has been ascribed to the biological nature of the human being—to fundamental physiologic, psychologic, and social needs [10]. From these universal attributes have sprung many cultural invariants pertaining to the relationship of the human being to the habitat, to fellow humans, to the world of symbolic thought, to self, and so forth [11].

Psychological anthropology attempts to focus on how a dynamic culture affects the personality and behavior of its component members. The interactions between the individual striving for self-gratification and the society whose goals and needs are consonant with that of its members result in a gradual mutual modulation that forms the base for prevailing attitudes and values [12]. The present study has demonstrated that U.S. and Japanese attitudes toward certain life events are significantly concordant. Studies cited by Berelson and Steiner

Table 5.3

Comparison of Ranking and Item Scores Derived from the SRRQ between
Japanese (*N* = 112) and U.S. (*N* = 168) Samples

SRRQ item number	Item name*	Americans		Japanese	
		Rank	Geometric mean	Rank	Geometric mean
4	Death of spouse†	1	880	1	1079
26	Divorce	2	630	3	637
22	Marital separation†	3	541	7	459
1	Marriage	4	500	6	500
6	Death of close family member	5	483	4	573
3	Detention in jail‡	6	474	2	721
35	Major personal injury or illness‡	7	426	5	542
39	Retirement from work§	8	401	11	289
25	Being fired from work	9	384	8	373
24	Marital reconciliation†	10	362	15	272
15	Sexual difficulties	11	326	10	311
14	Major change in health of family	12	325	9	327
19	Addition of new family member§	13	311	23	181
36	Major business readjustment	14	305	12	284
18	Major change in financial state‡	15	288	21	210
28	Major change in arguments with spouse§	16	281	33	118
10	Death of close friend	17	278	16	269
27	Changing to different line of work	18	276	13.5	274
13	Pregnancy	19	273	13.5	274
8	Mortgage foreclosure	20	248	19	225
29	Major change in work responsibilities	21	228	22	197
21	Son or daughter leaving home†	22	204	18	247
16	In-law troubles	23	195	20	221
30	Wife starting or ending work	24.5	192	25	165

[13] show that the Japanese do not differ from the peoples of Western Europe and
the United States in the manner in which they assign a prestige rank to comparable occupations nor do they differ in their rates of upward and downward social
mobility.

However, it is also evident that from these common bases are derived the
cultural variants that distinguish one society from another. In this study, 17 of the
42 life event items were found to be scored significantly different by Japanese
and Americans. These will be discussed in a categorical fashion.

Items 3 and 11—detention in jail, and minor violations of the law—were both
given higher scores by the Japanese. This is in keeping with one of the prime

Table 5.3, continued

SRRQ item number	Item name*	Americans		Japanese	
		Rank	Geometric mean	Rank	Geometric mean
43	Start or end of formal schooling§	24.5	192	32	126
2	Troubles with boss	26	174	27	145
12	Outstanding personal achievement	27	161	24	166
33	Mortgage loan over $10,000§	28	158	17	252
38	Major change in living conditions	29	153	26	162
31	Major change in working conditions	30	141	31	131
42	Changing to new school	31	126	34	108
9	Major revision of personal habits	32	124	29	135
20	Change in residence	33	114	37	91
32	Major change in recreation†	34	113	38	85
37	Major change in social activities†	35	105	39	72
23	Major change in church activities§	36	93	42	46
5	Major change in sleeping habits	37	83	35	94
7	Major change in eating habits	38.5	78	36	93
34	Mortgage loan less than $10,000§	38.5	78	30	170
17	Major change in family get-togethers	40	75	40	60
40	Vacation	41	54	41	56
41	Christmas	42	40	43	40
11	Minor violations of the law§	43	34	28	138

* Items listed in order of descending rank on Americans' geometric mean
Items scored significantly different:
† $p \leq 0.05$
‡ $p \leq 0.01$
§ $p \leq 0.001$

facets of Japanese culture, that of the concept of the obligation of the individual to his or her family, name, and position [14]. Going to jail because of a moral transgression imposes a great sense of shame for the family and a sense of guilt for loss of prestige and status. It has been indicated that one of the greatest motivations of Japanese behavior is the threat of external disapproval and sanctions [9]. Colby, in a study of narrative patterns in folktales, has described the concern of the Japanese with the external social situation [15].

The mortgage or loan of greater or less than $10,000 was considered by the Japanese to be more meaningful, but not necessarily because of the sums of money involved (note that the Americans considered major change in financial status to be of more consequence than did the Japanese). In Japan, going to a bank to borrow money is uncommon. Further, this act may be consonant with mortgaging one's honor until the debt is repaid.

Item 22 (marital separation), item 24 (marital reconciliation), and item 28 (change in number of arguments with spouse) all relate to conflictual transactions with the spouse. The Americans considered these items to have greater meaning than did the Japanese.

The U.S. family system is characterized by an emphasis on the conjugal family unit of parent and children. The trend in Western countries, as in Japan [16], is toward a relatively isolated, autonomous unit with little or no extended kinship network [17]. The factors of equality between spouses, free choice of mate, the propriety of isolated conjugal units, the devaluation of kinship networks, and extensive social mobility are associated with the concept of romantic love as a selective factor in marriage and a cohesive factor in marital relations. Both participants bring to the marriage a great spouse-dependent need for emotional security [18]. This greater emotional interdependence between U.S. spouses for love, affection, companionship, and esteem may have resulted in the finding that marital discord carries with it greater implications for the Americans.

The lesser meaning of marital discord among Japanese may also be due to the fact that in the Japanese culture the role of the wife and the role of the husband are more clearly delineated than they are in the U.S. society [16;17]. In the latter, the patterns of general equality between spouses, accentuated by the reduction in male dominance by job-holding wives, make less discrete the traditional role of the husband as the breadwinner and the role of the wife as homemaker and child-rearer.

Just as the traditional role of the Japanese male is dominance, the ideal role of the wife is devotion, respect, and duty to the husband. While the contemporary Japanese woman has greater freedom and power than before, her sphere of authority still remains in household duties and child-rearing. Although the husband's authority can override that of the wife at any time, the distinct separation of areas of responsibilities may make marital conflicts of less concern than in the U.S. culture. The skill of the wife in husband management is the adjustment of the wife to the husband's superior status, and success depends on how well she can adjust to the moods and behavior of her husband. These subtle maneuvers are carried out in such a way that in actuality the Japanese wife may have greater power over home activities than does the U.S. housewife [16].

In situations where marital discord arises, it is the Japanese wife who shoulders the blame for the poor behavior of her husband. His behavior is regarded as reflecting an improper discharge of wifely duties [9]. The erosion of these traditional roles in the contemporary Japanese middle class is still slow in spite of legal reforms and democratization [16]. Stoetzel [19] has shown in studies on Japanese youth that the most desirable quality by far that a spouse could have was "good temper." The emphasis on temperament rather than romantic love in the selection of mates may tend to insure marital harmony.

It is also noted that divorce, an end point of marital difficulties, was not rated differently in the two cultures. In all Western countries, changing social forces have produced definite increases in divorce rates in the past half century. It is interesting that, in spite of the industrialization, the urbanization, and the trend toward a less kinship oriented family group in Japan, there was a distinct downward trend in divorce rate per 1,000 marriages from 1900 to 1950: from 184 to 100. At the same time in the United States, this rate rose from 75 to 232. The complexity of the reasons for these data has been explored by Goode [17].

Death of spouse was rated by both the Americans and Japanese as requiring the most adjustment of all events. However, the Japanese gave a significantly greater weight to this event (1,079–880). There may be two reasons for this. It is conjectured that the loss of a life partner may well uncover needs that range beyond the emotions accompanying the death. In the case of the Japanese wife, although she is submissive, she is emotionally less dependent on the male. Her great dependence on the male lies in the security that attaches to his salary-making ability. The loss of the husband is a severe disruption of her stable family life and a change in status in the larger community; the loss of income is crucial to the Japanese woman in this middle-class stratum. She does not work, her abilities to work and support the family are almost nil, and remarriage is only a remote possibility. While the modern young couple may be less affected, the loss of a husband to the Japanese middle-class urban housewife results in complete disruption of family life and security [16].

The Japanese husband, on the other hand, has been shown to be more dependent on his wife than the converse [20]. This dependence presumably stems from the strong mother–child relationship that predominates in Japan. The Japanese husband relies heavily on the skill of the wife to preserve his ego and dominant status in the household by catering to his wants, forgiving his errant behavior, and managing the home. Thus, while not denying the emotion that is experienced by the Japanese at death of a spouse, it does appear to be different from the U.S. experience where loss of a love object and companion is paramount.

Major personal injury or illness was of greater concern to the Japanese. The meaning of this is obscure although it has been conjectured that the greater concern over illness and death by the Japanese could be interpreted as an introjection of guilt [21]. Economic security has been described as a more meaningful goal of life in Japan than in America [16;19]. A major illness or injury to the wage-earning husband is a serious threat to the well-being of the family, which then has to live in relative frugality. While there is health insurance, the income loss is a great blow. Financial security has been expressed by Japanese youth as being a primary aim in life, a major illness being greatly feared as jeopardizing this goal. For the wife, a major illness would work a similar hardship for she would be unable to take care of her husband and family for whom she has a great sense of devotion and responsibility.

The Japanese regarded changes in church activities to be less meaningful than did the Americans. The Japanese sample consisted primarily of Buddhists or those who expressed no religious preferences. The Buddhist temple in Japan is considerably different from the U.S. church with its Sunday worship and sociore-ligious activities. Religion in Japan is primarily one of self-observance and self-keeping of morals. The temple does not have the same kind of force and meaning in Japanese life that the church has in U.S. society [22]. Religious activities, as Americans define it, would be of less concern to the Japanese inasmuch as this facet of church religion is generally unknown. Christians constitute less than 5 percent of the total Japanese population, and religious activities play a negligible part in the interests of Japanese youth [19]. The comprehensive study by Vogel on Japan's new middle class [16] is striking in the fact that there is no mention of church or religious activities.

The Japanese have for centuries been oriented to the concept of the family unit as the basic unit of society. The family's name, status, and goals overrode all individual members' desires [14]. In view of this emphasis on family kinship and one's obligation to it [16;19;23], it was of interest to compare the five life event items that affected the family. Item 6 (death of close family member), item 14 (major change in health of family member), and item 17 (major change in family get-togethers) were not rated as significantly different. Two items, however, were scored significantly different. These were item 19 (addition of a new member to the family), which the Americans rated as more meaningful, and item 21 (son or daughter leaving home), which the Japanese rated higher.

These findings indicate the family kinship items of the SRRQ are concerned only with intrafamily relationships; and, in this sense, the magnitude of the kinship and affection that exists between family members is not different be-tween the Americans and the Japanese. The Japanese concept of filial piety and family kinship is bound up in a system of obligations and responsibilities of each of its members to the family group. In such a system, the individual's transgres-sion is reflected upon all family members. The family items of the SRRQ do not concern themselves with this concept of the family, which must relate its behav-ior to an external society that is its invisible but ethical judge.

There are two items that relate to schooling: item 42 (changing to a new school), and item 43 (start or end of formal schooling). The former was not scored significantly different between the Japanese and the Americans, but the latter was scored higher by the Americans. These results are interesting inasmuch as the emphasis of the Japanese on education and schooling is considered to be a very traumatic experience for the family [16]. There is tremendous pressure placed on youth to achieve academically, since this is an essential step leading to life security. The whole family is involved in the student's enterprise, financially and emotionally. High rates of suicides and mental disturbances occur in the student age group. The strain of *shiken jigoku* (examination hell) is a phenome-non that hits Japanese families in their striving for financial security. Our findings indicate that the Americans are just as concerned as the Japanese as regards the value of education.

In view of the greater concern of the Japanese for financial security one might expect that items concerning the husband and his work would be viewed as having greater meaning [16]. This was not so, for of the seven items that relate to this area (items 39, 25, 36, 27, 2, and 31), none was scored significantly higher by the Japanese. As a matter of fact, the Americans scored three of these items higher: item 39 (retirement from work), item 29 (major change in work responsibilities), and item 2 (troubles with boss).

The Japanese middle-class family's leisure, social, and recreational activities are quite different from those of the U.S. middle class [16]. These are severely limited by the family budget and qualified by the fact that the husband and wife generally do not share in recreational activities as do many Americans. Although they aspire to a greater leisure in scope and time, this is restricted to the simpler entertainments. The ownership of a car, for example, as economical as a Japanese car is, must still be considered as a semiluxury rather than a necessity as it is in the United States. The Japanese therefore devote a lesser share of time and money in external society and recreational pursuits. It is no surprise, then, that item 32 (major change in recreation) and item 37 (major change in social activities) were rated lower by the Japanese.

SUMMARY

Data from two Japanese samples of Hiroshima ($N = 55$) and Sendai ($N = 57$) were collected on the Social Readjustment Rating Questionnaire. The two groups were homogeneous in terms of relative order of ranking of the 43 items and the magnitude of the item scores. However, Sendai males were found to differ in some respects from the other subgroups. The two samples were from an urban, university, and middle socioeconomic background.

A comparison of the combined Japanese sample and a selected U.S. sample ($N = 168$) indicated essential similarities in their attitudes towards life events, but with some interesting differences that reflect cultural variation.

REFERENCES

1. Holmes, T.H., and R. H. Rahe. "The Social Readjustment Rating Scale." *Journal of Psychosomatic Research* 11 (1967):213–18. Reprinted in this volume, Chapter 2.

2. *1960 Population Census of Japan, Hiroshima-ken.* Vol. 4, pt. 34. Bureau of Statistics, Office of the Prime Minister, 1963.

3. *1960 Population Census of Japan and Miyagi-ken.* Vol. 4, pt. 4. Bureau of Statistics, Office of the Prime Minister, 1963.

4. Taeber, I. B. *The Population of Japan.* Princeton: Princeton University Press, 1958.

5. Masuda, M., and T. H. Holmes. "Magnitude Estimations of Social Readjustments." *Journal of Psychosomatic Research* 11 (1967):219–25. Reprinted in this volume, Chapter 3.

6. Siegel, S. *Nonparametric Statistics for the Behavioral Sciences.* New York: McGraw-Hill, 1956.

7. Arkin, H., and R. R. Colton. *Statistical Methods*. 4th ed. New York: Barnes and Noble, 1959, p. 26.

8. Edwards, A. E. *Statistical Analysis*. New York: Rinehart, 1958, p. 44.

9. De Vos, G. "The Relation of Guilt towards Parents to Achievement and Arranged Marriage among the Japanese." *Psychiatry* 23 (1960):287–301.

10. Kluckhohn, C. "Universal Categories of Culture." In *Anthropology Today,* edited by A. L. Kroeber, pp. 507–23. Chicago: University of Chicago Press, 1953.

11. Keesing, F. *Cultural Anthropology*. New York: Rinehart, 1958.

12. Spiro, M. E. "An Overview and a Suggested Reorientation." In *Psychological Anthropology: Approaches to Culture and Personality,* edited by F. L. K. Hsu, pp. 459–92. Homewood, Ill.: Dorsey Press, 1961.

13. Berelson, B., and G. A. Steiner. *Human Behavior: An Inventory of Scientific Findings*. New York: Harcourt, Brace, and World, 1964.

14. Benedict, R. *The Chrysanthemum and the Sword: Patterns of Japanese Culture*. Boston: Houghton Mifflin, 1946.

15. Colby, B. N. "Cultural Patterns in Narrative." *Science* 151 (1966):793–98.

16. Vogel, E. F. *Japan's New Middle Class: The Salary Man and His Family in a Tokyo Suburb*. Berkeley: University of California Press, 1963.

17. Goode, W. J. *World Revolutions and Family Patterns*. Glencoe, Ill.: Free Press, 1963.

18. Williams, R. M. *American Society*. New York: Alfred Knopf, 1959, pp. 36–37.

19. Stoetzel, J. *Without the Chrysanthemum and the Sword: A Study of the Attitudes of Youth in Post-War Japan*. New York: Columbia University Press, 1955.

20. Caudill, W. "Japanese-American Personality and Acculturation." *Genetic Psychology Monographs* 45 (1952):3–102.

21. Norbeck, E., and G. De Vos. "Japan." In *Psychological Anthropology: Approaches to Culture and Personality,* edited by F. L. K. Hsu, pp. 19–47. Homewood, Ill.: Dorsey Press, 1961.

22. Moberg, D. O. *The Church as a Social Institution*. Englewood Cliffs, N.J.: Prentice-Hall, 1962.

23. Bennett, J. W., and M. Nagai. "Echoes: Reactions to American Anthropology—Japanese Critique of the Methodology of Benedict's *Chrysanthemum and the Sword*." *American Anthropologist* 55 (1953):404–11.

6

The Social Readjustment Rating Scale: A Comparative Study of Black, White, and Mexican Americans

Anthony L. Komaroff, Minoru Masuda, and Thomas H. Holmes

The studies that most directly led to the current investigation began with the work of Hinkle and his coinvestigators [1–4]. In their studies of telephone workers over a 20-year period, they found that in most individuals illness tended to occur in "clusters" during periods of "increased environmental load with disturbances of mood, behavior, physical activity, sleep patterns, appetite, and various bodily processes." The great majority of illnesses occurred at times when the subjects perceived their lives as unsatisfying, threatening, overdemanding, or conflictual, and felt that they could not adapt.

Holmes et al. [5] studied employees of a tuberculosis sanatorium who developed tuberculosis during their employment. Holmes and his colleagues retrospectively examined the lives of their subjects with respect to certain "life change events" described in their research questionnaire, and found, like Hinkle et al., that life change events tended to cluster in the 12–24 months preceding the onset of tuberculosis. No such clustering occurred in the healthy control group.

Rahe et al. [6;7] analyzed the occurrence of life change events in certain patients and found that a similar clustering of events appeared in the two years preceding the onset of cardiac disease, skin disease, hernia, and pregnancy. These authors further attempted to determine if a more clear and predictable relationship between these life change events and disease onset could be obtained if the events could be individually weighted in terms of the amount of readjustment they required. In order to quantify the readjustment required by the life change

---

This chapter is reprinted with permission from Anthony L. Komaroff, Minoru Masuda, and Thomas H. Holmes, "The Social Readjustment Rating Scale: A Comparative Study of Negro, White, and Mexican Americans," *Journal of Psychosomatic Research* 12 (1968):121–28. Copyright 1968 by Pergamon Press, Ltd.

events, Holmes and Rahe [8] sought the opinions of 394 subjects, predominantly a white, urban, middle-income group, using a Social Readjustment Rating Questionnaire (SRRQ). There was a striking degree of correlation between the subjects in their quantitative judgments about psychosocial phenomena. Age, sex, educational background, religious affiliation, and generation American appeared not to influence the evaluation. There was less correlation between whites and blacks sampled than between other groups.

Masuda and Holmes [9] administered the SRRQ to a sample in Japan and found, on comparison with white Americans, that there was a significant agreement in the mean rank ordering of the items and a significant concordance in the interindividual rankings. There was a high consensus in the attitudes of middle-class Japanese and white middle-class Americans on the magnitude of personal readjustments required when faced with common life events.

The consistency of the quantitative responses among the white middle-class subjects, the consensus between the Japanese and the Americans, and the consistently lower correlations between the black and white subjects evidenced in the previous studies, raised the following questions: (1) Could the same attitude testing instrument be applied to members of two urban U.S. subculture groups: black Americans and Mexican Americans? (2) Would these subculture groups differ significantly from the white American group and from each other in their assessment of the amount of adaptation required by certain life change events? This study attempts to answer these questions.

METHODS

The two subculture groups sampled lived in the "poverty areas" of a southern section of Los Angeles. These poverty areas were designated as such by the federal government, as is apparent by the many programs and local organizations established by the government's Office of Economic Opportunity. Access to the members of these subculture communities was obtained by working through these local organizations, whose membership consisted entirely of residents of the poverty areas. Groups of from 5 to 15 people gathered together by these organizations were presented with the SRRQ by the investigator.

With the increased emphasis in recent years on problems of U.S. subculture groups, the citizens in these areas have for several years been sought out by graduate students, social workers, and social scientists. Most of these interviewers have requested personal information and opinions. Consequently, members of these subculture communities have become reluctant to participate in questionnaire research of any type, and are particularly sensitive to questions regarding their race, education, marital status, and income. After initial interviews indicated that many people would not answer the instrument if asked these types of questions, it was decided only to make questionnaire inquiries about age, sex, and religion. Identification of the subjects as black American or Mexican American was based on the judgment of the investigator.

Since the local organizations sampled included youth training programs and adult community-cooperation programs, the sample included rebellious young people (some of whom had participated in riot activity the previous summer) and passive adults who spoke of social harmony and slow progress toward improvement of their social condition. All ages, from teenagers through octogenarians, were represented. The black Americans showed a female/male ratio of 3.6; and the Mexican Americans, a ratio of 2.4 (Table 6.1).

The SRRQ, as originally worded, contained some language that, in trial runs, was not understood by many of those asked to read and complete it. For this reason, the wording was simplified on certain items: For example, "marital reconciliation with spouse" was changed to "getting back together with your husband or wife." Some examples of the original and revised items of the SRRQ are shown in Table 6.2.

Each group of individuals sampled was given a verbal synopsis of the instructions for completing the SRRQ rather than written instructions such as had been given to the white American group. This was done because many subjects balked at having to read detailed instructions. The verbal instructions were essentially as follows.

This is a list of certain things that happen in people's lives. Each of these things changes a person's life, causes a person a certain amount of stress and strain. For instance, this first one, "getting married," that's something that changes a person's life, isn't it? Now, what I'd like you to do is compare each of these things on the list with getting married. Think to yourself, is this thing more or less of a change in someone's life than getting married is; does it take a longer or shorter time for a person to get used to this change than it does to get used to getting married? It doesn't matter whether you think something is better or worse than getting married. That's not what we're interested in. It's whether you think it's more or less of a change than getting married is.

Now, if you look over by "getting married" you'll see that we've put down 500 points. What that means is that if you think something else on the list is more of a change than

Table 6.1
Breakdown of Population Groups

Group	Male	Female	Age < 30	Age ≥ 30	Single	Married
White American (N = 394)*	179	215	206	188	171	223
Black American (N = 64)	14	50	31	33	†	†
Mexican American (N = 78)	23	55	51	27	†	†

* Data from Holmes and Rahe [8]

† Few subjects were willing to give information on marital status.

getting married, you put down more than 500 points. You put down however many points you want, depending on how much more of a change than getting married it is. If you think something is less of a change than getting married, you put down less than 500 points. It's as simple as that.

In all of these things, think about how much of a change these things are for all people, the average person, not just for you.

Now, are there any questions?

Stevens [10] has discussed the general advantage of using geometric means in social science questionnaire data. Masuda and Holmes [11] have demonstrated the cogency of the use of the geometric mean with the SRRQ. The geometric mean was computed as the antilogarithm of the mean of the logs of the scores. Subsequent mention of mean values refers to geometric mean values.

RESULTS

The mean scores and rank order of the 43 SRRQ items for the Mexican Americans and black Americans are compared with the scores of the white American middle-income group of Holmes and Rahe [8] in Table 6.3. A comparison of the mean item score rank orders of the white American group and the black American group showed a correlation coefficient (Spearman's rho) of 0.798 ($p = 0.001$); the white American versus Mexican American correlation was 0.735 ($p = 0.001$); the Mexican American versus black American correlation was

Table 6.2
Some Examples of Revised Wording of SRRQ Used in Subculture Groups

Item 3	Original:	Detention in jail
	Revised:	Being kept in jail
Item 12	Original:	Outstanding personal achievement
	Revised:	Achieving an outstanding goal
Item 18	Original:	Major change in financial state (e.g., a lot worse off or a lot better off than usual)
	Revised:	Major change in having money (a lot more or a lot less than usual)
Item 22	Original:	Marital separation from spouse
	Revised:	Splitting up with husband or wife
Item 36	Original:	Major business readjustment (e.g., merger, reorganization, bankruptcy, etc.)
	Revised:	Major business change (e.g., like going into business with someone else, changing your business, going broke)

0.892 ($p = 0.001$). In short, the three population groups ranked the items in a very similar fashion. The coefficients also indicate that the two subgroups are more closely related to each other than to the white American middle-income group.

In general, the black American responses tended to be higher than the white American responses, while the Mexican American responses tended to be lower (see column totals in Table 6.3). One possible explanation for this could have been that the black Americans regarded the mode item—getting married—with which all other items had to be compared, as requiring less adjustment than did the white American group, thus elevating their responses to other items. The converse argument would explain the generally lower responses obtained from the Mexican American group.

To determine the validity of this explanation, representatives of each of the three population groups, similar in age and sex to those in the questionnaire study—none of whom was familiar with the questionnaire or the study—were asked the following question.

If 1,000 points were the most change and adjustment that anything could cause a person, and zero points meant no change or adjustment at all, how much change and adjustment do you think most people have to make when they get married? In other words, if 1,000 points were the most you could give for the biggest change in a person's life, and zero points meant no change at all, how many points would you give for the amount of change required by a person getting married?

A total of 75 subjects were questioned, and the following mean values were obtained: white Americans ($N = 22$), 479; black Americans ($N = 30$), 492; and Mexican Americans ($N = 23$), 506. Analysis of variance demonstrated no significant differences between the attitudes of the three groups towards the mode item, getting married. Thus, it appears that, apart from any difference in their assessment of the mode item, the black Americans simply thought that more life change event items required more adjustment than did getting married. Likewise, the Mexican Americans thought that no items required as much change as did marriage.

Table 6.3 also shows the rankings of the life event items in each of the three comparison groups. The three groups agreed on five of the 43 items as ranking in the first ten. These five were: death of spouse, marital separation from spouse, marriage, death of a close family member, and major personal injury or illness. Items ranked in the first ten by the white Americans but not by both subculture groups included marital reconciliation with spouse and retirement from work. On the other hand, both subculture groups ranked the item "mortgage greater than $10,000" in the first ten items, in distinction to the white American group.

Because the scores were not true interval scores, it was decided to use nonparametric statistical methods. Each of the 43 items was subjected to an analysis of variance. The Kruskal-Wallis one-way analysis of variance [12] uses all the responses given by every member of each population group, rather than consider-

Table 6.3
SRRQ Item Mean Scores and Rank Order* for White, Mexican, and
Black Americans

Life Event	White Americans		Mexican Americans		Black Americans	
	Score	Rank	Score	Rank	Score	Rank
Death of spouse	771	1	341	5	652	1
Divorce	593	2	312	10	383	13
Marital separation from spouse	516	3	365	2	447	7
Marriage	500	4	500	1	500	5
Death of a close family member	469	5	339	6	553	2
Detention in jail	439	6	253	19	422	8
Major personal injury or illness	416	7	348	3	518	4
Being fired from work	378	8	325	9	341	16
Marital reconciliation with spouse	366	9	309	11	345	14
Retirement from work	361	10	266	18	333	17
Gaining a new family member	337	11	232	22	289	22
Major change in health of a family member	335	12	296	13	475	6
Sexual difficulties	316	13	288	16	401	11
Major business readjustment	308	14.5	332	7	326	18
Major change in financial state	308	14.5	328	8	401	12
Changing to a different line of work	287	16	191	32	247	26
Major change in arguments with spouse	286	17	296	14	307	21
Pregnancy	284	18	307	12	403	10
Death of close friend	270	19	199	28	261	24
Major change in work responsibilities	243	20	271	17	344	15
Foreclosure on a mortgage or loan	231	21	211	27	248	25
Son or daughter leaving home	219	22	197	29	236	28
Trouble with in-laws	213	23	174	36	231	30
Mortgage greater than $10,000	210	24	342	4	544	3

ing the mean value of rank order for each item. When a significant variance was found to exist among the responses of all three population groups, a more precise examination of the variance was determined by the Mann-Whitney U-test [12]. This test examines the variance between pairs of population groups in their responses to a single item.

The results of these analyses of variance are shown in Table 6.4. Only those Mann-Whitney U comparisons between pairs were considered significant if the Kruskal-Wallis H among the three groups was significant ($p < 0.05$). The majority of these differences were significant at the 0.01 and 0.001 levels.

It will be noted that 29 of the 43 items demonstrated a significant variance among the three population groups. On 14 items (items 5, 7, 9, 11, 13, 17, 20, 23,

Table 6.3, continued

Life Event	White Americans		Mexican Americans		Black Americans	
	Score	Rank	Score	Rank	Score	Rank
Wife beginning or ending work	204	25	214	25	235	29
Outstanding personal achievement	192	26	214	26	405	9
Beginning or ending formal schooling	191	27	236	21	287	23
Major change in living conditions	186	28	216	24	313	19
Trouble with the boss	178	29	108	43	200	36
Revision of personal habits	149	30	239	20	224	31
Major change in working conditions	148	31	183	33	213	33
Change in residence	140	32	177	35	217	32
Changing to a new school	135	33	141	40	170	42
Major change in recreation	127	34	228	23	196	37
Major change in social activities	125	35	132	42	177	40
Major change in church activities	112	36	157	38	202	35
Mortgage or loan less than $10,000	105	37.5	293	15	310	20
Major change in sleeping habits	105	37.5	164	37	192	39
Major change in number of family get-togethers	103	39	151	39	194	38
Major change in eating habits	98	40	213	27	211	34
Vacation	74	41	182	34	174	41
Christmas	59	42	194	31	243	27
Minor violations of the law	54	43	133	41	150	43
Total	11,340		10,597		13,520	

* Items listed according to white American rank order

26, 31, 32, 34, 40, and 41) the white American group scored the items significantly differently from both of the other two subgroups. In similar analyses, the Mexican Americans scored only three items (items 2, 3, and 4) differently from the other two, while the black Americans scored five items in this manner (items 14, 18, 29, 35, and 38).

Table 6.4 also shows that the white Americans scored 20 items differently as compared to the Mexican Americans and 26 items differently as compared to the black Americans. The latter and the Mexican Americans scored only 11 items differently from each other. There were only three items (items 6, 12, and 33) in which the scoring was significantly different between all three pairs of subgroups.

Table 6.4
Significant* Differences between Groups on Mean Item Scores†

No.	Item	White Americans	Mexican Americans	Black Americans
1	Marriage	500	500	500
2	Trouble with the boss	178———	—108———	—200
3	Detention in jail	439———	—253———	—422
4	Death of spouse	771———	—341———	—652
5	Major change in sleeping habits	105———	—164	192
6	Death of a close family member	469———	—339———	—553
7	Major change in eating habits	98———	—213	211
8	Foreclosure on a mortgage or loan	231	211	248
9	Revision of personal habits	149———	—239	224
10	Death of a close friend	270	199	261
11	Minor violations of the law	54———	—133	150
12	Outstanding personal achievement	192———	—214———	—405
13	Pregnancy	284———	—307	403
14	Major change in health of a family member	335	296—	—475
15	Sexual difficulties	316	288	401
16	Trouble with in-laws	213	174	231
17	Major change in number of family get-togethers	103———	—151	194
18	Major change in financial state	308	328—	—401
19	Gaining a new family member	337	232	289
20	Change in residence	140———	—177	217
21	Son or daughter leaving home	219	197	236
22	Marital separation from spouse	516	365	447
23	Major change in church activities	112———	—157	202

DISCUSSION

This study demonstrates two things: (1) the apparently sophisticated intellectual task of quantifying life change events can be executed with significant consistency by a population of academically unsophisticated and partially illiterate people; and (2) although the subculture population groups scored many life change items significantly differently from the previously examined white American middle-income population, all three groups established the same general hierarchy of change for the 43 items.

It is important to know that these subculture groups are capable of responding to the questionnaire consistently. Hopefully, with the establishment of these mean values in the two subculture groups, studies can be done in these groups to investigate the link between the adjustment to life change events and the natural history of disease.

The present sample of black Americans and Mexican Americans from South

Table 6.4, continued

No.	Item	White Americans	Mexican Americans	Black Americans
24	Marital reconciliation with spouse	366	309	345
25	Being fired from work	378	325	341
26	Divorce	593———312		383
27	Changing to a different line of work	287	191	247
28	Major change in arguments with spouse	286	296	307
29	Major change in work responsibilities	243	271———344	
30	Wife beginning or ending work	204	214	235
31	Major change in working conditions	148———183		213
32	Major change in recreation	127———228		196
33	Mortgage greater than $10,000	210———342———544		
34	Mortgage or loan less than $10,000	105———293		310
35	Major personal injury or illness	416	348———518	
36	Major business readjustment	308	332	326
37	Major change in social activities	125	132	177
38	Major change in living conditions	186	216———313	
39	Retirement from work	361	266	333
40	Vacation	74———182		174
41	Christmas	59———194		243
42	Changing to a new school	135	141	170
43	Beginning or ending formal schooling	191	236	287

* Mann-Whitney U-test [12]

† Bars connect significantly different item scores

Los Angeles is seen to be heavily weighted toward females (Table 6.1). The urban black male virtually disappears from the statistics in the middle years. He has been described by Moynihan [13] as the "invisible" man because of his truancy from life via unemployment, welfare, and so on. The matricentricity of the ghetto black family structure is associated with the "disappearing" black male. The preponderance of females in the study may well be a reflection of this phenomenon. A similar but lesser predominance of females seen in the Mexican American sample may indicate a tendency of the Mexican American male to emulate his male black American neighbor in South Los Angeles.

In order to examine the data in more detail the questionnaire items that involve related attitudes are considered together. The discussion is subdivided into certain socioeconomic categories to facilitate such a consideration.

Fourteen life change event items are related to the area of labor and income. Eight of these (items 2, 18, 29, 31, 33, 34, 40, and 41) were evaluated with a significant difference, in terms of the amount of adjustment they required, between the two subculture groups and the white American group. In every case the subculture groups regarded the items as requiring more of an adjustment than did the white Americans. The Mexican American group generally scored lower on these items than did the black Americans. These items included mortgage greater than $10,000, mortgage or loan less than $10,000, major change in financial state, major change in work responsibilities, major change in working conditions, vacation, and Christmas.

Two items apply directly to housing: change in residence, and major change in living conditions. Both items were evaluated as significantly more difficult adjustments by the subculture groups. Two items—major change in sleeping habits, and major change in eating habits—were scored significantly higher by both subculture groups than by white Americans.

It is not surprising that people in the subculture groups should find it harder to adjust to changes affecting their economic well-being. They live in what Lewis [14] has called a "culture of poverty." This involves more than being impoverished; it is being impoverished while living in a cash economy, having neither the personal nor social tools necessary for advancing in the larger society. Perhaps the higher change scores that both subculture groups gave to the items mentioned reflect the heightened strain among the poor when the securities of life are threatened.

Being fired from work and retirement from work were not assessed differently by the subculture and white American groups. Perhaps this is a manifestation of some degree of financial security provided to the subculture groups by welfare programs.

Two items relate to education—changing to a new school, and beginning or ending formal schooling. The black Americans, but not the Mexican Americans, regarded these items as requiring significantly more adjustment. Thus it appears that, despite the language difficulties that interfere with education in many Mexican Americans, it is the black Americans who may experience more difficulty adjusting to the school situation.

The Mexican American responses are lower and the black American responses are higher than those of white Americans to death of a close family member and major personal injury or illness. The Mexican American response is lower than either the black American or white American response to death of spouse. It is possible that the security of the extended family, found in Mexican American communities, cushions the adjustment required when ill health or death comes to a close family member. In conflict with this explanation is the fact that both black Americans and Mexican Americans regarded major change in health of a family member as requiring more adjustment that did the white American group. The fact that black Americans regard death of a close family member as requiring more adjustment than do white Americans may indicate that, however loosely the family is organized, its integrity is more important in promoting a sense of stability among blacks than it is among whites. Neither subculture group responded with a significant difference from white Americans to death of a close friend.

Trouble with the boss and detention in jail were not regarded as requiring more adjustment by the subculture groups; in fact, the Mexican Americans regarded both items as requiring significantly less adjustment. This is surprising, especially in view of recent demonstrations of anger on the part of blacks against the prevailing authority. The lower responses of the Mexican American group may indicate that, at the present time, the Mexican American community is less responsive and volatile in reacting to the prevailing authority. The lack of recent ferment in urban Mexican American society comparable to that in black American society may support this assumption.

Neither subculture group regarded sexual difficulties as requiring more or less adjustment than did white Americans. Both subculture groups regarded pregnancy as requiring more adjustment than did white Americans. Both subculture groups regarded divorce as requiring less adjustment than did white Americans. These data seem to indicate that sexual difficulties and pregnancy are not taken lightly by these subculture groups as is sometimes thought, although actual union with the opposite sex is something that can be dissolved more easily than in the larger society.

There were considerably more significantly different responses between the white Americans and the two subculture groups in this study than were found between the white American and the urban Japanese samples reported by Masuda and Holmes [9]. It appears, therefore, that the people who live within pockets of poverty in the United States are less similar to white American middle-class society than are the urban Japanese.

SUMMARY

This study investigated two U.S. subculture groups—urban black Americans and Mexican Americans—in their assessment of the adjustment required by certain specified life change events. A questionnaire for quantifying the adjustment required by these life events was employed. It was found that, in the great majority of life change items, the numerical responses of the two subculture groups and the responses of a previously examined white American middle-income group differed significantly. The responses of the two subculture groups differed more from the white American group, in fact, than did a previously studied Japanese sample. Despite these differences, however, all three population groups ranked the life change items in a significantly concordant manner.

ACKNOWLEDGMENT

Our special thanks to William R. Larson, Ph.D., and the Computer Center of the University of Southern California for their assistance in handling the data.

REFERENCES

1. Hinkle, L. E., N. Plummer, R. Metraux, P. Richter, J. W. Gittinger, W. N. Thetford, A. M. Ostfeld, F. D. Kane, L. Goldberger, W. E. Mitchell, H. Leichter, R. H. Pinsky, D. Goebel, I. D. J. Bross, and H. G. Wolff. "Studies in Human Ecology: Factors Relevant to the Occurrence of Bodily Illness and Disturbances in Mood, Thought and Behavior in Three Homogeneous Population Groups." *American Journal of Psychiatry* 114 (1957): 212–20.

2. Hinkle, L. E., and H. G. Wolff. "Ecologic Investigations of the Relationship between Illness, Life Experiences and the Social Environment." *Annals of Internal Medicine* 49 (1958):1373–88.

3. Hinkle, L. E., and H. G. Wolff. "The Nature of Man's Adaptation to His Total Environment and the Relation of This to Illness." *Archives of Internal Medicine* 99 (1957):442–60.

4. Hinkle, L. E., W. N. Christenson, F. D. Kane, A. Ostfeld, W. N. Thetford, and H. G. Wolff. "An Investigation of the Relation between Life Experience, Personality Characteristics, and General Susceptibility to Illness." *Psychosomatic Medicine* 20 (1958):278–95.

5. Holmes, T. H., N. G. Hawkins, C. E. Bowerman, E. R. Clarke, Jr., and J. R. Joffe. "Psychosocial and Psychophysiological Studies of Tuberculosis." *Psychosomatic Medicine* 19 (1957):134–43.

6. Rahe, R. H., M. Meyer, M. Smith, G. Kjaer, and T. H. Holmes. "Social Stress and Illness Onset." *Journal of Psychosomatic Research* 8 (1964):35–44. Reprinted in this volume, Chapter 12.

7. Rahe, R. H., and T. H. Holmes. "Social, Psychologic and Psychophysiologic Aspects of Inguinal Hernia." *Journal of Psychosomatic Research* 8 (1965):487–91.

8. Holmes, T. H., and R. H. Rahe. "The Social Readjustment Rating Scale." *Journal of Psychosomatic Research* 11 (1967):213–18. Reprinted in this volume, Chapter 2.

9. Masuda, M., and T. H. Holmes. "The Social Readjustment Rating Scale: A Cross-cultural Study of Japanese and Americans." *Journal of Psychosomatic Research* 11 (1967):227–37. Reprinted in this volume, Chapter 5.

10. Stevens, S. S. "A Metric for the Social Consensus." *Science* 151 (1966):530–41.

11. Masuda, M., and T. H. Holmes. "Magnitude Estimations of Social Readjustments." *Journal of Psychosomatic Research* 11 (1967):219–25. Reprinted in this volume, Chapter 3.

12. Siegel, S. *Nonparametric Statistics for the Behavioral Sciences.* New York: McGraw-Hill, 1956.

13. Moynihan, D. P. "Employment, Income, and the Ordeal of the Negro Family." *Daedalus* 94 (1965):745–70.

14. Lewis, O. "The Culture of Poverty." *Scientific American* 215, no. 4 (1966):19–25.

7

Impact of a Natural Catastrophe on Life Events

James G. Janney, Minoru Masuda, and Thomas H. Holmes

INTRODUCTION

On May 30, 1970, a devastating *terremoto* (earthquake) rocked Peru's Callejon de Huaylas, an alpine valley bounded by the more than 20,000-foot Cordillera Blanca mountains. An estimated 60,000 persons perished as a result of the earthquake; innumerable others were displaced from home, land, and loved ones. One of the authors (JGJ) had the opportunity to assist the *damnificados* as a member of the American Alpine Club Peruvian Relief Mission [1]. He was impressed that the life changes induced by the earthquake had profound social, economic, and medical implications. Using the Social Readjustment Rating Questionnaire (SRRQ) [2] and the Schedule of Recent Experience (SRE) [3], this study quantifies the importance of these changes. The questionnaires were administered in Huaráz, the largest city struck by the earthquake, and in Arequipa, a comparable city untouched by the *terremoto*, one year after the earthquake.

METHODS

Questionnaires

The SRRQ and the SRE were designed by Holmes and Rahe [2;3] as a means of quantifying evidence that life events evoke psychophysiologic reactions that play a causative role in the natural history of disease processes [4–8]. The SRRQ elicits from the sample a scale of mean scores of 43 life event items. These original scores are divided by 10 for convenience to form the Social Readjust-

This chapter is reprinted with permission from *Journal of Human Stress* 3, no. 2 (June 1977):22–34. Copyright 1977 by Heldref Publications.

ment Rating Scale (SRRS) [2]. The item event happenings as recorded on the SRE are then multiplied by the scale values from the SRRS to derive life change scores as life change units (LCU). The temporal association between life change and health change [9–13], the reliability of the questionnaires [2;14], as well as striking intercultural and international correlation of the SRRS [15–21] have been demonstrated.

The SRRQ was administered in both cities. The SRRQ items dealing with magnitude of mortgages and loans were altered. The $10,000 figure on the United States questionnaire was changed to the appropriate Peruvian equivalent of 100,000 soles (U.S. $2,200). One item properly read, "Loan or mortgage greater than 100,000 soles"; another mistakenly read, "Loan or mortgage less than 1,000,000 soles," and will not be considered in the discussion.

The SRE was modified, arranging the years from June 1 to June 1 so that the earthquake of May 30, 1970, would be included in the June 1, 1969, to June 1, 1970, year—leaving an entire year designated as the post-earthquake year. Death of spouse was inadvertently omitted from the SRE; however, mean annual LCU varied so much between cities that this item would not have changed the results. In fact, there were probably more spouses killed in Huaráz during the earthquake year; and had this item been included, the intercity difference would probably have been much greater. LCU from Huaráz and Arequipa were calculated using the SRRS values derived from each population group to eliminate any bias that a combined-city score might have made.

The Samples

The city of Huaráz, having a pre-earthquake population of 40,000, was chosen as the primary study area. The 10,000-foot valley of Huaráz is primarily agricultural, producing potatoes, wheat, and corn. While the majority of rural inhabitants are Quechua Indians, the majority of urban dwellers are mestizos, of mixed Spanish and Indian blood. There are two high schools, and the adult population of the city is approximately 75 percent literate [22]. The Huaráz region has been called Peru's "Little Switzerland," for some of the world's most spectacular peaks, including the massive Nevado Huascaran, rise from the city to above 20,000 feet.

The 1970 *terremoto* leveled 90 percent of this adobe city. H. Adams Carter [1] writes that in the

valley's largest city, Huaráz, over half of the inhabitants, some 20,000 people . . . were killed when the highly unstable adobe-brick houses toppled. Houses of these sunbaked clay and straw bricks with tile roofs supported by the wooden beams offer little earthquake resistance. Most of the [houses] were built on deep, poorly compacted, alluvial deposits with high water tables, which tend to magnify the intensity of the shaking. The earthquake began with gentle swaying, followed by hard shaking which lasted for more or less a minute. There were pronounced side to side movements. Adobe buildings began to fall after about 15 seconds of hard shaking. In the whole region an estimated 1,000,000 people were left homeless. Rockfall on steep slopes also accounted for many deaths and injuries. Strong tremors continued in the region for weeks.

Medical teams arrived from many countries to assist the Peruvians. The seriously injured were cared for in makeshift tent hospitals. Though typhoid fever especially was feared, no infectious diseases become epidemic [23]. People were housed in temporary tent villages. Reconstruction began very slowly.

Arequipa, a city of 100,000 in southern Peru, was chosen as a control area. Arequipa is more metropolitan than Huaráz, having a university and a higher degree of industrialization. However, both Huaráz and Arequipa are primarily agricultural, and Arequipa's 7,800-foot elevation dictates an agricultural pattern similar to that of Huaráz.

Questionnaire Administration

The SRRQ, previously translated into Spanish [18] and the SRE, translated specifically for this study, were distributed to night school students from Huaráz (SRRQ, $N = 69$; SRE, $N = 53$) and Arequipa (SRRQ, $N = 78$; SRE, $N = 81$) in June and early July 1971, one year after the earthquake. The SRRQ previously had been administered to samples of convenience in San Salvador, El Salvador ($N = 197$) [19], Alicante, Spain ($N = 212$) [18], and Seattle, Washington, U.S.A. ($N = 394$) [2;24]. The questionnaires were administered in night schools to insure intersample uniformity and because the students were willing and able to complete the forms. Verbal instructions and repeated explanations supplemented written instructions. The samples obtained were not meant to be representative of the total population of Huaráz and Arequipa, for they were predominantly young and unmarried.

Data Analysis

The data were analyzed by the use of the geometric mean and nonparametric statistics inasmuch as subjective magnitude estimations do not produce true interval scales nor a normal distribution [24].

RESULTS AND DISCUSSION

Sample Characteristics

The comparison of sample characteristics of the two Peruvian cities, El Salvador, Spain, and the United States is presented in Table 7.1. Compared to other surveys, the Peruvian subjects were single. As a result, close similarity in age and marital status was achieved between the two Peruvian cities. The large majority

Table 7.1

Comparison of Sample Characteristics

Demographic Category	Groups	Huaráz (N = 69)	Arequipa (N = 78)	El Salvador* (N = 197)	Spain* (N = 212)	United States* (N = 394)
Sex	Male	58.0%	50.0%	65%	66%	45%
	Female	42.0%	50.0%	35%	34%	55%
Marital Status	Single	75.4%	89.6%	64%	40%	43%
	Married	24.6%	10.4%	35%	60%	57%
Race	Caucasian		1.3%	20%	100%	92%
	Mestizo	100.0%	98.7%	58%		
	Indian			4%		
	Negro					5%
	Other			18%		3%
Religion	Catholic	98.6%	100.0%	87%	99%	11%
	Other	1.4%		3%		77%
	None			10%	1%	12%
Age	0–30 years	95.7%	92.3%	76%	49%	52%
	31–59 years	4.3%	7.7%	22%	43%	35%
	60+ years			2%	7%	13%
Education	0–9 years	4.4%		38%	32%	46%**
	10–12 years	95.6%	53.8%	30%	27%	
	12+ years		46.2%	30%	41%	54%

* El Salvador [19]; Spain [18]; United States [2]
** 0–12 years

of Peruvians, Spaniards, and El Salvadorians were Roman Catholics, whereas there was diverse religious distribution in the United States.

The Arequipa population was receiving English instruction and had wider educational experience than the Huaracinos. Ninety-five percent of the Huaráz group, as opposed to 100 percent of the Arequipa group, had completed high school. While no Huaráz student had attended university, 46 percent of the Arequipa students had attended university for one or more years. This educational difference was the greatest disparity measured between the two groups.

Social Readjustment Rating Scale (SRRS)

Table 7.2 presents the geometric means and the comparative SRRS rankings of the five groups. Significant differences in mean values of SRRS items between

Huaráz and other population groups are indicated. There are marked differences in rank ordering as well. The earthquake victims placed relatively more importance on events of an economic nature than did the Arequipa group. They ranked foreclosure of a loan or mortgage, change of responsibilities at work, and trouble with the boss considerably higher than did Arequipeños. Items indicative of interpersonal dynamics, in contrast, were ranked lower by Huaráz subjects. Marriage, for example, was placed 11 ranks lower in Huaráz than in Arequipa. In addition, the people of Huaráz ranked divorce, marital reconciliation, outstanding personal achievement, and pregnancy clearly lower than all three other countries as well as Arequipa. Certainly, this signifies a marked reevaluation of these events post-earthquake. An increased perception in significance of economic events might be expected from people who have suffered a natural catastrophe. The decrease in perception of personal and interpersonal events probably evolved because emotional needs were superseded by physical needs.

Peruvian SRRS magnitudes (Figure 7.1) were markedly higher than values assigned by populations from El Salvador, Spain, and the United States. Generally speaking, the Arequipa values were about 200 points greater, while the Huaráz values were about 300 points greater than the similarly ranked items in the other three countries. The higher values are accompanied by a successive shift of the modulus item (marriage) from 1st in El Salvador, 4th in the United States, and 8th in Spain, to 18th in Arequipa and 29th in Huaráz. As shown in Figure 7.1, only in the Huaráz group does death of a spouse assume such a low rank (15th). The higher values assigned by the Huaracinos to life events on the SRRS are considered to be products of the impact of the earthquake. This experience has altered their perception to produce a generalized increase in sensitivity to life events.

The most specific physical need destroyed by the earthquake was shelter, because approximately 90 percent of Huaráz homes were leveled by the earthquake. At the time of this study, the town center had been bulldozed flat. No one had been allowed to begin reconstruction because of poorly defined, yet rigid building regulations. As a result, the entire populace of Huaráz had been relocated north in small, temporary housing. Unlike houses, crops and the majority of livestock survived the earthquake. Thus, secondary to the initial readjustment to the loss of loved ones, the major long-term adjustment concerned shelter. Not surprisingly, change in living conditions was the event listed as requiring the most readjustment by the people of Huaráz. This event was ranked 7–27 ranks higher in Huaráz than by all other population groups. Change in residence, accordingly, was ranked 9 higher than in Arequipa. Similarly, the Huaráz subjects, most of whom still live in their parents' houses, ranked son or daughter leaving home at least 12 ranks higher than all other groups. The fact is clearly pointed out that the earthquake caused much disruption in the living situations of the Huaracinos.

Another impressive change in rank ordering attributable to the earthquake was a marked decrease in ranking of health-related items. Most salient was a drop in

Table 7.2
Life Event Items on the SRRS (Comparative Ranks and Geometric Means)#

Life Event Items	Huaráz		Arequipa		El Salvador@		Spain@		United States@	
	Rank	Mean	Rank	Mean	Rank	Mean	Rank	Mean	Rank	Mean
Change in living conditions	1	1,331	14	588	8	321*	21	212***	28	186***
Fired at work	2	1,139	6	680	7	324	5	622**	8	378
Mortgage less than $10,000	3	1,114	4	712	25	215	24	187**	37	105***
Mortgage more than $10,000	4	990	13	608	9	292	13	340	24	210***
Christmas	5	968	28	389	34	164***	35	81***	42	59***
Foreclosure of loan or mortgage	6	938	25	421**	16	263***	12	389*	21	231***
Begin or end formal school	7	865	7	661	6	339***	22	195***	27	191***
Change in financial status	8	848	16	525	4	352**	14	327**	15	308
Son or daughter leaving home	9	775	21	459	26	213**	27	128***	22	219
Retirement	10	773	12	616	18	235	19	220**	10	361
Sexual difficulties	11	769	17	517	12	273	9	496**	13	316
Marital separation	12	724	8	645	19	232	3	664**	3	516
Change in responsibility at work	13	689	24	422	10	290	25	155***	20	243*
Change to a different line of work	14	677	22	454	28	192**	18	234	16	287
Death of spouse	15	643	1	874	2	436	1	1,524***	1	771***
Business readjustment	16	598	3	737*	11	286	10	419	14	308
Death of close family member	17	579	29	378*	13	272	16	284*	5	469
Minor law violation	18	577	38	313	43	116***	43	44***	43	54***
Personal injury or illness	19	575	2	777	3	389	2	1,339***	7	416
Change in church activities	20	553	20	471*	38	151***	36	75***	36	112***
Trouble with the boss	21	544	41	283**	36	159***	28	125***	29	178***
Divorce	22	543	5	708*	14	265	6	516***	2	593***
Vacation	23	543	11	618	33	183*	30	102***	41	74***
Change in personal habits	24	538	32	368	22	224***	32	84*	30	149***

92

Event										
Gaining a new family member	25	526	23	451	17	241	15	293	11	337
Trouble with in-laws	26	523	33	361	41	143	39	64***	23	213
Pregnancy	27	515	19	475	15	264	7	516	18	284***
Wife begins or stops work	28	508	31	369	27	198**	29	104***	25	204***
Marriage	29	500	18	500	1	500	8	500	4	500
Change in social activities	30	486	26	410	32	184	41	60***	35	125***
Change in residence	31	482	40	284*	40	145*	26	142***	32	140***
Change in recreation	32	482	36	319	29	191	40	63***	34	127**
Change in health of family member	33	480	27	405	20	230**	23	192***	12	335
Marital reconciliation	34	446	10	633	23	223	20	216	9	366
Detention in jail	35	433	9	636*	24	221	4	655***	6	439*
Outstanding personal achievement	36	418	15	543*	5	348	11	390	26	192***
Change in eating habits	37	401	39	305*	35	164***	38	73***	40	98***
Change in work hours or conditions	38	392	42	281	31	186	37	74***	31	148***
Change in number of arguments with spouse	39	359	30	377	30	188	31	98***	17	286
Death of a close friend	40	343	35	352	21	230	17	249	19	269
Change in sleeping habits	41	338	43	236*	37	152*	34	82***	38	105***
Change to a new school	42	337	34	353	39	150	33	83**	33	135**
Change in number of family get-togethers	43	323	37	314	42	132*	42	51***	39	103***

* Significant differences from Huaráz scores. Mann–Whitney U-test

@ El Salvador [19]; Spain [18]; United States [2;24]

    * $p \leq 0.05$

  ** $p \leq 0.01$

*** $p \leq 0.001$

the position of death of spouse, ranked first or second in all other groups, to 15th. Similarly, Huaráz ranked personal injury or illness, change in health of family member, death of a close friend, and death of a close family member lower than El Salvador, Spain, and the United States. Seemingly inconsistent, however, death of a close family member was ranked 12 higher in Huaráz than in Arequipa.

The general picture emerging, then, is that people of Huaráz felt they needed less readjustment to matters of death, injury, and illness than population groups not traumatized by natural catastrophe. This may be accounted for either because of denial, or because of an adjustment and desensitization to the facts of death, injury, and illness. While denial is certainly a very real occurrence following death, the reaction is usually worked through after a period of one year, the time between the earthquake and this study. The aftermath of the Huaráz disaster left many weeks of cleaning of debris. Gruesome tasks of dealing with the corpses for this long period of time possibly did help desensitize these people to death.

Another earthquake-induced change in SRRS ranking is reflected in increased emphasis on religious events. While both Huaráz and Arequipa perceived change in church activities as being of greater relative importance than in the other three countries, Huaráz, in addition, assigned an increased rank to Christmas. This item was judged at least 23 ranks higher by Huaracinos than by all other groups, including Arequipeños. This increase in rank order might well reflect a renewed emphasis on religion following this natural catastrophe.

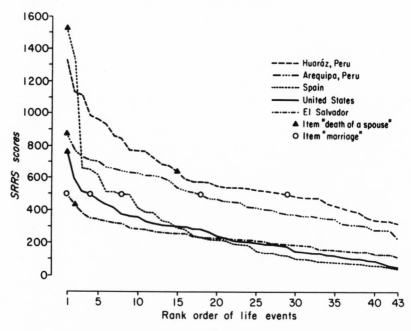

Figure 7.1   Rank order and SRRS values.

Table 7.3
Cross-cultural Comparisons of SRRS Rank Order Correlations*

	Arequipa	El Salvador	Spain	United States
Huaráz	0.54	0.45**	0.36**	0.18***
Arequipa		0.69	0.73	0.57
El Salvador			0.81	0.69
Spain				0.83

* Based on Spearman's rho. All comparisons significant at $p \leq 0.001$, except:
** $p \leq 0.01$
*** $p \leq 0.20$

The rank order correlations of the SRRS life-event item scores among the two Peruvian cities and El Salvador, Spain, and the United States are shown in Table 7.3. Comparison of Huaráz with El Salvador revealed Spearman's rho equal to 0.45; Huaráz with Spain, $r_s = 0.36$; and Huaráz with the United States, $r_s = 0.18$ (not significant). In contrast, Arequipa compared more closely with all three countries: $r_s = 0.69$, 0.73, and 0.57, respectively.

Huaráz correlated with El Salvador more closely; Spain next; and finally the United States. Arequipa correlated more closely with Spain than with El Salvador. In turn, El Salvador correlated more closely with Spain (0.81) than with the United States (0.69). These data point to a progressive decrease in consensus about the salience of cultural variation relative to perceptions of life change events from the United States to the less industrialized countries.

In the United States, at one end of the industrial spectrum, items of need such as mortgage greater than $10,000, foreclosure of loan or mortgage, and change in living conditions are ranked low; and matters of interpersonal dynamics such as marriage, marital separation, marital reconciliation, and divorce are ranked high. Arequipa and Huaráz, at the other end of the industrial spectrum, tend to rank items of need higher; and items of interpersonal dynamics, lower. Correlations are closer between similar, less developed cultural groups than with the United States and reflect their common judgment about the importance of food, clothing, and shelter.

Previous cross-cultural studies on the SRRS had shown high coefficients of correlation. Spearman's rho ranged from 0.70 to 0.97 when populations from the United States [2], Japan [15], El Salvador [19], Spain [18], France, Belgium, Switzerland [20], and Sweden and Denmark [17] were compared. Consensus was also very high between different intracultural groups—black versus white, male versus female, various age groups, and different religions within Seattle—Pearson's coefficient of correlation being between 0.82 and 0.97 [2]. In addition,

Table 7.4

Comparison of Mean LCU between Huaráz and Arequipa

Year	LCU		Significant Differences* Between Huaráz and Arequipa
	Huaráz	Arequipa	
June 1970–June 1971 (A)	360.00	203.53	$p \leq 0.01$
June 1969–June 1970 (B) Earthquake	692.62	281.18	$p \leq 0.001$
June 1968–June 1969 (C)	250.28	195.00	N.S.
June 1967–June 1968 (D)	190.45	113.60	$p \leq 0.05$
June 1966–June 1967 (E)	155.94	119.16	N.S.

* Mann-Whitney U-test

COMPARISONS OF MEAN LCU WITHIN A GIVEN CITY

Huaráz	Year B from A, C, D and E	$p \leq 0.001$
	Year A from D	$p \leq 0.01$
	Year A from E	$p \leq 0.001$
	Year C from E	$p \leq 0.01$
Arequipa	Year B from D and E	$p \leq 0.001$
	Year B from C and A	$p \leq 0.01$
	Year A from D	$p \leq 0.01$
	Year A from E	$p \leq 0.05$
	Year C from D and E	$p \leq 0.001$

consensus between cities from the same culture was high, Spearman's rho between Honolulu and Seattle being 0.97 [25].

Contrary to these very close correlations, the comparison between Huaráz and Arequipa revealed a striking disparity, Spearman's rho being only 0.54. While the rank order correlation of the SRRS between Huaráz and Arequipa is still statistically significant, the value is the lowest intracultural correlation yet observed. Indeed, the Huaráz–Arequipa correlation is lower than that between Arequipa and the United States. Huaráz, in the aftermath of the earthquake, shows not only a progression in the cultural shift from interpersonal dynamics to items of need (cited above) but also some very striking shifts in items that previously had been uniform in all Latin American groups.

Life Change Units (LCU)

Table 7.4 presents the mean annual LCU for the two Peruvian cities. Huaráz scores are higher than Arequipa scores in every year, with significant differences

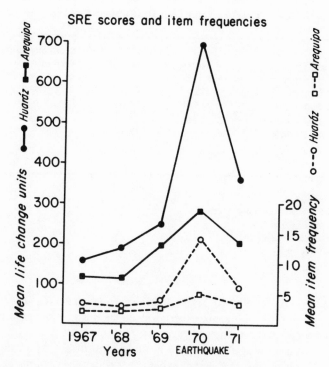

Figure 7.2 Mean annual LCU and total item frequencies.

two years pre-earthquake, the year of the earthquake, and in the post-earthquake year. In addition, comparison of LCU within each city through the five years shows that significant differences existed in both Huaráz and Arequipa. The mean LCU in Huaráz between the pre-earthquake year and the post-earthquake year were significantly different from the earthquake year itself. These same differences were noted in Arequipa. Thus, in both cities there was a gradual rise in mean LCU pre-earthquake with a peak in the earthquake year. In the post-earthquake year, Arequipa returned to its pre-earthquake level; the Huaráz mean LCU lessened but remained significantly higher than the pre-earthquake level.

Figure 7.2 shows the mean number of life events per individual in each year as well as the mean annual LCU discussed above. It is clear that both increased sharply during the earthquake year for Huaráz. However, for Arequipa, the rise in LCU is not matched by a rise in the mean number of life events.

The higher LCU scores seen in Huaráz were due to a combination of both higher SRRS values and increased number of life changes. One would expect the LCU to go up in the earthquake year; more traumatic events and life changes transpired in that year, secondary to the earthquake. In the subsequent year, with many of the effects of the earthquake still present, it is not surprising that the

Table 7.5
Comparison of Mean Annual LCU for Four Health Items* on the SRE

| Year | LCU | | Significant Differences** |
	Huaráz	Arequipa	Between Huaráz and Arequipa
June 1970–June 1971	45.17	29.44	0.05
June 1969–June 1970	215.50	53.09	0.001
June 1968–June 1969	34.64	44.54	N.S.
June 1967–June 1968	45.24	16.15	N.S.
June 1966–June 1967	23.06	19.73	N.S.

* Personal injury or illness
Change in health of family member
Death of close friend
Death of a close family member
** Mann-Whitney U-test (one tailed)

Huaráz score was significantly higher than the Arequipa score. In 1967, 1968, and 1969, prior to the earthquake, there was no significant change in the mean item incidence for the two cities.

In the earthquake year, the Arequipa mean LCU also rose significantly compared to the previous year. A partial explanation is that the earthquake affected all Peruvians. It received extensive national and international press coverage. Photographs were posted throughout the country calling attention to the catastrophe; all Peruvians were urged to help the *damnificados*.

However, there were also other national events that might have increased life change in Arequipa and contributed to the rise in Huaráz. In September 1968, a military regime headed by Juan Velasco Alvarado overthrew the existing Peruvian government. Velasco Alvarado instituted several potent reforms including the *reforma agraria*, a working program to distribute the *hacienda* land to the farmers. Although unevenly applied, the *reforma agraria* especially affected middle-class landholders, including many Arequipeños. Upheavals at all levels of local government took place that would have affected equally both Huaráz and Arequipa. Thus, the pressures of revolution and land reform might well explain the progress in LCU in Arequipa, as well as in Huaráz in the year prior to the earthquake. These increases, while statistically significant, contribute to but do not override the higher life change scores in Huaráz in both the earthquake and post-earthquake years.

Four health items listed on the SRE include personal injury or illness, death of a close family member, death of a close friend, and change in the health of a family member. The sums of the mean annual LCU for these health items for the two cities are shown in Table 7.5. As predicted, there was a significant difference between the two cities not only during the earthquake year but also during the post-earthquake year.

There was no epidemic of infectious disease following the earthquake to account for this difference. Though SRRS values for health-related items were not different for the two cities, except for Huaráz's higher score for death of a family member, the incidence of these events in Huaráz was much higher. Direct injury from the earthquake no doubt contributed to increased health-item totals in the earthquake year. The consequences of the earthquake led to an increased incidence in health-related items both during the earthquake year and also in the post-earthquake year. These findings corroborate our postulate that a natural catastrophe would increase life change and subsequently health change.

SUMMARY

The Social Readjustment Rating Questionnaire (SRRQ) and the Schedule of Recent Experience (SRE) were administered one year following the May 30, 1970, earthquake in Peru. The study was done in an earthquake-devastated city, Huaráz, and in a comparison city, Arequipa. Data analysis of the rankings of perceptions of life events on the Social Readjustment Rating Scale (SRRS) between the two Peruvian cities, as well as international cross-cultural comparisons, was specifically earthquake centered: Events dealing with shelter and religious experience were ranked higher, while events dealing with death and illness were ranked lower. The second conclusion reflected a generalized increase in ranking of items dealing with bodily necessities and decreased ranking of items dealing with the personal and interpersonal dynamics as one sampled progressively less industrialized cultures.

During the earthquake year and subsequent year the Huaráz population had significantly higher mean annual life change units (LCU), as did Arequipa, though not so great as those in Huaráz. In the case of Arequipa, this may be explained by the national nature of the catastrophe and by the effects of recent government revolution and land reform. As predicted, the added stresses of this natural catastrophe led to a marked increase in health change as reflected in the four SRE health items. The Huaráz population experienced a significant rise in health change, in the earthquake year and in the subsequent year as well.

REFERENCES

1. Carter, H. A. "The Earthquake in Peru." *American Alpine Journal* 17 (1971):241–60.

2. Holmes, T. H., and R. H. Rahe. "The Social Readjustment Rating Scale." *Journal of Psychosomatic Research* 11 (1967):213–18. Reprinted in this volume, Chapter 2.

3. Holmes, T. H., and R. H. Rahe. *Booklet for Schedule of Recent Experience (SRE)*. Seattle: University of Washington, 1967.

4. Wolff, H. G., S. Wolf, and C. C. Hare, eds. *Life Stress and Bodily Disease*.

Research Publications of the Association for Research in Nervous and Mental Disease, vol. 29. Baltimore: Williams and Wilkins, 1950.

5. Holmes, T. H., H. Goodell, S. Wolf, and H. G. Wolff. *The Nose: An Experimental Study of Reactions within the Nose in Human Subjects during Varying Life Experiences.* Springfield, Ill.: Charles C Thomas, 1950.

6. Wolf, S. *The Stomach.* New York: Oxford University Press, 1965.

7. Wolf, S., P. V. Cardon, E. M. Shepard, and H. G. Wolff. *Life Stress and Essential Hypertension.* Baltimore: Williams and Wilkins, 1955.

8. Grace, W. J., S. Wolf, and H. G. Wolff. *The Human Colon.* New York: Paul B. Hoeber, 1951.

9. Hawkins, N. G., R. Davies, and T. H. Holmes. "Evidence of Psychosocial Factors in the Development of Pulmonary Tuberculosis." *American Review of Tuberculosis and Pulmonary Diseases* 75 (1957):768–80. Reprinted in this volume, Chapter 11.

10. Rahe, R. H., M. Meyer, M. Smith, G. Kjaer, and T. H. Holmes. "Social Stress and Illness Onset." *Journal of Psychosomatic Research* 8 (1964):35–44. Reprinted in this volume, Chapter 12.

11. Rahe, R. H., and T. H. Holmes. "Social, Psychologic and Psychophysiologic Aspects of Inguinal Hernia." *Journal of Psychosomatic Research* 8 (1965):487–91.

12. Rahe, R. H., and T. H. Holmes. "Life Crisis and Disease Onset. I. Qualitative and Quantitative Definition of the Life Crisis and Its Association with Health Change." First published as pt. 2 of R. H. Rahe, "Life Crisis and Health Change." In *Psychotropic Drug Response: Advances in Prediction*, edited by P. R. A. May and J. R. Wittenborn, pp. 92–125. Springfield, Ill.: Charles C Thomas, 1969. Reprinted in this volume, Chapter 13.

13. Rahe, R. H., and T. H. Holmes. "Life Crisis and Disease Onset. II. A Prospective Study of Life Crises and Health Changes." First published as pt. 3 of R. H. Rahe, "Life Crisis and Health Change." In *Psychotropic Drug Response: Advances in Prediction*," edited by P. R. A. May and J. R. Wittenborn, pp. 92–125. Springfield, Ill.: Charles C Thomas, 1969. Reprinted in this volume, Chapter 14.

14. Casey, R. L., M. Masuda, and T. H. Holmes. "Quantitative Study of Recall of Life Events." *Journal of Psychosomatic Research* 11 (1967):239–47. Reprinted in this volume, Chapter 10.

15. Masuda, M., and T. H. Holmes. "The Social Readjustment Rating Scale: A Cross-cultural Study of Japanese and Americans." *Journal of Psychosomatic Research* 11 (1967):227–37. Reprinted in this volume, Chapter 5.

16. Komaroff, A. L., M. Masuda, and T. H. Holmes. "The Social Readjustment Rating Scale: A Comparative Study of Negro, Mexican and White Americans." *Journal of Psychosomatic Research* 12 (1968):121–28. Reprinted in this volume, Chapter 6.

17. Rahe, R. H. "Multi-cultural Correlations of Life Change Scaling: America, Japan, Denmark, and Sweden." *Journal of Psychosomatic Research* 13 (1969):191–95.

18. Celdrán, H. H. "The Cross-cultural Consistency of Two Social Consensus Scales: The Seriousness of Illness Rating Scale and the Social Readjustment Rating Scale in Spain." Medical thesis, University of Washington, 1970.

19. Seppa, M. T. "The Social Readjustment Rating Scale: A Comparative Study of Salvadorans, Spanish and Americans." Medical thesis, University of Washington, 1970.

20. Harmon, D. K., M. Masuda, and T. H. Holmes. "The Social Readjustment Rating Scale: A Cross-cultural Study of Western Europeans and Americans." *Journal of Psychosomatic Research* 14 (1970):391–400.

21. Holmes, T. H., and M. Masuda. "Life Change and Illness Susceptibility." In *Sepa-*

ration and Depression: Clinical and Research Aspects, edited by J. P. Scott and E. C. Senay, pp. 161–86. AAAS Publication no. 94. Washington, D.C.: American Association for the Advancement of Science, 1973.

22. Doughty, P. L. *Huaylas*. Ithaca, N.Y.: Cornell University Press, 1968.

23. Rennie, D. "After the Earthquake." *Lancet* 2 (1970):704–7.

24. Masuda, M., and T. H. Holmes. "Magnitude Estimations of Social Readjustments." *Journal of Psychosomatic Research* 11 (1967):219–25. Reprinted in this volume, Chapter 3.

25. Ruch, L. O., and T. H. Holmes. "Scaling of Life Change: A Comparison of Direct and Indirect Methods." *Journal of Psychosomatic Research* 15 (1971):221–27. Reprinted in this volume, Chapter 4.

Introduction

Quantifying the Seriousness of Illness

In the course of our early studies of the relationship of life change magnitude to the onset of health changes, we noticed—but could not measure—an apparent relationship between the magnitude of life change and the seriousness of illness. Subjects with lower life change scores seemed to have less serious illnesses, while those with higher life change scores seemed to have the more serious illnesses.

We knew the question to ask: Is there a relationship between the seriousness of illness experienced and the magnitude of life change present at the onset of illness? But we could not answer the question until we could quantify the seriousness of illness. There was no satisfactory measure available (notice that we were distinguishing "severity" of illness from "seriousness" of illness), so we had to devise one.

The Seriousness of Illness Rating Questionnaire employs the method of subjective magnitude estimation to produce a rank ordering of 126 diseases ranging from dandruff and warts to cancer and heart attacks. We found that U.S. non-physicians and physicians both basically agree about the seriousness of illnesses. Studies in Spain, El Salvador, and Ireland (see discussion in Chapter 21) further demonstrated a broad, cross-cultural consensus in perceptions of the seriousness of illness.

The Seriousness of Illness Rating Scale—like the Social Readjustment Rating Scale—was developed as a means to an end. Chapter 8 shows the development of this new instrument. In a subsequent study (*Journal of Psychosomatic Research* 14 [1970]:59–64), we established the reproducibility of the instrument using the test-retest method. Chapter 16 in Part III of this book shows how we put the Seriousness of Illness Rating Scale to work.

8

Seriousness of Illness Rating Scale

Allen R. Wyler, Minoru Masuda, and Thomas H. Holmes

In 1960 Hinkle et al. [1] defined seriousness of illness as "the likelihood that this episode of illness, or its sequelae, if untreated, will lead to the death of a subject." Thus, their scale of seriousness was a function of an estimated epidemiologic probability of death. They then distinguished "seriousness" from "severity" by defining the second concept as "degree of disability—the extent to which a person is unable to carry out his social life." They were able to quantitate severity by such measurements as the number of days missed from work due to any one illness. Both of these definitions, therefore, minimized subjective components of seriousness. In the present study, seriousness was considered from a different vantage point—the gestalt view of illness. The concept of "seriousness of illness" for this study, although difficult to define, included such factors as prognosis, duration, threat to life, degree of disability, and degree of discomfort.

Since the early 1950s many studies have shown a relationship between life stress and the onset of specific illnesses [2–13]. In 1964 Rahe et al. [14] showed that a cluster of "social stress" events was significantly associated with the onset of illness. Readjustments to psychosocial events were quantified by the development of the Social Readjustment Rating Scale [15], and the Schedule of Recent Experience [10] was developed to record the chronology of all events. Subsequent study by Rahe et al. [16] showed that illness clusters appeared after increases in one's "basal" social stress level. Rahe also found a relationship between the amount of social stress and the seriousness of one's illness.

This study hopes to discriminate further the relationship between the social

This chapter is reprinted with permission from Allen R. Wyler, Minoru Masuda, and Thomas H. Holmes, "Seriousness of Illness Rating Scale," *Journal of Psychosomatic Research* 11 (1968): 363–74. Copyright 1968 by Pergamon Press, Ltd.

stress and seriousness of illness by establishing a magnitude estimation of the seriousness of illness. The chapter describes a rank order of 126 diseases on this basis and the magnitude estimations of these as they relate to a given modulus disease item. In addition, the illness scores were scrutinized as to whether physicians with knowledge of disease would rank or score disease items in a grossly different manner from the general public.

METHODS

A list of diseases was compiled in the following manner. The admitting diagnoses of all the patients who had entered Doctors Hospital during the year June 1965–June 1966 were collected and, in addition, the diagnostic records of all patients of a Seattle general practitioner. From this primary list, 150 of the most frequent diagnoses were selected. The list was then increased to 250 diseases by selection from *Principles of Internal Medicine* (Harrison) and the American Medical Association's *Standard Nomenclature of Disease and Operations*. The list of 250 diseases was submitted to ten physicians who practice in ten different specialties. These doctors were asked to eliminate those illnesses that were thought not to be commonly seen in medical practice, or those diseases that would not be familiar to the majority of the people. This medical screening helped ensure a final disease list that could be evaluated by people in general on diseases that could be easily recognized by the majority of respondents. The diseases picked in this manner by the ten physicians numbered 175. Several diseases not seen by the public, such as multiple sclerosis, were left on the list since such widespread publicity has been given them that most respondents would have had some familiarity with them. Shark bite was left on the list because of personal interest.

The list was pretested on 35 patients from a private practice. The results indicated that the disease list contained illnesses that could not be discriminated. For example, pyelonephritis and glomerulonephritis—or meningitis and encephalitis—were not seen as being different. A second pretest using another group of 22 nonmedically educated persons showed further that many of the medical terms for diseases were not familiar to the respondents. In this same oral pretest the respondents were questioned as to terminology they could readily identify. Taking into account the results from the above two pretests, diseases were combined into one heading and/or changed into simpler language. At times the two processes were used simultaneously. For example, pyelonephritis and glomerulonephritis were combined into the heading of "kidney infection." The final list contained 126 disease items.

The questionnaire was constructed as follows: The first page asked for biographical information and gave instructions for scoring the disease items. Each questionnaire contained two additional pages of disease items. Pretesting had shown that a list of 63 diseases could be easily rated within 15 minutes, and was of such length that the respondent would not fatigue. Therefore, every respondent evaluated only half of the complete list of diseases. The two sheets of disease items used for each questionnaire were such that there would be an equal number of questionnaires of each possible combination and order of pages. The instruction page made the following request of the respondents:

Please rate the following list of illnesses as to their relative seriousness. In scoring, use all of your experience in arriving at your answer. This means personal experience where it applies as well as what you have learned to be the case for others. Strive to give your opinion of the average degree of seriousness for each illness rather than the extreme. There is no right or wrong answer.

The mechanics of rating are these: The seriousness of the disease Peptic Ulcer has been given an arbitrary value of 500. You are asked to compare the seriousness of each of the remaining diseases to peptic ulcer. As you rate each of the remaining diseases think to yourself, "Is this disease more or less serious than a peptic ulcer?" If, for example, you decide the disease is more serious than a peptic ulcer, then choose a proportionately larger number than 500 (as an example, you may wish to rate it as 501, 600, 725, 888, etc., points). Place this number in the blank directly opposite the disease in the column marked "VALUES." If you decide the disease is less serious, indicate how much less serious by placing a proportionately smaller number than 500 in the column marked "VALUES." If the disease is equal in seriousness, record the number 500 in the column marked "VALUES."

Distribution of the questionnaires was as follows: Of the nonmedical sample, 150 were distributed directly to University Hospital outpatients, and to patients from three private practices located in widely different areas of Seattle; and 150 were sent to the wives of the University of Washington faculty. Of the medical sample, 100 were mailed to practicing physicians and 50 to residents and interns, all at the University Hospital.

A letter of introduction accompanied the mailing, but there were no further instructions other than what appeared on the front sheet of the questionnaire. For the questionnaires handed out at the outpatient clinic, instructions were given to the receptionist to say only that the questionnaire was for a research project and it was not mandatory that the patient fill it out, but it would be appreciated if he or she did so; that the patient need not give his or her name on the questionnaire; and also that the patient should fill it out during the time spent in the clinic and return it when leaving.

RESULTS

Of the 300 questionnaires given to the nonmedical sample, 141 were returned. From the physician group of 150, 117 were returned. The characteristics of the two groups are seen in Table 8.1. The medical group was virtually only between the ages 21–65, while the nonmedical sample had a few respondents on either side of this range. The medical group had few females and few nonmarried respondents. However, those in the medical group who were not married were males. In both groups the respondents were primarily Caucasian and Protestant, about 10 percent of each group being Roman Catholic. The medical group paralleled the nonmedical group with respect to generation American, but was very much biased with respect to years of education.

The geometric mean scores for each disease item in both the medical and the nonmedical groups, as well as the rankings of these diseases, are shown in Table

Table 8.1
Characteristics of Medical and Nonmedical Samples

		Medical sample	Nonmedical sample
Age			
	Less than 21 years	0	13
	21 to 34 years	50	75
	35 to 65 years	66	44
	Greater than 65 years	1	9
Sex			
	Male	114	58
	Female	3	83
Religion			
	Roman Catholic	12	15
	Protestant	70	62
	Other	35	44
Race			
	Caucasian	116	130
	Negro	1	2
	Other	0	9
Marital status			
	Married	113	91
	Not married	4	50
Years of education			
	Less than 12 years	0	15
	12 to 16 years	0	108
	Greater than 16 years	117	18
Generation American			
	1st	17	8
	2nd	26	29
	3rd	74	104
Total number		117	141

8.2. The rationale for using the geometric mean has been discussed recently by Masuda and Holmes [17]. Spearman's rank order correlation coefficient (rho) was used to compare the mean rank orders of the two groups. Spearman's rho was computed to be a highly significant 0.947. The high degree of correlation may be seen in Table 8.2, which gives the mean and rank for each disease in both groups.

Because of the high degree of correlation the scores for the two groups were combined and a new "grand" rank order and mean were found for each disease. These grand values are also shown in Table 8.2. For the medical and nonmedical samples, means of all the disease item scores were found to be 368 and 374, respectively, which was not significantly different by the t-test. The parallelism in the ranking and the scoring of the two groups is shown graphically in Figure 8.1. It should be noted that in Figure 8.1 the abscissa is the medical rank ordering.

The physicians scored the diseases of lesser magnitude consistently lower than did the nonmedical group, while scoring consistently higher the diseases of greater magnitude. The intersection of the two scoring curves is at a point of disease magnitude just prior to the modulus disease item of peptic ulcer.

Kendall's coefficient of concordance (W) is a statistic that signifies the extent of individual agreement existing in the rank ordering of the disease items. Inasmuch as not all respondents had evaluated the complete list of disease items, but only one of six possible combinations, it was decided to test agreement among individual raters in the nonmedical group for each of the four pages. For pages 1–4, Kendall's W was 0.702, 0.669, 0.688, and 0.594, respectively. The chi-square values are significant at a p of < 0.0005.

Item analyses of individual diseases were done using the Kruskal-Wallis

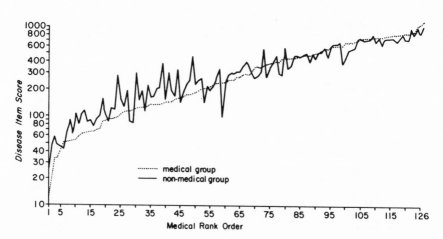

Figure 8.1   A comparison of disease item scores between medical and nonmedical groups.

Table 8.2
Rank Order and Geometric Mean Scores of Disease Items

Grand rank	Disease item	Grand mean	Medical sample		Nonmedical sample	
			Rank	Mean	Rank	Mean
1	Dandruff	21	1	14	1	27
2	Warts	32	2	20	4	47
3	Cold sore, canker sore	43	4	35	5	48
4	Corns	46	5	43	3	46
5	Hiccups	48	6	50	2	43
6	Bad breath	49	3	34	6	59
7	Sty	59	9	53	7	64
8	Common cold	62	7	51	8	67
9	Farsightedness	72	11	60	10	81
10	Nosebleed	73	8	52	16	91
11	Sore throat	74	16	68	9	78
12	Nearsightedness	75	14	66	12	86
13	Sunburn	80	10	54	22	109
14	Constipation	81	15	67	15	90
15	Astigmatism	83	17	71	17	94
16	Laryngitis	84	12	64	21	107
17	Ringworm	85	13	65	23	111
18	Headache	88	21	92	14	89
19	Scabies	89	18	72	19	104
20	Boils	96	20	89	20	105
21	Heartburn	98	29	117	11	85
22	Acne	103	28	115	13	88
23	Abscessed tooth	108	22	93	26	124
24	Colorblindness	109	23	96	25	119
25	Tonsillitis	117	19	87	32	156
26	Diarrhea	118	33	125	24	115
27	Carbuncle	122	26	113	27	126
28	Chicken pox	134	25	105	33	160
29	Menopause	140	31	123	30	150
30	Mumps	148	27	113	37	191
31	Dizziness	149	35	134	34	161
32	Sinus infection	150	41	146	31	155
33	Bed sores	153	59	240	18	97
34	Increased menstrual flow	154	45	163	29	146
35	Fainting	155	36	135	35	165
36	Measles	159	32	124	41	196
37	Painful menstruation	163	43	155	36	168
38	Infection of the middle ear	164	37	136	42	204

cont'd

Table 8.2, continued

Grand rank	Disease item	Grand mean	Medical sample		Nonmedical sample	
			Rank	Mean	Rank	Mean
39	Varicose veins	173	42	147	40	195
40	Psoriasis	174	53	205	28	141
41	No menstrual period	175	38	139	43	208
42	Hemorrhoids	177	34	130	46	224
43	Hay fever	185	46	164	38	192
44	Low blood pressure	189	24	98	56	281
45	Eczema	204	55	218	39	193
46	Drug allergy	206	47	172	48	231
47	Bronchitis	210	50	186	47	230
48	Hyperventilation	211	30	121	61	307
49	Shingles	212	54	208	45	219
50	Mononucleosis	216	40	142	60	306
51	Infected eye	220	56	226	44	215
52	Bursitis	222	48	174	51	258
53	Whooping cough	230	52	201	52	264
54	Lumbago	231	51	197	50	255
55	Fibroids of the uterus	234	39	140	76	380
56	Migraine	242	60	240	49	243
57	Hernia	244	44	163	69	339
58	Frostbite	263	57	238	59	272
59	Goiter	283	61	252	59	297
60	Abortion	284	62	256	64	311
61	Ovarian cyst	288	58	238	71	345
62	Heatstroke	293	63	256	62	308
63	Gonorrhea	296	49	180	83	463
64	Irregular heart beats	302	64	273	68	318
65	Overweight	309	70	351	53	267
66	Anemia	312	65	280	67	317
67	Anxiety reaction	315	71	356	57	288
68	Gout	322	74	387	55	274
69	Snake bite	324	69	322	66	313
70	Appendicitis	337	66	298	73	369
71	Pneumonia	338	68	298	75	375
72	Depression	344	79	441	58	292
73	Frigidity	347	72	358	65	312
74	Burns	348	78	414	63	309
75	Kidney infection	374	67	298	84	471
76	Inability for sexual intercourse	382	75	398	72	354

Table 8.2, continued

Grand rank	Disease item	Grand mean	Medical sample		Nonmedical sample	
			Rank	Mean	Rank	Mean
77	Hyperthyroid	393	81	456	70	343
78	Asthma	413	82	457	74	372
79	Glaucoma	426	76	398	79	441
80	Sexual deviation	446	88	495	78	416
81	Gallstones	454	77	414	86	485
82	Arthritis	468	90	507	80	444
83	Starvation	473	85	472	85	472
84	Syphilis	474	73	372	96	572
85	Accidental poisoning	480	83	459	87	487
86	Slipped disk	487	84	461	88	493
87	Hepatitis	488	86	485	89	494
88	Kidney stones	499	87	494	91	506
89	Peptic ulcer	500	89	500	90	500
90	Pancreatitis	514	99	624	77	390
91	High blood pressure	520	94	571	82	462
92	Smallpox	530	100	665	81	445
93	Deafness	533	91	526	92	524
94	Collapsed lung	536	80	450	99	597
95	Shark bite	545	92	545	93	535
96	Epilepsy	582	93	564	98	596
97	Chest pain	609	101	674	94	546
98	Nervous breakdown	610	95	601	100	604
99	Diabetes	621	102	675	95	570
100	Blood clot in blood vessels	631	97	610	102	640
101	Hardening of the arteries	635	96	602	103	649
102	Emphysema	636	103	687	97	593
103	T.B.	645	98	613	104	665
104	Alcoholism	688	112	770	101	635
105	Drug addiction	722	106	735	107	710
106	Coma	725	110	763	105	680
107	Cirrhosis of the liver	733	105	725	110	736
108	Parkinson's disease	734	104	705	113	744
109	Blindness	737	107	742	108	716
110	Mental retardation	745	108	752	111	739
111	Blood clot in the lung	753	117	820	106	681
112	Manic depressive psychosis	766	114	800	114	745
113	Stroke	774	111	766	116	752
114	Schizophrenia	776	120	852	109	724

cont'd

Table 8.2, continued

Grand rank	Disease item	Grand mean	Medical sample		Nonmedical sample	
			Rank	Mean	Rank	Mean
115	Muscular dystrophy	785	116	820	115	746
116	Congenital heart defects	794	118	835	112	740
117	Tumor in the spinal cord	800	115	811	117	791
118	Cerebral palsy	805	109	759	119	834
119	Heart failure	824	113	774	122	849
120	Heart attack	855	119	850	121	843
121	Brain infection	872	122	885	120	836
122	Multiple sclerosis	875	123	910	118	830
123	Bleeding in brain	913	121	880	124	978
124	Uremia	963	125	1090	123	869
125	Cancer	1020	124	1050	125	1000
126	Leukemia	1080	126	1160	126	1009
Mean		370		368		374

analysis of variance and the Mann-Whitney U-test. These statistics seek out significant differences in the mean scores of each disease among or between sample subgroups. In the subgroups with three or more divisions—for example, age—the Kruskal-Wallis test (with an α-level of 0.05) was first used to screen for differences in scoring among the subgroups of individual disease items. If differences were detected by the Kruskal-Wallis test, then the Mann-Whitney test (with an α-level of 0.01) was used to determine which specific pair(s) was significantly different. Tables 8.3–8.8 list the disease items that were scored as significantly different by subgroups of the nonmedical sample according to category. Age and years of education were variables that showed the greatest numbers of differences in disease item scoring.

In sharp contrast, the medical sample subgroups showed few disease items scored differently. The diseases rated as significantly different within subgroups of the physicians were as follows: Sexual deviation was rated higher by second-generation American than by third-generation American; bronchitis was rated lower by those physicians under the age of 35 than physicians older than this age, but the reverse was found for blood clot in the lungs. Also, slipped disk was rated higher by Protestant physicians than the physicians in the "other" religious division. Sex, marital status, and years of education were not treated as variables inasmuch as the sample sizes were not large enough. In the narrowly selected medical group, the other variables of age, religion, and generation American were not important factors in disease item scoring. Those diseases that were related as significantly different in the physicians subgroup were not the same diseases that appeared in the same subgroups of the nonmedical samples.

Between the medical and nonmedical samples, as shown in Table 8.9, there were 31 diseases that were scored as significantly different, or approximately 25 percent of the total disease items. Twenty-four of the 31 disease items were

Table 8.3
Significant* Differences in Disease Item Scores in the Nonmedical
"Religious" Subgroups†

Disease item	Direction of difference
Depression	Other > Catholic
Spinal cord tumor	Other > Catholic
	Protestant > Catholic
Anxiety reaction	Other > Protestant
Frigidity	Other > Protestant
Ovarian cyst	Catholic > Protestant
	Catholic > Other

* Kruskal-Wallis and Mann-Whitney tests
† Subgroups: Protestant, Catholic, Other

Table 8.4
Significant* Differences in Disease Item Scores in the Nonmedical
"Years of Education" Subgroups†

Disease item	Direction of difference
Color blindness	Group 1 > 2, 1 > 3
Nearsightedness	Group 1 > 3, 1 > 2
Farsightedness	Group 1 > 2, 1 > 3
Astigmatism	Group 1 > 2, 1 > 3
Spinal cord tumor	Group 3 > 1, 3 > 2
Alcoholism	Group 2 > 1, 3 > 1
Brain infection	Group 2 > 3
Burns	Group 2 > 3
Mononucleosis	Group 1 > 2, 2 > 3

* See Table 8.3.

† Group 1: less than 12 years of education; 2: 12–16 years of education; 3: 16 years or more of education

Table 8.5
Significant* Differences in Disease Item Scores in the Nonmedical "Age" Subgroups†

Disease item	Direction of difference
Hernia	Group 1 > 3
Multiple sclerosis	Group 2 > 1
Deafness	Group 1 > 3
Color blindness	Group 1 > 2, 1 > 3
Nearsightedness	Group 1 > 2, 3 > 2
Farsightedness	Group 1 > 2, 3 > 1
Uremia	Group 2 > 1, 3 > 1
Abortion	Group 1 > 2, 1 > 3
Pneumonia	Group 1 > 2, 1 > 3
Tonsillitis	Group 1 > 2, 1 > 3
T.B.	Group 1 > 2, 1 > 3
Appendicitis	Group 1 > 3, 2 > 3
Ringworm	Group 1 > 3, 2 > 3
Scabies	Group 1 > 2, 1 > 3
Collapsed lung	Group 1 > 3
Nosebleed	Group 3 > 1, 3 > 2

* See Table 8.3.
† Group 1: less than 21 years; 2: 21–34 years; 3: 35–65 years

Table 8.6
Significant* Differences in Disease Item Scores in the Nonmedical "Sex" Subgroups

Disease item	Direction of difference
Cerebral palsy	Except for bedsores, males
Painful menstruation	consistently scored these
Bedsores	items higher.
Frostbite	
Heart attack	

* See Table 8.3.

below the mean degree of seriousness (mean 370). As was previously indicated in Figure 8.1, the disease items on the lower half of the curves were scored lower by the physicians and the disease items on the upper half were scored higher by the physicians.

The homogeneity of disease item ranking within the medical and nonmedical groups is shown by Kendall's rank order coefficient (tau) when applied to the subgroups. The subgroups tested with this statistic were age, religion, and generation American for both the medical and nonmedical samples. In all cases, the correlation coefficient was significant to the 0.0003 level. In other words, in all subgroups, the concordance between the rank ordering of the various divisions could not have happened by chance alone.

Table 8.7
Significant* Differences in Disease Item Scores in the Nonmedical "Marital Status" Subgroups

Disease item	Direction of difference
Deafness	In all cases, the "not
Color blindness	married" group scored
T.B.	the items higher.
Appendicitis	
Fibroids of the uterus	
Congenital heart defects	

* See Table 8.3.

Table 8.8
Significant* Differences in Disease Item Scores in the Nonmedical "Generation American" Subgroups†

Disease item	Direction of difference
Gonorrhea	Group 1 > 2
Drug addiction	Group 1 > 2
Hyperventilation	Group 1 > 2
Blood clot in lungs	Group 2 > 1
Irregular heart beats	Group 1 > 2
Low blood pressure	Group 1 > 2

* See Table 8.3.
† Group 1: second generation; 2: third generation

DISCUSSION

In this study, unlike Hinkle's illness scaling, the overall interpretation of "seriousness" was left to the respondent. The respondent's emotional association to a disease was a factor in influencing his or her scoring of that disease. In

Table 8.9
Significant* Differences in Disease Item Scores between
Medical and Nonmedical Groups

Disease item	Item's grand rank	Group that scored item lower
Warts	2	Medical
Nosebleed	10	Medical
Sunburn	13	Medical
Laryngitis	16	Medical
Ringworm	17	Medical
Chicken pox	28	Medical
Mumps	30	Medical
Bedsores	33	Medical
Measles	36	Medical
Infection of middle ear	38	Medical
Varicose veins	39	Medical
Hemorrhoids	42	Medical
Hyperventilation	48	Medical
Mononucleosis	50	Medical
Bursitis	52	Medical
Lumbago	54	Medical
Fibroids of the uterus	55	Medical
Hernia	57	Medical
Abortion	60	Medical
Ovarian cyst	61	Medical
Gonorrhea	63	Medical
Gout	68	Nonmedical
Depression	72	Nonmedical
Kidney infection	75	Medical
Hyperthyroid	77	Nonmedical
Syphilis	84	Medical
Pancreatitis	90	Nonmedical
Low blood pressure	91	Nonmedical
Smallpox	92	Nonmedical
Collapsed lung	94	Medical
Uremia	124	Nonmedical

* See Table 8.3.

Hinkle's scale of five groups of illnesses, seriousness was determined by the probability that the illness, or its sequelae, would be fatal if untreated. Comparison of the disease items in Hinkle's study and the disease items of this study showed that 52 disease items were common to both lists. Of the 52 disease items, 29 were in agreement as to which quintile they appeared. Chi-square analysis indicates a significant correspondence ($p = 0.02$). Diseases that did not correspond in rankings were in large part infectious diseases. Since estimations of seriousness in this study were not predicated on the same considerations as Hinkle's on the basis of treatment, it is not surprising that a disease such as pneumonia (which can be, in a large number of cases, successfully treated) might have a lower rating than that found in Hinkle's list.

It is important at this point to consider the validity of having respondents subjectively rate the disease items, and then using their average rating for the construction of a disease seriousness scale. The method is taken from the field of psychophysics and the rationale and validity of such a procedure for the Social Readjustment Rating Scale have been investigated by Masuda and Holmes [17]. Stevens [18], in his comprehensive review of the field of psychosocial estimations, expounds on the validity of these metrics.

One striking facet of this study, as shown in Figure 8.1., is the highly significant degree of mean rank order correlation between the medical and nonmedical samples. The obvious conclusion to be drawn is that whether or not a person has had a medical education his or her view of the seriousness of illness remains essentially similar.

However, the physician looks at seriousness from ostensibly a more knowledgeable point of view. As Figure 8.1 and Table 8.9 show, the physicians rate less serious diseases lower, and more serious diseases higher on the scale. We might therefore attribute the wider range of the physicians' scale to their medical education.

The homogeneity of disease item rating within the medical subgroups is striking as compared to the relative heterogeneity within the nonmedical subgroups. A major reason for the homogeneity with the medical group may be due to their commonality of education, and their preference for and opportunity in the field of medicine. In addition, the medical group was not complicated by factors of sex and marital status although it is noted that those diseases rated as significantly different by the males in the nonmedical group are not the same as the diseases rated as significantly different by the medical group.

As referred to above, the heterogeneity of the nonmedical group applies to the scoring of individual disease items within subgroups. Forty-one disease items were rated as significantly different within all nonmedical subgroups. In comparison of similar subgroups (age, religion, and generation American) the total number of disease items scored as significantly different by the nonmedical subgroups was 30. This number remains strikingly different from the four disease items scored as significantly different within the medical subgroups. The nonmedical raters have been shown by Kendall's W to be highly concordant and thus to be in high interindividual agreement. Within the population of nonmedically educated, a person's view of the seriousness of any disease item may be affected by age, sex, race, generation American, marital status, and religion, but in varying degrees.

It is of interest that the males' perception of painful menstruation in the female leads to the judgment that it is a more serious disorder than it is considered to be by the females themselves. The females may regard the disorder as being a usual or normal accompaniment of the menstrual process and hence less serious. The males scored heart attack higher than females since it is the male who carries the higher risk of heart attacks. Deafness was scored higher by those respondents under 21 years of age than those respondents over the age of 35. An explanation might be that the older a person becomes, the more adjusted that person becomes to the fact that auditory acuity lessens as part of the natural aging process. Moreover—as Table 8.5 shows— color blindness, nearsightedness, and farsightedness were scored higher by respondents under 21 than by respondents over 21. The same reasoning may apply to this example as was applied to deafness. Also poor eyesight and/or wearing glasses may well interfere more in the action patterns and self-conceptions of younger subjects than of older subjects. Catholics rated ovarian cyst significantly higher than both Protestants and others. Such a rating could be due to Catholics viewing an ovarian cyst as a threat to reproductive potential. Gonorrhea and drug addiction were scored lower by third-generation Americans. Such a scoring might be a function of the changing morality of recent concern.

The grand mean for each disease item was computed in order to gain greater accuracy in attainment of an estimation of average degree of seriousness. The validity for such a computation rests on the highly significant degrees of concordance and correlation. The values of the statistical coefficients show that both groups (medical and nonmedical) with their respective subgroups are samples from the same population.

In light of the above discussion, what is the extent of the interaction of the variables between the nonmedical subgroups? For example, to what degree is the variable of years of education intertwined with the variable of age? There were nine disease items scored as significantly different among the "years of education" nonmedical subgroups, and 16 disease items scored as significantly different within the "age" nonmedical subgroups. Scrutiny of the two groups of disease items (Table 8.4) reveals three items that were present in both groups (color blindness, nearsightedness, and farsightedness). In each of the three cases the youngest group and the least educated group scored these items higher than the other age and education groups. However, reference to the actual questionnaires shows that, of the 13 respondents under the age of 21, seven were college students, three were high school graduates, and two were attending high school. Of the 15 respondents in the "less than 12 years of education" subgroup, only the two high school students were under the age of 21. It is evident that interaction between the subgroups for these diseases was minimal.

SUMMARY

A quantitative scale of seriousness of illness has been defined in this report. Two samples of 117 physicians and 141 nonphysicians scored 126 disease items according to the respondent's concept of relative seriousness. The mean rank order correlation coefficient for the disease items between samples was found to be highly significant (Spearman's rho = 0.947). There was a highly significant interindividual concordance (Kendall's W) in the ranking of disease items. A grand rank order and mean of the disease items were formed by combining the two groups. It was found that in the nonphysician sample, ratings were more affected by variables such as sex, marital status, age, and so on, than in the physician sample. The degree of homogeneity within the physician sample was felt to be in part a function of the medical education that they had all undergone. It was also shown that physicians tended to rate "less serious illness" lower, and "more serious illness" higher than the nonphysician group.

REFERENCES

1. Hinkle, L. E., Jr., R. Redmont, N. Plummer, and H. G. Wolff. "An Examination of the Relation between Symptoms, Disability, and Serious Illness, in Two Homogeneous Groups of Men and Women." *American Journal of Public Health* 50 (1960):1327–66.

2. Graham, D. T., and I. Stevenson. "Disease as Response to Life Stress." In *The Psychological Basis of Medical Practice*, edited by H. I. Lief, V. F. Lief, and N. R. Lief, pp. 115–36. New York: Harper and Row, 1963.

3. Greene, W. A., Jr. "Psychological Factors and Reticulo-endothelial Disease. I. Preliminary Observations on a Group of Males with Lymphomas and Leukemias." *Psychosomatic Medicine* 16 (1954):220–30.

4. Greene, W. A., Jr., L. E. Young, and S. N. Swisher. "Psychological Factors and Reticulo-endothelial Disease. II. Observations on a Group of Women with Lymphomas and Leukemias." *Psychosomatic Medicine* 18 (1956):284–303.

5. Greene, W. A., Jr., and G. Miller. "Psychological Factors and Reticulo-endothelial Disease. IV. Observations on a Group of Children and Adolescents with Leukemia: An Interpretation of Disease Development in Terms of the Mother–Child Unit." *Psychosomatic Medicine* 20 (1958):124–44.

6. Weiss, E., B. Dlin, H. R. Rollin, H. K. Fischer, and C. R. Bepler. "Emotional Factors in Coronary Occlusion." *Archives of Internal Medicine* 99 (1957):628–41.

7. Fischer, H. K., B. Dlin, W. Winters, S. Hagner, and E. Weiss. "Time Patterns and Emotional Factors Related to the Onset of Coronary Occlusion." Abstract. *Psychosomatic Medicine* 24 (1962):516.

8. Kissen, D. M. "Specific Psychological Factors in Pulmonary Tuberculosis." *Health Bulletin* (Edinburgh) 14 (1956):44–46.

9. Kissen, D. M. "Some Psychosocial Aspects of Pulmonary Tuberculosis." *International Journal of Social Psychiatry* 3 (1958):252–59.

10. Hawkins, N. G., R. Davies, and T. H. Holmes. "Evidence of Psychosocial Factors in the Development of Pulmonary Tuberculosis." *American Review of Tuberculosis and Pulmonary Diseases* 75 (1957):768–80. Reprinted in this volume, Chapter 11.

11. Smith, M. "Psychogenic Factors in Skin Disease." Medical thesis, University of Washington, 1962.

12. Rahe, R. H., and T. H. Holmes. "Social, Psychologic and Psychophysiologic Aspects of Inguinal Hernia." *Journal of Psychosomatic Research* 8 (1965):487–91.

13. Kjaer, G. "Some Psychosomatic Aspects of Pregnancy with Particular Reference to Nausea and Vomiting." Medical thesis, University of Washington, 1959.

14. Rahe, R. H., M. Meyer, M. Smith, G. Kjaer, and T. H. Holmes. "Social Stress and Illness Onset." *Journal of Psychosomatic Research* 8 (1964):35–44. Reprinted in this volume, Chapter 12.

15. Holmes, T. H., and Rahe, R. H. "The Social Readjustment Rating Scale." *Journal of Psychosomatic Research* 11 (1967):213–18. Reprinted in this volume, Chapter 2.

16. Rahe, R. H., J. D. McKean, and R. J. Arthur. "A Longitudinal Study of Life-change and Illness Patterns." *Journal of Psychosomatic Research* 10 (1966):355–66.

17. Masuda, M., and T. H. Holmes. "Magnitude Estimations of Social Readjustments." *Journal of Psychosomatic Research* 11 (1967):219–25. Reprinted in this volume, Chapter 3.

18. Stevens, S. S. "A Metric for the Social Consensus." *Science* 151 (1966):530–41.

PART III

CLINICAL APPLICATIONS:
LIFE CHANGE STUDIES

Introduction

The Clinical Tool: The Schedule of Recent Experience (SRE)

Turning the life chart into a self-administered questionnaire was the bright idea of Norman Hawkins, a sociologist working with me among tuberculosis patients at Firland Sanatorium in the early 1950s. Professor Hawkins later taught one of the first courses in medical sociology in the nation. He reproduces a complete version of the original Schedule of Recent Experience in his book, *Medical Sociology: Theory, Scope, and Method* (Springfield, Ill.: Charles C Thomas, 1958), and explains how it was used to document what we then called "the social taxis" of a patient. It is instructive to compare this early version of the SRE with later forms. The first SRE was noticeably different in content, format, and scoring from those reproduced in the appendixes at the end of Chapter 9.

The original SRE collected data for the preceding ten years, asking about a variety of demographic and social factors as well as the occurrence of life events. Here are several questions from the original Schedule of Recent Experience:

14. Check under any years where you had poor hours or working conditions.

15. Check when you had too much detail or responsibility in your work.

16. Check when you have been constantly uncertain about holding a good job, or when you had seniority rights, etc., denied to you.

Notice the difference between the wording in those questions and the wording of the SRE items after we had the Social Readjustment Rating Scale and its definition of the concept of life change. In the revised Schedule of Recent Experience we ask subjects to indicate the number of times they have experienced "A lot more or a lot less trouble with the boss" (item 1), "Major change in working hours or conditions" (item 29), and "Major change in responsibilities at work (e.g., promotion, demotion, lateral transfer)" (item 30). The new emphasis is on change itself, and not on the subject's interpretation of the event ("poor hours," "too much," "good job," "constantly uncertain").

We also learned the value of wording items in general terms that encompass a variety of related situations. In the original Schedule of Recent Experience, subjects were asked to specify "when you and your mate had difficulty because of: (1) Disagreement on rearing children; (2) Serious illness in the family; (3) In-law trouble; (4) Disagreement in choice of friends; (5) Each others' personal habits"—all in a single question (#22). The Schedule of Recent Experience today documents discrete, objective events such as "A major change in the number of arguments with spouse (e.g., either a lot more or a lot less than usual regarding child-rearing, personal habits, etc.)" (item 11).

Chapter 9 details the evolution of the SRE and presents the final form resulting from that process. Chapter 10 investigates the reliability of the instrument over time and describes experiments with item wording and recall of life events. The order, number, and wording of life event items in the Schedule of Recent Experience were not standardized until we had incorporated the SRRS scoring method into the SRE framework. At the time of the recall study described in Chapter 10, the SRE still covered a ten-year period and contained only 40 items (marital reconciliation and pregnancy were the missing items).

9

Manual for the Schedule of Recent Experience (SRE)

Marion E. Amundson, Cheryl A. Hart, and Thomas H. Holmes

PURPOSE AND HISTORY OF THE SCHEDULE OF RECENT EXPERIENCE (SRE)

The Schedule of Recent Experience (SRE) is a paper-and-pencil questionnaire that elicits information about the occurrence of particular events in an individual's recent life experience. It is designed for collecting quantitative and qualitative data about people's life-style and history, and thus serves as a standardized form for organizing such data in research and as a basis for subsequent interviews in the clinic.

Historically the SRE evolved from the "life chart" of Meyer [1]. To examine disease in the setting in which it occurred, the life chart documented biologic, psychologic, and sociologic processes in their relation to health and disease. Information provided by the patient was arranged chronologically, by year and age. Entries on the chart described life situations (experiences indicative of the life-style of the individual and those indicative of occurrences that involved the individual) as well as the patient's emotional responses to those situations. Related diseases were listed in a separate column.

Beginning in this laboratory in 1949, the life chart device was applied to the study of some 5,000 case histories, including tuberculosis, cardiac disease, skin disorders, pregnancy, and hernia [2;3]. From this systematic study, the life events of the SRE were selected for their observed occurrence prior to the onset of illness or clinical symptoms. During the developmental phase of this research, it was noted that the psychological significance of the events varied widely with the patient, and only certain of the events were negative or "stressful" in the conventional sense of the word, that is, "socially undesirable." Many of the events included in the SRE were socially desirable and were initiated by the patient. There was, however, one theme common to all life events. The occurrence of each event usually evoked or was associated with some change and adaptive behavior on the part of the involved individual. The wording of each SRE item thus emphasizes change from the existing steady state and not psychological meaning, emotion, or social desirability.

DESCRIPTION OF THE SRE QUESTIONNAIRE

As the SRE evolved, the format has undergone considerable change. The present SRE questionnaire solicits identifying data and information about recent experience with 42 life events (see Appendixes 9.1 and 9.2 at the very end of this chapter). These life events generally refer to ordinary, but sometimes extraordinary, social and interpersonal transactions and major areas of dynamic significance in the social structure: family constellation, marriage, occupation, economics, residence, peer relations, education, religion, recreation, and health.

Respondents are asked to record the number of times each event occurred in specified time periods. In earlier editions of the SRE the first 12 questions required "yes" or "no" answers rather than "number of times," but the present versions request number of times for *all* 42 items.

TIME PERIODS RECORDED IN THE SRE

In the development of the SRE, life event information has been requested for a variety of time periods such as for ten years, three years, one year, or even daily reports [4]. In some research, a specific event has been used as a point of departure—for example, imprisonment [5]—and the subject is asked about a given number of years before and after the specified event. The time intervals recorded by the SRE can be further modified to meet the needs of the individual researcher or clinician (see Appendix 9.3).

DEVELOPMENT OF THE SOCIAL READJUSTMENT RATING SCALE (SRRS)

In its early applications, the SRE data were used to tally the total *number* or *frequency* of life events experienced by the patient. These data showed clearly that many diseases had their onset in a setting of mounting social change [2]. In an attempt to add precision to the measurement, the Social Readjustment Rating Scale (SRRS) was developed [6]. The method for assigning a magnitude to each of the items was that used in psychophysics for measuring sensation magnitude and intensity [7]. A sample of 394 subjects completed the Social Readjustment Rating Questionnaire (SRRQ) (comprised of 42 SRE items plus Christmas).

They provided magnitude estimations for the amount of change and readjustment associated with each of the events, relative to marriage, which was given the arbitrary value of 500. The mean score, divided by 10, of each item for the entire sample was calculated and arranged in rank order. The results of this study are the Social Readjustment Rating Scale (SRRS) (see Appendix 9.4), and these values are used to weight the relative impact of the SRE life events.

ADMINISTERING THE SRE

The SRE is designed as a self-report questionnaire and has been tested for both clarity and the reliability of self-report data obtained with it. It has also been used as a framework for structured interviews. Satisfactory data have been obtained by interview when it has been thought that the individual could not complete a paper-and-pencil report.

An interview administration of the SRE may take several forms. The interviewer might ask the respondent how many times each of the SRE events has occurred in the recent past. Alternatively, the interviewer might obtain the history in a less structured manner with the goal of completing the SRE for the respondent at a later date. In one study where the interview technique was used, interviewers noted that the information obtained by questionnaire was a valid, though conservative, estimate of the recent life change reported during interview sessions [8].

SCORING THE SCHEDULE OF RECENT EXPERIENCE

In scoring the SRE (see Appendix 9.5), items identified by the subjects are assigned their values from the Social Readjustment Rating Scale. The life change score for *each time period*, in life change units (LCU), is calculated as a weighted item frequency:

$$LCU = \Sigma \text{ (Item frequency x Scale value)}$$

For example, if an individual has experienced two vacations (13 LCU each), one change in eating habits (15 LCU), and the death of a close friend (37 LCU) in one year, the life change score for that year is calculated as follows:

$$2 \times 13 = 26$$
$$1 \times 15 = 15$$
$$1 \times 37 = \underline{37}$$

Total   78 LCU

The data suggest that the more life change that occurs the greater the likelihood of illness. The following criteria have been established to evaluate the LCU scores for the previous year:

1. 300 or more LCU = 80 percent chance of illness in the near future
2. 150–299 LCU = 50 percent chance of illness in the near future
3. Less than 150 LCU = 30 percent chance of illness in the near future

The temporal association of an illness or health change with LCU events appears to be as follows: The reported change in health must occur within the two-year period following the occurrence of a cluster of life changes. This two-year period is the time when the subject is at risk after the life change clustering. A technique for achieving self-report information about a subject's illness is the Illness History form (see Appendix 9.6).

The following retrospective and prospective studies were used to define the predictability of a health change occurring after life changes [9].

Rahe [10] studied the association between health changes and life changes in a sample of 88 young resident physicians. He found that those individuals who experienced a mild life crisis (150–199 LCU) in one year showed a 37 percent chance of health change the following year. Those who experienced a moderate life crisis (200–299 LCU) showed a 51 percent chance of a health change the following year. And those who experienced a major life crisis (300 or more LCU) showed a 79 percent chance of a health change during the next year.

T. S. Holmes [11] followed 54 medical students from the beginning of their freshman year to the end of their sophomore year. They completed the SRE before their entrance to medical school, and their LCU scores were used to predict disease occurrence for a full two-year period at risk. At the end of that time the SRE was administered a second time, so the retrospective data could be compared with the prospective data. The outcome of both approaches was essentially the same: 52 percent of the subjects experienced major health changes during the two-year period at risk. Of these, 86 percent with high life-change scores (300 or more LCU), 48 percent with moderate life-change scores (150–299 LCU), and 33 percent with low life-change scores (less than 150 LCU) experienced major health changes.

VALIDITY AND RELIABILITY OF THE SRE

The SRE is unique among the life event questionnaires in wide use today in that each event was selected for its observed occurrence prior to the onset of illness. Thus, during the developmental phase of the SRE research, close examination of the setting in which illness developed revealed a particular selection of life events. These events are the content of the SRE.

Recent interest in research with life event checklists has produced a variety of instruments for measuring life change experience. These lists vary in length and item wording. In many cases, the lists are modifications of the original SRE and are intended to customize the device for particular samples (see section below, "Modifications of the SRE for Special Populations").

The SRE was developed in a tuberculosis sanatorium, cross-validated on two samples totaling 165 admissions, and pretested for readability and clarity; its maximal validity was established as lying in the age range from 25 to 55 years. A reliability coefficient of 0.831 was obtained between first and second administrations of the form at five-month intervals in a group of 40 newly admitted white patients (age 25–60) with pulmonary tuberculosis [2].

Casey, Masuda, and Holmes [12] studied the ten-year SRE response of 54 resident physicians who completed the form at two separate administrations, spaced nine months apart. A coefficient of reliability (Pearson's r) between the two administrations was calculated, based on the total LCU scores for each subject, for each of three years. For the period of time eight years prior to the first SRE administration, the correlation between consecutive reports was 0.67 ($p = 0.0005$). For the period five years prior to the initial SRE, the correlation between SRE reports separated by nine months was 0.74 ($p = 0.0005$).

Further examination of the individual events on the SRE showed a highly significant relation between the values of the events and the percentage of consistent responses ($r = 0.59$; $p = 0.0005$). The more salient life events were most consistently recalled.

Although there was strong agreement between reports from the two administrations, differences did exist. Close analysis of each year showed that 44 of 54 subjects contributed to the total of 91 discrepant reports. Mean total LCU scores indicated that significantly less material was recalled for the more distant time periods included in the SRE.

Another parameter studied by Casey et al. [12] was the item phrasing. Many of the SRE items contain words that qualify or clarify the items. It appeared that an individual might assign different magnitudes to these qualifiers when confronted with them on two separate occasions. This fluctuation in the subject's interpretation of these key words might contribute to inconsistent recall. Since only the items qualified by the word "substantial" were significantly associated with inconsistent responses, these seven items were eliminated in a second analysis, and a Pearson correlation was done between the score values of the remaining items and percent consistency of recall ($r = 0.55$; $p = 0.005$). This highly significant correlation indicates that it is the saliency of the items and not the presence of qualifying words that most affects the consistency of recall.

In another study, Thurlow [13] administered a five-year SRE to two samples of respondents. One sample of 21 college students (mean age 27 years) completed the SRE twice, with a two-week interval between the administrations. The test–retest reliability after a two-week interval was highly significant ($r = 0.78$; $p = 0.005$). The other sample of 111 brewery employees (mean age 46 years) completed the five-year SRE on two occasions, with an interval of two years between administrations. For the three years included in both administrations, there was significant concordance between reports for only the most recent year

($r = 0.34$; $p = 0.01$). Consistency of recall dropped dramatically in the four- and five-year reports but "objective" changes were rated more consistently than "subjective" ones.

Rahe et al. [8] studied a different type of report reliability in 116 patients with coronary heart disease. Patients and their spouses were asked to complete a two-year SRE that divided each year into quartiles. Spouses were further asked to complete the SRE as if they were the patient. Interpair correlations were strongest for the most recent quarter ($r = 0.47$; $p = 0.01$) and were slightly diminished for the most distant quarter, two years past ($r = 0.31$). Another study by Brown et al. [14] indicated that, when life events were carefully dated by the interviewers and confined to the events with which both spouses would be familiar, interpair correlations improved substantially.

To summarize, several factors have been seen to affect the recall reliability of the SRE. Diminished reliability seems to be related primarily to:

1. the time interval between successive administrations;
2. the age, education, and probable intelligence of the subjects;
3. the time interval over which subjects' recent life changes are summed;
4. the wording and format of the life event items; and
5. the relative salience of the SRE events.

STATISTICAL CONSIDERATIONS

Life change data obtained with the SRE can be approached statistically in one of two ways: item frequency counts or LCU composite scores. These measures are, necessarily, highly correlated so that individuals with high item-frequency totals will tend also to have high LCU scores [15]. Both simple counts of life events and LCU measures are expected to show the same relation to dependent measures, such as symptoms, illness onset, accidental injury, and so forth.

Life event frequencies and life change scores in LCU have different frequency distributions and may be approached with different statistical methods. The frequency distribution for any single event of the SRE is highly skewed so that very few individuals experience each event many times. The frequency distribution of one item, change in eating habits, is shown in Figure 9.1. Thurlow [13] has suggested that this distribution should be transformed to a logarithmic scale prior to any statistical analysis. Logarithmic transformations somewhat normalize these highly skewed distributions.

The distribution of LCU scores in a sample is also skewed and becomes progressively more normal as larger time intervals are included. Thus, the distribution of LCU scores obtained from a period of one year is more skewed than the distribution of LCU scores summed over a three-year period (see Figure 9.2).

Skewed distribution functions such as these caution the researcher about using

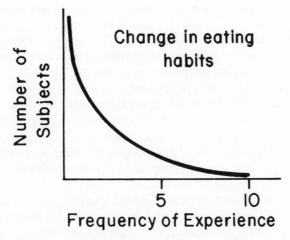

Figure 9.1   Frequency distribution of one item in the SRE.

standard techniques for statistical inference with life change data from the SRE. It is not uncommon to find that the standard deviations of highly skewed distributions are larger than the mean values of these distributions. Nonparametric statistics offer an appropriate alternative to standard parametric techniques here because they do not depend on distribution assumptions.

VARIABILITY IN THE FREQUENCY OF LIFE EVENTS

Masuda and Holmes [16] have examined the variability among different groups in their reports of the frequency of occurrence of 40 SRE life events. Their data were collected from prisoners, pregnant women, fracture patients, football

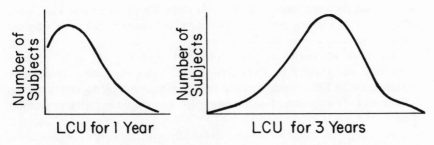

Figure 9.2   Distribution of LCU scores for one-year and three-year periods.

players, college students, general hospital patients, medical students, medical residents, alcoholics and heroin addicts in treatment centers, and two large groups of subjects drawn from a wide segment of the U.S. population. Comparing these 12 different samples, they found consistency in the rank order of life event frequencies in spite of differences in the absolute frequency of events. Kendall's coefficient of concordance between these groups was 0.65 ($p = 0.001$). Although young subjects tended to report higher SRE frequencies than elderly subjects, there tended to be a similarity between all the groups in that changes in residence, sleeping, eating, and recreation were the most commonly experienced events. Life events reported least frequently by all groups were death of spouse, divorce, mortgage foreclosure, retirement, and mortgage for a major purchase (greater than $10,000).

Age, sex, marital status, education, social class, and race factors were also explored to determine whether each influenced the relative frequency of experience with life events. As indicated above, age was an important factor, in that young people accumulate more life events and elderly people accumulate fewer. Sexual status did not affect the occurrence of the total number of life events, but there were differential life event occurrences between men and women. The analysis of marital status, education, social class, and race was more difficult to interpret since these factors imparted different effects from group to group.

MODIFICATIONS OF THE SRE FOR SPECIAL POPULATIONS

Since the SRE was first derived, modifications of the original items have been produced to accommodate the life experiences of special populations. Frequently these listings evolve from sampling techniques that differ from those used for the original SRE.

In 1968, Coddington [17] developed a life event questionnaire for children, with specific categories of events for preschool, grammar school, and junior and senior high school students, respectively. These questionnaires contain events that, in some cases, overlap with the SRE. Other events were added because they were seen to require significant amounts of change/readjustment by children. A survey of professional workers in child guidance provided magnitude estimates for the amount of change/readjustment that a child would experience with each of these events. By using these magnitude estimates for each item, the child's life change score on Coddington's questionnaire is calculated by the same weighted frequency technique as in the SRE.

A listing of life events, clinically observed to occur prior to the onset of depression, was derived by Paykel et al. [18]. This list shows considerable overlap with the SRE events, but has been screened for events that are either indicative or symptomatic of depression, such as changes in eating or sleeping habits.

In an attempt to customize the SRE to the life experiences of college athletes, Bramwell et al. [19] developed the Athletic Schedule of Recent Experience

(ASRE). This is a life event questionnaire including many items of unique importance to this sample, such as troubles with the coach or change to a new playing status. Magnitude estimations for these events were given by a sample of football players, and this is the Social and Athletic Readjustment Rating Scale (SARRS). This scaling result shows a highly significant rank order correlation with the SRRS on the shared items ($r_s = 0.84$; $p = 0.001$).

The College Schedule of Recent Experience (CSRE) was produced by Marx et al. [20] to include concerns expressed by college students. Students were sampled to obtain a list of events that were seen to have caused change in recent life patterns, and then a separate sample rated the events using the magnitude estimation technique. Many of the events provided by the student sample were the same as those in the SRE. A comparison of the scaling results from college students and those in the SRRS again showed substantial agreement on the shared items.

Over the years, Rahe [21] has gradually modified the SRE to suit a military population. Thirteen items have been added to the original 42 of the SRE, and some response possibilities have been made more specific. This questionnaire is the Recent Life Changes Questionnaire (RLCQ). In addition to this he has developed the subjective life change unit (SLCU) scaling system in an attempt to study the relation between an individual's perceptions and illness susceptibility. On an interval scale (1–100) an individual completing the RLCQ is asked also to estimate the amount of life change and readjustment he or she *personally* experienced secondary to each life event. Thus, the respondent indicates the frequency of recent experience with each event and then gives a number estimate for the relative intensity of that experience. The life change score is calculated as the sum of all the subjective estimates in a given time interval.

REFERENCES

1. Meyer, A. "The Life Chart and the Obligation of Specifying Positive Data in Psychopathological Diagnosis." In *Contributions to Medical and Biological Research*, vol. 2, pp. 1128–33. New York: Paul B. Hoeber, 1919.

2. Hawkins, N. G., R. Davies, and T. H. Holmes. "Evidence of Psychosocial Factors in the Development of Pulmonary Tuberculosis." *American Review of Tuberculosis and Pulmonary Diseases* 75 (1957):768–80. Reprinted in this volume, Chapter 11.

3. Rahe, R. H., M. Meyer, M. Smith, G. Kjaer, and T. H. Holmes. "Social Stress and Illness Onset." *Journal of Psychosomatic Research* 8 (1964):35–44. Reprinted in this volume, Chapter 12.

4. Holmes, T. S., and T. H. Holmes. "Short-term Intrusions into the Life Style Routine." *Journal of Psychosomatic Research* 14 (1970):121–32. Reprinted in this volume, Chapter 15.

5. Masuda, M., D. L. Cutler, L. Hein, and T. H. Holmes. "Life Events and Prisoners." *Archives of General Psychiatry* 35 (1978):197–203. Reprinted in this volume, Chapter 20.

6. Holmes, T. H., and R. H. Rahe. "The Social Readjustment Rating Scale." *Journal of Psychosomatic Research* 11 (1967):213–18. Reprinted in this volume, Chapter 2.

7. Stevens, S. S. *Psychophysics: Introduction to Its Perceptual, Neural, and Social Prospects*, edited by G. Stevens. New York: John Wiley and Sons, 1975.

8. Rahe, R. H., M. Romo, L. Bennett, and P. Siltanen. "Recent Life Changes, Myocardial Infarction, and Abrupt Coronary Death." *Archives of Internal Medicine* 133 (1974):221–28.

9. Holmes, T. H., and M. Masuda. "Life Change and Illness Susceptibility." In *Separation and Depression: Clinical and Research Aspects*, edited by J. P. Scott and E. C. Senay, pp. 161–86. AAAS Publication no. 94. Washington, D.C.: American Association for the Advancement of Science, 1973.

10. Rahe, R. H. "Life Crisis and Health Change." In *Psychotropic Drug Response: Advances in Prediction*, edited by P. R. A. May and J. R. Wittenborn, pp. 92–125. Springfield, Ill.: Charles C Thomas, 1969. Pts. 2 and 3 reprinted in this volume, Chapters 13 and 14.

11. Holmes. T. S. "Adaptive Behavior and Health Change." Medical thesis, University of Washington, 1970.

12. Casey, R. L., M. Masuda, and T. H. Holmes. "Quantitative Study of Recall of Life Events." *Journal of Psychosomatic Research* 11 (1967):239–47. Reprinted in this volume, Chapter 10.

13. Thurlow, H. J. "Illness in Relation to Life Situation and Sick-role Tendency." *Journal of Psychosomatic Research* 15 (1971):73–88.

14. Brown, G. W., F. Sklair, T. O. Harris, and J. L. T. Birley. "Life-Events and Psychiatric Disorders. Part 1. Some Methodological Issues." *Psychological Medicine* 3 (1973):74–87.

15. Rahe, R. H. "The Pathway between Subjects' Recent Life Changes and Their Near-Future Illness Reports: Representative Results and Methodological Issues." In *Stressful Life Events: Their Nature and Effects*, edited by B. S. Dohrenwend and B. P. Dohrenwend, pp. 73–86. New York: John Wiley and Sons, 1974.

16. Masuda, M., and T. H. Holmes. "Life Events: Perceptions and Frequencies." *Psychosomatic Medicine* 40 (1978):236–61. Reprinted in this volume, Chapter 21.

17. Coddington, R. D. "The Significance of Life Events as Etiologic Factors in Diseases of Children. I. A Survey of Professional Workers." *Journal of Psychosomatic Research* 16 (1972):7–18.

18. Paykel, E. S., B. A. Prusoff, and E. H. Uhlenhuth. "Scaling of Life Events." *Archives of General Psychiatry* 25 (1971):340–47.

19. Bramwell, S. T., M. Masuda, N. N. Wagner, and T. H. Holmes. "Psychosocial Factors in Athletic Injuries: Development and Application of the Social and Athletic Readjustment Rating Scale (SARRS)." *Journal of Human Stress* 1, no. 2 (1975):6–20. Reprinted in this volume, Chapter 19.

20. Marx, M. B., T. F. Garrity, and F. R. Bowers. "The Influence of Recent Life Experience on the Health of College Freshmen." *Journal of Psychosomatic Research* 19 (1975):87–98.

21. Rahe, R. H. "Epidemiological Studies of Life Change and Illness." *International Journal of Psychiatry in Medicine* 6 (1975):133–46.

Appendix 9.1
Schedule of Recent Experience (SRE)

CARD NO. 1   DATE_____ ___ ___
         1   4   5
GROUP NO.___ ___   ID NO.___ ___ ___ ___ ___
            2   3   6   7   8   9   10

NAME_____ ADDRESS _____

AGE _____   SEX: Male ____ Female ____
    11, 12   13
MARITAL STATUS: Married_ Divorced_ Separated_ Widowed_ Never Married_
      14
EDUCATION: Grade school_ High school_ Trade school_ College_ Advanced Degree_
      15

Instructions:

For each life event listed below please do the following:
     Think back on the event and decide if it happened during the last 12 months. If the
     event did happen, indicate the *number of times* it happened by placing a number in
     the column labeled 0–12 months ago.

	0–12 months ago
1. A lot more or a lot less trouble with the boss.	_____ 16
2. A major change in sleeping habits (sleeping a lot more or a lot less, or change in part of day when asleep).	_____ 17
3. A major change in eating habits (a lot more or a lot less food intake, or very different meal hours or surroundings).	_____ 18
4. A revision of personal habits (dress, manners, associations, etc.).	_____ 19
5. A major change in your usual type and/or amount of recreation.	_____ 20
6. A major change in your social activities (e.g., clubs, dancing, movies, visiting, etc.).	_____ 21
7. A major change in church activities (e.g., a lot more or a lot less than usual).	_____ 22

cont'd

	0–12 months ago
8. A major change in number of family get-togethers (e.g., a lot more or a lot less than usual).	23
9. A major change in financial state (e.g., a lot worse off or a lot better off than usual).	24
10. Trouble with in-laws.	25
11. A major change in the number of arguments with spouse (e.g., either a lot more or a lot less than usual regarding child-rearing, personal habits, etc.).	26
12. Sexual difficulties.	27
13. Major personal injury or illness.	28
14. Death of a close family member (other than spouse).	29
15. Death of spouse.	30
16. Death of a close friend.	31
17. Gaining a new family member (e.g., through birth, adoption, oldster moving in, etc.).	32
18. Major change in the health or behavior of a family member.	33
19. Change in residence.	34
20. Detention in jail or other institution.	35
21. Minor violations of the law (e.g., traffic ticket, jaywalking, disturbing the peace, etc.).	36
22. Major business readjustment (e.g., merger, reorganization, bankruptcy, etc.).	37
23. Marriage.	38
24. Divorce.	39
25. Marital separation from spouse.	40

	0–12 months ago
26. Outstanding personal achievement.	
	41
27. Son or daughter leaving home (e.g., marriage, attending college, etc.).	
	42
28. Retirement from work.	
	43
29. Major change in working hours or conditions.	
	44
30. Major change in responsibilities at work (e.g., promotion, demotion, lateral transfer).	
	45
31. Being fired from work.	
	46
32. Major change in living conditions (e.g., building a new home, remodeling, deterioration of home or neighborhood).	
	47
33. Wife beginning or ceasing work outside the home.	
	48
34. Taking out a mortgage or loan for a major purchase (e.g., purchasing a home, business, etc.).	
	49
35. Taking out a mortgage or loan for a lesser purchase (e.g., purchasing a car, TV, freezer, etc.).	
	50
36. Foreclosure on a mortgage or loan.	
	51
37. Vacation.	
	52
38. Changing to a new school.	
	53
39. Changing to a different line of work.	
	54
40. Beginning or ceasing formal schooling.	
	55
41. Marital reconciliation with mate.	
	56
42. Pregnancy.	
	57

Appendix 9.2
Schedule of Recent Experience (SRE)

CARD NO. 1
       1

GROUP NO.___ ___
      2   3

DATE_____ ___ ___
              4   5

ID NO.___ ___ ___ ___ ___
     6 7 8 9 10

NAME_____ ADDRESS _____

AGE _____   SEX: Male ____ Female ____
   11, 12   13

MARITAL STATUS: Married_ Divorced_ Separated_ Widowed_ Never Married_
   14

EDUCATION: Grade school_ High school_ Trade school_ College_ Advanced Degree_
   15

Instructions:

For each life event listed below please do the following:

Think back on the event and decide if it happened to you and when it happened. If the event did happen, indicate the *number of times* it happened by placing a number in each of the appropriate time periods. The columns are as follows:

0 to 6 months ago 6 months to 1 year ago 1 to 2 years ago 2 to 3 years ago

---

	0–6 mo ago	6 mo– 1 yr ago	1–2 yrs ago	2–3 yrs ago
1. A lot more or a lot less trouble with the boss.	16	17	18	19
2. A major change in sleeping habits (sleeping a lot more or a lot less, or change in part of day when asleep).	20	21	22	23
3. A major change in eating habits (a lot more or a lot less food intake, or very different meal hours or surroundings).	24	25	26	27
4. A revision of personal habits (dress, manners, associations, etc.).	28	29	30	31
5. A major change in your usual type and/or amount of recreation.	32	33	34	35

138

Appendix 9.2, continued

	0–6 mo ago	6 mo– 1 yr ago	1–2 yrs ago	2–3 yrs ago
6. A major change in your social activities (e.g., clubs, dancing, movies, visiting, etc.).	36	37	38	39
7. A major change in church activities (e.g., a lot more or a lot less than usual).	40	41	42	43
8. A major change in number of family get-togethers (e.g., a lot more or a lot less than usual).	44	45	46	47
9. A major change in financial state (e.g., a lot worse off or a lot better off than usual).	48	49	50	51
10. Trouble with in-laws.	52	53	54	55
11. A major change in the number of arguments with spouse (e.g., either a lot more or a lot less than usual regarding child-rearing, personal habits, etc.).	56	57	58	59
12. Sexual difficulties.	60	61	62	63
13. Major personal injury or illness.	64	65	66	67
14. Death of a close family member (other than spouse).	68	69	70	71
15. Death of spouse.	72	73	74	75
16. Death of a close friend.	76	77	78	79

END CARD 1

CARD NO. 2
1
REPEAT
COL. 2–10

17. Gaining a new family member (e.g., through birth, adoption, oldster moving in, etc.).	11	12	13	14

cont'd

139

Appendix 9.2, continued

	0–6 mo ago	6 mo–1 yr ago	1–2 yrs ago	2–3 yrs ago
18. Major change in the health or behavior of a family member.	15	16	17	18
19. Change in residence.	19	20	21	22
20. Detention in jail or other institution.	23	24	25	26
21. Minor violations of the law (e.g., traffic tickets, jaywalking, disturbing the peace, etc.).	27	28	29	30
22. Major business readjustment (e.g., merger, reorganization, bankruptcy, etc.).	31	32	33	34
23. Marriage.	35	36	37	38
24. Divorce.	39	40	41	42
25. Marital separation from spouse.	43	44	45	46
26. Outstanding personal achievement.	47	48	49	50
27. Son or daughter leaving home (e.g., marriage, attending college, etc.).	51	52	53	54
28. Retirement from work.	55	56	57	58
29. Major change in working hours or conditions.	59	60	61	62
30. Major change in responsibilities at work (e.g., promotion, demotion, lateral transfer).	63	64	65	66
31. Being fired from work.	67	68	69	70
32. Major change in living conditions (e.g., building a new home, remodeling, deterioration of home or neighborhood).	71	72	73	74

	0–6 mo ago	6 mo– 1 yr ago	1–2 yrs ago	2–3 yrs ago
33. Wife beginning or ceasing work outside the home.				
	75	76	77	78

END CARD 2

CARD NO. 3
1
REPEAT
COL. 2–10

34. Taking out a mortgage or loan for a major purchase (e.g., purchasing a home, business, etc.).				
	11	12	13	14
35. Taking out a mortgage or loan for a lesser purchase (e.g., purchasing a car, TV, freezer, etc.).				
	15	16	17	18
36. Foreclosure on a mortgage or loan.				
	19	20	21	22
37. Vacation.				
	23	24	25	26
38. Changing to a new school.				
	27	28	29	30
39. Changing to a different line of work.				
	31	32	33	34
40. Beginning or ceasing formal schooling.				
	35	36	37	38
41. Marital reconciliation with mate.				
	39	40	41	42
42. Pregnancy.				
	43	44	45	46

END CARD 3

Appendix 9.3
Modifications of Time Periods Recorded in the SRE

10-Year SRE

---

1. List the number of times under the years when there has been either a lot more or a lot less trouble with the boss.

1970	1971	1972	1973	1974	1975	1976	1977	1978	1979

Monthly SRE

---

1. List the number of times under the months when there has been either a lot more or a lot less trouble with the boss.

1968	1969
Sept. Oct. Nov. Dec.	Jan. Feb. Mar. Apr. May June July Aug. Sept. Oct. Nov. Dec.

Daily SRE

---

1. List the number of times under the days when there has been either a lot more or a lot less trouble with the boss.

Mon. Tue. Wed. Thur. Fri. Sat. Sun.

Specific Event as Point of Departure

---

1. List the number of times under the time periods when there has been either a lot more or a lot less trouble with the boss.

2 yrs before to 1 yr before this pregnancy	1 yr before to 6 mon before pregnancy	6 mon before to beginning of pregnancy	From beginning of this pregnancy to now

---

Before and After a Specific Event (0 Point is Imprisonment or Surgery, e.g.)

---

1. List the number of times under the time periods when there has been either a lot more or a lot less trouble with the boss.

5 yrs before	4 yrs before	3 yrs before	2 yrs before	1 yr before	0	1 yr after	2 yrs after	3 yrs after	4 yrs after	5 yrs after

Appendix 9.4
The Social Readjustment Rating Scale

	Life Event	Mean Value
1.	Death of spouse	100
2.	Divorce	73
3.	Marital separation from mate	65
4.	Detention in jail or other institution	63
5.	Death of a close family member	63
6.	Major personal injury or illness	53
7.	Marriage	50
8.	Being fired at work	47
9.	Marital reconciliation with mate	45
10.	Retirement from work	45
11.	Major change in the health or behavior of a family member	44
12.	Pregnancy	40
13.	Sexual difficulties	39
14.	Gaining a new family member (e.g., through birth, adoption, oldster moving in, etc.)	39
15.	Major business readjustment (e.g., merger, reorganization, bankruptcy, etc.)	39
16.	Major change in financial state (e.g., a lot worse off or a lot better off than usual)	38
17.	Death of a close friend	37
18.	Changing to a different line of work	36
19.	Major change in the number of arguments with spouse (e.g., either a lot more or a lot less than usual regarding child-rearing, personal habits, etc.)	35
20.	Taking out a mortgage or loan for a major purchase (e.g., for a home, business, etc.)	31
21.	Foreclosure on a mortgage or loan	30
22.	Major change in responsibilities at work (e.g., promotion, demotion, lateral transfer)	29
23.	Son or daughter leaving home (e.g., marriage, attending college, etc.)	29
24.	Trouble with in-laws	29
25.	Outstanding personal achievement	28
26.	Wife beginning or ceasing work outside the home	26
27.	Beginning or ceasing formal schooling	26
28.	Major change in living conditions (e.g., building a new home, remodeling, deterioration of home or neighborhood)	25
29.	Revision of personal habits (dress, manners, associations, etc.)	24
30.	Trouble with the boss	23
31.	Major change in working hours or conditions	20
32.	Change in residence	20
33.	Changing to a new school	20

cont'd

Appendix 9.4, continued

	Life Event	Mean Value
34.	Major change in usual type and/or amount of recreation	19
35.	Major change in church activities (e.g., a lot more or a lot less than usual)	19
36.	Major change in social activities (e.g., clubs, dancing, movies, visiting, etc.)	18
37.	Taking out a mortgage or loan for a lesser purchase (e.g., for a car, TV, freezer, etc.)	17
38.	Major change in sleeping habits (a lot more or a lot less sleep, or change in part of day when asleep)	16
39.	Major change in number of family get-togethers (e.g., a lot more or a lot less than usual)	15
40.	Major change in eating habits (a lot more or a lot less food intake, or very different meal hours or surroundings)	15
41.	Vacation	13
42.	Christmas	12
43.	Minor violations of the law (e.g., traffic tickets, jaywalking, disturbing the peace, etc.)	11

Source: Holmes, T. H., and Rahe, R. H., "The Social Readjustment Rating Scale," *Journal of Psychosomatic Research* 11 (1967):213–18.

Appendix 9.5
Administering and Scoring the Schedule of Recent Experience (SRE)

Subjects complete the SRE questionnaire beginning with NAME. They may date it also.

To keypunch directly from the form, use the CODING INFORMATION and complete GROUP NO. and ID NO., circle last two digits of the year under DATE, and code the items on SEX, MARITAL STATUS, and EDUCATION.

To hand score the SRE, multiply the number of times each event occurred by the value listed for each event from the following ordered list. Then total the results for a score for *each* time period. A template is available for hand scoring.

Please note: Responses of 4+ are scored as 4.

Values* for the Items on the SRE

No.	SRE Event	Mean Value		No.	SRE Event	Mean Value
1.	Trouble with boss	23		24.	Divorce	73
2.	Change in sleeping habits	16		25.	Marital separation	65
3.	Change in eating habits	15				
4.	Revision of personal habits	24		26.	Outstanding personal achievement	28
5.	Change in recreation	19		27.	Son or daughter leaving home	29
6.	Change in social activities	18				
7.	Change in church activities	19		28.	Retirement	45
8.	Change in number of family get-togethers	15		29.	Change in work hours or conditions	20
9.	Change in financial state	38		30.	Change in responsibilities at work	29
10.	Trouble with in-laws	29				
11.	Change in number of arguments with spouse	35		31.	Fired at work	47
12.	Sex difficulties	39		32.	Change in living conditions	25
13.	Personal injury or illness	53		33.	Wife begin or end work	26
14.	Death of close family member	63		34.	Mortgage or loan for major purchase (home, business, etc.)	31
15.	Death of spouse	100		35.	Mortgage or loan for lesser purchase (car, TV, etc.)	17
16.	Death of close friend	37		36.	Foreclosure of mortgage or loan	30
17.	Gain of new family member	39		37.	Vacation	13
18.	Change in health of family member	44		38.	Change in schools	20
19.	Change in residence	20		39.	Change to different line of work	36
20.	Jail term	63		40.	Begin or end school	26
21.	Minor violations of the law	11				
22.	Business readjustment	39		41.	Marital reconciliation	45
23.	Marriage	50		42.	Pregnancy	40

*From Holmes, T.H., and Rahe, R.H.: "The Social Readjustment Rating Scale," *Journal of Psychomatic Research* 11 (1967):213–18.

Appendix 9.5, continued
Coding Information for the SRE

Card 1
ITEM   COLUMN
NO.   NO.
      1   Individual card no. 1. (One card for 1-year SRE.)
      2–3   Identification code for particular group, 01 through 99.
      4–5   Date: last two digits of year.
      6–10 Subject number, 00001 through 99999.
      11–12 Age
      13   Sex   0 = male
                                     1 = female
      14   Marital status 0 = married
                                     1 = divorced
                                   2 = separated
                                   3 = widowed
                                   4 = never married
      15   Education   0 = grade school
                                     1 = high school
                                   2 = trade school
                                   3 = college
                                   4 = advanced degree
  1   16   Item number 1, occurrences during 0–12 months period.
             Response of 4+ = 4
             And so forth through
 42   57   Item number 42, occurrences during 0–12 months period.

Three-year version

Card 1
ITEM   COLUMN
NO.   NO.
      1   Individual card no. 1. (Three cards for 3-year SRE.)
      2–3   Identification code for particular group, 01 through 99.
      4–5   Date: last two digits of year.
      6–10 Subject number, 00001 through 99999.
      11–12 Age
      13   Sex   0 = male
                                       1 = female
      14   Marital status 0 = married
                                     1 = divorced
                                   2 = separated
                                   3 = widowed
                                   4 = never married

Appendix 9.5, continued

Card 1, continued

ITEM NO.	COLUMN NO.		
	15	Education	0 = grade school
			1 = high school
			2 = trade school
			3 = college
			4 = advanced degree
1	16	Item number 1, occurrences during 0–6 months period. Response of 4+ = 4	
	17	Item number 1, occurrences during 6–12 months.	
	18	Item number 1, occurrences during 1–2 years.	
	19	Item number 1, occurrences during 2–3 years. And so forth through	
16	76	Item number 16, 0–6 months.	
	77	Item number 16, 6–12 months.	
	78	Item number 16, 1–2 years.	
	79	Item number 16, 2–3 years.	

Card 2

ITEM NO.	COLUMN NO.	
	1	Individual card no. 2.
	2–10	Same as card 1, Columns 2–10.
17	11	Item number 17, 0–6 months.
	12	Item number 17, 6–12 months.
	13	Item number 17, 1–2 years.
	14	Item number 17, 2–3 years. And so forth through
33	75	Item number 33, 0–6 months.
	76	Item number 33, 6–12 months.
	77	Item number 33, 1–2 years.
	78	Item number 33, 2–3 years.

Card 3

ITEM NO.	COLUMN NO.	
	1	Individual card no. 3.
	2–10	Same as card 1, Columns 2–10.
34	11	Item number 34, 0–6 months.
	12	Item number 34, 6–12 months.
	13	Item number 34, 1–2 years.
	14	Item number 34, 2–3 years. And so forth through
42	43	Item number 42, 0–6 months.
	44	Item number 42, 6–12 months.
	45	Item number 42, 1–2 years.
	46	Item number 42, 2–3 years.

Appendix 9.6
Illness History

Instructions

On this page you are to list in column 1 the "Health Changes" you have had in the *past three years*. By health changes are meant things like illness, disease, sickness, nervous breakdown, surgery, accidents, injuries, pregnancy, etc. In column 2, "Date of Occurrence" is important so that the *time* of illness can be matched with the *time* on the Schedule of Recent Experience. In column 3, "Time Lost" gives some idea of the seriousness of the health change. The last 3 columns, on "Treatment" and "Hospitalization," give some idea of how your illness was taken care of.

List Health Changes	Date of Occurrence		Time Lost Due to Illness	Treatment by Self		Treatment by Doctor		If Hospitalized Number of Days Stay
	Month	Year		Yes	No	Yes	No	

10

Quantitative Study of Recall of Life Events

Robert L. Casey, Minoru Masuda, and Thomas H. Holmes

Questionnaire and interview protocols designed to elicit information about an individual's personal and social history (as in the medical or psychiatric interview) are usually assumed to derive valid information from the subject. Recent studies [1;2] questioning this assumption have been fraught with difficulties including the bias of report by proxy and the lack of adequate standardization of question administration; but most importantly, these studies were devoid of an approach to the validity of recall. The concept that validity of recall is related to the saliency of illness has been well established in health interview studies [3–5]. This investigation establishes that consistency of recall is similarly related to the saliency of life events and infers that if an event is recalled consistently, it is salient to the individual and may indirectly reflect validity of recall.

METHODS AND MATERIALS

The present Schedule of Recent Experience (SRE) questionnaire is self-administered and contains three parts. The face sheet documents personal information pertaining to residence, occupational, social, and marital status, and so on. A separate attached sheet asks for information concerning the health of the individual over a ten-year period. The body of the instrument consists of 40 items (Table 10.1) to which the subjects are asked to respond. The 40 items refer to life events, either indicative of the life-style of the individual or indicative of occurrences involving the individual. In previous studies [6–8] a method was defined

This chapter is reprinted with permission from Robert L. Casey, Minoru Masuda, and Thomas H. Holmes, "Quantitative Study of Recall of Life Events," *Journal of Psychosomatic Research* 11 (1967):239–47. Copyright 1967 by Pergamon Press, Ltd.

Table 10.1
Values of Questions on SRE

Item No.	SRE question	Mean value (LCU)
13.	Trouble with boss	23
14.	Change in sleeping habits	16
15.	Change in eating habits	15
16.	Revision of personal habits	24
17.	Change in recreation	19
18.	Change in social activities	18
19.	Change in church activities	19
20.	Change in number of family get-togethers	15
21.	Change in financial state	38
22.	Trouble with in-laws	29
23.	Change in number of arguments with spouse	35
24.	Sex difficulties	39
25.	Personal injury or illness	53
26.	Death of close family member	63
27.	Death of spouse	100
28.	Death of close friend	37
29.	Gain of new family member	39
30.	Change in health of family member	44
31.	Change in residence	20
32.	Jail term	63
33.	Minor violations of the law	11
34.	Business readjustment	39
35.	Marriage	50
36.	Divorce	73
37.	Marital separation	65
38.	Outstanding personal achievement	28
39.	Son or daughter leaving home	29
40.	Retirement	45
41.	Change in work hours or conditions	20
42.	Change in responsibilities at work	29
43.	Fired at work	47
44.	Change in living conditions	25
45.	Wife begin or stop work	26
46.	Mortgage over $10,000	31
47.	Mortgage or loan less than $10,000	17
48.	Foreclosure of mortgage or loan	30
49.	Vacation	13
50.	Change in schools	20
51.	Change to different line of work	36
52.	Begin or end school	26

for assigning a magnitude of significance to these events. The values are defined as life change units (LCU). It is clear that some items have more significance or salience than others, ranging from 11 to 100 LCU. Twelve of the 40 items in the SRE ask the subject to place a mark for the year the item occurred, while 28 of the items ask the subject to respond with a number: That is, they ask the subject to list the number of times that an item occurred for each year (example in Table 10.2). If the response to an item is positive, the subject places a mark or number under the year or years in which they event occurred. If the item does not apply, the subject marks the "does not apply" space.

In the summer of 1964, 88 resident physicians in the University of Washington integrated residency program completed and returned the questionnaire. In the spring of 1965, the same instrument was again completed by 54 of the 88 subjects. Thus, 54 paired sets of records were obtained, with the time interval of approximately nine months between the initial response (Time 1, or T1) and the second response (Time 2, or T2).

The questionnaire was scored in the following manner. The number of marks or numbers for each item were tabulated, multiplied by the value of the item (item LCU), and then summed to obtain the subject's total life change units (total LCU) for each year. Figure 10.1 shows the total LCU scores of one individual obtained over the ten-year period for the two administrations of the questionnaire. Similar data for the 54 subjects showed that the results obtained from the first administration of the questionnaire (T1) often differed from those of the second administration of the questionnaire (T2). For the purpose of this study, if the score difference between the total Time 1 and Time 2 LCU for the year was 40 LCU or greater, that score difference was labeled "discrepant." A score difference less than 40 LCU was labeled "nondiscrepant." The criterion point of 40 LCU score difference as discrepant was based on the fact that the standard deviation of the mean score difference between T1 and T2 was 40 LCU. Further, inspection of the distribution of the score differences of the 54 subjects (Figure 10.2) also indicates such an apparent cutoff point.

Three years (1957, 1960, and 1963) were arbitrarily chosen for detailed investigation. In studying in detail the factors affecting recall, the responses of one year, 1963, were chosen. This represented the most recent year completed at the two response times.

In the examination of individual items, a "consistent" response means that the individual marked, numbered, or left blank the item at both Time 1 and Time 2 in a similar way, and is designated *consistency of recall*. An "inconsistent" response occurred when an individual marked or numbered the item differently at Time 1 than at Time 2, and is designated *inconsistent recall*.

Percent consistency is derived from the actual number of paired consistent responses to an item in relation to the total possible number of paired responses to the item.

Table 10.2.
Two General Types of Phrasing

---

(1) *Mark under the years* that you have had either a lot more or a lot less financial problems:

| 1956 | 1957 | 1958 | 1959 | 1960 | 1961 | 1962 | 1963 | 1964 | 1965 |

Does not apply _____

(2) *List the number of times each year* that you have been fired:

| 1956 | 1957 | 1958 | 1959 | 1960 | 1961 | 1962 | 1963 | 1964 | 1965 |

Does not apply _____

RESULTS

Questionnaire Stability

A coefficient of stability (Pearson's r) for the two administrations (T1 and T2) of the questionnaire was calculated, based on total LCU scores for each subject for the years 1957, 1960, and 1963. Pearson product moment correlations were high ($r = 0.669$ for 1957; $r = 0.638$ for 1960; and $r = 0.744$ for 1963), the t-test showing these correlations to be significant at the 0.0005 level of confidence.

The Nature of the Variability over Time

Although there was statistically high score agreement between T1 and T2, differences between a subject's T1 and T2 total scores did exist. While ten subjects had stable scores for the three years studied, 12 had discrepant scores for the three years. Most subjects (32) scored with stability (nondiscrepantly) for one or two years and discrepantly for the remainder. Forty-four subjects, then, scored discrepantly to some degree for one or more of the three years.

Some subjects scored higher the second time—some lower— when compared with the Time 1 score. The sign test [9] showed that there was no consistency in the direction of change (neither a uniform increase nor decrease in the total LCU scores) among the subjects from Time 1 to Time 2, for all three years.

The 44 subjects contributed a total of 91 discrepant scores in all three years. The fairly equal distribution of these scores for each year is shown in Table 10.3. The mean differences of the scores, reflecting the magnitudes of the discrepancy,

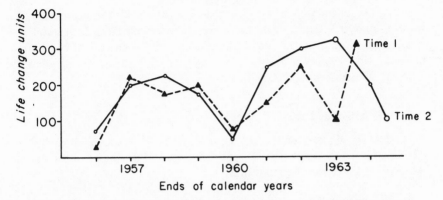

Figure 10.1 Yearly LCU over ten consecutive years as judged at two different times: T1 and T2.

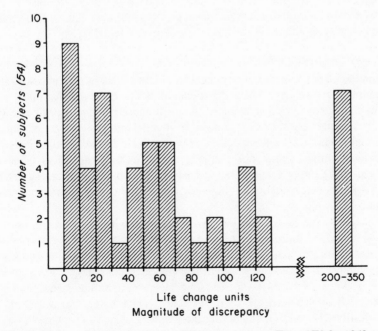

Figure 10.2 Magnitude of score differences between T1 and T2 for 1963.

increased slightly from 1957 to 1963 (Table 10.3). These differences among the three years were not significant ($X^2 = 4.4$; $p = 0.10$).

The distinct change among the three years is manifested in the mean total LCU scores (Table 10.3). These total LCU score values indicate that less material was recalled for the more distant time periods, almost 50 percent less when comparing 1957 with 1963. The mean total scores for each year were significantly different ($X^2 = 36.2$; $p = 0.0005$).

Factors Affecting Recall

The first step undertaken to study the consistency of recall was an analysis of individual items for 1963. The skewed distribution of the discrepant scores for the year 1963 is shown in Figure 10.2.

Recall and Saliency

The percents of consistent responses to each item by the 33 subjects who had discrepant total scores for 1963 were compiled. Some items were recalled with more consistency than others, the range of consistent responses per item extending from 36 percent to 100 percent. A curve of the percent consistency of responses for each of the items as they relate to the item values is shown in Figure 10.3. Items, placed in the order of increasing item value, are represented by the bar graph. The items responded to more consistently had higher item values—that is, had higher magnitudes of significance or salience—while the items responded to less consistently had lower (less salient) item values. This relationship is highly significant (Pearson's $r = 0.586$; $p < 0.0005$).

Recall and Item Qualifiers

Another item parameter investigated for 1963 was that of item phraseology. In examining the language of the questionnaire it was observed that many of the items contained words that attempted to qualify or clarify the items (Table 10.4). These qualifiers are adjectives and can be divided into four categories: substantial, major–minor, a lot more–a lot less, unusual–close–special. It appeared that individuals might assign different magnitudes to these qualifiers when confronted with them on two separate occasions (T1 and T2). Such a fluctuation in the subjective interpretation of these key words might contribute to inconsistent recall.

The items were categorized into two classes: those items with qualifiers (22 of the 40 items) and those without (18 of the 40 items). A point biserial correlation between qualifiers associated with low percentage consistency responses and nonqualifiers associated with a high percentage of consistency was significant ($r_{pb} = 0.358$; $F = 5.62$; $p < 0.05$). The four categories of individual qualifiers were then examined separately. Each of the four qualifier categories was dealt with statistically (chi-square), comparing the numbers of items (containing the particular qualifier) that appeared above and below the median percent consistency

Table 10.3
Distribution of Discrepant Scores and Mean Total Scores over Time

	1957	1960	1963
Number of subjects with discrepant scores Differences greater than 40 ($N = 44$)	27	31	33
Mean difference of discrepant scores	90	100	119
Mean total LCU scores* ($N = 54$)	102	132	202

* $X^2 = 36.2$; $p = 0.0005$

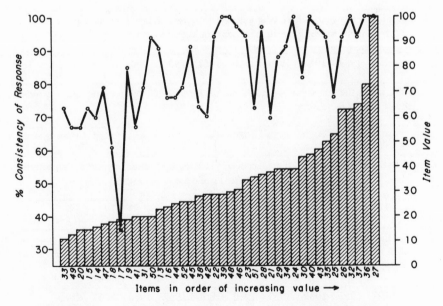

Figure 10.3   Item value and consistency of recall qualifiers and consistency of recall.

Table 10.4
Sample Items from SRE Questionnaire

Items with Qualifiers

20. Mark under the years that there has been a *substantial* change in family get-togethers (picnics, holidays, etc.):

1956	1957	1958	1959	1960	1961	1962	1963	1964	1965

30. List the number of times each year that there has been a *major* change in the health or behavior of a family member:

1956	1957	1958	1959	1960	1961	1962	1963	1964	1965

13. Mark under the years where there has been either *a lot more or a lot less* trouble with the boss:

1956	1957	1958	1959	1960	1961	1962	1963	1964	1965

Items with "Double Question" Plus Qualifiers

14. Mark under the years where your usual sleeping pattern was changed (sleeping *a lot more or a lot less, or change* in part of day when asleep):

1956	1957	1958	1959	1960	1961	1962	1963	1964	1965

15. Mark under the years where your eating habits were changed (either *a lot more or a lot less* eating, *or very different* meal hours or surroundings):

1956	1957	1958	1959	1960	1961	1962	1963	1964	1965

17. Mark under the years that there has been *substantial* change in your *usual amount and/or type* of recreation:

1956	1957	1958	1959	1960	1961	1962	1963	1964	1965

19. Mark under the years that there has been a *substantial* change in your church activity (either *a lot more or a lot less, or a change* in denomination):

1956	1957	1958	1959	1960	1961	1962	1963	1964	1965

25. List the number of times each year that you experienced *major illness, injury or substantial health change* (for example, pregnancy, menopause, large weight gain or loss, etc.):

1956	1957	1958	1959	1960	1961	1962	1963	1964	1965

---

of 86 percent. Only the items with the qualifier "substantial" had a distribution that differed significantly from the expected, these items clustering below the median. Similarly the chi-square test was performed between the numbers of items containing a particular qualifier that were above and below the median item value of 29. None of the four categories analyzed differed significantly from the expected, although the items with the qualifier "substantial" showed a trend toward an association with low item values ($p = 0.10$).

Of the qualifiers, it seems that the items with "substantial" are the only ones associating qualifiers with percent consistency, and to some extent with item score value. To determine the degree of influence of the items containing this qualifier, these seven items were deleted, and a Pearson correlation was done between the score values of the remaining items and percent consistency of recall ($r = 0.546$; $p = 0.005$). This highly significant correlation indicates that it is the saliency of the items and not the presence of qualifying words that most affect the consistency of recall.

Recall and Item Phraseology

Other factors related to the structure and syntax of the items may play a role in determining the magnitude of consistent responses. Items 14, 15, 17, 19, and 25 (Table 10.4) contain a double statement—that is, asking whether a subject is eating a lot more or a lot less, *and* whether meal hours or surroundings are different. These items were all associated with item recall consistency below the median percentage (86 percent) (Figure 10.3).

Recall and the Individual

The data were next analyzed to test whether recall was affected by the level of life change (LCU score) at the times of questionnaire administration. Since Time 1 and Time 2 occurred 5–7 months following the first of January, 1964 and 1965, respectively, the 1964 and 1965 scores were used as indicators of the amount of change that the individual was undergoing in his or her life situation at the times of questionnaire administration. The higher of the two life change scores at the time (either T1 or T2) of administration of the questionnaire was compared to the higher of that individual's two scores for 1963. It was found that there was no relationship between the LCU scores at the time that the questionnaire was taken and the magnitude of the scores for 1963.

DISCUSSION

The stability coefficients (Pearson's r) for the three representative years were statistically significant at less than 0.0005 level of confidence (t-tailed). These correlations are especially significant in light of the long interval (nine months) between the two administrations of the questionnaire, and they reflect a high level of consistent scores for all three years as well as a reliable instrument.

A significant difference in the total mean scores among the three years was noted, with less material being recalled for the more distant time periods. It appears that time influences the volume of material remembered. With the passing of time, many events that the individual once recalled were no longer recalled, while certain events were retained longer and became reliably fixed in memory. Just how much time is required for this process to occur is not certain. The mean total scores of T1 and T2 for 1963 are of approximately equal magnitude, indicating that it takes a period of time greater than nine months to affect the magnitude of recall.

In exploring the variability of the scores between T1 and T2 for 1957, 1960, and 1963, it was apparent that most of the individuals with discrepant scores did not have a consistent pattern of discrepancy for all three years, but rather for one or two of the three time periods. Further, the discrepant scores did not cluster around one time period more than another, but rather were evenly distributed throughout the three years. The magnitudes of the discrepant score differences did not significantly change among the three years. These data plus the close approximation in Pearson's r among the three years would infer that, for the nine months elapsed between T1 and T2, recall for the more distant time periods is as consistent as recall for the more recent years, indicating that time may not affect the consistency of recall.

The hypothesis, that the higher LCU scores of each of the subjects at the time of the recall task (T1 and T2) might result in a skewing of the magnitude of the 1963 LCU scores in a uniform direction, was not confirmed. The lack of influence of the only parameter in the data that involves change in the individual's life situation confirms the work of other investigators [1;2] who have not been able to relate definitive individual factors to the consistency of recall.

The relationship between items containing qualifying words associated with low consistency of recall and items without qualifiers associated with high item consistency was significant ($r_{pb} < 0.05$). In examining the categories of item qualifiers separately, it appeared that the qualifier "substantial" was significantly related to inconsistency of recall, while the other qualifiers were not. This finding reflects the inability of individuals to assign the same subjective magnitude to the word "substantial" on two separate test occasions. The use of qualifiers and the posing of more than one question in an item are techniques often used to help clarify items that are nebulous in nature and difficult to communicate. It is ironic that they should compound clarity and foster inconsistency of recall.

It has been shown that both mean item value and qualifiers (particularly the qualifier "substantial") were related significantly to percent consistency of recall. When the items containing the qualifier "substantial" were deleted from the correlation between mean item value and percent consistency, the correlation diminished slightly but remained significant at the 0.005 level.

Thus the most significant determinant affecting the consistency of recall was mean item value (LCU). The parallel relationship between increasing item value (LCU) and increasing consistency of recall has been stated. The association between these two variables was significant at the 0.0005 level of confidence.

The mean item value (LCU) has been discussed in two previous papers [6;7] and is indicative of the magnitude of significance or salience that the item has for the individual in terms of the degree of change and adaptability required by the individual to meet the event in the life situation. The influence of the event depends on change in the pattern of living rather than on psychological meaning, emotions, or social desirability [6].

Investigators in the field of health studies have been concerned with the validity of recall and have set forth some valuable findings. Mechanic [3] pointed out that there are various factors unrelated to personality or demographic characteristics that seem to be related to the validity of reporting. He mentioned that the most persistent factor underlying health interview studies was that serious disorders that require repeated attention were more salient than less serious ones and were more likely to be reported accurately. Investigators associated with the National Health Survey [10] indicate that minor illnesses were subject to considerably more memory bias and recall variability than those affecting the life of the individual to the extent that one or more specific forms of action had been taken. The forms of action included restriction of usual activities, disability, work loss, the seeking of medical advice, or the taking of medicines. These actions required a significant change in the ongoing life pattern of the individual, with their influence on recall coming from an alteration in the existing state of adjustment, rather than on psychological meaning or emotion.

It appears that similar relationships are at work in two universes of discourse—reporting of illness, and recall of life events—that are usually considered separately but that will now be studied together. Validity of recall is possible to determine in studying medical illnesses, but it is more difficult to assess in relation to life events. Consistency of recall, however, is readily measurable when studying the individual in the life setting. Since validity of recall cannot be feasibly studied in the life situation, is it possible that consistency of recall is a reflection of recall validity? It has been shown that both validity of recall and consistency of recall are related to the same variable: the saliency of the illness or the saliency of the life event. It has also been shown that "saliency" is defined in terms of change in the ongoing life pattern of the individual in both universes of discourse and has approximately the same meaning in both settings. In this conceptual framework, if an individual responds consistently to the same item on two separate occasions, nine months apart, it is apparent that the item event has salience for that individual and the consistent recall may indirectly be a reflection of validity of recall. The consistency of recall may well be an indicator that the event or some facsimile did (or did not) occur in the life situation.

This chapter has shown that item value or saliency is the single factor most affecting consistency of recall. There are other factors, however, that may influence consistency of recall: item qualifiers and item phraseology. It would seem that these factors associated with lower recall consistency should be used cautiously and possibly deleted from questions having low item value or low salience. Lastly, the concept introduced in this chapter that consistency of recall is significantly determined by saliency of life events can be applied to the 40 life event items of the SRE. The high median percentage of recall consistency (86 percent) for the 40 items is an indicator that these particular life events are salient to the lives of the respondents and infers that clusters of such significant events might indeed contribute to illness onset. Further, the patterns of consistency of recall to the various items, reflecting the saliency of the life events, confirms and substantiates the rating of these life events by the 394 subjects reported in an earlier study [6].

SUMMARY

A self-administered questionnaire, the Schedule of Recent Experience (SRE), containing events pertinent to the life situation, was completed by a group of 54 resident physicians on two occasions, nine months apart. The data were analyzed to determine the stability of the questionnaire and for factors affecting consistency of recall.

The correlation coefficients (coefficient of stability) for the two administrations of the questionnaire based on the total life change unit scores (LCU) were significant for the three years examined. The passage of time was found to affect the magnitude of individual scores but apparently had no effect on the consistency of the scores. Items containing qualifying words (particularly the word "substantial") significantly affected recall consistency.

However, the most potent factor affecting consistency of recall was the saliency of the life event items, reflected by their mean item values (LCU). This relationship between saliency of the life event and consistency of recall was highly significant. The relationship between saliency and consistency of recall found in this study was then compared to a similar concept established in health interview studies, to make the inference that consistency of recall may indirectly reflect recall validity.

REFERENCES

1. Haggard, E. A., A. Brekstad, and A. G. Skard. "On the Reliability of the Anamnestic Interview." *Journal of Abnormal and Social Psychology* 61 (1960):311–18.

2. Wenar, C., and J. B. Coulter. "A Reliability Study of Developmental Histories." *Child Development* 33 (1962):453–62.

3. Mechanic, D., and M. Newton. "Some Problems in the Analysis of Morbidity Data." *Journal of Chronic Diseases* 18 (1965):569–80.

4. U.S. National Health Survey. *Health Interview Responses Compared with Medical Records.* Public Health Service, Series D-5. Washington, D.C.: Government Printing Office, 1961 (June).

5. U.S. National Health Survey. *Comparison of Hospitalization Reporting in Three Survey Procedures.* Public Health Service, Series D-8. Washington, D.C.: Government Printing Office, 1963 (January).

6. Holmes, T. H., and R. H. Rahe. "The Social Readjustment Rating Scale." *Journal of Psychosomatic Research* 11 (1967):213–18. Reprinted in this volume, Chapter 2.

7. Rahe, R. H., and T. H. Holmes. "Life Crisis and Disease Onset. I. Qualitative and Quantitative Definition of the Life Crisis and Its Association with Health Change." First published as pt. 2 of R. H. Rahe, "Life Crisis and Health Change." In *Psychotropic Drug Response: Advances in Prediction*, edited by P. R. A. May and J. R. Wittenborn, pp. 92–125. Springfield, Ill.: Charles C Thomas, 1969. Reprinted in this volume, Chapter 13.

8. Rahe, R. H., and T. H. Holmes. "Life Crisis and Disease Onset. II. A Prospective Study of Life Crises and Health Change." First published at pt. 3 of R. H. Rahe, "Life Crisis and Health Change." In *Psychotropic Drug Response: Advances in Prediction*, edited by P. R. A. May and J. R. Wittenborn, pp. 92–125. Springfield, Ill.: Charles C Thomas, 1969. Reprinted in this volume, Chapter 14.

9. Siegel, S. *Nonparametric Statistics for the Behavioral Sciences.* New York: McGraw-Hill, 1956.

10. National Concept for Health Statistics. *Health Survey Procedure: Concepts, Questionnaire Development, and Definitions in the Health Interview Study.* Public Health Service, Series 1–2. Washington, D.C.: Government Printing Office, 1964 (May).

Introduction

Developing the Paradigm: Life Change and Illness Susceptibility

The following six chapters form the core of the Holmes laboratory's life change research. First in retrospective studies and then in prospective work, we collected data that culminated in our formulation of a basic paradigm for the relation of life change to illness onset. Put simply, we found that, the greater the magnitude of life change (or life crisis), the greater the probability that the life change would be associated with disease onset, and the greater the probability that the population at risk would experience disease.

The beauty of the retrospective case-control study reported in Chapter 11 is that the time of disease onset was determined from routine quarterly chest X-rays done on all employees at Firland Sanatorium. It is not often that one can so precisely date the onset of disease; with many diseases (and especially those that develop quietly over a number of years, such as cancer) the best we can do is to date the time of diagnosis.

Chapter 12 brings together data from five studies in which we used a similar research design. In these studies of health changes as different as hernia, heart disease, skin disease, and pregnancy, we again found that the accumulation of many life changes was an important factor in determining the time of disease onset.

Enter the Social Readjustment Rating Scale, providing a unique method for a quantitative definition of a "life crisis." In Chapters 13 and 14—our pilot studies—Richard Rahe and I used the Social Readjustment Rating Scale for the first time to score the Schedule of Recent Experience. In the retrospective study described in Chapter 13, we plotted each subject's annual life change score for the past ten years and superimposed on that profile the occurrence of reported illnesses. In Chapter 14, on the prospective study, we began with the amount of life change, predicted what was going to happen, and then studied what actually did happen in the following two years. In both studies we demonstrated a direct relationship between magnitude of life crisis and risk of health change in the following two years.

By the time the pilot studies appeared in print, Dr. Rahe had moved to San Diego and had begun his now-famous studies of life change and illness in military populations. While he experimented with using a six-month life change unit (LCU) score to predict near-future illness in navy men aboard ships, T. Stephenson Holmes in Seattle modified the Schedule of Recent Experience for a prospective study of daily life change and health changes. And so with the findings in Chapter 15, we had a complete time span for our paradigm studies: We had demonstrated that life change scores can predict the *occurrence* of health changes for periods of 1–2 years, for six months, and on a daily basis.

Only one element in our paradigm remained to be established: the relation of magnitude of life change to *magnitude* (or seriousness) of health change. The study in Chapter 16—using the newly developed Seriousness of Illness Rating Scale—provided the necessary data. We were able to confirm statistically what we had observed empirically in our other studies. Not only are people more likely to get sick when they experience increased life change—but also, the greater the magnitude of the life change, the more serious the illness is likely to be if they do get sick.

11

Evidence of Psychosocial Factors in the Development of Pulmonary Tuberculosis

Norman G. Hawkins, Roberts Davies, and Thomas H. Holmes

INTRODUCTION

The literature concerning psychic phenomena in tuberculosis is extensive [1–5]. For 2,500 years or more some physicians have believed that tuberculosis was frequently initiated by unhappy or stressful experiences. The discovery of the tubercle bacillus discouraged this belief, but it never disappeared [6–9]. The demonstration of marked variations in resistance to tuberculosis between species and between individuals of the same species has suggested that infection alone is an incomplete explanation of progressive disease.

A number of investigators have presented evidence of physiologic mechanisms whereby life stresses may adversely affect human resistance. At an early date it was noted that certain autonomic phenomena associated with chronic emotional stress were prominent among tuberculous patients [9–11]. Strong similarities have been found between persons suffering from pulmonary tuberculosis and cases of effort syndrome [12–14]. A number of studies have shown deviations in hormones related to resistance, and association between these deviations and emotional states [15–18].

Studies of patients at Firland Sanatorium in Seattle have established that they are typically unstable and socially marginal, and had experienced apparently critical patterns of life stresses prior to the detection of their disease [19;20]. From these findings it was logical to draw the hypothesis that a life-organizational stress situation of significant proportions typically appears shortly before the onset of the disease.

This chapter is reprinted from *American Review of Tuberculosis and Pulmonary Diseases* 75 (1957):768–80. Copyright 1957 by the American Lung Association. Reprinted by permission of the *American Review of Respiratory Disease*.

PLAN OF INVESTIGATION

The Problem

It was proposed to test the above hypothesis by relating crisis to onset of the disease. A thoroughly scientific test would have involved the selection of well people at random, assignment of these to an experimental and a control group, and application of stress to the experimental group. This was manifestly out of the question.

At first glance it would seem that the next best approach would have been to sample tuberculous patients at random and to make an ex post facto comparison with a random sample of the population. However, the following difficulties immediately presented themselves:

1. As already noted, patients are distinctly *not* representative in connection with economic, racial, and other factors intimately related to the question of situational crisis.
2. Only rarely can the approximate time of onset be established.
3. Even if a random sample of the population could be induced to have chest films, the replacement of any having questionable films would raise a serious question concerning the randomness of the final choice of sample.
4. Since crisis is postulated as a precipitating cause—not an exclusive cause—a valid comparison would require evidence of infection in the normative sample.

These considerations made it necessary to seek a comparison of two groups matched on a number of background items, including chest films and skin tests, both of which groups had been consistently examined roentgenographically for evidence of tuberculosis so that time of onset and time of detection would be in close agreement. Furthermore, since matching from otherwise distinct groups tends to exaggerate differences of the investigated variables, it was considered advisable to draw both samples from a presumably homogeneous population.

Method

The only available population from which two samples could be obtained that would conform to these requirements consisted of all persons employed at Firland Sanatorium from its establishment at the present location in June 1947. Each of these had been given skin tests with PPD (purified protein derivative) in graded strengths, an initial chest film at the time of employment, and subsequent chest films at intervals of three months.

The tuberculous sample consisted of all employees at work between the specified dates who were found eligible for compensation as a result of tuberculosis in connection with their employment. The sample used for comparison consisted of other employees matched *individually* by age, sex, race, marital status, education, time of employment, job classification, income, skin test reading, appearance of chest film, and previous record of chronic conditions possibly related to pulmonary tuberculosis.*

The employees who had contracted tuberculosis were first classified with respect to age, sex, race, job classification, and time of employment. From questionnaires the education, income, and marital status were determined. Department heads were then asked for the names of employees who would closely approximate the various criteria. Those of the same sex, race, and job classification, hired within six months of the same day as the tuberculous employee, and within the same decade of age, were accepted as the pool from which further matching would be done. The names of these and of the persons to be matched were turned over to the medical director of the sanatorium for comparison of the chest films and medical data.

A total of 31 employees had been found to have compensable pulmonary tuberculosis. Seven had terminated employment, moved, and left no forwarding addresses; one refused to participate; one was from too small a job classification to select a satisfactory comparison; and two could not be matched on physiologic variables. This left 20 cases for study.

Two of the cases of tuberculosis were first diagnosed in 1949; six, in 1950; four, in 1951; four, in 1952; two, in 1953; and two, in 1954. Time of detection ranged from 4 months to 73 months after employment, the mean being 26.5 months. Of the 11 patients not in the study, six had become ill prior to 1950.

The previous occurrence of psychosocial stresses was measured by means of the Schedule of Recent Experience, a form for registering a uniform list of difficulties and hardships by year of occurrence. Entries are always made by the person under study, and the response pattern represents a measure of the frequency and location of experiences. The Schedule of Recent Experience was developed in the sanatorium, cross-validated on two samples totaling 165 admissions, and pretested for readability and clarity; the maximal validity was established as lying in the age range from 25 to 55 years. A reliability coefficient of 0.831 was obtained between first and second administrations of the form at five-month intervals in a group of 40 newly admitted white patients with pulmonary tuberculosis between the ages of 25 and 60 years.

The level of personal integration (a phenomenon assumed to be related to experience of crisis) was measured by the Cornell Medical Index, a standardized list of 195 items used for screening psychoneurotic suspects by quantitative criteria. The Cornell Medical Index had been pretested for use by the semiliterate and is reliably interpreted by clinicians, nurses, medical students, and social workers, as well as by psychiatrists [21]. The reliability of response was 0.805 when tested in the same manner as described above for the Schedule of Recent Experience.

For the purposes of the study, "situational crisis" was defined as a uniformly

---

* Chronic conditions included diabetes, hypothyroidism, asthma, pulmonary emphysema, mitral stenosis, pulmonic stenosis, silicosis, hypertension, and alcoholism.

and sharply rising frequency of the dislocative factors in the life history that are measured by the Schedule of Recent Experience. A significantly greater number of patients in the sick group who registered such a concentration in the two years preceding onset of the disease compared with the same period for the well group, and a significantly higher level of cumulative experience among the sick than among the well, would confirm the hypothesis.

It was unnecessary to postulate a connection between the extent of crisis and the degree of personal disintegration reflected on the Cornell Medical Index. On the other hand, the general conception of crisis is such that a relationship between the two phenomena would certainly strengthen the theory.

In view of the small numbers compared and the fact that they were matched rather than randomized, it was essential that analysis be confined to statistical measures applicable to these precise conditions. The *t*-test of differences between means has a sampling distribution that changes according to the sample size, so that a larger difference is required for smaller samples in order to achieve the same level of significance as in larger samples. Most of the current texts on social and psychologic statistics give specific instructions for the use of this test in a matched design. The chi-square test likewise corrects for the sample size by requiring increasingly greater proportional differences from increasingly smaller samples. The latter test ordinarily requires random sampling but, when used as a test for homogeneity, it requires only that the groups be equal and that the factor tested shall occur under conditions of equal opportunity. These were the tests employed. Since the only chi-square comparison employed a four-place table, the calculations were corrected for continuity.

OBSERVATIONS

The matched groups numbered 20 each, of whom 3 were male and 17 were female. The final matching was such that all were white. Each of the groups contained one physician, four registered nurses, and twelve subordinate nursing and auxiliary personnel. Two of the employees who were ill had had inactive tuberculosis at the time of employment and were matched with employees having inactive disease of similar extent who remained well. With these two exceptions, all were cases of minimal tuberculosis. None of the control subjects had developed tuberculosis when we monitored at six months after completion of the study.

The matching by sex and marital status was necessarily exact. Race was constant. None of the control subjects was hired more than six months earlier or later, but no more exact measure was computed. Job classification was judged by department heads and medical data by the medical director.

Income means were $3,485 for the ill and $3,815 for the well, with standard deviations of $95.20 and $121.18, respectively, demonstrating that the match was consistently very close for all 20 pairs. The tuberculous group had a mean age of 45.15 years and standard deviation of 14.24 years; the controls, a mean of

46.40 years and standard deviation of 14.20 years. On this variable there was again a uniformly good match. The means of education were 12.00 years for the tuberculous and 11.95 years for the control subjects, but respective standard deviations were 2.55 years and 1.57 years, a difference significant at the 0.05 level.

There was also a very close agreement on the number in the household (a factor not consciously controlled), with an average of 2.90 for the ill and 3.00 for the well employees and standard deviations of 3.59 and 3.50.

The distribution of stressful situations, such as financial hardship, changes of jobs and residences, and domestic problems, was markedly different for the two groups, as shown in Figures 11.1 and 11.2. It will be noted that two broad classes of events progress in concomitant fashion in Figure 11.1, while in Figure 11.2 they are unrelated. Calculation of straight line regressions of the combined frequencies revealed a positive slope of 0.275 for the tuberculous sample and a negative slope of 0.009 (practically horizontal) for the control subjects. The groups thus exhibited the predicted phenomenon of uniformly accelerating stress frequencies among those who became tuberculous.

The total incidence of such stressful occurrences during the ten years, however, was on the average higher for the control subjects. In Table 11.1 the incidence for the two groups is shown. In view of their relatively meager total experience of these stressful events, the very high frequency among the tuberculous employees in the final period is the more remarkable by way of contrast.

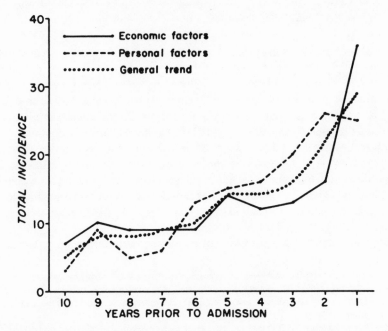

Figure 11.1   Incidence of social taxis in the ten years prior to illness among 20 tuberculous employees at Firland Sanatorium.

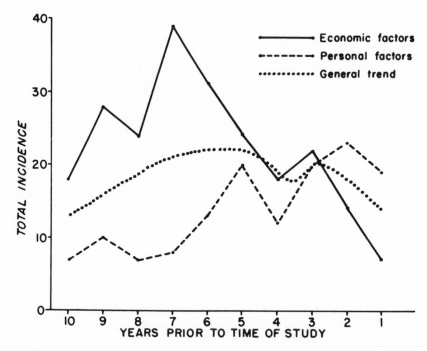

Figure 11.2   Incidence of social taxis in the ten years prior to time of study among 20 nontuberculous employees at Firland Sanatorium.

It had been predicted that, whatever the highest frequency of stress in a given case, a significantly greater number of the tuberculous employees would record that highest frequency as occurring either one or two years prior to onset (detection) of their illness. The comparison is shown in Table 11.2. The difference between nine tuberculous employees and one control subject resulted in a corrected chi-square value of 6.55, significant at the 0.02 level of confidence.

It was also predicted that in the peak year the tuberculous employees would have recorded a significant concentration of disturbing events. That is, the proportion of the total ten years' experience appearing in a single year would be significantly higher. The means and standard deviations for this percentage concentration are shown in Table 11.3.* The t-ratio for the difference is 3.32, significant at the 0.005 level of confidence.†

In view of the fact that the group of ill subjects went through a significantly

---

* In this comparison the peak-year frequency for each case was divided by the total ten-year frequency for that case. These quotients were then used as score distributions in the same fashion as density or rate levels might be used, and means and variances were computed from the distribution for each group.

† In a one-tailed test of pairs it would be customary to use 19 degrees of freedom and take half the tabled value of probability. The present study employed 38 degrees of freedom and the actual tabled value, thus obtaining a more conservative estimate of significance.

Table 11.1
Total Experience of Social Stresses Recorded for the Ten-year Period Covered in the SRE by 20 Tuberculous and 20 Matched Nontuberculous Employees of Firland Sanatorium

Group	Ten-year Frequency of Social Forces	
	Mean	Standard Deviation
Tuberculous	16.7	15.5
Nontuberculous	23.5	10.3

disturbed phase at the predicted time and yet had less hardship in the long run, it was essential that the distribution of factors be examined in more detail to see whether the differences occurred only in a few areas or were quite general throughout the life organization. The findings from this analysis are reported in Table 11.4, showing the average contribution from each type of disturbance during the ten years, and in Table 11.5, which gives the percentage of each type that occurred in the final two of those ten years.

The tendency toward concentration is consistent in all areas of experience for the group of ill subjects. While the absolute concentration was quite marked in some instances in which the factors had been unimportant in the long-term experience of this group (for example, personal crisis and marital stress), the concentration was significant only for financial hardship, job changes, resident changes, and work stress. With the exception of the last, these had all been of greater importance in the histories of the group of those who were ill. On the

Table 11.2
Location of Year of Peak Frequency of Social Stresses among 20 Tuberculous and 20 Matched Nontuberculous Employees of Firland Sanatorium Shown in the SRE

	Time of Occurrence		Total
	Final Two Years	Prior	
Tuberculous	9	11	20
Nontuberculous	1	19	20
Total cases	10	30	40

Note: The chi-square test of homogeneity, corrected for continuity, has a value of 6.55 in this table. The value is significant at the 0.02 level of confidence.

Table 11.3

Proportion of Ten-year Experience of Social Stresses Concentrated within the Peak Year of Such Experience as Recorded on the SRE by 20 Tuberculous and 20 Nontuberculous Matched Employees of Firland Sanatorium

Group	Percentage of Experience Recorded in Peak Year	
	Mean	Standard Deviation
Tuberculous	36.4	13.1
Nontuberculous	25.2	7.4

Note: The value of the *t*-ratio for this table is 3.32; with 38 degrees of freedom, it is significant at the 0.005 level of confidence.

whole, then, the critical cumulation had been consistent in all areas of the life organization and significant in the areas of long-term disturbance.

Five dimensions of pathologic response may be judged from the Cornell Medical Index: total affirmative responses, affirmative responses on the last page (manifest personality items), ambiguous responses, number of written comments, and dispersion throughout the various sections representing bodily systems and emotional moods. These are two cutting points for the number of total affirmatives, making six criteria of classification.

As shown in Table 11.6, the number referable as psychoneurotic suspects by two or more of these criteria was 13 among the tuberculous and 5 among the controls. The corrected chi-square value is significant at the 0.05 level of confidence. The ill employees were significantly more often classifiable as pathologically disturbed according to the standard interpretation of the index.

The two groups were also compared on each of the five dimensions of pathology. The tabulations are given in Table 11.7. It is at once evident that the tuberculous employees exceeded their healthy counterparts on all except manifest personality items. These are items with psychologic implications that are clear to both naive and sophisticated respondents, whereas other measures of pathology are not likely to be suspected except by one familiar with the manual of interpretation [21]. All differences were significant, the most definitive being the number of comments, which was significant at the 0.01 level of confidence.

An examination of the separate items of manifest personality disturbance was extremely interesting. There are six sections in all, with items indicative of inadequacy, depression, anxiety, sensitivity, hostility, and tension. In five of these sections the group differences were not significant, but in reference to hostility the ill group expressed significantly less at the 0.001 level. That one section accounted for the negative, though not significant, finding with respect to this criterion.

Table 11.4
Proportion of the Total Frequency of Social Stresses Contributed from Each Class of Disturbing Events in the SRE by 20 Tuberculous and 20 Matched Nontuberculous Employees of Firland Sanatorium

	Mean Percentage of Total During 10 Years	
Item Group	Tuberculous	Nontuberculous
Financial hardship	15.7	12.4
Job changes	13.5	10.1
Residence changes	12.8	9.4
Changes in social relations	17.9	16.8
Irregular habits	9.5	8.2
Personal crisis*	6.8	11.3
Work stress	7.4	14.9
Marital stress	3.5	8.3

* A residual item aimed at showing any gross failure of the instrument to measure critical disturbance. No such failure was evident. Four other item groups are not shown because response from both groups was absent or meager.

Table 11.5
Proportion of the Frequency of Each Item Group of the SRE Appearing in the Final Two Years for 20 Tuberculous and 20 Matched Nontuberculous Employees of Firland Sanatorium

	Mean Percentage Recorded in the Final Two Years	
Item Group	Tuberculous	Nontuberculous
Financial hardship	29.8	8.1
Job changes	30.1	6.2
Residence changes	31.7	4.9
Changes in social relations	35.5	22.7
Irregular habits	28.8	9.4
Personal crisis*	68.1	20.0
Work stress	33.3	11.3
Marital stress	40.0	33.3

* A residual item aimed at showing any gross failure of the instrument to measure critical disturbance. No such failure was evident. Four other item groups are not shown because response from both groups was absent or meager.

Table 11.6
Number of Cases among 20 Tuberculous and 20 Matched Nontuberculous
Employees of Firland Sanatorium Whose Answers to the Cornell Medical Index
Classify Them as Pathologically Disturbed

	Pathologic*	Others
Tuberculous	13	7
Nontuberculous	5	15

* Judged by the standard of demonstrating two or more evaluative criteria for referral to a psychiatrist. The chi-square value of the frequencies, corrected for continuity, was found to be 4.95. This was significant at the 0.05 confidence level.

The total scores on the Schedule of Recent Experience and those on the Cornell Medical Index correlated negatively. However, a number of other features of the two instruments exhibited positive association. These are listed in Table 11.8. While these results are far from conclusive they do present some grounds for supposing that stressful experiences and pathologic signs were two aspects of a single process.

Certain by-products of the study throw further light on the differences in group performance. There were two questions in the Schedule of Recent Experience relating to changes of residence, the answers to which should have been identical. Similarly, the Cornell Medical Index contains two adjacent sections: one showing the self-concept as a sickly or robust person; the other showing an actual list of common ailments. In both these comparisons the tuberculous employees were significantly more discrepant when the relevant items were compared and the quantitative difference was tabulated. Likewise the tuberculous group was more variable in their scores and subscores on the two instruments, their distributions being typified by significantly extreme separations into high and low and the various individuals being typified by erratic fluctuations of these extremes for the various life factors and the different indexes of pathology.

DISCUSSION

As previously noted, the small size of the samples represents no serious drawback if treated by the methods used in the present study.* As a matter of fact there is a valid reason for preferring the small sample in such research. The same level of significance is of greater practical importance when it is achieved in a small sample than when it requires a very large sample, for the smaller the number the closer must be the approach to the ideal of invariable difference.

* See the final paragraph under the section "Method," above.

Table 11.7

Differences in Occurrence of Clinical Criteria of the Cornell Medical Index among 20 Tuberculous and 20 Matched Nontuberculous Employees at Firland Sanatorium

Criteria	Mean Occurrence		Significance*
	Tuberculous	Nontuberculous	
Total "yes" answers	28.20	17.35	0.05
"Yes" answers to page 4†	4.85	6.45	
Ambiguous response‡	1.45	0.70	0.05
Comments§	3.85	1.10	0.01
Dispersion‖	5.65	3.95	0.02

  * Probability that such a difference would occur by chance, as measured by t-test with 38 degrees of freedom.

  † This page consists of "manifest" personality items, that is, items whose emotional tone is obvious to the respondent.

  ‡ Marking either both or neither of the two possible answers.

  § All changes that would qualify the response.

  ‖ The average number of sections, of a total of 18, through which affirmative answers were scattered.

A real limitation is presented by the fact that the study was retrospective. There are the inherent dangers of overlooking cases, losing cases that cannot be matched, and failing to match variables essential for the homogeneity of the samples. The fallibility of memory is also a matter to be considered, although the high reliability of the questionnaire over a period of five months is consistent with prevailing evidence that memory is most dependable in matters of organized personal experience, such as family and economic life [22]. In connection with matching, a very prominent source of error lies in the fact that important factors, such as chest films and medical histories, are not quantitative variables but qualitative clinical judgments.

Even if these limitations could be ignored, it does not necessarily follow that social crisis was causal even to the degree of being a precipitant. The effects of the disease process, the shock of diagnosis, or both, may have distorted the subsequent reactions of the group of those who were ill by giving the immediately preceding experiences a heightened emotional tone. The results in terms of psychoneurotic signs could be explained very well in similar terms.

On the positive side it can be pointed out that the theory was not constructed in retrospect but that the instruments were chosen with a specific consequence of that theory in mind; that the validity and reliability of the instruments were established beforehand; and that both instruments are quantitative and hence not dependent on personal bias or clinical impression for their interpretation. Moreover, the test was so designed as to take into account the crucial evidence concerning prior chest films and presence of tubercle bacilli.

Other pertinent data were available. The group used in testing reliability contained 20 males and 20 females. When the frequencies of stressful events were graphed separately for the sexes, it was seen that the graph rose continuously for females up to the time of admission while that for males rose and then dropped sharply. This phenomenon has a possible connection with the circumstances of male hospitalization: Treatment is more frequently delayed, the disease is more frequently advanced, and the delay and stage of disease are probably associated phenomena. Further evidence of the concomitance of traumatic experience, emotional reaction, and disease status was shown in the Firland study of adrenocortical activity [18].

SUMMARY

A group of sanatorium employees who became ill with tuberculosis was compared with an individually matched group of employees who remained well. The matching included age, race, sex, marital status, education, time of employment, job classification, income, skin test reading, appearance of chest roentgenograms, and previous record of certain chronic conditions.

Those who became ill had experienced a concentration of disturbances, such as domestic strife, residential and occupational changes, and personal crises during the two years preceding the change in a series of quarterly chest films

Table 11.8
Linear Correlations Indicating Relationship between Life Situation Revealed in the SRE and Personality Status Measured by the Cornell Medical Index, among 20 Tuberculous and 20 Matched Well Employees at Firland Sanatorium

Factors		Coefficient
Schedule of Recent Experience	Cornell Medical Index	
Relative concentration of social forces	Relative dispersion of response	+0.57
Proportion of total comprising financial hardship	Extent of prior disease	−0.73
Proportion of total comprising domestic trouble	Number of comments	+0.59
Change of residence	Response ambiguity	+0.63
Relative concentration of social forces	Number of pathologic criteria demonstrated	+0.71

leading to determination of pulmonary tuberculosis. This concentration of disturbance, or situational crisis, was significant in comparison with the experience of the group of subjects who were well. The tuberculous group also evidenced a significant degree of psychoneurotic pathology and did not recognize or could not admit their personality deficit on questions in which this recognition was obvious.

The conclusion appears reasonable that many of the employees who became ill did so in a situation of stress that would be conducive to lowered resistance. It is not suggested that stress must invariably accompany infection in order to produce progressive tuberculosis in humans, or that stress, if present, must be psychic in nature. Within the acknowledged limitations of the test, however, the postulation of psychosocial crisis as one of the precipitant causes is tenable.

REFERENCES

1. Berle, B. B. "Emotional Factors and Tuberculosis: A Critical Review of the Literature." *Psychosomatic Medicine* 10 (1948):366–73.

2. Miller, P. "Medical Social Service in a Tuberculosis Sanatorium." *Public Health Report* 66, nos. 31 and 36 (1951):987–1008, 1139–57.

3. Turk, O. *Concepts of Emotional and Psychological Aspects of Tuberculosis Patients.* New York: National Tuberculosis Association, 1952.

4. Merrill, B. R. "Some Psychosomatic Aspects of Pulmonary Tuberculosis: A Review of the English Language Literature." *Journal of Nervous and Mental Disease* 117 (1953):9–28.

5. Wittkower, E. D. "Psychological Aspects of Tuberculosis." *American Review of Tuberculosis* 67 (1953):869–73.

6. Minor, C. L. "The Psychological Handling of the Tuberculosis Patient." *American Review of Tuberculosis* 2 (1918):459–69.

7. Service, W. C. "Insomnia in Tuberculosis." *American Review of Tuberculosis* 23 (1931):440–55.

8. Davis, M. *Practical Manual of Diseases of the Chest.* London: Oxford University Press, 1948, p. 351.

9. Fahnestock, W. M. "Case of Concealed Phthisis, Illustrative of Sympathetic Irritation." *American Journal of the Medical Sciences* 5 (1830):366–69.

10. Klebs, A. C. *Tuberculosis: A Treatise by American Authors.* New York: Appleton, 1909, p. 663.

11. Pottenger, F. M. "The Antagonistic Action of the Vagus and Sympathetic Division of the Autonomic System in Pulmonary Tuberculosis." *Journal of Laboratory and Clinical Medicine* 1 (1916):234–43.

12. Boas, E. P. "Functional Cardiovascular Disturbances in Tuberculosis." *American Review of Tuberculosis* 4 (1920):455–63.

13. Crile, G. W. *Diseases Peculiar to Civilized Man.* Edited by A. Rowland. New York: MacMillan, 1934, p. 53.

14. Murray, G. *Some Common Psychosomatic Manifestations.* 2nd ed., chap. 4. London: Oxford University Press, 1951.

15. Ishigami, T. "The Influence of Psychic Acts on the Progress of Pulmonary Tuberculosis." *American Review of Tuberculosis* 2 (1918):470–84.

16. Heise, F. H., and L. Brown. "Adrenalin Hypersensitiveness in Definite and Unproved Pulmonary Tuberculosis." *American Review of Tuberculosis* 4 (1920):609–15.

17. Peterson, W. F., and S. A. Levinson. "A Study of Adrenalin Reaction in Tuberculosis Patients." *American Review of Tuberculosis* 18 (1928):616–25.

18. Clarke, E. R., Jr., D. W. Zahn, and T. H. Holmes. "The Relationship of Stress, Adrenocortical Function, and Tuberculosis." *American Review of Tuberculosis* 69 (1954):351–69.

19. Hawkins, N. G. "A Research Application of Case Materials in the Sociology of Tuberculosis." Master's thesis, University of Washington, 1953.

20. Hawkins, N. G., and T. H. Holmes. "Environmental Considerations in Tuberculosis: Ecologic Factors in Tuberculosis Morbidity." *Transactions 50th Anniversary Meeting National Tuberculosis Association* 50 (1954):233–38.

21. Brodman, K., I. Lorge, A. J. Erdmann, and H. G. Wolff. *Manual for the Cornell Medical Index Health Questionnaire.* Rev. ed. New York: Cornell University Medical College, 1953.

22. Faris, R. E. L. *Social Psychology.* New York: Ronald Press, 1952.

12

Social Stress and Illness Onset

Richard H. Rahe, Merle Meyer, Michael Smith, George Kjaer, and Thomas H. Holmes

Alteration in social status preceding onset of particular diseases has recently been reviewed by Graham [1]. Greene has specifically dealt with losses preceding recognizable symptoms of leukemia and lymphoma [2–4]. Changes in social situations prior to coronary occlusion have been described by Fischer [5;6]. Furthering the scientific approach to such material, Kissen used a standard questionnaire method to elicit social stresses preceding onset of tuberculosis [7;8].

The purpose of the research to be reported has been to examine systematically the relationships of environmental variables to the time of illness onset. Despite the obvious biases and limitations involved in the method, the data have been gathered retrospectively by a standardized questionnaire developed originally to study psychosocial phenomena and onset of tuberculosis [9;10]. Since then its use has been extended to patients with cardiac disease, skin disease, inguinal hernia, and pregnancy [11–13]. This chapter makes use of data from all of these studies in order to examine the proposition that many, if not all, diseases have their onset in a setting of mounting frequency of social stress.

METHOD AND MATERIALS

The instrument employed, the Schedule of Recent Experience, is self-administered and is in multiple choice and sentence completion form. The questionnaire documents information pertaining to residence, occupation, social and marital

This chapter is reprinted with permission from Richard H. Rahe, Merle Meyer, Michael Smith, George Kjaer, and Thomas H. Holmes, "Social Stress and Illness Onset," *Journal of Psychosomatic Research* 8 (1964):35–44. Copyright 1964 by Pergamon Press, Ltd.

status, personal and economic factors, and health status. In a separate section, major social readjustments are identified by year of occurrence over a ten-year period.

With one exception, illness onset is dated by initial recognition of symptoms judged by experts to be associated with the particular diseases.

Seven patient samples, representing five distinct medical entities, and two control groups were studied. Six hospitals in the Seattle area were used. Table 12.1 gives a detailed comparison of all groups.

Two of the patient samples had been diagnosed and hospitalized at Firland Sanatorium with pulmonary tuberculosis. One of the tuberculous samples was drawn from employees who developed the disease while working at the sanatorium. In this sample the onset of disease was known to have occurred within the three-month interval since the last routine chest X-ray examination. The other sample was chosen randomly from patients discharged to the outpatient department.

A closely matched control group was constructed for the Firland employee sample. On the Schedule of Recent Experience, the control group identified changes in social status over the ten-year period prior to the study. These subjects were also employees at Firland with identical risk of exposure to tuberculosis, but who did not develop the disease. The 20 members in each group were individually matched for sex, age, race, marital status, income, education, length of employment, tuberculin skin test, number in household, and previous record of chronic disease that might possibly be related to causation of pulmonary tuberculosis (for example, diabetes, hypothyroidism, nontuberculous pulmonary disease, and alcoholism). None of the control subjects had developed tuberculosis at follow-up six months after the study.

The Firland outpatient sample of 40 tuberculous patients was studied along with a group of 40 patients with newly diagnosed cardiac disease and 40 control subjects. The cardiac disease patients were gathered from persons attending the cardiology diagnostic laboratories at the University of Washington School of Medicine and King County Hospital. Disorders included were rheumatic, coronary, hypertensive, and congenital heart disease. The control population was similar in sex, race, age, education, and occupation. There was some variance in marital status, social class, and city area of residence. As in the Firland employee control group, these controls had experienced no recent major disease. They had never been diagnosed as having either tuberculosis or cardiac disease.

New outpatients seen in the dermatology clinics of University Hospital and King County Hospital provided a group of 39 subjects with newly acquired skin disease.

Thirty-seven consecutive admissions for inguinal hernia repair to the surgical services of King County Hospital, U.S. Public Health Service Hospital, and Veterans Administration Hospital provided a group in which 25 subjects gave complete information.

From the King County Hospital outpatient obstetric clinic, a sample of conve-

Characteristics of the Seven Patient Samples and Two Control Groups Examined with the SRE

	Study 1		Study 2			Study 3	Study 4	Study 5	Study 6
	Tuberculous employees	Non-tuberculous employees	Tuberculous outpatients	Cardiac sample	Control group	Hernia sample	Skin disease sample	Pregnancy sample	Unwed mothers
Selection	Matched	Matched	Random	Random	Matched	Consecutive hospital admissions	Consecutive clinic admissions	Consecutive hospital admissions	Random
Sex	3 males, 17 females	3 males, 17 females	18 males, 22 females	19 males, 21 females	18 males, 22 females	23 males, 2 females	Predominantly females	All females	All females
Race	All white	All white	34 white 3 black 3 Asian Amer.	37 white 3 black	39 white 1 black	24 white 1 black	25 white 14 black	31 white 4 black	18 white 13 black 1 Filipino 1 Amer. Indian
Age (yr)	45 (mean)	46 (mean)	40 (mean)	39 (mean)	39 (mean)	58 (average)	45 (average)	27 (average)	22 (average)
Occupation	5 in professions; 15 subordinate personnel	5 in professions; 15 subordinate personnel	Housewives and trades people	Housewives and trades people	Housewives and trades people	Predominantly unskilled	Housewives and unemployed	Housewives	Predominantly unemployed
Average education (yr)	12	12	11	12	12	10	10	12	11
Predominant social class	Middle	Middle	Lower	Middle	Middle	Lower	Lower	Middle	Lower
Married (%)	Matched	Matched	48	60	92	76	Approx. 40	All	None
Predominant residence	Urban	Urban	Urban	Suburban	Suburban	Suburban	Urban	Suburban	Urban
Total number	20	20	40	40	40	25	39	35	33

nience was gathered of 33 unwed pregnant females. In each case, data were collected within a month of delivery.

From the obstetric service of Madigan Army Hospital, 35 subjects, either prenatal or postpartum, were obtained over a two-month period (Table 12.1).

RESULTS

Significant differences in the temporal occurrence of changes in social status were found between the 20 Firland employees, for whom the time of onset of tuberculosis was known within three months, and their matched controls. Frequency of change in social status was generally dispersed throughout the ten years measured in the 20 nontuberculous Firland employees, and the total number of changes was greater than occurred in the tuberculous sample (Table 12.2). However, half of the tuberculous subjects demonstrated peak frequency of changes in social status during the final two premorbid years. The difference between the two groups in this respect (using the *t*-test) is significant at the 0.02 level of confidence (Table 12.3). Changes in personal and economic status dominate the social alterations found. These categories of social stress include personal health, loss or change of status of close friends or relatives, and severe financial hardship. These data are presented by year of occurrence in Figures 12.1 and 12.2.

Comparison of the temporal patterns of social stress in the ten years preceding onset of symptoms in the Firland outpatient tuberculous group and the cardiac disease sample revealed no difference. Both groups had similar clustering of stresses into the final two years before symptom onset. In this study, Firland outpatients and heart disease subjects were compared to a matched control group. The mounting frequency of change in social status during the final two years in both disease samples differed significantly from the control group. The *t*-test showed the differences to be significant at the 0.05 level of confidence (Figures 12.3 and 12.4). The cardiac disease sample displayed a high incidence of change in family constellation in the final two premorbid years.

The other disease categories studied showed similar clustering of social alterations in the two years prior to onset.

Skin disease patients demonstrated that between one-quarter and two-thirds of all changes in social status experienced in the ten years antedating illness onset were encountered in the final two and a half years (Table 12.4). Personal factors and residential changes were the most apparent.

The data from patients with inguinal hernia indicated that, if these subjects were to experience changes of a personal nature in the ten years preceding onset of symptoms, the probability was 2–4 times as great that it would occur in the final two-year period than at any other time. Change in residence was 2–3 times more frequent in the final two premorbid years. This is shown in Figure 12.5. Changes in social status of a similar degree and nature were also found in the two-year period preceding elective or emergency surgery for hernia repair.

Table 12.2
Total Experience of Social Stresses Recorded for the Ten-year Period Covered in
the SRE by 20 Tuberculous and 20 Matched Nontuberculous Employees of Firland
Sanatorium

	Ten-year frequency of social forces	
Group	Mean	Standard deviation
Tuberculous	16.7	15.5
Nontuberculous	23.5	10.3

Table 12.3
Location of Year of Peak Frequency of Social Stresses among 20 Tuberculous and
20 Matched Nontuberculous Employees of Firland Sanatorium Shown in the SRE

	Time of occurrence		
Group	Final 2 yr	Prior	Total cases
Tuberculous	9	11	20
Nontuberculous	1	19	20
Total cases	10	30	40

Table 12.4
Mean Percentage of Total Social Stresses Shown in the SRE Encountered during
the 2.5-Year Period Prior to Clinic Visit for 39 Patients with Newly Acquired Skin
Disease

Category of stress	University Hospital patients %	King County Hospital patients %
Personal stress	41.5	51.3
Marital stress	66.7	24.7
Social stress	46.9	35.6
Change in residence	41.3	52.1
Work stress	38.9	32.6

Unwed mothers experienced a steady rise in frequency of social stresses up to the year of delivery studied (Figure 12.6). Married mothers were examined in terms of percentage of sample experiencing at least one major stress per year. A progressive increase in percentage affected was detected as the year of pregnancy studied was approached (Figure 12.7).

DISCUSSION

In this study an attempt has been made to examine critically the nature of the life situation in which disease occurs. The data adduced indicate that different disease entities and pregnancy occur in a setting characterized by a significant clustering of changes in social status. This clustering has been termed the *psychosocial life crisis*. These findings are supported by other investigations in which a variety of methods has been used [1]. Kissen investigated "emotional factors" (social stresses) existing prior to initial visit to a diagnostic chest clinic, using a sample of 267 patients [7]. A standard questionnaire was completed before any investigation of the patient's presenting complaints was done. On completion of the diagnostic workup, the subject's records were assigned to one of four subgroups. One subgroup was composed of those having tuberculosis detected; another subgroup was found to have "psychosomatic disease," but no

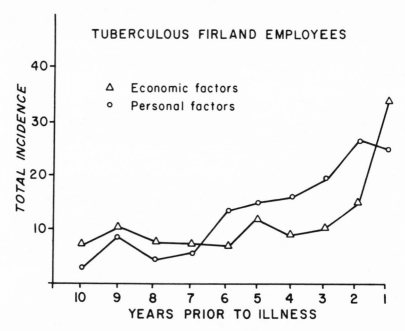

Figure 12.1   Incidence of two categories of social stress in the ten years prior to onset of symptoms among 20 tuberculous employees at Firland Sanatorium.

tuberculosis. A third subgroup had no abnormality discovered, and the remaining patients were labeled "others." Tuberculosis and psychosomatic subjects demonstrated social stresses preceding illness onset in 64.4 and 55 percent of cases, respectively. The "no abnormality discovered" and "others" subgroups registered social stresses preceding clinic visit in 23.5 and 22 percent of cases, respectively.

Greene and associates have published data pertaining to real or threatened losses experienced by patients in the two-year period prior to onset of leukemia or lymphoma [2-4]. This material was gained by interview. The incidence of real or threatened loss is seen to increase progressively over the two premorbid years in a condensed "life crisis" fashion. Of all losses encountered or threatened over the 24 months prior to illness onset, 50 percent of them are clustered into the final six months.

Fischer and others have studied, by interview, changes in social situations and bodily complaints for five years prior to disease onset in patients experiencing nonfatal coronary occlusion [5;6]. Attention was focused on the pattern of stress in the five years preceding heart attack. The data demonstrate peaks of events and bodily symptoms at three years, one year, and two months prior to attack. According to a recalculation of these data, of all significant events present in the five premorbid years, 70 percent of them fall into the final two years. The event most frequently described was alteration in the patient's close personal associations. Death of a family member or illness of a mate was outstanding. This

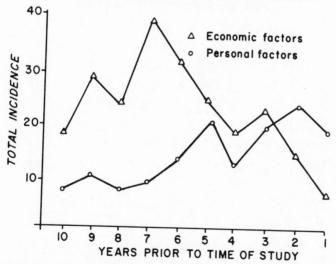

Figure 12.2   Incidence of two categories of social stress in the ten years prior to time of study among 20 nontuberculous employees at Firland Sanatorium.

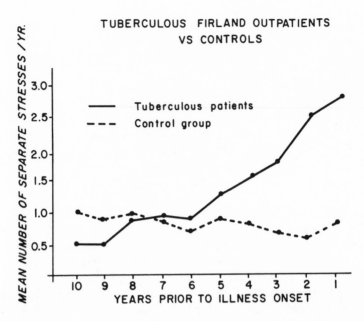

Figure 12.3 Incidence of social stress in the ten years prior to onset of symptoms among 40 tuberculous outpatients and 40 matched control subjects.

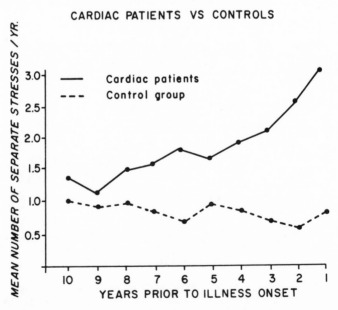

Figure 12.4 Incidence of social stress in the ten years prior to onset of symptoms among 40 cardiac patients and 40 matched control subjects.

HERNIA PATIENTS

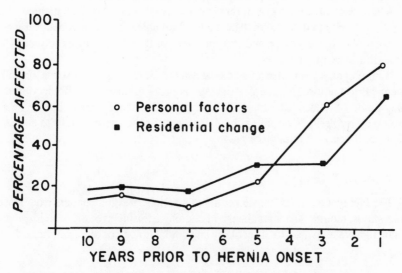

Figure 12.5   Incidence of two categories of social stress in the ten years prior to onset of symptoms among 25 hernia patients.

UNWED MOTHERS

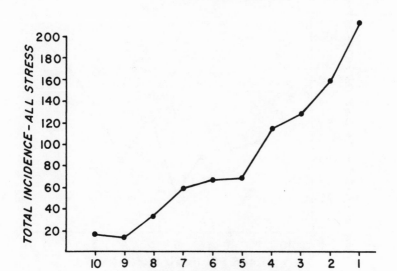

Figure 12.6   Incidence of social stress in the ten years prior to year of delivery among 33 unwed mothers.

finding is remarkably similar to the high incidence of change in family constellation preceding onset of symptoms found in the cardiac disease sample.

In assessing the limitations of retrospective study and reliance on memory, the final years prior to illness should be the most reliable. The significant differences between the illness groups and controls were in the years immediately prior to time of disease onset.

Both pregnancy samples revealed patterns of increasing social stress virtually identical to the disease groups. Marriage appears to make no difference in the magnitude of antecedent stress. This suggests that the changes observed may well play a role in determining the planning of or the susceptibility to conception—and hence, the timing of pregnancy.

FORMULATION

The fact that onset of disease occurs in a setting of significant environmental alterations, requiring a major change in ongoing adjustment of the individual, appears to have relevance to the ecology and epidemiology of disease. The body of

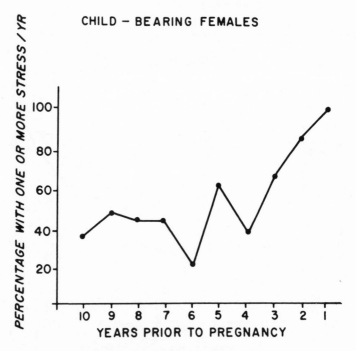

Figure 12.7   Incidence of social stress in the ten years prior to pregnancy among 35 married mothers.

data derived from a variety of psychophysiologic investigations provides the biological basis for this relevance [14–38]. These psychophysiological studies indicate that when both naturally occurring and experimentally induced life situations threaten the security of the individual and evoke attempts at adaptive behavior, they also evoke significant alterations in the function of most bodily tissues, organs, and systems. When sustained, these changes in function, in addition to engendering disturbing symptoms and tissue damage, often enhance the body's vulnerability or susceptibility to the noxious effects of a wide spectrum of etiologic agents.

Thus, any set of environmental factors significantly altering the steady state of the individual increases the probability that bodily resistance to disease will be lowered.

The studies reported in this chapter have focused attention on some of the characteristics of the environment of the individual that constitute the stimulus situation initiating the psychophysiologic response that lowers bodily resistance to disease. Thus, changes in social status achieve the significance of etiologic parameters. As such, they become a necessary, but not sufficient, cause of disease and help explain the specificity of the time of onset.

SUMMARY

Seven patient samples, representing five distinct medical entities, and two control groups were investigated using a standardized questionnaire yielding information about the quantity and timing of social stresses experienced over a ten-year period.

A sample of tuberculosis sanatorium employees who developed tuberculosis on the job was compared to an individually matched control sample of healthy employees. The temporal pattern of social stresses experienced in the ten years prior to illness was the differentiating feature between the two groups. The tuberculous group showed a skewing of social stresses into the final two of the ten premorbid years. The difference between the tuberculous group and their controls in this regard was significant at the 0.02 level of confidence.

A sample of tuberculous outpatients and a group of patients with cardiac disease were compared to a control group of similar but healthy subjects, and to one another. Both disease groups demonstrated clustering of social stresses in the final two years before disease onset. The difference of either patient sample from the control group was significant at the 0.05 level of confidence.

Patients with newly acquired skin disease, subjects with inguinal hernia, and married and unmarried females experiencing pregnancy demonstrated similar increases in social stresses in the final two years preceding symptom onset.

The mounting frequency of changes in social status in the two years preceding disease onset was termed the *psychosocial life crisis*. It is postulated that the life crisis represents a necessary but not sufficient precipitant of major health changes.

REFERENCES

1. Graham, D. T., and I. Stevenson. "Disease as Response to Life Stress." In *The Psychological Basis of Medical Practice,* edited by H. I. Lief, V. F. Lief, and N. R. Lief, pp. 115–36. New York: Harper and Row, 1963.

2. Greene, W. A., Jr. "Psychological Factors and Reticulo-endothelial Disease. I. Preliminary Observations on a Group of Males with Lymphomas and Leukemias." *Psychosomatic Medicine* 16 (1954):220–30.

3. Greene, W. A., Jr., L. E. Young, and S. N. Swisher. "Psychological Factors and Reticulo-endothelial Disease. II. Observations on a Group of Women with Lymphomas and Leukemias." *Psychosomatic Medicine* 18 (1956):284–303.

4. Greene, W. A., Jr., and G. Miller. "Psychological Factors and Reticulo-endothelial Disease. IV. Observations on a Group of Children and Adolescents with Leukemia: An Interpretation of Disease Development in Terms of the Mother–Child Unit." *Psychosomatic Medicine* 20 (1958):124–44.

5. Weiss, E., B. Dlin, H. R. Rollin, H. K. Fischer, and C. R. Bepler. "Emotional Factors in Coronary Occlusion." *Archives of Internal Medicine* 99 (1957):628–41.

6. Fischer, H. K., B. Dlin, W. Winters, S. Hagner, and E. Weiss. "Time Patterns and Emotional Factors Related to the Onset of Coronary Occlusion." Abstract. *Psychosomatic Medicine* 24 (1962):516.

7. Kissen, D. M. "Specific Psychological Factors in Pulmonary Tuberculosis." *Health Bulletin* (Edinburgh) 14 (1956):44–46.

8. Kissen, D. M. "Some Psychosocial Aspects of Pulmonary Tuberculosis." *International Journal of Social Psychiatry* 3 (1958):252–59.

9. Hawkins, N. G. *Medical Sociology.* Springfield, Ill.: Charles C Thomas, 1958.

10. Hawkins, N. G., R. Davies, and T. H. Holmes. "Evidence of Psychosocial Factors in the Development of Pulmonary Tuberculosis." *American Review of Tuberculosis and Pulmonary Diseases* 75 (1957):768–80. Reprinted in this volume, Chapter 11.

11. Smith, M. "Psychogenic Factors in Skin Disease." Medical thesis, University of Washington, 1962.

12. Rahe, R. H. "Psychosocial and Psychophysiologic Aspects of Abdominal Hernia." Medical thesis, University of Washington, 1961.

13. Kjaer, G. "Some Psychosomatic Aspects of Pregnancy with Particular Reference to Nausea and Vomiting." Medical thesis, University of Washington, 1959.

14. Dorpat, T. L., and T. H. Holmes. "Mechanisms of Skeletal Muscle Pain and Fatigue." *Archives of Neurology and Psychiatry* 74 (1955):628–40.

15. Engel, G. L., F. Reichsman, and H. L. Segal. "A Study of an Infant with a Gastric Fistula." *Psychosomatic Medicine* 18 (1956):374–98.

16. Grace, W. J., and D. T. Graham. "Relationship of Specific Attitudes and Emotions to Certain Bodily Diseases." *Psychosomatic Medicine* 14 (1952):243–51.

17. Grace, W. J., S. Wolf, and H. G. Wolff. *The Human Colon.* New York: Paul P. Hoeber, 1951.

18. Graham, D. T. "The Pathogenesis of Hives: Experimental Study of Life Situations, Emotions and Cutaneous Vascular Reactions." In *Life Stress and Bodily Disease,* edited by H. G. Wolff, S. Wolf, and C. C. Hare, pp. 987–1009. Research Publications of the Association for Research in Nervous and Mental Disease, vol. 29. Baltimore: Williams and Wilkins, 1950.

19. Graham, D. T. "Cutaneous Vascular Reactions in Raynaud's Disease and in States of Hostility, Anxiety, and Depression." *Psychosomatic Medicine* 17 (1955):200–207.

20. Graham, D. T., J. A. Stern, and G. Winokur. "Experimental Investigation of the Specificity of Attitude Hypothesis in Psychosomatic Disease." *Psychosomatic Medicine* 20 (1958):446–57.

21. Graham, D. T., and S. Wolf. "The Relation of Eczema to Attitude and to Vascular Reactions of the Human Skin." *Journal of Laboratory and Clinical Medicine* 42 (1953):238–54.

22. Hardy, J. D., H. G. Wolff, and H. Goodell. *Pain Sensations and Reactions.* Baltimore: Williams and Wilkins, 1952.

23. Hinkle, L. E., Jr., W. N. Christenson, F. D. Kane, A. Ostfeld, W. N. Thetford, and H. G. Wolff. "An Investigation of the Relation between Life Experience, Personality Characteristics, and General Susceptibility to Illness." *Psychosomatic Medicine* 20 (1958):278–95.

24. Holmes, T. H., H. Goodell, S. Wolf, and H. G. Wolff. *The Nose: An Experimental Study of Reactions within the Nose in Human Subjects during Varying Life Experiences.* Springfield, Ill.: Charles C Thomas, 1950.

25. Holmes, T. H., T. Treuting, and H. G. Wolff. "Life Situations, Emotions and Nasal Disease: Evidence on Summative Effects Exhibited in Patients with 'Hay Fever.' " In *Life Stress and Bodily Disease,* edited by H. G. Wolff, S. Wolf, and C. C. Hare, pp. 545–65. Research Publications of the Association for Research in Nervous and Mental Disease, vol. 29. Baltimore: Williams and Wilkins, 1950.

26. Holmes, T. H., and H. G. Wolff. "Life Situations, Emotions and Backache." In *Life Stress and Bodily Disease,* edited by H. G. Wolff, S. Wolf, and C. C. Hare, pp. 750–72. Research Publications of the Association for Research in Nervous and Mental Disease, vol. 29. Baltimore: Williams and Wilkins, 1950.

27. Mittelmann, B., and H. G. Wolff. "Affective States and Skin Temperature: Experimental Study of Subjects with 'Cold Hands' and Raynaud's Syndrome." *Psychosomatic Medicine* 1 (1939):271–92.

28. Mittelmann, B., and H. G. Wolff. "Emotions and Gastroduodenal Function." *Psychosomatic Medicine* 4 (1942):5–61.

29. Mittelmann, B., and H. G. Wolff. "Emotions and Skin Temperature: Observations on Patients during Psychotherapeutic (Psychoanalytic) Interviews." *Psychosomatic Medicine* 5 (1943):211–31.

30. Sparer, P. J., ed. *Personality, Stress and Tuberculosis.* New York: International Universities Press, 1956.

31. Stern, J. A., G. Winokur, D. T. Graham, and F. K. Graham. "Alterations in Physiological Measures during Experimentally Induced Attitudes." *Journal of Psychosomatic Research* 5 (1961):73–82.

32. Stevenson, I., and C. H. Duncan. "Alterations in Cardiac Function and Circulatory Efficiency during Periods of Life Stress as Shown by Changes in the Rate, Rhythm, Electrocardiographic Pattern and Output of the Heart in Those with Cardiovascular Disease." In *Life Stress and Bodily Disease,* edited by H. G. Wolff, S. Wolf, and C. C. Hare, pp. 799–817. Research Publications of the Association for Research in Nervous and Mental Disease, vol. 29. Baltimore: Williams and Wilkins, 1950.

33. Stevenson, I., C. H. Duncan, and H. G. Wolff. "Circulatory Dynamics before and

after Exercise in Subjects with and without Structural Heart Disease during Anxiety and Relaxation." *Journal of Clinical Investigation* 28 (1949):1534–43.

34. Stewart, A. H., I. H. Weiland, A. R. Leider, C. A. Mangham, T. H. Holmes, and H. S. Ripley. "Excessive Infant Crying (Colic) in Relation to Parent Behavior." *American Journal of Psychiatry* 110 (1954):687–94.

35. Wolf, S., P. V. Cardon, E. M. Shepard, and H. G. Wolff. *Life Stress and Essential Hypertension: A Study of Circulatory Adjustments in Man.* Baltimore: Williams and Wilkins, 1955.

36. Wolf, S., and H. G. Wolff. "Studies on the Nature of Certain Symptoms Associated with Cardiovascular Disorders." *Psychosomatic Medicine* 8 (1946):293–319.

37. Wolf, S., and H. G. Wolff. *Human Gastric Function.* New York: Oxford University Press, 1947.

38. Wolff, H. G. *Headache and Other Head Pain.* 2nd ed. New York: Oxford University Press, 1963.

13

Life Crisis and Disease Onset: Qualitative and Quantitative Definition of the Life Crisis and Its Association with Health Change

Richard H. Rahe and Thomas H. Holmes

This chapter deals with the pilot application of a unique quantitative method for investigating the relationship of life events to illness onset. In another report [1] a method was defined for assigning a magnitude of significance to 43 life events and occurrences empirically observed to cluster at the time of disease onset. The resulting scale, the Social Readjustment Rating Scale (SRRS), reflected the magnitude of change required in ongoing life adjustment by each event, and the values were defined in terms of life change units (LCU). The scale ranged from 11 LCU for a minor violation of the law to 100 LCU for death of spouse. The Social Readjustment Rating Scale has since been validated by cross-cultural studies [2–6] and by comparison with other scaling methods [7].

The life events used in the SRRS were originally used at the University of Washington to construct a Schedule of Recent Experience (SRE). This instrument, a self-administered questionnaire, allows the respondent to document over the past ten years of his or her life the occurrence or absence of the various life event items. In previous retrospective studies, the SRE has been used to adduce data that the life events cluster significantly in the two-year period preceding onset of tuberculosis, heart disease, skin disease, hernia, and pregnancy [8]. These findings are similar to those of other investigations using different methods to study a variety of disease entities [9–17].

The title of this chapter and its first paragraph have been reinstated from a mimeographed version of the paper prepared by Dr. Rahe and Dr. Holmes in 1966. The study was first published as pt. 2 (pp. 99–106) of Richard H. Rahe, "Life Crisis and Health Change," in *Psychotropic Drug Response: Advances in Prediction,* edited by Philip R. A. May and J. R. Wittenborn (1969), pp. 92–125. Reprinted courtesy of Charles C Thomas, Publisher, Springfield, Illinois.

METHOD

The Schedule of Recent Experience was mailed to 200 resident physicians in the University of Washington's integrated hospital system. The cover letter requested the participation of residents in a research project but did not disclose the project's purpose. A separate page was attached to the SRE, asking the subject to list all "major health changes," by year of occurrence, over the past ten years. In this pilot study, it was assumed that the subjects were sophisticated in matters of health and disease, and no systematic attempt was made to verify the report of their health changes. The 88 subjects (86 males and 2 females, aged 22–38 years) who completed and returned the questionnaire provided retrospective data that were analyzed for the relationship of health changes to life changes.

The items subscribed to in the SRE by the subjects were assigned their respective values from the Social Readjustment Rating Scale. The values, which were labeled *life change units* (LCU) of the life events indicated to have occurred, were summed over each of the past ten years; these yearly LCU totals were plotted for each subject. On a subject's LCU profile were superimposed the health change data. (For examples, see Figures 13.1, 13.2, and 13.3.)

RESULTS

A total of 96 diseases or changes in health status were reported by the 88 subjects for the previous ten years. The 34 varieties reported were classified into seven categories (Table 13.1). Infectious and allergic, psychosomatic, and musculoskeletal disorders composed the majority of reported health changes.

Based on the previous studies [8], an arbitrary criterion was established for the temporal association of an illness or health change with life change events. A reported change in health must have occurred within a two-year period following the occurrence of a cluster of life changes in order to be defined as associated with the life change cluster. Eighty-nine of the 96 health changes clearly met this criterion. Thus, 93 percent of the health changes reported were associated temporally with a clustering of life changes whose values summed at least to 150 LCU per year. The health change itself was not counted as one of the life changes making up the LCU total for the year.

In some instances the peaks of life changes mounted to greater than 500 LCU. Only two of the several hundred life change events reported had an individual LCU value of 63, and no other reported life change had a value greater than 44 LCU. The magnitude for most of the reported life changes was 18–25 LCU. Thus, the number of life changes making up a peak of 150–500 LCU ranged between 7 and 25.

From these data a *life crisis,* a term used loosely in previous reports [8;16;18–21], could be quantitatively and qualitatively defined. A life crisis was therefore stipulated to mean any clustering of life change events whose individual values summed to 150 LCU or more in one year. The duration of a life crisis

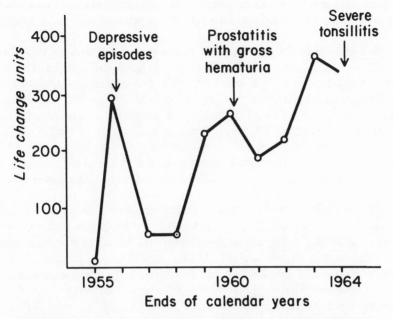

Figure 13.1   Subject A: Temporal relationship of life crisis and disease occurrence.

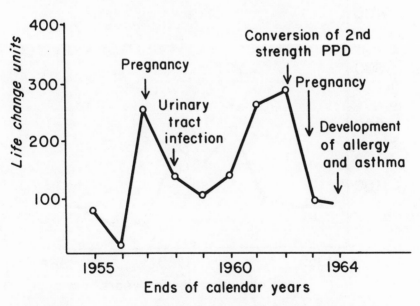

Figure 13.2   Subject B: Multiple health changes associated with separate life crises.

was found to be generally 1–2 years; rarely, it was longer. This was the case when three, and occasionally four, successive years had separate LCU totals greater than 150.

Further analysis of the data indicated that a linear relationship appeared to exist between the magnitude of the life crisis and the risk of associated health change. As the life change units increased, so did the percentage of subjects with an associated health change at that LCU magnitude. For subjects with scores between 150 and 199 LCU, 37 percent had an associated health change. This association rose to 51 percent for subjects with scores between 200 and 299 LCU, and to 79 percent for those with scores greater than 300 LCU. Table 13.2 summarizes these data. These three ranges of scores have been used to define a mild (150–199 LCU), moderate (200–299 LCU), and major (300 or more LCU) life crisis.

In some subjects, two or more health changes occurred during a time at risk. This accounts for the fact that, in Table 13.2, the 89 health changes were associated with only 72 life crises. The mean for the life crises associated with two or more health changes was 303 LCU, or a major life crisis. The mean for the life crises followed by one health change was 276 LCU, or a high-moderate life crisis. The majority of the 58 life crises without an associated health change were of low-moderate magnitude, with a mean of 227 LCU.

To present some concrete examples of an LCU profile over a ten-year period,

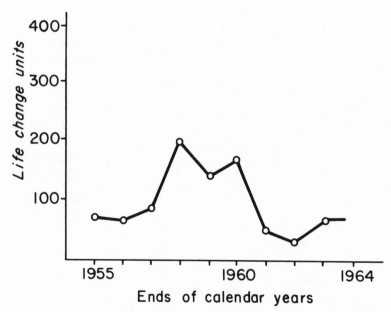

Figure 13.3   Subject C: Occurrence of a life crisis with no accompanying illness.

and to illustrate graphically the relation between a life crisis and major health change, three subjects' data sheets are presented in Figures 13.1, 13.2, and 13.3. The solid line connects points that indicate yearly LCU totals. Reported health changes are indicated over their year of occurrence. In Figure 13.1, the subject's depressive episodes in 1956 coincided with a life crisis, whereas his episodes of prostatitis in 1960 and tonsillitis in 1964 occurred about one year after the appearance of the life crisis with which they were associated. On the average, associated health changes followed a life crisis by about a year. Figure 13.2 provides an example of multiple health changes associated with two life crises of major magnitude. Figure 13.3 is the profile of a subject who reported no major health changes during the past ten years. The life crises in this figure, 1958 and 1960, are both of low-moderate magnitude.

DISCUSSION

In previous retrospective studies using the SRE, the specific disease entity was the point of departure [8]. Analysis of the data demonstrated that the association of a cluster of life events with onset of each disease was typical for these subjects compared to nonsick control subjects. By contrast, the point of departure in the present retrospective study is the population of 88 resident physicians. Life events were collected, assigned a magnitude (LCU), and observed for their temporal association with any disease or health change reported.

The life crises observed encompassed a wide variety of life changes, and the health changes associated with the life crises were heterogeneous. The latter included acute illnesses, exacerbations of chronic diseases, decision for elective surgical procedures, large gains or reductions in body weight, and pregnancy. Accidents, with concomitant body trauma, composed yet another category. Thus the term *health change* has been chosen so that a wide variety of medical entities could be included under one heading.

The subjects in this study completed the SRE for a second time eight months later. Preliminary analysis of the data indicates highly significant agreement between the items subscribed to in the first and second questionnaires. Thus, while it is still not possible to estimate the completeness of recall, it does seem that what is being recalled by these subjects is consistent.

The high degree of association between health changes and life crises demonstrated in this investigation confirms the findings of the previous studies and reinforces the previous conclusion that the life crisis may well be of etiologic significance in the genesis of major health change. In the process of human reaction and readjustment to a variety of significant life situations, many body systems (for example, cardiovascular, neuroendocrine, respiratory, musculoskeletal, and autonomic nervous) have been shown to become physiologically activated, some with sustained and eventually injurious effects [13;18;22–39]. The findings from this study suggest the possibility that, the greater the magnitude of the crisis, the greater the probability that the involved subject's psychophysiologic activation will result in tissue, organ, and body system dysfunction. When so affected, a person may become vulnerable to available pathogens, which, under conditions of less life change, might not overcome the body's resistance. Not only does the body appear to become more vulnerable to illness, but pregnancy, elective decisions leading to alterations in health status, and accidents with associated body trauma seem to appear, as well, during a life crisis period.

Table 13.1
Ninety-six Major Health Changes Reported by 88 Subjects over a Ten-year Period

Infectious and Parasitic	
Appendicitis	1
Genitourinary	7
Upper respiratory	7
Systemic (bacterial)	3
Pneumonia (viral and bacterial)	3
Gastrointestinal	4
Hepatitis	3
Mononucleosis	4
Mumps	1
Chickenpox	3
Influenza	5
Vesicular stomatitis	2
Filariasis	1
Malaria	2
Total	46

Allergic	
Hives	1
Onset or exacerbation of allergies	5
Onset or exacerbation of asthma	4
Conversion of tuberculin skin test to positive	2
Total	12

Psychosomatic	
Onset or exacerbation of ulcer symptoms	4
Amenorrhea	1
Onset of paroxysmal atrial tachycardia	1
Total	6

Musculoskeletal	
Herniated nucleus pulposus	1
Severe muscle sprains and ligamentous tears	4
Broken bones	3
Bursitis	1
Diffuse polyarthritis with joint effusion	1
Total	10

Miscellaneous	
Surgical procedures	9
Wisdom teeth extractions	1
Large (20 lbs.) weight gains or losses	3
Pregnancies	2
Total	15

Psychiatric	
Psychoneurotic depressive reactions	4
Total	4

Accidents Associated with Body Trauma	
Severe laceration of tendons	1
Pneumothorax, traumatic	1
Internal injuries due to auto accident	1
Total	3

Table 13.2
Relationship of Life Crisis Magnitude to Percentage of Life Crises
Associated with Health Changes

	Number of Life Crises Associated with Health Changes	Number of Life Crises Not Associated with Health Changes	Total Number of Life Crises	Life Crises Associated with Health Changes (%)
Mild life crisis (150–199 LCU)	13	22	35	37
Moderate life crisis (200–299 LCU)	29	28	57	51
Major life crisis (300 or greater LCU)	30	8	38	79
Totals	72*	58	130	55

* Some life crises were associated with more than one change.

Not all persons experiencing a life crisis report a health change that year or the next. This may well be a manifestation of high resistance to health change. It may be assumed to have been the case for those subjects (21 percent) who had major life crises (greater than 300 LCU) and good health for the succeeding two years. Such a population deserves special study to elucidate further the nature of resistance to disease.

REFERENCES

1. Holmes, T. H., and R. H. Rahe. "The Social Readjustment Rating Scale." *Journal of Psychosomatic Research* 11 (1967):213–18. Reprinted in this volume, Chapter 2.

2. Komaroff, A. L., M. Masuda, and T. H. Holmes. "The Social Readjustment Rating Scale: A Comparative Study of Negro, Mexican and White Americans." *Journal of Psychosomatic Research* 12 (1968):121–28. Reprinted in this volume, Chapter 6.

3. Masuda, M., and T. H. Holmes. "The Social Readjustment Rating Scale: A Cross-cultural Study of Japanese and Americans." *Journal of Psychosomatic Research* 11 (1967):227–37. Reprinted in this volume, Chapter 5.

4. Harmon, D. K., M. Masuda, and T. H. Holmes. "The Social Readjustment Rating Scale: A Cross-cultural Study of Western Europeans and Americans." *Journal of Psychosomatic Research* 14 (1970):391–400.

5. Celdrán, H. H. "The Cross-cultural Consistency of Two Social Consensus Scales: The Seriousness of Illness Rating Scale and the Social Readjustment Rating Scale in Spain." Medical thesis, University of Washington, 1970.

6. Rahe, R. H. "Multi-cultural Correlations of Life Change Scaling: America, Japan, Denmark and Sweden." *Journal of Psychosomatic Research* 13 (1969):191–95.

7. Ruch, L. O., and T. H. Holmes. "Scaling of Life Change: Comparison of Direct and Indirect Methods." *Journal of Psychosomatic Research* 15 (1971):221–27. Reprinted in this volume, Chapter 4.

8. Rahe, R. H., M. Meyer, M. Smith, G. Kjaer, and T. H. Holmes. "Social Stress and Illness Onset." *Journal of Psychosomatic Research* 8 (1964):35–44. Reprinted in this volume, Chapter 12.

9. Fischer, H. K., B. Dlin, W. Winters, S. Hagner, and E. Weiss. "Time Patterns and Emotional Factors Related to the Onset of Coronary Occlusion." Abstract. *Psychosomatic Medicine* 24 (1962):516.

10. Graham, D. T., and I. Stevenson. "Disease as Response to Life Stress. I. The Nature of the Evidence." In *The Psychological Basis of Medical Practice,* edited by H. I. Lief, V. F. Lief, and N. R. Lief, pp. 115–36. New York: Harper and Row, 1963.

11. Greene, W. A., Jr. "Psychological Factors and Reticulo-endothelial Disease. I. Preliminary Observations on a Group of Males with Lymphomas and Leukemias." *Psychosomatic Medicine* 16 (1954):220–30.

12. Greene, W. A., Jr., L. E. Young, and S. N. Swisher. "Psychological Factors and Reticulo-endothelial Disease. II. Observations on a Group of Women with Lymphomas and Leukemias." *Psychosomatic Medicine* 18 (1956):284–303.

13. Greene, W. A., Jr., and G. Miller. "Psychological Factors and Reticulo-endothelial Disease. IV. Observations on a Group of Children and Adolescents with Leukemia: An Interpretation of Disease Development in Terms of the Mother–Child Unit." *Psychosomatic Medicine* 20 (1958):124–44.

14. Kissen, D. M. "Specific Psychological Factors in Pulmonary Tuberculosis." *Health Bulletin* (Edinburgh) 14 (1956):44–46.

15. Kissen, D. M. "Some Psychosocial Aspects of Pulmonary Tuberculosis." *International Journal of Social Psychiatry* 3 (1958):252–59.

16. Rahe, R. H., and A. E. Christ. "An Unusual Cardiac (Ventricular) Arrhythmia in a Child: Psychiatric and Psychophysiologic Aspects." *Psychosomatic Medicine* 28 (1966): 181–88.

17. Weiss, E., B. Dlin, H. R. Rollin, H. K. Fischer, and C. R. Bepler. "Emotional Factors in Coronary Occlusion." *Archives of Internal Medicine* 99 (1957):628–41.

18. Holmes, T. H., N. G. Hawkins, C. E. Bowerman, E. R. Clarke, and J. R. Joffe. "Psychosocial and Psychophysiologic Studies of Tuberculosis." *Psychosomatic Medicine* 19 (1957):134–43.

19. Kjaer, G. "Some Psychosomatic Aspects of Pregnancy with Particular Reference to Nausea and Vomiting." Medical thesis, University of Washington, 1959.

20. Rahe, R. H., and T. H. Holmes. "Social, Psychologic and Psychophysiologic Aspects of Inguinal Hernia." *Journal of Psychosomatic Research* 8 (1965):487–91.

21. Smith, M. "Psychogenic Factors in Skin Disease." Medical thesis, University of Washington, 1962.

22. Dudley, D. L., T. H. Holmes, C. J. Martin, and H. S. Ripley. "Changes in Respiration Associated with Hypnotically Induced Emotion, Pain, and Exercise." *Psychosomatic Medicine* 26 (1964):46–57.

23. Dudley, D. L., C. J. Martin, and T. H. Holmes. "Psychophysiologic Studies of Pulmonary Ventilation." *Psychosomatic Medicine* 26 (1964):645–60.

24. Dudley, D. L., M. Masuda, C. J. Martin, and T. H. Holmes. "Psychophysiological

Studies of Experimentally Induced Action Oriented Behavior." *Journal of Psychosomatic Research* 9 (1965):209–21.

25. Dudley, D. L., T. H. Holmes, C. J. Martin, and H. S. Ripley. "Hypnotically Induced Facsimile of Pain." *Archives of General Psychiatry* 15 (1966):198–204.

26. Grace, W. J., S. Wolf, and H. G. Wolff. *The Human Colon.* New York: Paul B. Hoeber, 1951.

27. Grace, W. J., and D. T. Graham. "Relationship of Specific Attitudes and Emotions to Certain Bodily Diseases." *Psychosomatic Medicine* 14 (1952):243–51.

28. Graham, D. T., J. A. Stern, and G. Winokur. "Experimental Investigation of the Specificity of Attitude Hypothesis in Psychosomatic Disease." *Psychosomatic Medicine* 20 (1958):446–57.

29. Graham, D. T. "Cutaneous Vascular Reactions in Raynaud's Disease and in States of Hostility, Anxiety, and Depression." *Psychosomatic Medicine* 17 (1955):200–207.

30. Graham, D. T. "The Pathogenesis of Hives: Experimental Study of Life Situations, Emotions, and Cutaneous Vascular Reactions." In *Life Stress and Bodily Disease,* edited by H. G. Wolff, S. Wolf, and C. C. Hare, pp. 987–1007. Research Publications of the Association for Research in Nervous and Mental Disease, vol. 29. Baltimore: Williams and Wilkins, 1950.

31. Graham, D. T. "The Relation of Psoriasis to Attitude and to Vascular Reactions of the Human Skin." *Journal of Investigative Dermatology* 22 (1954):379–88.

32. Graham, D. T., J. D. Kabler, and L. Lunsford, Jr. "Vasovagal Fainting: A Diphasic Response." *Psychosomatic Medicine* 23 (1961):493–507.

33. Hinkle, L. E., Jr., W. N. Christenson, F. D. Kane, A. Ostfeld, W. N. Thetford, and H. G. Wolff. "An Investigation of the Relation between Life Experience, Personality Characteristics, and General Susceptibility to Illness." *Psychosomatic Medicine* 20 (1958):278–95.

34. Holmes, T. H., T. Treuting, and H. G. Wolff. "Life Situations, Emotions and Nasal Disease: Evidence on Summative Effects Exhibited in Patients with 'Hay Fever.' " *Psychosomatic Medicine* 13 (1951):71–82.

35. Holmes, T. H., and H. G. Wolff. "Life Situations, Emotions and Backache." *Psychosomatic Medicine* 14 (1952):18–33.

36. Lorenz, T. H., D. T. Graham, and S. Wolf. "The Relation of Life Stress and Emotions to Human Sebum Secretion and to the Mechanism of Acne Vulgaris." *Journal of Laboratory and Clinical Medicine* 41 (1953):11–28.

37. Stevenson, I., and C. H. Duncan. "Alterations in Cardiac Function and Circulatory Efficiency during Periods of Life Stress as Shown by Changes in the Rate, Rhythm, Electrocardiographic Patterns and Output of the Heart in Those with Cardiovascular Disease." In *Life Stress and Bodily Disease,* edited by H. G. Wolff, S. Wolf, and C. C. Hare, pp. 799–817. Research Publications of the Association for Research in Nervous and Mental Disease, vol. 29. Baltimore: Williams and Wilkins, 1950.

38. Wolf, S., and H. G. Wolff. *Human Gastric Function.* New York: Oxford University Press, 1947.

39. Wolff, H. G. *Headache and Other Head Pain.* 2nd ed. New York: Oxford University Press, 1963.

14

Life Crisis and Disease Onset:
A Prospective Study of Life Crises
and Health Changes

Richard H. Rahe and Thomas H. Holmes

A qualitative and quantitative definition of a life crisis and its association with disease has been presented in detail in previous reports [1;2]. In brief, a ratio scale was generated for 43 familiar life change events empirically found to cluster in the settings in which illness occurred. Each life change reported by subjects was assigned a numerical value from the Social Readjustment Rating Scale. These numerical values were called *life change units* (LCU). This unique method provided a qualitative and quantitative definition of the amount of change in ongoing life adjustment required for each subject in any given year. Subjects with a yearly total of less than 150 LCU were classified as having no life crisis. Yearly totals from 150 to 199 LCU were defined as *mild* life crisis, yearly totals from 200 to 299 LCU were defined as *moderate* life crisis, and yearly totals greater than 299 LCU were defined as *major* life crisis. Any major health change reported the same year or up to two years following a life crisis was defined as associated with that life crisis. Application of this method to a recent retrospective study demonstrated that 93 percent of the reported health changes were associated with a life crisis. Also, a direct relationship was discovered between life crisis magnitude, expressed by the LCU value, and percentage of life crises with an associated health change.

This chapter contains the results of a pilot project in which the new quantitative method for defining a life crisis is applied to a prospective study of the

The title of this chapter and its first two paragraphs have been reinstated from a mimeographed version of the paper prepared by Dr. Rahe and Dr. Holmes in 1966. The study was first published as pt. 3 (pp. 106–12) of Richard H. Rahe, "Life Crisis and Health Change," in *Psychotropic Drug Response: Advances in Prediction*, edited by Philip R. A. May and J. R. Wittenborn (1969), pp. 92–125. Reprinted courtesy of Charles C Thomas, Publisher, Springfield, Illinois.

occurrence of disease or health change. The data-gathering instrument, the Schedule of Recent Experience (SRE), is a self-administered questionnaire. It documents, by year of occurrence, changes in residence, occupation, finances, personal status, family, social activities, and health status over the past ten years. The subjects for the study were the same 88 resident physicians who composed the population for the retrospective investigation of the association of life change and health change [2].

The sample of 88 University of Washington resident physicians was then used to test the predictability of near-future health changes by using data on recent life changes. All other information accumulated about the subjects was ignored in making predictions concerning their relative risks of developing health changes during the follow-up period. Up to this point, the life crisis hypothesis had never been tested for its merits, or lack of them, as a predictive tool.

METHOD

The final one and a half years of the work with the SRE was used to derive LCU scores to serve as the base for the prospective study. Thus, the LCU values for the year of 1963 and for the first six months of 1964 (time of completion of SRE) were used to divide the subjects into risk categories for future health change occurrence.

Eight months after completion of the SRE, the 88 subjects were canvassed for information regarding their health experience during the interval. Eighty-four of the original sample of residents were successfully contacted; all of this number gave information pertaining to their state of health during the eight-month interim. These data were then examined for their correlations with the life change data.

RESULTS

The 84 subjects reported 32 major health changes during the follow-up period. Thirty-one of the health changes, or 97 percent, were associated with, and clearly followed, a life crisis of at least mild (LCU 150 or greater) magnitude (Table 14.1). (The report of laryngitis by one subject was associated with a score of 130 LCU.) In Table 14.1, the major health changes reported during the follow-up year are grouped into 21 varieties. The health changes are listed by rank order of the life crises with which they were associated.

The correlation of the life crises data and health change data from the follow-up period was analyzed by dividing the subjects into two groups: those who, from 1963 to mid-1964, had LCU totals of 250 or more; and those who, for the same time period, had totals below 250 LCU. As shown in Table 14.2, health changes in the follow-up period are significantly associated with the higher LCU totals. In a second analysis, the subjects were divided by their one-and-a-half-year LCU totals into groups of high, moderate, and low risk. Table 14.3 also indicates that

Table 14.1
Major Health Changes Experienced by the 84 Subjects
during the Follow-up Period

No. Variety	LCU, or Mean LCU Value
1 Gross hematuria secondary co-Coumadin® reaction, taken for recent diagnosis of paroxysmal atrial tachycardia	500
1 Diagnosis of von Willebrand's disease	450
2 Major surgical procedures	418*
1 Approximately 20 lb. weight loss	365
1 Thrombophlebitis	360
1 Tonsilitis	360
2 Severe flu	340*
1 Renal calculi and colic	315
1 Spontaneous abortion	275
3 Ulcer symptoms	275*
1 Fever of unknown origin	270
3 Exacerbations or onset of allergies or asthma	263*
1 Pregnancy	260
2 Severe muscle strains	257*
1 Amenorrhea	245
2 Accidents with moderate body trauma	245*
2 Mononucleosis and/or hepatitis	240*
1 Pneumonia	235
3 Upper respiratory infections or laryngitis	220*
1 Wisdom teeth extraction	205
1 Initial refraction for glasses	170

32 Total

* Mean LCU

Note: Coumadin®, a preparation of sodium warfarin, is manufactured by Endo Laboratories, Inc.

the risk of occurrence of near-future health change is directly related to the magnitude of the LCU total.

A third analysis of the data involved the 41 subjects in the high-risk group. Twenty-four of this number had experienced one or more illnesses during the time interval that provided the base LCU scores for the prospective study. Table 14.4 indicates that for the follow-up period there was no significant difference in the near-future experience of health change between the group of 24 previously ill subjects and the group of 17 previously healthy individuals.

Table 14.2
Association of LCU with Health Change

	Life Change Units (250 or more)	Life Change Units (less than 250)
Mean life change units	392	188
Number of subjects	41	43
Number of health changes	24	9*
Number of subjects with health changes	20	9
Percent of subjects with health changes	49	21**

$* p < 0.001$
$** p < 0.01$

Table 14.3
Association of Health Change with Life Change Intensity
of Major, Moderate, and Mild Magnitude

	Major	Moderate	Mild
Mean LCU Values:	380	211	121
Number of subjects	41	32	11
Number of health changes	24	8	1*
Number of subjects with health changes	20	8	1
Percent of subjects with health changes	49	25	9*

* Differences between major, moderate, and mild risk groups significant at $p < 0.01$

DISCUSSION

This study was designed to examine the probability of occurrence of disease and other health changes in a group of subjects homogeneous with respect to most physical and social dimensions but dissimilar in regard to recent life changes. The data indicate a powerful association between life crisis magnitude and occurrence of disease or other health change.

The life crisis concepts adduced by these pilot studies are felt to have distinct advantages over a more general terminology, such as "life stress." First, the life

Table 14.4
Relationship of Prior Illness to the Occurrence of Future Illness
in High-risk Subjects

| | Previous Health Change | |
	Yes	No
Mean life change units	452	307
Number of subjects	24	17
Number of health changes	12	12*
Number of subjects with health changes	10	10
Percent of subjects with health changes	42	59

* $p = 0.20$ (NS)

crisis data allow for a certain amount of life change to be experienced without risk to health. Second, although an individual experiences a life crisis, different health change risks are reflected at different life crisis magnitudes. A third advantage of the life crisis concepts is that the life changes measured draw from both the exceptional and from the commonly experienced changes in social status for an individual. This lends more universal application to these data.

It is of interest to compare these prospective data with the findings of the retrospective study [2]. For the eight follow-up months in the present study, 49 percent of those subjects with a major life crisis experienced health changes. For those subjects with moderate and mild life crises, 25 percent and 9 percent, respectively, experienced health changes. In the retrospective study, the subjects were at risk for two years following the advent of the life crisis; the association with health change was 79 percent, 51 percent, and 37 percent, respectively, for the three magnitudes of life crisis. When both sets of data are plotted, the slope of the two lines is similar. This suggests that when the subjects in the prospective study have been at risk the full two years, the yield of health changes may well approximate that observed in the retrospective study.

The reported health changes were listed according to the magnitudes of the life crises with which they were associated in order to investigate the possibility that, the higher an individual's life crisis magnitude, the more likely he or she is to develop a serious disorder. The difficulty in establishing such a relationship is twofold. First, there is as yet no quantitative ratio scale of a major health change with which the results of this study can be compared. Second, a life crisis of high magnitude often had more than one associated health change. A large weight loss, for instance, may be associated with a life crisis of 400 LCU, but it may be only one of three health changes associated with that life crisis. By itself, the large weight loss would appear a relatively minor health change to be associated with a life crisis of such high magnitude. Nevertheless, the rank order in Table 14.1 does suggest a direct relationship between LCU magnitude and relative seriousness of the health change.

As with the data from the retrospective study, the present findings suggest some inferences concerning resistance to disease, and those with the greatest resistance to health changes appear to be those 17 subjects in the high-risk group having an average LCU of 307. (See Table 14.4.) Although highly stressed, this group reported no major health changes during the eight months of the prospective study and none during the 18 months prior to the prospective study. On the other hand, the 24 subjects in the high-risk group in Table 14.4, with an average LCU of 452, composed the majority of persons most susceptible to health change. This group contained only 28 percent of the total sample; but, counting the health changes that occurred during both the 18 months before and the eight months after the completion of the SRE, these subjects accounted for 58 percent of all health changes. These data are consistent with the findings of Hinkle [3], which demonstrate that illness is not randomly distributed throughout a population; rather, most illness occurrence is condensed into a small percentage of a given population. Since the group of 24 previously ill subjects experienced a similar illness rate in the follow-up period as did the 17 previously healthy individuals, in the high-risk group the occurrence of an illness during a high-risk period does not appear to lessen the probability of experiencing a closely following subsequent illness.

The prospective design of this study partially resolves some methodologic problems of the retrospective studies. The methodological requirement of this study, that a life crisis be present before the subject was placed in a category of near-future illness risk, insured that the subsequent health changes clearly followed the life crises, and not vice versa. Also, since the health changes followed the life crises, the illness experience could not have biased the recall of the life events composing the life crisis. Although this study still does not document the accuracy of what is recalled, the important thing appears to be that the subject does make a meaningful judgment about whether or not the SRE items apply to his or her recent life.

The final unresolved methodologic issue in this pilot study is the way in which the health change data were collected. Allowing the subjects to decide what, if any, health changes to report introduces an obvious bias. Some of the factors influencing the self-report of illness have been reviewed and discussed by Mechanic [4]. In a prospective study of injury among college athletes, the report of injury was objectively determined. The results [5] are almost identical to those contained in this chapter.

REFERENCES

1. Holmes, T. H., and R. H. Rahe. "The Social Readjustment Rating Scale." *Journal of Psychosomatic Research* 11 (1967):213–18. Reprinted in this volume, Chapter 2.

2. Rahe, R. H., and T. H. Holmes. "Life Crisis and Disease Onset. I. Qualitative and Quantitative Definition of the Life Crisis and Its Association with Health Change." First published as pt. 2 of R. H. Rahe, "Life Crisis and Health Change." In *Psychotropic Drug Response: Advances in Prediction*, edited by P. R. A. May and J. R. Wittenborn, pp. 92–125. Springfield, Ill.: Charles C Thomas, 1969. Reprinted in this volume, Chapter 13.

3. Hinkle, L. E., Jr., W. N. Christenson, F. D. Kane, A. Ostfeld, W. N. Thetford, and H. G. Wolff. "An Investigation of the Relation of Life Experience, Personality Characteristics, and General Susceptibility to Illness." *Psychosomatic Medicine* 20 (1958):278–95.

4. Mechanic, D., and M. Newton. "Some Problems in the Analysis of Morbidity Data." *Journal of Chronic Diseases* 18 (1965):569–80.

5. Holmes, T. H. "Psychologic Screening." In *Football Injuries: Papers Presented at a Workshop*, pp. 211–14. Sponsored by Subcommittee on Athletic Injuries, Committee on the Skeletal System, Division of Medical Sciences, National Research Council, February 1969. Washington, D.C.: National Academy of Sciences, 1970.

15

Short-term Intrusions into the Life-style Routine

T. Stephenson Holmes and Thomas H. Holmes

The Social Readjustment Rating Questionnaire (SRRQ) was developed by Holmes and Rahe [1;2] as a scaling instrument for the life changes empirically determined to precede major health changes, such as illness onset or exacerbation, injury, surgery, and pregnancy [3–16]. These life changes involve modifications of an individual's sleeping, eating, social, recreational, personal, and interpersonal habits—events that require or are indicative of varying amounts of adjustment. The Social Readjustment Rating Scale assigns magnitudes to each of 42 life change items, according to the amount, severity, and duration of adjustment that each is perceived to require. The scaling instrument was found to be concordant among various segments of the U.S. population [1;17;18] and between Americans and people of other cultures as well [19–21].

The Schedule of Recent Experience (SRE), a self-administered paper-and-pencil survey, lists these life changes by year of occurrence. By assigning to the life changes the empirically determined magnitudes of the SRRQ, it was found that, the higher a person's life change score for a given year, the greater the chances of that person's experiencing a major health change within the near future [22;23].

The present study considers these variables over a shorter time period: It examines the occurrence of daily life changes and possible correlations with daily health changes.

This chapter is reprinted with permission from T. Stephenson Holmes and Thomas H. Holmes, "Short-term Intrusions into the Life Style Routine," *Journal of Psychosomatic Research* 14 (1970):121–32. Copyright 1970 by Pergamon Press, Ltd.

METHOD

From the SRE, a Schedule of Daily Experience (SDE) was derived. The 42 life change items were recorded on a daily basis. The instructions printed on the survey sheet are as follows:

Each of the following items has a space beside it for each day of the coming week. If, during the course of the week, any of the items applies to you, check the appropriate box. If one should apply more than once in a single day, indicate by the appropriate number in that box. Begin the chart on the day you receive it, and indicate the day by circling it and writing in the date. Do not mark in any space which does not apply.

And following the life change items is printed:

In the spaces below, record briefly the day-to-day health changes which you may experience. These might include minor accidents, injuries, cuts, bruises, eyestrain, backache, headache, toothache, earache, stomach ache, muscle strain, coughing, sneezing, running nose, bloody nose, allergic reactions, nausea, vomiting, diarrhea, shortness of breath, skin rash, acne, athlete's foot, hay fever, sunburn, and the like. If you can, try to give some brief reason for a symptom, such as "Sore eye due to irritation of contact lens" or "Sore muscles due to swimming yesterday."

Also try to give some indication of your general state of thought, feeling, and behavior, for example, nervousness, tension, elation, moodiness, irritability, anxiety, anger, fatigue, etc. In general, include the signs, symptoms, and inconveniences of everyday life which usually pass unnoticed. Try to be as complete as possible.

The magnitudes of the life changes, expressed in life change units (LCU), were summed for each day, and the total correlated in various ways with the signs and symptoms experienced during that day.

The SDE was distributed to a sample of convenience of 80 individuals, fairly homogeneous in age and peer status. They comprised graduate students, laboratory technicians, secretaries, and medical students. The general mechanics of the study and the printed instructions on the form were explained to each participant in the same way, and each was asked to follow the survey for at least two weeks, preferably three or four. The range for participation in the study was from two weeks to nine weeks.

Due to nonresponse and incomplete response, the total usable sample comprises 55 persons (69 percent). They include 37 males and 18 females, whose ages range from 16 to 60 years, with a median of 23 years, primarily due to the 28 medical students in the survey. The median education of 17 years is due to the same bias.

The investigator retained at least weekly personal contact with as many subjects as possible. These informal interviews sometimes provided additional information about the subjects not reported in the survey sheet. Of the final sample, only one person had not been in such contact with the investigator.

RESULTS

Table 15.1 is a ranking of the 42 life change items according to their frequency of occurrence in the entire sample. There was a negative correlation between the magnitude of life change events and the frequency of their occurrence (r_s = –0.706; $p < 0.001$). A relatively small number of life changes, those of the least magnitude (15–20 LCU), were the most frequently reported. Seventy-nine percent of all the life changes are among the first eight items in Table 15.1, all with magnitudes less than 25 LCU. The next 13 items, all less than 45 LCU, account for another 19 percent. Thus, half the life change events account for 98 percent of all the life changes reported, leaving all the other half responsible for only 2 percent.

The health changes most frequently reported were those related to the following arbitrary categories: skin; eye, ear, nose, and throat; central nervous system; gastrointestinal system; and musculoskeletal system (Table 15.2). Together they account for 95 percent of all the health changes reported.

Only two individuals reported visits to a physician, and these were for routine examinations. Three individuals reported five visits to the dentist: Four were routine visits, and one was for the repair of a broken tooth. Thus, the latter was the only instance of a health change requiring professional attention. In more than 1,300 man-days, fewer than half a dozen absences from work or disruptions of personal schedules were reported. These health changes are, then, the signs and symptoms of everyday life, which reflect in varying degrees each individual's life-style. They include headaches, backaches, stomach aches, sore throats, diarrhea, skin infections, and nearly 100 other assorted aches and pains.

There are subjects in the survey who managed to be free or very nearly free of signs and symptoms for as long as a month; there are also those who experienced in the same length of time no day, or very few days, without signs and symptoms. Most people, however, fall in the middle—so much so, in fact, that there is an almost equal distribution of symptomatic days, on which any sign or symptom at all occurred (47 percent), and nonsymptomatic days, on which none occurred (53 percent).

On the whole, signs and symptoms form such an integral part of daily life that, for the entire period of 1,300 man-days, there is on the average nearly one symptom per day for each of the 55 subjects, and more than two per person on each symptomatic day.

In order to examine possible relationships between the occurrence of these signs and symptoms and the magnitude of daily life change, several statistical tests were employed. The Wilcoxon Signed Rank test for matched pairs demonstrates clearly that the two are directly related ($z = -3.25$; $p < 0.001$). That is, a person is much more likely to experience signs and symptoms on a day of high life change than on one of low life change.

Figure 15.1 shows the data of one subject on 18 consecutive days. During that time he experienced a variety of symptoms on six days. Of these days, five have

Table 15.1
Life Change Frequency and Magnitude

Life change	Magnitude	Number of occurrences
Change in eating habits	15	417
Change in sleeping habits	16	417
Change in social activities	18	340
Change in recreational habits	19	298
Change in personal habits	24	190
Change in working hours or conditions	20	150
Vacation	13	130
Change in family get-togethers	15	117
Change in financial state	38	80
Change in living conditions	25	70
Outstanding personal achievement	28	62
Change in responsibilities at work	29	39
Change in number of arguments with spouse	35	38
Change in residence	20	34
Change in health or behavior of family member	44	34
Change in line of work	36	30
Change in church activities	19	28
Troubles with the boss	23	23
Sexual difficulties	39	22
Son or daughter leaving home	29	21
Gaining a new family member	30	20
Personal injury or illness	53	15
Wife beginning or ceasing work	26	8
Minor violations of the law	11	7
Beginning or ceasing formal schooling	26	7
In-law troubles	29	6
Mortgage or loan less than $10,000	17	3
Marital reconciliation	45	3
Marital separation	65	2
Changing to a new school	20	1
Mortgage or loan greater than $10,000	31	1
Major business readjustment	39	1
Marriage	50	1
Death of a close family member	63	1
Foreclosure of mortgage or loan	30	0
Death of a close friend	37	0
Pregnancy	40	0
Retirement from work	45	0
Being fired from work	47	0
Detention in jail	63	0
Divorce	73	0
Death of spouse	100	0

Table 15.2
Symptom Frequency by Organ System

Organ system	Number of symptoms
Skin	293
Eye, ear, nose, throat	278
Gastrointestinal system	214
Musculoskeletal and connective tissue system	201
Central nervous system	164
Respiratory system	24
Miscellaneous	21
Endocrine system	14
Genitourinary system	5
Cardiovascular system	2
Total	1216

life change scores above the mean for that person (15.6 LCU) and only one has a score below. Similarly, Figure 15.2 shows 21 days of another subject. Again, there are six symptomatic days, of which five have scores above the mean (27.8 LCU) and only one has a score below. Figure 15.3 shows a subject with 12 symptomatic days out of 14. Of these, nine have scores above the mean (65.1 LCU) and only three have scores below.

The amount of life change was found to be higher on the day before and the day after signs and symptoms are experienced ($z = -1.75$ and -1.66, respectively; $p < 0.05$) as well as on the day of occurrence. This establishes a clustering of high LCU totals about symptomatic days (Figure 15.4).

Figure 15.4 also shows a similar clustering of low amounts of life change about days in which no signs and symptoms occur. There is approximately twice as much life change on symptomatic days (mean score 49.8 LCU) as on nonsymptomatic days (mean score 25.5 LCU).

A different method of assessing the relationship of these parameters is the biserial coefficient test, which in effect distributes signs and symptoms along a continuum of life change. This test again demonstrates ($r_b = 0.327$; $p < 0.01$) that signs and symptoms are found associated with days with the highest LCU scores.

Spearman's rank order correlations (r_s) were computed between pairs of the following variables: mean LCU score, proportion of days symptomatic, mean symptom frequency, and coefficient of variation of LCU score (standard deviation as a percent of the mean) (Table 15.3).

The correlation between mean LCU score and mean symptom frequency implies that the individuals with the greatest magnitudes of life change have the

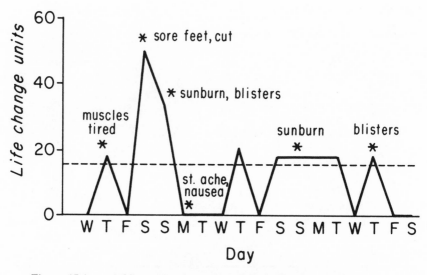

Figure 15.1 A 23-yr-old male medical student with low overall mean LCU score.

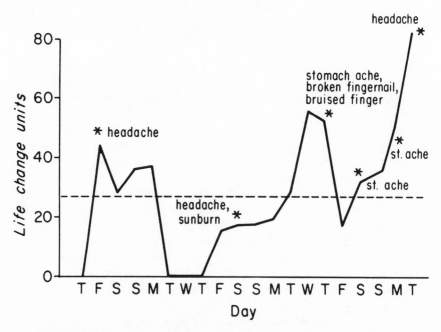

Figure 15.2 A 23-yr-old female laboratory technician with intermediate overall mean LCU score.

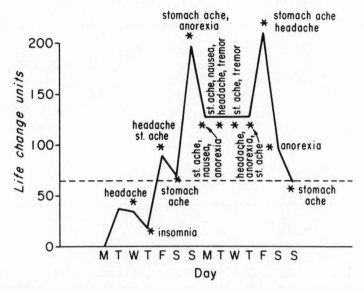

Figure 15.3 A 23-yr-old male medical student with high overall mean
LCU score.

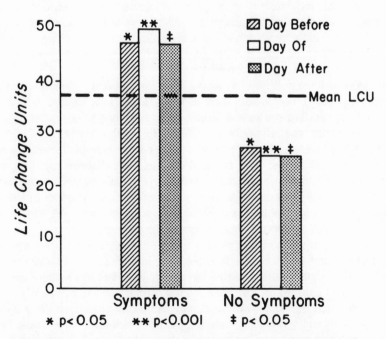

Figure 15.4 Clustering of life change about days on which signs and
symptoms occur.

Table 15.3

Correlations between Life Change and Symptoms (Spearman's rho)

	Coefficient of variation LCU Score	Mean symptom frequency	Proportion of days symptomatic
Mean LCU Score	$r_s = -0.784$ $p < 0.001$	$r_s = 0.447$ $0.001 < p < 0.01$	$r_s = 0.480$ $p < 0.001$
Proportion of days symptomatic	$r_s = -0.266$ $0.05 < p < 0.10$	$r_s = 0.963$ $p < 0.001$	
Mean symptom frequency	$r_s = -0.201$ $p > 0.01$		

most signs and symptoms. The 30 percent of the sample with the highest LCU scores demonstrate 50 percent of all the signs and symptoms experienced by the entire sample (Figure 15.5). The women in the survey demonstrate 58 percent more signs and symptoms than the men.

The correlation between mean LCU score and proportion of days symptomatic implies that the individuals with the greatest magnitudes of life change also are the most chronically symptomatic (that is, have signs and symptoms most of the time). The very high correlation of mean symptom frequency with proportion of days symptomatic indicates that people with many signs and symptoms experience them chronically rather than all at once.

Subjects with the highest LCU scores have the least daily variability in their values ($p < 0.001$). People with these more stable LCU scores tend to have the highest symptom frequencies and largest proportions of days symptomatic, but these correlations are statistically inconclusive ($p > 0.05$) (Table 15.3).

Of ten individuals in the study known to have some kind of chronic disorder (four, psychiatric illness; two, atopic dermatitis; one, diabetes mellitus; one, rheumatoid arthritis; one, ovarian cyst; and one, pilonidal cyst), seven rank in the upper 30 percent by proportion of days symptomatic, mean symptom frequency, and mean LCU scores (not necessarily the same seven in each case). Most of the signs and symptoms reported are unrelated to the chronic disorders.

Four of the subjects with chronic illness (one, diabetes mellitus; one, rheumatoid arthritis; and two, atopic dermatitis) were in a single family and together experienced a significant amount of life change attendant to the marriage of a daughter (see Figure 15.6). The bride did not participate. The five family members experienced peaks of both life change and health change on the wedding day. The signs and symptoms collectively experienced on the day of the ceremony were: one report each of headache, backache, acne, bursitis, heartburn, bruise, skin burn, stomach ache, diarrhea, hemorrhoid bleeding, tremor, skin abrasion, and sore muscles; and two reports each of tears, athlete's foot, and sunburn. There are 19 signs and symptoms—16 different, and all unrelated to the chronic illnesses.

An example of the contribution of a particular life setting to the onset of one of the signs and symptoms of everyday life is seen in the report of a young secretary, who emphasizes her emotional reactions as well as life events:

8/2: Woke feeling depressed with my life and decided not to go to work. Spent the morning finishing [correspondence] lesson and mailed it. Received letter from N.Y. (haven't heard from *him* since July 13th). Really became frustrated about my feelings for this man—terrible loving someone that can never be yours to really love and belong to. Spent a few hours soul searching—I seem to be suffering from feelings of love, hate, *guilt*, and I am most likely a little sexually frustrated! (Old Maid syndrome.) After feeling sorry for myself I wrote him a letter trying to explain my feelings, but after I mailed the letter I

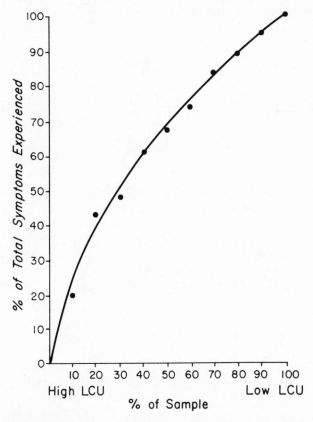

Figure 15.5   Distribution of signs and symptoms in the sample. Subjects are ranked by deciles from highest LCU to lowest LCU.

was very angry with myself for having weaken[ed] and not just said goodbye. Developed a real beautiful tension headache! (None of this would have happened if I went to work—Ha!). Went to bed very early and slept very soundly which really surprised me.

DISCUSSION

This investigative method produces a brief qualitative and quantitative medical history, spanning a limited length of time and minimizing the problems of recall and experimenter bias, since the survey is filled out daily by the subject. A subject may report a hay fever attack and a backache, perhaps on the same day that his wife's mother comes to visit. This is an event that requires a certain degree of adjustment on his part. The SDE substitutes for the event a number whose value is greater or lesser depending on his perception of the number and kinds of changes requiring adjustment that are related to the visit.

For example, he may check "Gaining a new family member," "In-law troubles," and "Change in number of arguments with spouse" for that particular day. If his personal routine is more severely upset, he may also check "Change in

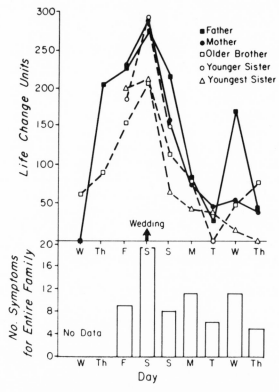

Figure 15.6   Family's response to marriage of 20-yr-old girl.

sleeping habits," "Change in eating habits," or "Change in living conditions." The combinations are many, but his daily point total reflects his individual perception of the number of the day's events, and provides a number opposite which his symptoms can be recorded.

Though filling out the SDE requires very little time, it must be kept up every day for maximum validity. It has been shown that longer periods of time between data gathering result in a decrease in information reported [24–27]. The frequent personal contact of the investigator with the subjects was an attempt to encourage and reinforce regular and accurate reporting of data as well as to minimize the notoriously poor return of questionnaires in general [28].

That a very few life change events should account for the bulk of all those reported is a measure of their universality in human experience. The 21 most salient events (for example, marriage, divorce, detention in jail, and death of spouse) together comprise only 2 percent of the total reports, while four items (change in eating habits, sleeping habits, social activities, and recreational habits) comprise more than half (56 percent). It is a common observation of clinical management that the three most subtle indicators of a patient's current state of adjustment are changes in eating, sleeping, and sexual habits. It is thus of more than passing interest that two of these rank highest in the present frequency breakdown. The three together comprise a third of all the changes reported.

The skin may be visualized as the body's first line of defense against the environment, and has been shown to be a sensitive barometer of the system of thought, feeling, and behavior [29;30]. It is not surprising, then, that cutaneous signs and symptoms were most frequently reported in this study. The eyes, ears, nose, and throat, and the gastrointestinal and musculoskeletal systems are similarly in close and constant contact with the environment, and together with the skin account for more than 95 percent of all the signs and symptoms reported.

Hinkle [31;32] reported in studies of industrial absence that respiratory infections were the most frequent illnesses responsible. The number of signs and symptoms referable to the respiratory system in the present study is partially due to the classification system. The respiratory system category includes only signs and symptoms originating from structures below the larynx, such as cough and dyspnea. The eye, ear, nose, and throat category includes those above the larynx, such as colds and hay fever. Combination of the respiratory signs and symptoms of each category yields nearly 200 reports. Thus it is evident that respiratory signs and symptoms are also among those most frequently reported.

Systems such as the genitourinary, endocrine, and cardiovascular are almost entirely internal and may be thought to be buffered against direct environmental assault. Though the central nervous system is likewise internal, it carries the full responsibility of mediating the response of every system to every stimulus, and the constant demands for adaptation may account for the large number of signs and symptoms related to it.

A hypothesis that can be examined from the data of the SDE is that the appearance of signs and symptoms may depend not only on the magnitude of life change, but also on the variability of life change. The proposal is that people with a great deal of daily variation in the LCU point totals may have a high incidence of signs and symptoms due to constant demands for adaptation to the different amounts of life change.

The findings are inconclusive, but the tendency is actually in the opposite direction. High symptom frequencies and large proportions of days symptomatic tend to indicate the least daily variability in LCU score rather than the most, as would be expected if there were direct relationships among mean LCU score, mean symptom frequency, and variability coefficient.

The present chapter completes a spectrum of health changes studied in relation to the life changes of the Social Readjustment Rating Questionnaire. Originally, Rahe and Holmes [22;23] found that the magnitude of life change establishes the probability of occurrence of a major health change within a one- or two-year period. In a later study of a population selected to be young and healthy, Rahe [12] examined six-month intervals and obtained similar results. The health changes were of lesser consequence, but they were still serious enough to receive attention by a physician. In the present study the association between life change and health change is once again borne out. The time scale in this case is in days, and the health changes are minor and do not require medical attention.

A number of the other present findings are also in accord with previous studies involving long time intervals and major health changes. Hinkle [31–35] found that a small number of people account for the majority of illness in several populations, and that a small number account for the majority of health. He also reported that the people most chronically absent from work due to illness have more illnesses involving more bodily systems than a low-absence control. Most frequently reported in his studies were respiratory and gastrointestinal disorders. Both of these systems are well represented in the present frequency list. Baetjer [36] found that industrial absence due to illness is far more frequent in women than in men. Recently Rahe and Arthur [12] have shown a clustering of greater than average life change before and after major health changes.

Many psychophysiologic studies have been carried out on a daily basis. While physiological measurements have been sophisticated and precise, the measurement of psychosocial factors has been empirical and qualitative [37–67]. The present report indicates the utility of the magnitudes of the Social Readjustment Rating Questionnaire in such day-to-day studies.

SUMMARY

1. A relatively small number of life change events account for most of the day-to-day life change, and a few bodily systems account for the majority of the signs and symptoms ofeveryday life.

2. A person is much more likely to experience the signs and symptoms of everyday life on days of greater than average life change, as reflected by his or her LCU point total. Life changes tend to cluster around health changes.

3. Conversely, a person is much less likely to experience signs and symptoms on days of less than average life change, and low amounts of life change tend to cluster around symptom-free days.

4. Individuals with the highest amounts of life change demonstrate the most signs and symptoms, as do those with some form of chronic illness, though most of the signs and symptoms are unrelated to the chronic disorders.

5. Women have more signs and symptoms than men.

6. Those people with many signs and symptoms have them more or less continuously and not all at once.

7. Of any given number of days, half are symptomatic and half are nonsymptomatic; but when the everyday signs and symptoms reported in this study occur, they do not affect work capacity or productivity and they do not require medical attention.

8. There is a negative correlation between variability and magnitude of mean life change.

9. There is no demonstrable relationship between occurrence of signs and symptoms and variability of life change.

10. These data are consistent with several long-term studies of life change and health change and suggest that minor health changes may be causally related to events requiring adaptive behavior.

REFERENCES

1. Holmes, T. H., and R. H. Rahe. "The Social Readjustment Rating Scale." *Journal of Psychosomatic Research* 11 (1967):213–18. Reprinted in this volume, Chapter 2.

2. Masuda, M., and T. H. Holmes. "Magnitude Estimations of Social Readjustments." *Journal of Psychosomatic Research* 11 (1967):219–25. Reprinted in this volume, Chapter 3.

3. Fischer, H. K., B. M. Dlin, W. L. Winters, S. B. Hagner, and E. Weiss. "Time Patterns and Emotional Factors Related to the Onset of Coronary Occlusion." Abstract. *Psychosomatic Medicine* 24 (1962):516.

4. Greene, W. A., Jr. "Psychological Factors and Reticulo-endothelial Disease. I. Preliminary Observations on a Group of Males with Lymphomas and Leukemias." *Psychosomatic Medicine* 16 (1954):220–30.

5. Greene, W. A., Jr., and G. Miller. "Psychological Factors and Reticulo-endothelial Disease. IV. Observations on a Group of Children and Adolescents with Leukemia: An Interpretation of Disease Development in Terms of the Mother–Child Unit." *Psychosomatic Medicine* 20 (1958):124–44.

6. Greene, W. A., Jr., L. E. Young, and S. N. Swisher. "Psychological Factors and Reticulo-endothelial Disease. II. Observations on a Group of Women with Lymphomas and Leukemias." *Psychosomatic Medicine* 18 (1956):284–303.

7. Hawkins, N. G., R. Davies, and T. H. Holmes. "Evidence of Psychosocial Factors in the Development of Pulmonary Tuberculosis." *American Review of Tuberculosis and Pulmonary Diseases* 75 (1957):768–80. Reprinted in this volume, Chapter 11.

8. Holmes, T. H., J. Joffe, J. W. Ketcham, and T. F. Sheehy. "Experimental Study of Prognosis." *Journal of Psychosomatic Research* 5 (1961):235–52.

9. Kissen, D. M. "Specific Psychological Factors in Pulmonary Tuberculosis." *Health Bulletin* (Edinburgh) 14 (1956):44–46.

10. Kissen, D. M. "Some Psychological Aspects of Pulmonary Tuberculosis." *International Journal of Social Psychiatry* 3 (1958):252–59.

11. Rahe, R. H. Personal communication.

12. Rahe, R. H., and R. J. Arthur. "Life-change Patterns Surrounding Illness Experience." *Journal of Psychosomatic Research* 11 (1968):341–45.

13. Rahe, R. H., and A. E. Christ. "An Unusual Cardiac (Ventricular) Arrhythmia in a Child: Psychiatric and Psychophysiologic Aspects." *Psychosomatic Medicine* 28 (1966): 181–88.

14. Rahe, R. H., J. D. McKean, Jr., and R. J. Arthur. "A Longitudinal Study of Life-change and Illness Patterns." *Journal of Psychosomatic Research* 10 (1967):355–66.

15. Rahe, R. H., M. Meyer, M. Smith, G. Kjaer, and T. H. Holmes. "Social Stress and Illness Onset." *Journal of Psychosomatic Research* 8 (1964):35–44. Reprinted in this volume, Chapter 12.

16. Weiss, E., B. Dlin, H. R. Rollin, H. K. Fischer, and C. R. Bepler. "Emotional Factors in Coronary Occlusion." *Archives of Internal Medicine* 99 (1957):628–41.

17. Komaroff, A. L., M. Masuda, and T. H. Holmes. "The Social Readjustment Rating Scale: A Comparative Study of Negro, Mexican, and White Americans." *Journal of Psychosomatic Research* 12 (1968):121–28. Reprinted in this volume, Chapter 6.

18. Ruch, L. O. "Scaling of Life Stress with Direct and Indirect Scaling Methods." Master's thesis, University of Hawaii, 1967.

19. Masuda, M., and T. H. Holmes. "The Social Readjustment Rating Scale: A Cross-cultural Study of Japanese and Americans." *Journal of Psychosomatic Research* 11 (1967):227–37. Reprinted in this volume, Chapter 5.

20. Parson, O. A. Personal communication.

21. Preston, C. E. Personal communication.

22. Rahe, R. H., and T. H. Holmes. "Life Crisis and Disease Onset. I. Qualitative and Quantitative Definition of the Life Crisis and Its Association with Health Change." First published as pt. 2 of R. H. Rahe, "Life Crisis and Health Change." In *Psychotropic Drug Response: Advances in Prediction*, edited by P. R. A May and J. R. Wittenborn, pp. 92–125. Springfield, Ill.: Charles C Thomas, 1969. Reprinted in this volume, Chapter 13.

23. Rahe, R. H., and T. H. Holmes. "Life Crisis and Disease Onset. II. A Prospective Study of Life Crises and Health Changes." First published as pt. 3 of R. H. Rahe, "Life Crisis and Health Change." In *Psychotropic Drug Response: Advances in Prediction*, edited by P. R. A. May and J. R. Wittenborn, pp. 92–125. Springfield, Ill.: Charles C Thomas, 1969. Reprinted in this volume, Chapter 14.

24. Casey, R. L., M. Masuda, and T. H. Holmes. "Quantitative Study of Recall of Life Events." *Journal of Psychosomatic Research* 11 (1967):239–47. Reprinted in this volume, Chapter 10.

25. Haggard, E. A., A. Brekstad, and A. G. Skard. "On the Reliability of the Anamnestic Interview." *Journal of Abnormal and Social Psychology* 61 (1960):311–18.

26. Mechanic, D., and M. Newton. "Some Problems in the Analysis of Morbidity Data." *Journal of Chronic Diseases* 18 (1965):569–80.

27. National Center for Health Statistics. *Health Survey Procedure: Concepts, Questionnaire Development, and Definitions in the Health Interview Survey*. Public Health Service, Series 1–2. Washington, D.C.: Government Printing Office, 1964 (May).

28. Linsky, A. S. "A Factorial Experiment in Inducing Responses to a Mail Questionnaire." *Sociology and Social Research* 49 (1965):183–89.

29. Ely, N., and S. C. Harris. Unpublished data.

30. Ely, N. E., J. W. Verhey, and T. H. Holmes. "Experimental Studies of Skin Inflammation." *Psychosomatic Medicine* 25 (1963):264–84.

31. Hinkle, L. E., Jr., and N. Plummer. "Life Stress and Industrial Absenteeism: The Concentration of Illness and Absenteeism in One Segment of a Working Population." *Industrial Medicine and Surgery* 21 (1952):365–73.

32. Hinkle, L. E., Jr., and H. G. Wolff. "The Nature of Man's Adaptation to His Total Environment and the Relation of This to Illness." *Archives of Internal Medicine* 99 (1957):442–60.

33. Hinkle, L. E., Jr., W. N. Christenson, F. D. Kane, A. Otsfeld, W. N. Thetford, and H. G. Wolff. "An Investigation of the Relation between Life Experience, Personality Characteristics, and General Susceptibility to Illness." *Psychosomatic Medicine* 20 (1958):278–95.

34. Hinkle, L. E., Jr., R. H. Pinsky, I. D. J. Bross, and N. Plummer. "The Distribution of Sickness Disability in a Homogeneous Group of 'Healthy Adult Men.' " *American Journal of Hygiene* 64 (1956):220–42.

35. Plummer, N., and L. E. Hinkle, Jr. "Medical Significance of Illness and Absence in an Industrial Population." *Annals of Internal Medicine* 39 (1953):103–15.

36. Baetjer, A. M. *Women in Industry*. Philadelphia: W. B. Saunders, 1948.

37. Clarke, E. R., Jr., D. W. Zahn, and T. H. Holmes. "The Relationship of Stress, Adrenocortical Function, and Tuberculosis." *American Review of Tuberculosis* 69 (1954):351–69.

38. Dudley, D. L., T. H. Holmes, C. J. Martin, and H. S. Ripley. "Changes in Respiration Associated with Hypnotically Induced Emotion, Pain, and Exercise." *Psychosomatic Medicine* 24 (1964):46–57.

39. Dudley, D. L., T. H. Holmes, C. J. Martin, and H. S. Ripley. "Hypnotically Induced Facsimile of Pain." *Archives of General Psychiatry* 15 (1966):198–204.

40. Dudley, D. L., T. H. Holmes, and H. S. Ripley. "Hypnotically Induced and Suggested Facsimile of Head Pain." *Journal of Nervous and Mental Disease* 144 (1967): 258–65.

41. Dudley, D. L., C. J. Martin, and T. H. Holmes. "Psychophysiologic Studies of Pulmonary Ventilation." *Psychosomatic Medicine* 26 (1964):645–60.

42. Dudley, D. L., C. J. Martin, and T. H. Holmes. "Dyspnea: Psychologic and Physiologic Observations." *Journal of Psychosomatic Research* 11 (1968):325–29.

43. Dudley, D. L., M. Masuda, C. J. Martin, and T. H. Holmes. "Psychophysiological Studies of Experimentally Induced Action Oriented Behavior." *Journal of Psychosomatic Research* 9 (1965):209–21.

44. Duncan, C. H., I. P. Stevenson, and H. S. Ripley. "Life Situations, Emotions, and Paroxysmal Auricular Arrhythmias." *Psychosomatic Medicine* 12 (1950):23–37.

45. Grace, W. J., and D. T. Graham. "Relationships of Specific Attitudes and Emotions to Certain Bodily Diseases." *Psychosomatic Medicine* 14 (1952):243–51.

46. Grace, W. J., S. Wolf, and H. G. Wolff. *The Human Colon*. New York: Paul B. Hoeber, 1951.

47. Graham, D. T. "The Pathogenesis of Hives: Experimental Study of Life Situations, Emotions and Cutaneous Vascular Reactions." In *Life Stress and Bodily Disease*, edited by H. G. Wolff, S. Wolf, and C. C. Hare, pp. 987–1009. Research Publications of the

Association for Research in Nervous and Mental Disease, vol. 29. Baltimore: Williams and Wilkins, 1950.

48. Graham, D. T. "The Relations of Psoriasis to Attitude and to Vascular Reactions of the Human Skin." *Journal of Investigative Dermatology* 22 (1954):379–88.

49. Graham, D. T. "Cutaneous Vascular Reactions in Raynaud's Disease and in States of Hostility, Anxiety, and Depression." *Psychosomatic Medicine* 17 (1955):200–207.

50. Graham, D. T., J. D. Kabler, and L. Lunsford. "Vasovagal Fainting: A Diphasic Response." *Psychosomatic Medicine* 23 (1961):493–507.

51. Graham, D. T., R. M. Lundy, L. S. Benjamin, J. D. Kabler, W. C. Lewis, N. O. Kunish, and F. K. Graham. "Specific Attitudes in Initial Interviews with Patients Having Different 'Psychosomatic' Diseases." *Psychosomatic Medicine* 24 (1962):257–66.

52. Graham, D. T., J. A. Stern, and G. Winokur. "Experimental Investigation of the Specificity of Attitude Hypothesis in Psychosomatic Disease." *Psychosomatic Medicine* 20 (1958):446–57.

53. Graham, D., and I. Stevenson. "Disease as Response to Life Stress. I. The Nature of the Evidence." In *The Psychological Basis of Medical Practice*, edited by H. I. Lief, V. F. Lief, and N. R. Lief, pp. 115–36. New York: Harper and Row, 1963.

54. Holmes, T. H., H. Goodell, S. Wolf, and H. G. Wolff. *The Nose: An Experimental Study of Reactions within the Nose in Human Subjects during Varying Life Experiences.* Springfield, Ill.: Charles C Thomas, 1950.

55. Holmes, T. H., N. G. Hawkins, C. E. Bowerman, E. R. Clarke, Jr., and J. R. Joffe. "Psychosocial and Psychophysiologic Studies of Tuberculosis." *Psychosomatic Medicine* 19 (1957):134–43.

56. Holmes, T. H., T. Treuting, and H. G. Wolff. "Life Situations, Emotions, and Nasal Disease: Evidence on Summative Effects Exhibited in Patients with 'Hay Fever.' " *Psychosomatic Medicine* 13 (1951):71–82.

57. Holmes, T. H., and H. G. Wolff. "Life Situations, Emotions, and Backache." *Psychosomatic Medicine* 14 (1952):18–33.

58. Lorenz, T. H., D. T. Graham, and S. Wolf. "The Relation of Life Stress and Emotions to Human Sebum Secretion and to the Mechanisms of Acne Vulgaris." *Journal of Laboratory and Clinical Medicine* 41 (1953):11–28.

59. Rahe, R. H., and T. H. Holmes. "Social, Psychologic, and Psychophysiologic Aspects of Inguinal Hernia." *Journal of Psychosomatic Research* 8 (1965):487–91.

60. Stern, J. A., G. Winokur, D. T. Graham, and F. K. Graham. "Alterations in Physiological Measures during Experimentally Induced Attitudes." *Journal of Psychosomatic Research* 5 (1961):73–82.

61. Stevenson, I. P., and C. H. Duncan. "Alterations in Cardiac Function and Circulatory Efficiency during Periods of Life Stress as Shown by Changes in the Rate, Rhythm, Electrocardiographic Pattern and Output of the Heart in Those with Cardiovascular Disease." In *Life Stress and Bodily Disease*, edited by H. G. Wolff, S. Wolf, and C. C. Hare, pp. 799–817. Research Publications of the Association for Research in Nervous and Mental Disease, vol. 29. Baltimore: Williams and Wilkins, 1950.

62. Stevenson, I. P., C. H. Duncan, S. Wolf, H. S. Ripley, and H. G. Wolff. "Life Situations, Emotions, and Extrasystoles." *Psychosomatic Medicine* 11 (1949):257–72.

63. Wolf, S. *The Stomach.* New York: Oxford University Press, 1965.

64. Wolf, S., P. V. Cardon, E. M. Shepard, and H. G. Wolff. *Life Stress and Essential Hypertension.* Baltimore: Williams and Wilkins, 1955.

65. Wolf, S., and H. G. Wolff. *Human Gastric Function*. New York: Oxford University Press, 1963.

66. Wolff, H. G. *Headache and Other Head Pain*. 2nd ed. New York: Oxford University Press, 1963.

67. Wolff, H. G., S. Wolf, and C. C. Hare, eds. *Life Stress and Bodily Disease*. Research Publications of the Association for Research in Nervous and Mental Disease, vol. 29. Baltimore: Williams and Wilkins, 1950.

16

Magnitude of Life Events and Seriousness of Illness

Allen R. Wyler, Minoru Masuda, and Thomas H. Holmes

The positive relationship between the occurrence of life events and onset of illness has been shown during the last two decades [1–13]. Readjustments to psychosocial events were quantified by the development of the Social Readjustment Rating Scale (SRRS) [14], and the Schedule of Recent Experience (SRE) [9] was developed to record the chronology of events. Further, Rahe et al. [15] showed that illness clusters appeared after increases in one's basal life change level. They also found an association between the amount of life change and the seriousness of one's illness. This relationship was uncovered with the use of a seriousness of illness scale that had been formulated in 1960 by Hinkle [16]. Hinkle's ordinal scale placed illnesses into five groups, each group of illnesses being determined by the degree of probability that a given disease or its sequelae, if untreated, would lead to death. In the Rahe study, Hinkle's illness groups had been combined into groups of minor and major illnesses. These data indicated that major illnesses were preceded by a greater magnitude of life changes than were minor illnesses.

Since Hinkle's study, a Seriousness of Illness Rating Scale (SIRS) has been developed by Wyler [17;18] and applied cross-culturally by Celdrán [19] and McMahon [20] to Spanish and Irish populations, respectively. It is the purpose of this study to use the SIRS and the SRE in an attempt to examine the relationship between the amount of life change prior to the onset of illness and the seriousness of that illness.

This chapter is reprinted from "Magnitude of Life Events and Seriousness of Illness," by Allen R. Wyler, Minoru Masuda, and Thomas H. Holmes. *Psychosomatic Medicine* 33 (1971):115–22. Copyright 1971 by the American Psychosomatic Society, Inc. Reprinted by permission of Elsevier Science Publishing Co., Inc.

METHODS

The Schedule of Recent Experience is a self-administered questionnaire. In addition to general biographic information, the items question the respondent about 42 life change situations during time periods of six months, one year, and two years prior to answering the questionnaire. Each life change situation has assigned to it a numerical score previously determined by Holmes and Rahe on the SRRS [14]. In scoring the SRE, the magnitude of each item was multiplied by the number of occurrences of that item within each time period.

Seriousness of illness was based on the Seriousness of Illness Rating Scale. The latter is a list of 126 illnesses, with each illness having a previously determined magnitude [17]. The magnitude attached to each item is an average of subjective estimations. The validity of the use of such a rating scale and the derivation of this method have been investigated by Masuda and Holmes [21], and by Stevens [22]. In this study, the primary disease responsible for the patient's admission to the hospital or clinic was chosen. Complications and/or secondary diagnoses were excluded.

The patients were obtained from the inpatient services of medicine, surgery, and psychiatry at the University of Washington Hospital; of medicine at the Veterans Administration Hospital; and of gynecology at Harborview Medical Center; and from the outpatient dermatology clinic at the University Hospital. The patients were chosen in a two-month period between June 15 and August 15, 1967. The patient selection was one of convenience, based on three requirements: (1) the patient's admitting diagnosis had to be one of the 126 disease items contained in the Seriousness of Illness Rating Scale; (2) the patient's illness had to be of recent onset or a recent exacerbation of a chronic illness; and (3) the resident physician of the service had to be certain that the patient was capable of filling out the questionnaire. The intent of the selection was to obtain a broad range of illnesses. Except for the dermatology patients ($N = 14$) who filled out the questionnaire during clinic hours, the questionnaire was left with the patient and collected at a later time.

RESULTS

A total of 232 questionnaires were obtained. Ten patients were from Harborview Medical Center; the others from University Hospital ($N = 212$) and the Veterans Administration Hospital ($N = 10$). The characteristics of the sample are shown in Table 16.1. The total sample was not biased as to sex, but the majority of the respondents were married. The age range was 18–69 years, with an average age of 41 years. The table indicates that the young and the aged were not well represented in the selection. Except for the Harborview Medical Center sample which was 90 percent Negro, all respondents were Caucasian. Most respondents had a high school education or greater, were third-generation American, and were Protestants.

Table 16.1
Characteristics of Patient Sample

Patient data	No. of patients
Age (yr)	
Less than 21	13
21–34	91
35–65	126
Greater than 65	2
Sex	
Male	131
Female	101
Religion	
Roman Catholic	37
Protestant	100
Other	95
Race	
Caucasian	223
Negro	9
Marital status	
Married	158
Single	30
Divorced	44
Years of education	
Less than 12	37
12 to 16	195
Generation American	
First	16
Second	58
Third	158
Total	232

The respondents displayed 42 different disease items. The disease and its seriousness magnitude and the number of patients represented by each item are listed in Table 16.2. The mean seriousness of illness score in this sample was 475; the mean of all disease items listed on the SIRS is 370 [17]. It is apparent that the patients in this study had disease scores that were skewed toward the upper half of the illness scale, reflecting illnesses requiring hospitalization.

The patients' mean cumulative scores on the SRE for the three time periods of six months, one year, and two years prior to admission are also shown in Table 16.2. They are 206, 386, and 585, respectively.

Spearman's rank order correlation coefficient (rho) [23] compared the indi-

Table 16.2
Illness Frequencies and Periodic SRE* Scores

Illness	No. of. patients†	SIRS‡ value	Mean SRE Scores		
			6 months	1 year	2 years
Dandruff	1	21	0	13	26
Headache	5	88	68	120	209
Acne	6	103	150	220	311
Fainting	1	155	75	143	206
Varicose veins	8	173	78	116	130
Psoriasis	6	174	115	237	317
Eczema	7	204	52	152	231
Bronchitis	8	210	215	311	322
Shingles	1	212	53	102	177
Mononucleosis	3	216	209	257	296
Hernia	9	244	208	367	457
Abortion	4	284	214	468	688
Gonorrhea	6	296	312	478	923
Irregular heart beats	9	302	235	321	411
Anemia	7	312	109	187	325
Anxiety reaction	4	315	287	310	482
Gout	2	322	105	215	336
Appendicitis	3	337	281	299	382
Pneumonia	4	338	107	218	456
Depression	9	344	362	560	833
Kidney infection	5	374	153	230	259
Hyperthyroid	2	393	417	673	816
Asthma	4	413	121	391	506
Gallstones	6	454	216	363	563
Arthritis	6	468	172	242	312
Hepatitis	1	488	69	82	95
Peptic ulcer	17	500	212	386	603
Pancreatitis	2	514	303	582	940
High blood pressure	4	520	170	286	405
Chest pain	7	609	205	321	638
Diabetes	6	621	320	500	599
Emphysema	7	636	103	240	357
Tuberculosis	1	645	295	325	475
Alcoholism	3	688	430	562	688
Cirrhosis	6	733	148	287	443
Manic depressive psychosis	4	766	381	566	753
Stroke	1	774	321	375	409
Schizophrenia	12	776	264	442	609
Heart failure	9	824	144	480	772
Heart attack	10	855	168	297	448
Meningitis	1	872	175	200	350
Cancer	15	1,020	305	461	777
Means		475	206	386	585

* SRE, Schedule of Recent Experience
† Total number, 232
‡ SIRS, Seriousness of Illness Rating Scale

viduals' three time-period SRE scores with the magnitudes of seriousness of illness. Rho for the six-month, one-year, and two-year periods was 0.302, 0.321, and 0.356, respectively. These were highly significant ($p \leq 0.005$).

For the three time periods of six months, one year, and two years prior to admission, correlation was highest with respect to the two-year period. Possibly the strength of the two-year period correlation over the other shorter time epochs may be due to the uncertainties that lie in determination of the time of actual onset of illness. From scanning the illness items included in the study (Table 16.2), it is apparent that there are many chronic and recurring illnesses that may fit the description of uncertainty of actual onset of illness.

The variable of uncertainty of onset of illness was investigated further. Six judges made independent classifications of the 42 illnesses encountered in the study into those with *chronic, ill-defined onset* and those with *acute, relatively well defined onset.* Absolute concurrence (six out of six) was found for 11 chronic and seven acute illnesses. With slightly less reliability (five out of six), there were 17 illnesses judged to be chronic and 11 judged to be acute. The chronic illnesses were dandruff, varicose veins, psoriasis, eczema, anemia, hyperthyroidism, gallstones, arthritis, peptic ulcer, high blood pressure, diabetes, emphysema, alcoholism, cirrhosis, schizophrenia, heart failure, and cancer. The acute illnesses were mononucleosis, abortion, gonorrhea, appendicitis, pneumonia, kidney infection, hepatitis, chest pain, stroke, heart attack, and meningitis. There were 122 patients with chronic illnesses and 45 with acute illnesses; 65 patients distributed among 14 illnesses were judged to be neither acute nor chronic (termed *others*).

Spearman's rank order correlation coefficients on the association of the seriousness of the illness to the magnitude of periodic life event accumulations in these classified groups are shown in Table 16.3. The data show that the positive relationship between the amount of life change and the seriousness of the illness

Table 16.3
Seriousness of Illness and Life Events (Spearman's correlation coefficients)

SRE scores	Chronic ($N = 122$)	Acute ($N = 45$)	Others ($N = 65$)	All nonacute ($N = 187$)
6 months	0.542*	−0.273	0.710†	0.648‡
1 year	0.681†	−0.318	0.776†	0.699‡
2 years	0.728‡	−0.191	0.822‡	0.729‡

* $p = 0.05$ (two-tailed)
† $p = 0.01$ (two-tailed)
‡ $p = 0.001$ (two-tailed)

demonstrated previously is separable into a highly significant association with chronic illness and a negative (but insignificant) correlation with acute illness.

Comparison of the ten infectious diseases with the 32 noninfectious diseases revealed similar correlations. Since seven of the ten infectious diseases were also previously labeled *acute*, it is apparent that the judgment that goes into acuteness of illness is influenced by the infectious nature of the disease. The three infectious nonacute illnesses were bronchitis, shingles, and tuberculosis.

Another reason for the strength of the correlation of the two-year period over the other two time periods indicated in Table 16.3 may relate to the saliency and recall of the items. The factors of item saliency, consistency of recall, and recall validity have recently been studied by Casey et al. [24] who used the SRE. In order to determine to what degree saliency affected the correlation, the present data were further analyzed by relating each time period of life change to illness magnitude separately, rather than cumulatively. Rho for the second six-month period prior to admission was 0.139, and the rho for the second year prior to admission was 0.230. The decrease in the magnitude of these coefficients by these statistical maneuvers would indicate that recall of apparently more salient items is not an important variable.

Inspection of the data revealed a group of patients representing two relatively less serious diseases, but having high SRE scores. The group consisted of ten patients from Harborview Medical Center. Of these, nine were Negro and one was Caucasian. All ten were of a lower socioeconomic class than were the patients from University Hospital and the Veterans Administration Hospital. The Harborview Medical Center patients had a seriousness of illness mean score of 292. The remainder of the sample had a seriousness of illness mean score of 475. For the three time periods, beginning with the six-month period, the Harborview Medical Center patients had a mean SRE total of 210, 376, and 575, respectively. Thus, they had higher mean life-change scores in the face of a lower seriousness of illness score. These high SRE scores were found to be due to an increased number of life changes within the six-month period, rather than to a small number of serious life changes. With the removal of this minority group, Spearman's coefficient of correlation was increased to 0.378, 0.415, and 0.480 for the six-month, one-year, and two-year periods, respectively.

It may well hold true that the more homogeneous the sample becomes with respect to socioeconomic class, the stronger the relationship between seriousness of illness and quantity of life change. In a recent study by Komaroff et al. [25], it was shown that the different ethnic groups evaluated the magnitude of life change events significantly differently. It is possible that different ethnic and/or socioeconomic groups have different basal levels of life change. Moreover, in the development of the SIRS, it had not been determined whether different ethnic groups might show differences in their assessment of seriousness of illness. This group of patients may view their illnesses as being more serious than would the group that determined the SIRS values.

DISCUSSION

The thrust of research in this and other laboratories [1–16] has documented the relationship of life change magnitude and disease onset. These life events assume etiologic significance by evoking attempts at adaptation that are often accompanied by psychophysiologic reactions. These alterations in bodily function may lead, in turn, to dysfunction, tissue damage, and discomfort. In addition, such psychophysiologic changes may render the body vulnerable to a variety of noxious or pathogenic environmental agents [26–41] and thus allow the emergence of disease that might otherwise have been resisted.

This research on a diseased population suggests—in addition—that, the greater the life change or adaptive requirement, the greater the disruption of bodily function, the greater the vulnerability or lowering of resistance to disease, and the more serious the disease that does develop. The concept of a variable threshold of resistance and the necessity of having a special pathogen present may help account for differences observed in the acute-infectious diseases.

Thus, the concept of life change appears to have relevance to the areas of causation of disease, time of onset of disease, and severity of disease. Despite the fact that life change magnitude is related to seriousness of illness and that *seriousness* of illness establishes a continuum along which individual diseases are distributed, the life change concept does not contribute much to an understanding of specificity of disease type.

SUMMARY

A study investigating the relationship between the quantity of life change that patients have undergone during the two years before the onset of their illness, and the seriousness of that illness, is described in this report. The sample represented 42 disease items and 232 patients. Thirty-six percent of the life change for the two-year period was found during the six-month period prior to onset of the illness. A significant positive relationship of life events to illness magnitude was found. For the three time periods of six months, one year, and two years prior to illness onset, the correlation was 0.302, 0.321, and 0.356, respectively. When the diseases were separated into acute and chronic categories, only the latter showed a highly significant positive correlation ($r_s = \geq 0.648$) in all time periods, while the former, contrastingly, did not. Two other variables that might affect the relationship of illness to life events were investigated. Ethnic and/or socioeconomic class raised the correlation, while saliency of life events of the patients was not relevant.

REFERENCES

1. Graham, D. T., and I. Stevenson, "Disease as Response to Life Stress." In *The Psychological Basis of Medical Practice*, edited by H. I. Lief, V. F. Lief, and N. R. Lief, pp. 115–36. New York: Harper and Row, 1963.

2. Greene, W. A., Jr. "Psychological Factors and Reticulo-endothelial Disease I. Preliminary Observations on a Group of Males with Lymphomas and Leukemias." *Psychosomatic Medicine* 16 (1954):220–30.

3. Greene, W. A., L. E. Young, and S. N. Swisher. "Psychological Factors and Reticulo-endothelial Disease. II. Observations on a Group of Women with Lymphomas and Leukemias." *Psychosomatic Medicine* 18 (1956):284–303.

4. Greene, W. A., and G. Miller. "Psychological Factors and Reticulo-endothelial Disease. IV. Observations on a Group of Children and Adolescents with Leukemia: An Interpretation of Disease Development in Terms of the Mother–Child Unit." *Psychosomatic Medicine* 20 (1958)124–44.

5. Weiss, E., B. Dlin, H. R. Rollin, H. K. Fischer, and C. R. Bepler. "Emotional Factors in Coronary Occlusion." *Archives of Internal Medicine* 99 (1957):628–41.

6. Fischer, H. K., B. Dlin, W. Winters, S. Hagner, and E. Weiss. "Time Patterns and Emotional Factors Related to the Onset of Coronary Occlusion." Abstract. *Psychosomatic Medicine* 24 (1962):516.

7. Kissen, D. M. "Specific Psychological Factors in Pulmonary Tuberculosis." *Health Bulletin* (Edinburgh) 14 (1956):44–46.

8. Kissen, D. M. "Some Psychosocial Aspects of Pulmonary Tuberculosis." *International Journal of Social Psychiatry* 3 (1958):252–59.

9. Hawkins, N. G., R. Davies, and T. H. Holmes. "Evidence of Psychosocial Factors in the Development of Pulmonary Tuberculosis." *American Review of Tuberculosis and Pulmonary Diseases* 75 (1957):768–80. Reprinted in this volume, Chapter 11.

10. Smith, M. "Psychogenic Factors in Skin Disease." Medical thesis, University of Washington, 1962.

11. Rahe, R. H., and T. H. Holmes. "Social, Psychologic and Psychophysiologic Aspects of Inguinal Hernia." *Journal of Psychosomatic Research* 8 (1965):487–91.

12. Kjaer, G. "Some Psychosomatic Aspects of Pregnancy with Particular Reference to Nausea and Vomiting." Medical thesis, University of Washington, 1959.

13. Rahe, R. H. "Life Crisis and Health Change." In *Psychotropic Drug Response: Advances in Prediction*, edited by P. R. A. May and J. R. Wittenborn, pp. 92–125. Springfield, Ill.: Charles C Thomas, 1969. Pts. 2 and 3 reprinted in this volume, Chapters 13 and 14.

14. Holmes, T. H., and R. H. Rahe. "The Social Readjustment Rating Scale." *Journal of Psychosomatic Research* 11 (1967):213–18. Reprinted in this volume, Chapter 2.

15. Rahe, R. H., J. D. McKean, and R. J. Arthur. "A Longitudinal Study of Life-Change and Illness Patterns." *Journal of Psychosomatic Research* 10 (1967):355–66.

16. Hinkle, L. E., Jr., R. Redmont, N. Plummer, and H. G. Wolff. "An Examination of the Relation between Symptoms, Disability, and Serious Illness, in Two Homogeneous Groups of Men and Women." *American Journal of Public Health* 50 (1960):1327–36.

17. Wyler, A. R., M. Masuda, and T. H. Holmes. "Seriousness of Illness Rating Scale." *Journal of Psychosomatic Research* 11 (1968):363–74. Reprinted in this volume, Chapter 8.

18. Wyler, A. R., M. Masuda, and T. H. Holmes. "The Seriousness of Illness Rating Scale: Reproducibility." *Journal of Psychosomatic Research* 14 (1970):59–64.

19. Celdrán, H. H. "The Cross-cultural Consistency of Two Social Consensus Scales: The Seriousness of Illness Rating Scale and the Social Readjustment Rating Scale in Spain." Medical thesis, University of Washington, 1970.

20. McMahon, B. J. "Seriousness of Illness Rating Scale: A Comparative Study of Irish and Americans." Medical thesis, University of Washington, 1971.

21. Masuda, M., and T. H. Holmes. "Magnitude Estimations of Social Readjustments." *Journal of Psychosomatic Research* 11 (1967):219–25. Reprinted in this volume, Chapter 3.

22. Stevens, S. S. "A Metric for the Social Consensus." *Science* 151 (1966):530–41.

23. Siegel, S. *Nonparametric Statistics for the Behavioral Sciences.* New York: McGraw-Hill, 1956.

24. Casey, R. L., M. Masuda, and T. H. Holmes. "Quantitative Study of Recall of Life Events." *Journal of Psychosomatic Research* 11 (1967):239–47. Reprinted in this volume, Chapter 10.

25. Komaroff, A. L., M. Masuda, and T. H. Holmes. "The Social Readjustment Rating Scale: A Comparative Study of Negro, Mexican, and White Americans." *Journal of Psychosomatic Research* 12 (1968):121–28. Reprinted in this volume, Chapter 6.

26. Holmes, T. H., N. G. Hawkins, C. E. Bowerman, E. R. Clarke, and J. R. Joffe. "Psychosocial and Psychophysiologic Studies of Tuberculosis." *Psychosomatic Medicine* 19 (1957):134–43.

27. Dudley, D. L., in collaboration with C. J. Martin, M. Masuda, H. S. Ripley, and T. H. Holmes. *The Psychophysiology of Respiration in Health and Disease.* New York: Appleton-Century-Croft, 1969.

28. Holmes, T. H., H. Goodell, S. Wolf, and H. G. Wolff. *The Nose: An Experimental Study of Reactions within the Nose in Human Subjects during Varying Life Experiences.* Springfield, Ill.: Charles C Thomas, 1950.

29. Holmes, T. H., T. Treuting, and H. G. Wolff. "Life Situations, Emotions and Nasal Disease: Evidence on Summative Effects Exhibited in Patients with 'Hay Fever.'" *Psychosomatic Medicine* 13 (1951):71–82.

30. Holmes, T. H., and H. G. Wolff. "Life Situations, Emotions and Backache." *Psychosomatic Medicine* 14 (1952):18–33.

31. Dorpat, T. L., and T. H. Holmes. "Mechanism of Skeletal Muscle Pain and Fatigue." *Archives of Neurology and Psychiatry* 74 (1955):628–40.

32. Grace, W. J., and D. T. Graham. "Relationship of Specific Attitudes and Emotions to Certain Bodily Diseases." *Psychosomatic Medicine* 14 (1952):243–51.

33. Mittelmann, B., and H. G. Wolff. "Affective States and Skin Temperature: Experimental Study of Subjects with 'Cold Hands' and Raynaud's Syndrome." *Psychosomatic Medicine* 1 (1939):271–92.

34. Mittelmann, B., and H. G. Wolff. "Emotion and Skin Temperature: Observations on Patients during Psychotherapeutic (Psychoanalytic) Interviews." *Psychosomatic Medicine* 5 (1943):211–31.

35. Graham, D. T. "The Pathogenesis of Hives: Experimental Study of Life Situations, Emotions and Cutaneous Vascular Reactions." In *Life Stress and Bodily Disease*, edited by H. G. Wolff, S. Wolf, and C. C. Hare, pp. 987–1009. Research Publications of the Association for Research in Nervous and Mental Disease, vol. 29. Baltimore: Williams and Wilkins, 1950.

36. Graham, D. T., and S. Wolf. "The Relation of Eczema to Attitude and to Vascular Reactions of the Human Skin." *Journal of Laboratory and Clinical Medicine* 42 (1953):238–54.

37. Graham, D. T. "Cutaneous Vascular Reactions in Raynaud's Disease and in States of Hostility, Anxiety, and Depression." *Psychosomatic Medicine* 17 (1955):200–207.

38. Mittelmann, B., and H. G. Wolff. "Emotions and Gastroduodenal Function." *Psychosomatic Medicine* 4 (1942):5–61.

39. Grace, W. J., S. Wolf, and H. G. Wolff. *The Human Colon.* New York: Paul B. Hoeber, 1951.

40. Wolf, S. *The Stomach.* New York: Oxford University Press, 1965.

41. Engel, G. L., F. Reichsman, and H. L. Segal. "A Study of an Infant with a Gastric Fistula." *Psychosomatic Medicine* 18 (1956):374–98.

Introduction

Expanding the Realm of Applications: Studies of the Natural History of Disease and Studies of Life-style and Performance

The studies in the previous section established a paradigm for the relationship of life change to time of disease onset and seriousness of illness. The studies in this section take that paradigm for granted, and go on to ask new questions. What can the concept of life change tell us about the course of acute and chronic diseases? Can life change predict performance and adjustment as well as health change? What can life change studies tell us about life-style and behavior? Can life change predict outcome as well as onset of illness?

Chapter 17 is a case study of diabetes. This case is of particular interest because the transient nature of the disease so beautifully illustrates the life change and illness paradigm demonstrated in group studies of illness onset. The disease first appeared in a setting of high life change, then slackened and eventually disappeared completely as the subject settled into a new life and routine and as his life change score decreased to a point below crisis level. This is an "all-purpose" life change study, combining as it does the qualitative description of an individual experiencing life crisis with the quantitative definition made possible by the Schedule of Recent Experience and the Social Readjustment Rating Scale.

In contrast to the acute disease process in Chapter 17, Chapter 18 focuses on chronic disease. Here we studied the relation of life change and psychosocial assets to the course of chronic intrinsic asthma. The Berle Index, which we used as our index of coping ability, is a nearly perfect instrument for use in studies of chronic disease. When we combined our measure of life change with the Berle measure of coping ability, we were able to predict which patients would require lower dosages of medication to deal with their disease.

Let me note three other life change studies conducted in the clinic that are of special interest. We established earlier (see Chapter 12) that the onset of pregnancy occurs in the setting of increased life change. In "Pregnancy and Life

Change," a study conducted a decade later with Cindy Cook Williams et al. *(Journal of Psychosomatic Research* 19 [1975]:123–29), we asked what effect life change magnitude has on the course of pregnancy. We found that, while life change does not appear to predict duration of pregnancy, it does show an association to diseases and complications experienced *during* pregnancy.

We shifted our attention even further along the course of disease in "Life Change and the Postoperative Course of Duodenal Ulcer Patients," a study with David K. Stevenson et al. *(Journal of Human Stress* 5, no. 1 [March 1979]: 19–28). The question asked in that study was "Does presurgery life change predict the course of recovery from surgery?" As we followed the patients over time, we found that those with high life change experienced the highest levels of signs and symptoms during the course of their recovery.

And in "Parental Adjustment to Childhood Leukemia" by Brenda D. Townes et al. *(Journal of Psychosomatic Research* 18 [1974]:9–14), we studied not the patient, but the patient's family. Using life change measurements we described, first, the setting in which a family receives the diagnosis of leukemia in its child and, second, the differences in the process of parental mourning as mother and father anticipate—and then respond to—the death of their child.

With Chapter 19 we make a dramatic change of scene, moving outside the clinic and hospital to study the occurrence of athletic injuries on the football field. This was our second try at predicting football injuries. In an earlier study ("Psychologic Screening," in *Football Injuries: Papers Presented at a Workshop* [Washington, D.C.: National Academy of Sciences, 1970], pp. 211–14), we had used the Schedule of Recent Experience and Social Readjustment Rating Scale developed for use with the general population. Here we experimented with a group-specific life events inventory and with group-specific life event ratings. The results were impressive: We significantly improved our ability to predict injuries.

The population under study in Chapter 20 is surely one of the most surprising in this collection: prisoners in federal and state penal institutions. In this study of life-styles, coping styles, and overt behaviors, the index event is incarceration in prison. Our findings, though necessarily tentative, remain tantalizing. It would appear that (at least for unsuccessful criminals) the pattern of committing a crime, getting caught, and being put in prison resembles the signs and symptoms of an illness. Incarceration in prison—like the onset of illness—occurs in the setting of escalating life change.

Both Chapters 21 and 22 are summary statements, bringing together a wealth of accumulated evidence for the purpose of consolidating and evaluating the state of our knowledge. Chapter 21 makes use of data from 19 studies conducted in the Holmes laboratory using the Schedule of Recent Experience and the Social Readjustment Rating Questionnaire. Published a full decade after the original Social Readjustment Rating Scale paper was published and a full two decades after the original Schedule of Recent Experience study was published, Chapter

21 reviews and takes into account the developments in life event methodology in the intervening years.

Chapter 22 is a different kind of summary and serves as a fitting close to this collection of research reports. Death is the health change under study—a new focus, but this chapter unites the two approaches with which we began our research. Chapter 22 asks, first, what accounts for the time of onset of death and, next, what are the psychophysiologic mechanisms by which death is achieved?

17

Transient Diabetes Mellitus Associated with Culture Change

Kang-E Michael Hong and Thomas H. Holmes

Since Thomas Willis in 1684 [1] stated that diabetes mellitus was caused by "prolonged sorrow," there has been much conflicting data concerning psychological factors as a possible etiology of diabetes [2–8].

Hinkle and Wolf in 1950 [9] carried out a monumental work on the psychophysiology of diabetes and generated a hypothesis that diabetes mellitus is a disorder of adaptation. However, the controversy still exists. Palmer [10] refused to accept any validity of a relation between onset of diabetes mellitus and psychological factors. After reviewing the literature, Treuting [11] felt that the possibility exists that emotional factors may be important in the onset of diabetes. Slawson et al. [12] found that 20 of 25 new diabetic adults gave a history of object loss preceding the onset of diabetes. In his review of the history of the etiology of diabetes mellitus, Levine [13] has made no single comment on emotional factors and stated that the present search for a unified primary etiology of diabetes is characterized by great uncertainty. Most recently, Kimball [14], in his discussion of emotional and psychosocial aspects of diabetes, concluded that both onset and exacerbation of the disease are frequently related to events in the broader psychosocial environment.

This chapter presents a case study of a diabetic subject who developed the disease when he faced cultural changes due to migration. The diabetic symptoms disappeared within three years when the patient adapted to the new culture.

History and data will be analyzed in detail, and the dynamics of the onset and the process of the disease will be discussed.

This chapter is reprinted with permission from *Archives of General Psychiatry* 29 (November 1973):683–87, under the title "A Case Study of Transient Diabetes Mellitus Associated with Culture Change." Copyright 1973. American Medical Association.

CASE HISTORY

This is the case of a 31-year-old married male Korean physician who, at the time of the study, had been in the United States for the previous four years for his medical clinical training. Apparently he was in his usual state of health until the latter part of June 1968 when, as a result of a urine test requested by the U.S. embassy just prior to his coming to this country, it was noted that he had a trace of glycosuria. Since only one of three urinalyses showed it, the patient did nothing about this. In the second month of his internship, two months after his arrival in the United States, he noticed that he tired easily and became drowsy and uncomfortable one or two hours after a heavy meal. The patient described two different kinds of discomfort experienced after meals: The one was a general, vague body discomfort, which appeared usually within 30–60 minutes after a meal and consisted of fatigue, haziness, sleepiness, and inability to concentrate especially during conferences. The other type of discomfort occurred occasionally and consisted of anxiousness and jitteriness and shakiness of body. The patient also noticed polyphagia, polydipsia, and weight loss. Subsequently he recalled the findings of the urinalysis just prior to his departure for the United States, checked his urine, and noted intermittent glycosuria.

He had two fastings and two 2-hour postprandial blood sugar tests done. The former were normal, and the latter were 96 mg/100 ml and 162 mg/100 ml. Thereafter, a three-hour glucose tolerance test (GTT) was done without any preparation with a carbohydrate diet. The results were as follows: fasting, normal; one-half hour, 280 mg/100 ml; one hour, 350 mg/100 ml; two hours, 56 mg/100 ml; and three hours, 60 mg/100 ml. At this time the patient went to his physician, who ordered a repeat GTT with a good preparation involving a 300-gm carbohydrate diet of three days' duration. Serum insulin was also measured at the same time. The results were as follows:

Time, hr	Blood Sugar, mg/ml	Insulin, µU/ml
Fasting	82	23
1/2	202	435
1	144	365
2	104	142
3	74	37
4	66	18
5	86	24

Since his serum insulin values at one-half hour, one hour, and two hours were extraordinarily high, a tolbutamide tolerance test was done to rule out insulinoma; this was normal. Blood count and an electrocardiogram were within normal limits. Blood chemistry showed: protein-bound iodine, 5.0 mg/100 ml; cholesterol, 290 mg/100 ml; and total lipids, 617 mg/100 ml.

There was no family history of diabetes or any other significant major illness on either his paternal or maternal side. The patient had an appendectomy four months prior to migration; and when under stress, he tended to have diarrhea.

The patient's physician put him on tolbutamide (Orinase), 500 mg twice a day, and a 2,800-calorie diabetic diet. One year later the tolbutamide dosage was reduced to one 500-mg tablet per day. The patient's symptoms gradually improved toward the end of his internship, and urine sugar tests were observed to be intermittently 2+ or 3+ as compared to the previously consistent 4+. However, the symptoms and glycosuria flared up when he moved to another city in July 1969 to start his residency training. The symptoms were milder than the ones at the onset and consisted of fatigue, somnolence, and thirst. These symptoms improved gradually, although he noted consistent postprandial glycosuria. He was ordered to discontinue taking tolbutamide in September 1970, at which time another GTT showed no significant changes. After that, he rarely noticed any symptoms although the glycosuria continued; and, to the patient's surprise, glycosuria stopped in March 1971, approaching almost the end of the third year of his stay in the United States.

Personal Background History

The patient was born in a city of South Korea and was the middle of three siblings. The patient's family was described as being very close and intimate. His father was a 61-year-old retired government officer who was quiet, reserved, and even tempered, and rarely expressed his emotions. His mother was described as being "smothering, overdevoted, overindulgent, and extremely bright." The patient stated that, whenever people talk about a "Jewish mother," he cannot help being reminded of his mother. Being the only son in the family, he was favored by both parents, as is common in Korean families. His mother frequently reminded the patient of her ceaseless affection and her self-sacrificing devotion to her only son, who used to resent these overt expressions of her affection. This resentment was more pronounced during his college years. The patient reported that much later in his life he learned that his mother had been married once before her present marriage and had left her previous husband as well as her son from that marriage. As far as the patient knew, she had never attempted to see her other son. The patient wondered whether this was the reason that she devoted herself so much to her children, particularly to him.

Up to the time he came to this country, the patient had never been separated from his family except for a brief time during military service at age 24. However, he visited the family every single weekend during this period. After having finished medical school, he joined the Korean Air Force and served as a medical officer for three years until he decided to come to the United States for further medical training.

Apparently his departure was very traumatic for his mother, and the patient felt that his mother had become quite depressed and her health had deteriorated since his departure. She still sent letters every so often reading, "Dear my only son: I cried and cried last night to miss you and I am afraid that I am going to die without seeing you again," and expressing her loneliness and depression, and the meaningless of her life because of her son's absence.

The patient described himself as being rather self-sufficient, independent, and confident, and stated that he had been very successful academically, and had gone through medical school on a scholarship. He also stated that he was indecisive quite often, sensitive to others' criticism, and "weak to affection."

Reactions to Migration

When he was planning to come to this country for his postgraduate medical training, the patient was full of ambition to become a great scholar and come back to his country to devote himself to his people, and he felt little anxiety. On his arrival in the United States in July 1968, the patient found himself plunged into a vastly different cultural milieu, in addition to the demanding work of his internship. He found himself experiencing the most extreme, constant high tension and pressure due to feelings of alienation and isolation, an inability to communicate, and injured pride from not being as competent an intern as he expected himself to be. He felt frustrated and lost. The patient stated that the most painful thing was that he could not understand what people said to him, although he heard them clearly, and he had to respond to people in a global, intuitive, and primitive way based on his own presumptions. "I felt as if I had to pick up new words and nonverbal communication cues one by one and had to learn behavioral patterns one by one as an infant does in his first few years of life." The patient stated that he felt he behaved in a half-awake and half-dreamlike state in which everything was distant and like seeing a slow silent movie. In fact, when he went to the auto license department to take the license examination the clerk asked him whether he was dreaming. He stated that it was most frustrating for him not to be able to respond appropriately and immediately to the situation even though he saw the circumstance clearly in front of his eyes. "I felt I could not reason and I could not think logically. I felt my brain did not function properly. It was as though my brain received the information but didn't know what to do with it and had forgotten which set of brain cells it should trigger to analyze the information." He also felt discouraged and isolated quite often and described frequent bouts of anxiety, feelings of insecurity, and feelings of helplessness

During these first few months of great frustration and tension, the patient experienced changes in sleeping pattern, total lack of sexual desire, and the full-blown diabetic symptoms described previously.

The amount of feeling of tension and pressure was gradually reduced over the year of his internship, and he invited his fiancée from Korea to get married in January 1969. He was also reassured by his advisor and medical director that he was doing an adequate job as an intern. However, when he started a new adventure for his residency in another city, the above-described sensations and feelings reappeared while he was under great pressure for the first six months of his residency. In the following two years, he began to adjust gradually but steadily to his new environment until he finally regained his "old self," his humor, and his old spirit. It took three years before be could think logically and reason effectively at a competent level, and not have to translate English into Korean and Korean into English. Now he could think in English and dream in English as well as in Korean. This was the time when he felt that he had become well adapted to this culture and he started to feel at ease in any social setting. The patient indicated that this was also the time when his diabetic symptoms all disappeared.

COMMENT

Migration as a Major Life Change

One can speculate that an individual would experience tremendous physical, psychological, and sociocultural changes when migrating to a totally different culture. As far as individual experiences are concerned, little can be added to this patient's vivid description of the tension and frustration that he went through. Instead, it was decided to measure the magnitude of life change that this patient experienced during this period as well as two years before and three years after the onset of the disease. The magnitude of life change every six months was measured by using the Schedule of Recent Experience (SRE) developed by Holmes and Rahe [15]. The results are shown in Figure 17.1, part C. The patient had 624 life change units (LCU) in the year when he moved to the United States and 440 LCU in the one-year period prior to the onset of diabetes mellitus. These scores were among the highest LCU that we have ever observed in our studies.

Rahe [16] defined a life crisis as any clustering of life change events whose individual values summed to 150 LCU or more in one year, and divided into mild (150–199 LCU), moderate (200–299 LCU), and major (300 or more LCU) life crises. Rahe found that these life crises were associated with health changes by 37 percent, 51 percent, and 79 percent, respectively. In Holmes's prospective study [17], 86 percent of the subjects with high life-change scores experienced major health changes within two years. These significant associations were confirmed by many investigators in both retrospective and prospective studies [18–20]. Further studies revealed that there was a highly significant correlation between the seriousness of illness and the magnitude of life change events [21]. These data suggest that, the greater the life change or adaptive requirement, the greater the vulnerability or lowered resistance to disease and the more serious the disease that does develop.

It is a well-known speculation that a change in living environment from one culture to another results in discord between a person's past experiences and the requirements of the new environment, and this sociocultural discontinuity may contribute to physical and behavior disorders [22]. Hinkle et al., in their studies of almost 3,000 people including Chinese immigrants [23] and Hungarian refugees [24], stated that illnesses appeared in a cluster and that this cluster of illness most often occurred in periods significantly stressful for the person striving to adapt to total environmental changes. Abramson's study of 7,109 adults in Jerusalem [25] found that foreign-born persons had higher Cornell Medical Index scores than the native-born Israelis and that emotional disorders were associated with social status, status inconsistency, and migration.

Several reports have been made about what kind of experiences an individual goes through when placed in a totally different culture. Oberg [26] identified the stress due to this cultural change as "cultural shock" and characterized the stress as fear, anxiety, a feeling of helplessness, longing to go back home, and feelings of frustration. Gullahorn and Gullahorn [27] reported the initial elation and optimism followed by confusion, depression, and negative attitude toward the host culture when the sojourners encounter frustrations. Spradley and Phillips [28], in their study of a Peace Corps volunteer and a Chinese foreign student,

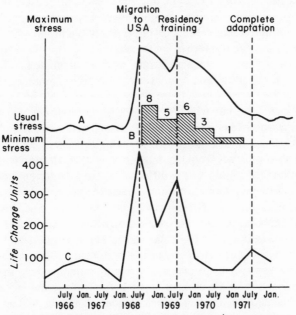

A: Intensity of subjective feeling of stress (the patient's own estimation).
B: Number of diabetic symptoms and progress in 6 month blocks.
C: Life Change Units in 6 month blocks by Schedule of Recent Experience.

Figure 17.1   Relationship among life events, life change magnitude, and the course of diabetes.

found that the language barrier requires more readjustment than any other aspect of a new culture. Taylor [29] reported on a Fijian overseas student who developed acute headache and inability to concentrate on his studies, and described his experience as "walk through time in dream." All these reports looked at some of the issues and experiences that migration created, and Holmes and his associates made it possible to evaluate these stresses in broader psychosocial terms.

Diabetes Mellitus as Adaptive Behavior to Life Crisis

Hinkle et al. [30] found that the onset of the symptoms of diabetes in all of three juvenile- and three adult-onset diabetics occurred in a setting of significant life stress, and exacerbations and remissions of the diabetes were observed to occur frequently in association with acutely stressful life situations and periods of relative security, respectively. In another study, Hinkle and Wolf [9] carefully reviewed the history of 27 random cases of diabetes and found that the onset of the disorder occurred after a period of environmental and interpersonal stress characterized by loss of persons, objects, relationships, or cultural values that the patient had regarded as indispensable to his or her total security. They also found that the situations that produced ketosis were all concerned with conflicts with parents and parent figures or symbolic representation of such conflict. They stated that each subject reacted to the situation as if he or she were being deprived of the affection and emotional support of the parent figure and as if the dependent relationship to this person were being threatened.

The present patient was separated from his close, intimate family for the first time in his life. His separation from his overaffectionate mother as well as from his mother culture was salient. There is much evidence that he had a very close and dependent relationship with his mother, who devoted herself to this patient in apparent expiation of her guilt for having abandoned a son from her previous unhappy marriage. In fact, the patient's moving to another country might have been an effort to get away from his smothering mother. Here he was thrown into a totally unfamiliar culture with a different language, different behavioral patterns, and a different interpersonal communication system. He became helpless and paralyzed. In this setting of cultural shock, he must have needed intense love and support from his parents more than at any time in his life. His feelings of helplessness, insecurity, anxiety, and shame can be understood easily. It is conceivable that to this "independent and confident," rather ambitious young physician the loss of a sense of security due to cultural shock, the subsequent inability to function at his optimal capability, and the resulting lowered self-esteem might have been a more significant trauma than the actual separation from his mother. It is most interesting to note that all the diabetic symptoms gradually disappeared as he regained his sense of security and once again exhibited his competence as a physician. As shown in Figure 17.1, the intensity of his feelings of stress, the diabetic symptoms, and the magnitude of the life changes followed a similar course. It is also interesting that a trace of glycosuria signaled the coming psychological reaction to migration, and that the feelings of complete adaptation to this new culture and a regaining of his sense of security were preceded by the return of normal physiological behavior, that is, disappearance of the diabetic symptoms.

Our extensive search of the literature on the remission of adult onset of diabetes revealed only one study done on a significant number of subjects. O'Sullivan and Hurwitz [31] studied 83 cases of early diabetes and found that 28 percent of the subjects became completely normal and 54 percent showed improvement with no treatment. However, they came to no acceptable explanation that can account for these striking spontaneous remissions.

Animal studies on diabetes mellitus are scanty, and Startsev [32] in the Soviet Union seems to be the only one who was able to produce a reliable animal model of diabetes mellitus. He produced hyperglycemia and other diabetic symptoms in both fed and unfed rhesus monkeys by forced immobilization, and the hyperglycemia lasted six months after the termination of the experiments.

Specificity: Why Diabetes Mellitus?

Although Hinkle and Wolf [9] claimed that situations associated with diabetes are concerned with losses, especially of parent figures, these associations do not seem to be particularly specific to diabetes mellitus. A variety of disorders have been reported in the literature to be precipitated by real or threatened loss. These include cancer, thyrotoxicosis, asthma, tuberculosis, ulcerative colitis, obesity, leukemia and lymphoma, rheumatoid arthritis, congestive heart failure, disseminated lupus erythematosus, Raynaud's disease, infectious hepatitis, functional uterine bleeding, as well as diabetes mellitus [33]. Schmale [33] stated that there was evidence for actual, threatened, or symbolic object loss prior to onset of disease in 41 of the 42 hospitalized patients he studied. Why then did this patient develop diabetes mellitus?

A series of interviews with this patient revealed that, as the only son in the family, he was the favorite of his parents. His parents, mother particularly, tended to save the best food for the children, and especially for him. They refrained from consuming meat, which was very expensive, in order that the patient would have more to eat since it was his favorite food. The patient stated that he used to consume a large amount of food at meals if there were meat dishes, and frequently refused to eat if meat or other "good" dishes were not available. This worried his mother a great deal when he refused to eat. The patient reported that his older sister does not like any kind of meat at all, and in fact is almost a strict vegetarian. Another significant point is that there was a two-year period in college when he did not like meat and frequently found it abhorrent to him. This was the time when he resented his mother's smothering affection most, as he stated in the case history.

When he came to this country, he found himself consuming a tremendous amount of meat at each meal, usually having a meat dish as a second dish as well, and sometimes eating only meat. He did not particularly care for sweets, and he rather avoided them because he was afraid that they would increase his blood sugar. He continued to consume a large amount of protein foods and avoid sweets and high carbohydrate foods until his physician gave an order to eat more carbohydrates.

It has been speculated that, in earliest infancy, the relation between food and mother love is so close that it is doubtful whether any distinction exists from the child's viewpoint [34]. So it seems that food, mother love, and emotional and physical security are intimately identified in infancy [9]. Hinkle and Wolf [9] stated that some persons in their later life respond to cumulative psychological, situational, and physical stresses, which involve the loss of love and security, as if they represented the threat of starvation. They also stated that diabetic glucose-tolerance curves are observed in starved individuals, and there is no qualitative difference between the metabolism of starvation and that of early, mild diabetes.

The patient in our study seems to be a good example of this kind of adaptive but inappropriate behavior to the separation from close family, especially mother. He equated food, meats in particular, as a symbolic representation of mother love, and he craved meat when he was in the situation in which he needed mother love and security so intensely. In other words, when he was psychologically starving for affection and security, he turned to the symbolic representation of this need—that is, meat—and he ate it voraciously as if it were affection from his mother, and it produced in him physiologic "starvation in the midst of plenty."

REFERENCES

1. Willis, T. *Practice of Physik: Treatise II, Pharmaceutice Rationalis.* London: Dring, Hayer and Leight, 1684, p. 74.

2. Neilson, C. H. "Emotional and Psychic Factors in Disease." *Journal of the American Medical Association* 89 (1927):1020–23.

3. Menninger, W. C. "Psychological Factors in the Etiology of Diabetes." *Journal of Nervous and Mental Disease* 81 (1935):1–13.

4. Dunbar, H. F., T. P. Wolfe, and J. McK. Rioch. "Psychiatric Aspects of Medical Problems: Psychic Component of Disease Process (including Convalescence) in Cardiac, Diabetic, and Fracture Patients." *American Journal of Psychiatry* 93 (1936):649–79.

5. Joslin, E. P. *The Treatment of Diabetes.* Philadelphia: Lea and Febiger, 1946, pp. 82–97.

6. Gendel, B. R., and J. T. Benjamin. "Psychogenic Factors in Etiology of Diabetes." *New England Journal of Medicine* 234 (1946):556–60.

7. Mirsky, I. A. "Emotional Factors in Patients with Diabetes Mellitus." *Bulletin of the Menninger Clinic* 12 (1948):187–94.

8. Bruch, H. "Physiologic and Psychologic Interrelationship in Diabetes in Children." *Psychosomatic Medicine* 11 (1949):200–210.

9. Hinkle, L. E., and S. Wolf. "Studies in Diabetes Mellitus: Changes in Glucose, Ketone, and Water Metabolism during Stress." In *Life Stress and Bodily Disease*, edited

by H. G. Wolff, S. Wolf, and C. C. Hare, pp. 338–89. Research Publications of the Association for Research in Nervous and Mental Disease, vol. 29. Baltimore: Williams and Wilkins, 1950.

10. Palmer, R. W. "The Diabetic Personality." *Journal of the Indiana Medical Association* 51 (1958):1399–1402.

11. Treuting, T. F. "The Role of Emotional Factors in the Etiology and Course of Diabetes Mellitus: A Review of the Recent Literature." *American Journal of Medical Science* 244 (1962):93–110.

12. Slawson, P. F., W. R. Flynn, and E. J. Kollar. "Psychological Factors Associated with the Onset of Diabetes Mellitus." *Journal of the American Medical Association* 185 (1963):166–70.

13. Levine, R. "History of Etiology of Diabetes Mellitus." *Archives of Pathology* 78 (1964):405–8.

14. Kimball, C. D. "Emotional and Psychosocial Aspects of Diabetes Mellitus." *Medical Clinics of North America* 55 (1971):1007–18.

15. Holmes, T. H., and R. H. Rahe. "The Social Readjustment Rating Scale." *Journal of Psychosomatic Research* 11 (1967):213–18. Reprinted in this volume, Chapter 2.

16. Rahe, R. H. "Life Crisis and Health Change." In *Psychotropic Drug Response: Advances in Prediction*, edited by P. R. A. May and J. R. Wittenborn, pp. 92–125. Springfield, Ill.: Charles C Thomas, 1969. Pts. 2 and 3 reprinted in this volume, Chapters 13 and 14.

17. Holmes, T. S. "Adaptive Behavior and Health Change." Medical thesis, University of Washington, 1970.

18. Rahe, R. H. "Life Change Measurement as a Predictor of Illness." *Proceedings of the Royal Society of Medicine* 61 (1968):1124–26.

19. Rubin, R. T., E. K. E. Gunderson, and R. J. Arthur. "Life Stress and Illness Pattern in the U.S. Navy: III. Prior Life Change and Illness Onset in an Attack Carrier's Crew." *Archives of Environmental Health* 19 (1969):753–57.

20. Holmes, T. S., and T. H. Holmes. "Short-term Intrusions into the Life Style Routine." *Journal of Psychosomatic Research* 14 (1970):121–32. Reprinted in this volume, Chapter 15.

21. Wyler, A. R., M. Masuda, and T. H. Holmes. "Seriousness of Illness Rating Scale." *Journal of Psychosomatic Research* 11 (1968):363–74. Reprinted in this volume, Chapter 8.

22. Reed, D., D. Labarthe, and R. Stallones. "Health Effects of Westernization and Migration among Chamarros." *American Journal of Epidemiology* 92 (1970):94–112.

23. Hinkle, L. E., Jr., and H. G. Wolff. "The Nature of Man's Adaptation to his Total Environment and the Relation of This to Illness." *Archives of Internal Medicine* 99 (1956):442–60.

24. Hinkle, L. E., F. D. Kane, W. N. Christenson, and H. G. Wolff. "Hungarian Refugees: Life Experiences and Features Influencing Participation in the Revolution and Subsequent Flight." *American Journal of Psychiatry* 116 (1959):16–19.

25. Abramson, J. H. "Emotional Disorder, Status Inconsistency and Migration: A Health Questionnaire Survey in Jerusalem." *Milbank Memorial Fund Quarterly* 44 (1966):23–48.

26. Oberg, K. *Culture Shock.* Indianapolis: Bobbs-Merrill, 1954.

27. Gullahorn, J. T., and J. E. Gullahorn. "An Extension of U-Curve Hypothesis." *Journal of Social Issues* 19 (1963):33–47.

28. Spradley, J. P., and M. Phillips. "Culture and Stress: A Quantitative Analysis." *American Anthropologist* 74 (1972):518–29.

29. Taylor, A. J. W. "A Fijian Student's Anxiety and Stress." *New Zealand Medical Journal* 68 (1968):161–63.

30. Hinkle, L. E., F. M. Evans, and S. Wolf. "Studies in Diabetes Mellitus: III. Life History of Three Persons with Labile Diabetes and Relation of Significant Experiences in Their Lives to the Onset and Course of the Disease." *Psychosomatic Medicine* 13 (1951): 160–202.

31. O'Sullivan, J. B., and D. Hurwitz. "Spontaneous Remissions in Early Diabetes." *Archives of Internal Medicine* 117 (1966):769–74.

32. Startsev, V. G. *Modelirovanie Neurogennykh Zabolevanii Cheloveka v Eksperimente na Obezianakh.* Moscow: Meditsina Press, 1971.

33. Schmale, A. H. "Relationship of Separation and Depression to Disease. I. A Report on a Hospitalized Medical Population." *Psychosomatic Medicine* 20 (1958):259–77.

34. Freud, A. *Normality and Pathology in Childhood: Assessments of Development.* New York: International Universities Press, 1965, p. 71.

18

Life Change, Coping Ability, and Chronic Intrinsic Asthma

Gilberto de Araujo, Paul P. Van Arsdel, Jr.,
Thomas H. Holmes, and Donald L. Dudley

Adverse environmental inputs may be directly associated with the precipitation of asthmatic attacks, influence the way the patient perceives the symptoms, and interfere in general with the response of the disease to medical treatment [1–7]. What determines the degree to which this occurs in a given patient, however, has been unclear. Long-term observations of chronic asthmatics, in our clinics, has led to the empirical observation that psychosocial factors may explain, at least in part, the variable response to medications and environmental changes. Although methods for a comprehensive evaluation of psychosocial factors have existed for many years, little use has been made of them in the study of chronic disease.

Berle et al. in 1952 [8] studied 736 patients with various chronic diseases. They isolated psychologic and social variables associated with improvement, or lack of improvement, in these patients. Based on these items, a relatively objective instrument for assessing "psychosocial assets" was developed and called the Berle Index (BI). Holmes et al. in 1961 [9] used the BI on a group of patients with pulmonary tuberculosis to predict outcome. They found that treatment failure was associated with low Berle values and that psychosocial assets (BI scores) remained relatively constant over time. Dudley et al. [10] observed that the probability of early death in a group of patients with emphysema increased in the presence of low psychosocial assets.

Hawkins et al. [11] and Rahe et al. [12] have found that a cluster of social events requiring change in life adjustment is significantly associated with the

This chapter is reprinted with permission from Gilberto de Araujo, Paul P. Van Arsdel, Jr., Thomas H. Holmes, and Donald L. Dudley, "Life Change, Coping Ability and Chronic Intrinsic Asthma," *Journal of Psychosomatic Research* 17 (1973):359–63. Copyright 1973 by Pergamon Press, Ltd.

time of illness onset. A quantitative method of scaling these environmental changes was devised (the Schedule of Recent Experience, or SRE) [13]. The SRE has been used to document the association of life changes with onset and seriousness of illness [14].

In this report, the association among psychosocial assets (BI score), life change (SRE score), and severity of chronic asthma (amount of steroid needed to control the asthma) was examined. This was done by: (1) using the Berle Index and the Schedule of Recent Experience for quantification of factors involving psychologic and social variables; and (2) relating the numerical value of these variables to the severity of chronic asthma, as indicated by the mean daily dose of adrenocorticosteroids required to control it. It was felt that patients with low psychosocial assets and high environmental changes would tend to pursue a more severe course and, consequently, require a higher dose of medication to control their disease. The data on psychosocial assets have been published, in part, elsewhere [15].

METHOD

The Berle Index is divided into three parts. Part 1 deals with data such as age, social status, and past medical history, and is worth 20 points. Part 2 relates items associated with the patient's family and interpersonal relationships as they are perceived by the patient (28 points for males; 20 points for females). Part 3 consists of the physician's evaluation of the patient's past performance, personality structure, and attitudes towards the illness (based on historical data and current mental status), and is worth 40 points. The numbers obtained by adding the scores are converted to a percentage of the maximum possible total score. The scores obtained on this instrument are positively related to the patient's ability to adjust to disease.

The Schedule of Recent Experience is a self-administered questionnaire that documents information pertaining to social changes, which are identified by the time of occurrence over a two-year period prior to the date of testing. Every item has a numerical value assigned. The result is given by the addition of all positive items and is expressed in life change units (LCU). Total LCU is an approximation of total social change or "environmental input" and is positively related to the probability of organ failure.

The subjects in this study were 36 chronic intrinsic asthmatic patients for whom corticosteroids were part of comprehensive, long-term treatment. There were 15 males and 21 females ranging from 19 to 74 years of age. All patients were maintained at the lowest possible steroid dose; during the study, five no longer required steroids continuously. None had significant symptoms related to extrinsic allergic factors.

The psychosocial evaluation was done on three or four visits to the allergy clinic of the University of Washington Hospital. It was performed by an investigator who was not involved in the medical management of the patients and was not aware of the steroid dosage. It should be emphasized that the presence or absence of an underlying psychiatric disorder was not a factor in the selection of the patients.

When the psychosocial evaluation was completed, the patients were arbitrarily divided into two groups according to their Berle score: low psychosocial assets for patients with Berle scores below 80 percent, and high psychosocial assets for patients with scores of 80 percent or above. They were also divided into two groups on the basis of their life change score: low life change for patients with less than 300 LCU, and high life change for those with 300 LCU or more.

One year later their medical records were reviewed, and the mean daily amount of prednisone or its equivalent used that year was calculated. The medical management, including adjustment of the steroid dose, was done independently by physicians unaware of the BI or LCU scores. It should be noted that the mean steroid dose did not change significantly in any patient during the year of the study.

RESULTS

Table 18.1 summarizes the data obtained in this group of patients regarding their Berle scores, life change units, and steroid dose used.

As a group, patients with low Berle scores required a higher prednisone dose (mean of 15.9 mg/day) than those with high scores (5.5 mg/day). By the Wilcoxon rank sum test, this was a significant difference ($p < 0.005$, one sided).

Considering all patients of both groups, there was a negative rank order correlation between psychosocial assets and steroid dosage. The correlation coefficient, $r_s = -0.564$, was significant ($p < 0.001$). The scores of each part of the three parts of the BI were also correlated with the steroid dose by rank order separately. Part 1 was not significant. Part 2 and part 3 were significant ($p < 0.005$) for each. The sections of part 3 evaluating past performance, attitudes toward illness, and modifiability of factors involved were not significant. The

Table 18.1
Comparison of Low ($N = 14$) and High ($N = 22$) Berle Patients

	Age	Duration (yr)	Steroid dose	Berle				LCU
				1	2	3	Total %	
Low Berle	45.43	16.64	15.87	11.21	20.57	26.64	65.21	547.93
High Berle	39.18	15.45	5.45*	15.55	26.55	34.86	86.86	518.18

* $p \leq 0.005$ (*t*-test, one tailed); significant differences are limited to steroid dose.

Table 18.2
Comparison of Steroid Dosage Levels in Patients with High and Low Life Change and High and Low Coping Ability as Quantified by LCU and BI, Respectively

Group			No.	BI Average	LCU Average	Steroid (mg/day)
1	↑ BI	↓ LCU	10	86%	154	5.0
2	↑ BI	↑ LCU	12	85%	685	5.6
3	↓ BI	↓ LCU	4	66%	158	6.7
4	↓ BI	↑ LCU	11	63%	738	19.6

Note: *t*-test comparisons (one tailed); groups 1 and 2, nonsignificant; groups 1 and 3, nonsignificant; groups 1 and 4, $p \leq 0.005$; groups 2 and 3, nonsignificant; groups 2 and 4, $p \leq 0.005$; groups 3 and 4, $p \leq 0.01$.

section evaluating personality structure was highly significant ($r_s = 0.651$; $p < 0.0005$).

The Berle scores did not seem to be influenced by the early onset of asthma. Ten patients had the first onset of asthma at an early age; seven of those had high Berle scores. There was no significant difference between age at onset of asthma in the high and low Berle group. Also, low Berle scores did not appear to be a function of the duration of asthma in years. Twenty-one patients had asthma for more than ten years, and 14 of those had high Berle scores. There was no significant difference between duration of asthma in the high and low Berle group.

As a whole, there was no apparent relationship between the numerical value of the Schedule of Recent Experience and the average dose of steroid used by the patients during the preceding year. However, as Table 18.2 illustrates, with addition of psychosocial assets to the evaluation it was found that: (1) patients with high psychosocial assets invariably required relatively small dosages of corticosteroids (5.6 mg/day or less), whatever their LCU was; (2) patients with low psychosocial assets and high life change required significantly higher doses of steroid (mean of 19.6 mg/day) when compared with those with low assets and low life change (6.7 mg/day). The Wilcoxon rank sum test used to compare these two groups was significant at $p < 0.01$ (one tailed).

DISCUSSION

This study supports the concept that development of certain enduring methods of living results in varying ability to adjust to life situations and has a significant influence on the clinical course of subsequently developed disease processes.

Previous studies have shown that successful adaptation to severely diminished pulmonary function in patients with clinical emphysema is in part dependent on a combination of good coping ability (high psychosocial assets as defined by the Berle Index) and adaptive psychologic defensive systems [15;16]. In those studies the limited use of repressive types of psychologic defenses combined with high psychosocial assets was found to be associated with good adaptation to disease. Similar findings have recently been reported in patients with chronic renal disease who are dependent on hemodialysis [17]. It was clinically observed that patients with low coping ability and high life change were continuously incapacitated and needed continuous medical care. Patients with high coping ability were noted to deal adequately with life change without activation of physiologic systems and subsequent emergence of symptoms. The relationship between the use of repressive-type defenses and psychosocial assets appeared to be positive. It was felt that both high psychosocial assets and the limited use of repressive-type psychologic defenses resulted in attenuation of the impact of environmental change in physiologic systems [16;18]. This was postulated to be a mechanism by which acute exacerbations might be avoided.

The present study also was concerned with patients who had chronically diminished pulmonary function secondary to airway obstruction. However, the obstruction was secondary to chronic intrinsic asthma, rather than clinical emphysema.

Patients with chronic intrinsic asthma and high psychosocial assets were found to require low doses of steroids to control their disease, regardless of the amount of life change present. Patients with low psychosocial assets and low life-change scores required low doses of steroids also. However, patients with low psychosocial assets and high life change required high doses of steroids to control their disease. It would appear that the same relationship that was clinically observed with the emphysema patients between psychosocial assets and life change is also present for this group of chronic asthmatics. The need for increased clinical attention and medications for control of the disease is related to the patient's ability to cope with life change and the total amount of life change present. It is difficult to know if this relationship is stable with time or if patients with low psychosocial assets and high life change need lower doses of steroid medication when they are able to reduce their life change scores. This type of longitudinal study has not been done. If so, therapeutic procedures aimed at reducing life change scores might have considerable relevance and pertinence to the treatment of chronic asthmatics. Although our clinical impression was that patients with strong repressive-type defenses did better clinically than those without such defenses, this variable was not quantified in this study.

It is interesting to note that the subjective portions of the Berle Index appear to have stood the test of time better than the objective portion. This was true of both the patient's subjective evaluation and of the physician's subjective evaluation. Quantification of this type of data is seen to be of equal importance to quantification of the usual physiologic variables.

In general this study is seen as substantiating the premise that patients with low psychosocial assets have limited options for dealing with environmental change and disease. They are, therefore, more likely to have to rely on medications. Patients with high psychosocial assets have potential to use many resources in an appropriate way to deal with life change and disease and thereby have less need for specific medical therapy.

SUMMARY

Quantification of environmental change and psychosocial assets in this group of patients was useful in understanding variations in severity of chronic asthma. Patients with high psychosocial assets required limited steroid medication, regardless of the amount of life change present. On the other hand, patients with low psychosocial assets required high doses of steroids when experiencing high life change. Those with low psychosocial assets and low life change did not require high doses of steroids. This was assumed to be secondary to a lower demand on the patient in terms of the need for adaptive behavior. They could put more effort into adapting to their disease if they were not confronted with other life changes at the same time.

Based on the above observations, it would seem reasonable to help patients with low psychosocial assets and chronic asthma to modify their behavior in order to avoid high life change. A desirable long-term goal is the elevation of the patient's psychosocial assets or coping ability. At the present time this would appear to be beyond the capability of the currently fashionable psychiatric treatment modalities, at least as they apply to this patient population.

REFERENCES

1. Bastiaans, J., and J. Groen. "Psychogenesis and Psychotherapy of Bronchial Asthma." In *Modern Trends in Psychosomatic Medicine*, vol. 1, edited by O. Desmond. London: Butterworth, 1955.

2. Kleeman, S. T. "Psychiatric Contributions in the Treatment of Asthma." *Annals of Allergy* 25 (1967):611–19.

3. Knapp, P. H. "The Asthmatic and His Environment." *Journal of Nervous and Mental Disease* 149 (1969):133–51.

4. Luparello, T. J., N. Leist, C. H. Lourie, and P. Sweet. "The Interaction of Psychologic Stimuli and Pharmacologic Agents on Airway Activity in Asthmatic Subjects." *Psychosomatic Medicine* 32 (1970):509–13.

5. Rees, L. "The Importance of Psychological, Allergic and Infective Factors in Childhood Asthma." *Journal of Psychosomatic Research* 7 (1964):253–62.

6. Treuting, T. F., and H. S. Ripley. "Life Situations, Emotions and Bronchial Asthma." *Journal of Nervous and Mental Disease* 108 (1948):380–98.

7. Wright, G. L. "Asthma and Emotions: Aetiology and Treatment." *Medical Journal of Australia* 1 (1965):961–67.

8. Berle, B. B., R. H. Pinsky, S. Wolf, and H. G. Wolf. "Berle Index: A Clinical Guide

to Prognosis in Stress Disease." *Journal of the American Medical Association* 149 (1952): 1624–28.

9. Holmes, T. H., J. Joffe, J. W. Ketcham, and T. F. Sheehy. "Experimental Study of Prognosis." *Journal of Psychosomatic Research* 5 (1961):235–52.

10. Dudley, D. L., J. W. Verhey, M. Masuda, C. J. Martin, and T. H. Holmes. "Long Term Adjustment, Prognosis and Death in Irreversible Diffuse Obstructive Pulmonary Syndromes." *Psychosomatic Medicine* 31 (1969):310–25.

11. Hawkins, N. G., R. Davies, and T. H. Holmes. "Evidence of Psychosocial Factors in the Development of Pulmonary Tuberculosis." *American Review of Tuberculosis and Pulmonary Disease* 75 (1957):768–80. Reprinted in this volume, Chapter 11.

12. Rahe, R. H., M. Meyer, M. Smith, G. Kjaer, and T. H. Holmes. "Social Stress and Illness Onset." *Journal of Psychosomatic Research* 8 (1964):35–44. Reprinted in this volume, Chapter 12.

13. Holmes, T. H., and R. H. Rahe. "The Social Readjustment Rating Scale." *Journal of Psychosomatic Research* 11 (1967):213–18. Reprinted in this volume, Chapter 2.

14. Holmes, T. H., and M. Masuda. "Life Change and Illness Susceptibility." In *Separation and Depression: Clinical and Research Aspects*, edited by J. P. Scott and E. C. Senay, pp. 161–86. AAAS Publication no. 94. Washington, D.C.: American Association for the Advancement of Science, 1973.

15. De Araujo, G., D. L. Dudley, and P. P. Van Arsdel, Jr. "Psychosocial Assets and Severity of Chronic Asthma." *Journal of Allergy and Clinical Immunology* 50 (1972): 257–63.

16. Dudley, D. L., C. J. Martin, J. W. Verhey, and T. H. Holmes. "Response to Noxious Stimulation as an Indication of Successful Psychologic Defense Mechanisms in the Diffuse Obstructive Pulmonary Syndrome." *American Review of Respiratory Disease* 100 (1969):572–74.

17. Sviland, M. A. P. "Quantitative Denial and Home Hemodialysis Success: Implication for Psychotherapeutic Intervention." Abstract. *Psychosomatic Medicine* 35 (1973): 451.

18. Dudley, D. L., and E. M. Pattison. "Group Psychotherapy in Patients with Severe Diffuse Obstructive Pulmonary Syndrome." *American Review of Respiratory Disease* 100 (1969):575–76.

19

Psychosocial Factors in Athletic Injuries: Development and Application of the Social and Athletic Readjustment Rating Scale (SARRS)

Steven T. Bramwell, Minoru Masuda,
Nathaniel N. Wagner, and Thomas H. Holmes

Athletics is an area in which injuries occur frequently, resulting in loss of time, money, and games. Players, as well as management, have an important stake in minimizing these losses. Injuries in all sports are increasing despite technological advances in safety equipment. No doubt this is due in part to the increasing number of participants, to a greater emphasis on athletics, and to an increasing amount of leisure time available, particularly in the Western world. It is likely that the number of participants and injuries in athletics will continue to increase. It is important, therefore, to develop and increase our knowledge of possible etiological factors in the complex injury process, with hopes of reductions in personal debilitation.

In the past 20 years it has been found by several investigators [1–3] that onset of illness is significantly associated with an increase in the number of social events that require some adaptive or coping behavior on the part of the involved individual. These social events often are life situations that the individual has perceived as overwhelming, threatening, unsatisfying, or conflictual. It has been shown that the onset of certain diseases occurs at such times [2]. While most investigations have been concerned with various disease states, we have wondered whether acute trauma and injuries may also be associated with an increased perception of stressful events. Anyone who has experienced an accident or close miss remembers the strong emotional response following it and can appreciate the immediate effects that stressful events may have on one's ability to adapt and react appropriately and safely.

This chapter reports two phases in ongoing research on the relationship of

This chapter is reprinted with permission from *Journal of Human Stress* 1, no. 2 (June 1975): 6–20. Copyright 1975 by Heldref Publications.

psychosocial events to injuries in athletes. Part 1 describes the development of the Social and Athletic Readjustment Rating Scale (SARRS) and Part 2 describes the application of the newly derived SARRS to the varsity football players of a major university.

PART 1

The initial step in this investigation was to examine college football players and their perception of certain life events as compared to a general U.S. sample of 167 male subjects under the age of 30, measured by the Social Readjustment Rating Scale (SRRS) developed by Holmes and Rahe [3]. It appears that there are significant and important life events unique to athletes, which are not included in the SRRS and which necessitate a major life adjustment by the athlete. This study attempts to identify and quantify these athletic events in relation to those measured in the SRRS.

Method

In order to examine the athlete's view of certain life events, modifications were made in the Social Readjustment Rating Questionnaire (SRRQ). The basis for these modifications was derived from:

- preliminary questionnaires sent to athletes, both collegiate and professional, asking them to list events in their careers that influenced their personal and athletic life;
- questionnaires given previously to football players, asking them to list factors that they thought would or did influence their performance and behavior; and
- the athletic experience of one of the authors.

The modifications to the SRRQ made in developing the Social and Athletic Readjustment Rating Questionnaire (SARRQ) included certain deletions and additions, which are listed in Table 19.1. These changes were made, in part, to increase the credibility of the instrument with a male athlete sample. Pregnancy was dropped for obvious reasons. Retirement was deleted because these athletes have not yet begun their lifework and our focus was to be on their playing days and injuries. Christmas was dropped because in this college population it is redundant with vacation. Son or daughter leaving home was dropped since this population had no children. Troubles with the boss also was dropped.

Twenty additional items were included. Table 19.1 lists these additional athletic and social events that were determined to be unique events generally encountered by the athlete during his competitive days.

The reference item of the SRRQ—marriage—used to compare other life events was changed in view of the fact that only a small percentage of college football players are married. While those not married may well be able to estimate the amount of adjustment in one's life required by marriage, it was felt that an easier evaluation of the life events could be made if the reference base was an event that all individuals of the sample had experienced. Accordingly, a new modulus item—entering college—was chosen and assigned an arbitrary score of 500, as marriage had been in developing the SRRQ [3].

The change of the modulus item (that is, entering college), the incorporation of the new items, and the deletions as listed in Table 19.1 constituted a new 57-item, life event questionnaire termed the Social and Athletic Readjustment Rating Questionnaire (SARRQ).

Seventy-nine varsity college football players at the University of Washington

Table 19.1
Deletions and Additions to the SRRQ

	Life Event
Deletions	
	Pregnancy
	Retirement
	Christmas
	Troubles with boss
	Son or daughter leaving home
	Change in schools
Additions	
	Entering college
	Troubles with head coach
	Brother or sister leaving home
	Troubles with athletic director or general manager
	Troubles with assistant coaches
	Change in level of performance—high school to college; frosh to varsity; college to pro
	Major change in playing hours or conditions
	Major change in responsibility on team—captain, signals caller, seniority, etc.
	Change to a new position
	Being dropped from team
	Being dropped to a lesser playing status
	Changing to a new school or team
	Playing time lost due to injury or illness
	Difficulties with trainer or team physician
	Difficulties with eligibility—scholastic, transfer credits, etc.
	Discrimination from coaches or team
	Discrimination in community, at home, or away
	Major errors in ball games
	Difficulties in demonstrating athletic ability
	Separation from girl friend

were selected as the football sample. This sample included 66 white, 12 black, and one Mexican American team member ranging from 18 to 22 years of age. The comparative sample was the 167 male subjects under the age of 30 used in the development of the Social Readjustment Rating Scale (SRRS) by Holmes and Rahe [3]. This included 162 white, three black, and two Asian Americans. The geometric means were computed as the antilog of the mean of the logs of the scores. The use of the geometric mean in the SRRQ has been described previously by Masuda and Holmes [4].

Instructions to the athlete subjects for assigning a magnitude of change to the items to be scaled were the same as those used by Holmes and Rahe in developing the SRRS.

Results

The mean scores and rank order, as determined by the entire football team, were computed for all 57 items on the SARRQ and are listed in Table 19.2 as the Social and Athletic Readjustment Rating Scale (SARRS). The scale score is derived as in the SRRS when the geometric mean score is divided by 10 and assigned to the item as indication of magnitude [4].

Two new items were ranked in the first ten. Being dropped from team (mean value, 52) was ranked seventh. Entering college, the modulus item, was ranked ninth by the football players, with the assigned score of 50. Two new items were ranked in the second ten. Players ranked change in level of performance 17th (mean value, 35) and troubles with head coach next (mean value, 35). Six more athletic events were in the fourth ten; two new events, in the fifth ten; and one new item, in the last seven events.

The rank order as determined by the mean scores of the 37 like items in the SARRS was compared to that of the SRRS as scored by the general U.S. sample [3]. Table 19.3 lists the rank comparison. A Spearman rho of 0.843 ($p < 0.001$) was obtained. These results indicate a high consensus between the college football players and the general sample in the way in which they view the amount of readjustment needed to adapt to these events. The two samples agreed on eight items to be ranked in the first ten. The two items that the football players did not rank in the first ten were jail term and marital reconciliation. They rated, instead, death of close friend and begin or cease formal schooling. The two samples agreed on eight items to be ranked in the second ten. The football players ranked death of close friend higher and business readjustment lower. They included jail term, which the general sample rated higher, and outstanding personal achievement, which the general sample rated lower. The two samples agreed on five items in the third ten and agreed on five of the last seven items.

Scores and rank order of items were determined for both the white and black player subgroups of the football team. An r_s of 0.854 ($p < 0.001$) was obtained when the rank order of the 37 like items of the white football players was compared with that of the general U.S. sample. However, a comparison of the

Table 19.2
Social and Athletic Readjustment Rating Scale (SARRS)

Rank	Life Event	Mean Value
1	Death of spouse	101
2	Death of close family member	88
3	Marriage	72
4	Death of close friend	64
5	Divorce	64
6	Marital separation	60
*7	Being dropped from team	52
8	Being fired from work	52
*9	Entering college	50
10	Personal injury or illness	46
11	Change in health of family member	44
12	Begin or cease formal schooling	43
13	Change in financial state	42
14	Jail term	42
15	Outstanding personal achievement	36
16	Changing to different kind of work	36
*17	Change in level of performance	35
*18	Troubles with head coach	35
19	Gaining new family member	35
20	Sexual difficulties	34
21	Change in responsibility at work	34
22	Foreclosure on mortgage or loan	33
23	Change in number of arguments with spouse	33
*24	Being dropped to lesser playing status	32
25	Taking mortgage or loan greater than $10,000	32
*26	Changing to new school or team	31
*27	Discrimination from coaches or team	29
*28	Difficulties with eligibility	29
*29	Difficulties in demonstrating athletic ability	29

black players with the general group yielded a lower rank order coefficient ($r_s =$ 0.502; $p < 0.01$).

Comparison of the entire 57-item rank order between the white and black players yielded an even lower Spearman rho ($r_s = 0.420$; $p < 0.01$). Significant mean score differences on individual items (Table 19.4) showed that blacks ranked marriage and death of spouse significantly lower, while ranking changing to new school or team, discrimination from coaches, discrimination in community, and major errors in ball games significantly higher than the white players.

Table 19.2, continued

Rank	Life Event	Mean Value
*30	Troubles with assistant coaches	29
31	Wife begins or ceases work	28
32	Marital reconciliation	27
*33	Troubles with athletic director or general manager	27
*34	Major errors in ball games	27
35	Change in living condition	26
*36	Playing time lost due to injury	26
*37	Separation from girl friend	26
*38	Changing to a new position	24
39	Change in social activities	24
40	Trouble with in-laws	23
41	Business readjustment	23
42	Revision of personal habits	23
*43	Discrimination in community	23
44	Change in work hours or conditions	23
45	Mortgage or loan less than $10,000	22
*46	Change in team responsibility	21
*47	Change in playing hours or conditions	20
*48	Brother or sister leaving home	19
49	Change in eating habits	19
50	Change in sleeping habits	19
*51	Difficulties with trainer or physician	17
52	Vacation	17
53	Change in residence	16
54	Change in family get-togethers	14
55	Minor violation of the law	12
56	Change in church activities	12
57	Change in recreation	4

* New items

Discussion

As one might expect in light of previous social readjustment rating studies done on other U.S. subcultures [5], college football players do not differ in their assessment of the significance of life events from the middle-class U.S. population. Comparison of the SRRS and SARRS not only shows a high correlation in the relative order of magnitude of the perception of certain like life events, but also indicates that football players maintain the same general hierarchy of change. This is less true of members of the black minority group who, in this study, showed a reduced rank order correlation coefficient when compared to the white players. Nevertheless, the influence of a common U.S. cultural experience again is supported in that football players, despite demonstrable personality differences [6] and notable differences in living and competitive situations, reflect the attitudes and values of the larger society.

Individual differences in the rank order of life events may reflect some subcultural variations. However, in view of the fact that college students today are a unique portion of our society, it is difficult to determine if the individual items are characteristic of a young college sample rather than specifically those of football players. For example, higher ranking of begin or cease formal schooling would be expected in a college population, which is faced with leaving the sanctuary of the academic institution to earn a living. Higher ranking of death of close friend may well reflect the significance of friendship in a population that is generally unmarried and living away from home. The higher ranking of outstanding personal achievement in terms of adjustment is not surprising in that the college population, particularly football players, generally is regarded as achievement oriented. The lower ranking of marital reconciliation might be expected in a largely unmarried population within an increasingly divorce-oriented society. The lower rating of jail term is interesting in that it suggests that football players and college students view jail detention as less of a threat to occupational considerations and as less embarrassing than does the general population. The mood of today's campus would suggest that the experience of jail is more commonplace than previously.

The individual item differences between the white and black players (Table 19.4), as well as the rank order correlations, illustrate some important cultural differences. It is not surprising that black players would rate discrimination from both coaches and community higher than whites. The black community, with impetus largely from a younger, more vocal section, is deeply angered at the historical racist practices of our society and is deeply involved in the attempt to eliminate all such discriminatory practices.

In addition, as noted in other works [7], the great need of the young black male athlete to achieve is suggested in that he rates major errors in ball games (that is, fumbles, dropped passes, and so on) as an event requiring significantly more adjustment than it does for white male players. Major errors are certainly an obstacle to achievement and a source of frustration. The lower ranking of marriage and death of spouse by the black players was also observed by Komaroff, Masuda, and Holmes in 1968 [5]. This may reflect the greater importance of athletic achievement for the black male players and the consequent diminishing of marital concerns at this time in their lives. These differences also may reflect the subculture from which the black player comes, where divorce, broken homes, and shorter life expectancy are part of the black experience [8]. In addition, there is a difference in the sexual patterns of the black and white subcultures [9]. Thus the young black, subject to both historical and present social patterns different from those of the white society, rates these items differently.

Table 19.3
Comparison of Ranking of 37 Like Items in the SRRS and the SARRS

Life Events	American (N = 167) Rank	College Football (N = 79) Rank
Death of a spouse	1	1
Divorce	2	5
Death of close family member	3	2
Marital separation	4	6
Jail term	5	12
Personal injury or illness	6	8
Marriage	7	3
Marital reconciliation	8	22
Change in health of family member	9	9
Being fired	10	7
Death of close friend	11	4
Sexual difficulties	12	16
Gaining a new family member	13	15
Business readjustment	14	26
Changing to different kind of work	15	14
Change in number of arguments with spouse	16	19
Change in financial state	17	11
Taking mortgage or loan greater than $10,000	18	20
Foreclosure on mortgage or loan	19	18
Change in responsibility at work	20	17
In-law problems	21	24
Begin or cease formal schooling	22	10
Revision of personal habits	23	27
Change in living conditions	24	23
Wife begins or stops work	25	21
Outstanding personal achievement	26	13
Change in recreation	27	37
Change in work hours or conditions	28	28
Change in residence	29	33
Change in church activities	30	36
Mortgage or loan less than $10,000	31	29
Change in social activities	32	25
Change in sleeping habits	33	31
Change in eating habits	34	30
Change in family get-togethers	35	34
Vacation	36	32
Minor violation of the law	37	35

Table 19.4
Life Events That Differ between the White and Black Football Players

Life Event	White ($N = 66$) Geometric Mean	Black ($N = 12$) Geometric Mean	Significance* Level
Marriage	87.5	63.7	$p < 0.02$
Death of spouse	130.5	79.2	$p < 0.02$
Changing to new school or team	54.3	67.1	$p < 0.02$
Discrimination from coach	53.9	86.3	$p < 0.001$
Discrimination in community	39.4	81.7	$p < 0.01$
Major errors in ball games	59.6	68.3	$p < 0.02$

* Student's t-test

Also, the results from the SARRS demonstrate that there are unique events experienced by football players that are perceived as requiring significant degrees of adaptive behavior. The new items included in the SARRQ represent a special focus on the peer group and on educational and occupational (athletic) areas of college life. Examination of the magnitude of most events rated by football players is of interest. For example, being dropped from team is rated the same as its counterpart—being fired from work—in the original SRRS, and barely less than marital separation. Troubles with the head coach and change in level of performance (for example, freshman to varsity) needed more readjustment than sexual difficulties or foreclosure on mortgage or loan, certainly situations not taken lightly in our society. Most of the other new items representing athletic events also were given significant magnitudes as listed in the SARRS (Table 19.3).

PART 2

The second part of this investigation was aimed specifically at the possible relationship between athletic injuries and the magnitude of the perceived life change events that constituted the setting in which injuries were experienced.

Method

Members of a university varsity football team that played a major college schedule were selected for study because of their availability and the frequency of occurrence of salient injuries in this sport. Practice and game injuries were well documented by the Division of Sports Medicine at the university. The judgment of injury was made independently by Sports Medicine personnel who were unaware of the life change magnitudes of the individual players.

An Athlete Schedule of Recent Experience (ASRE) was constructed to include the items scaled in the Social and Athletic Readjustment Rating Scale (SARRS) (Table 19.3). This paper-and-pencil test allowed the subjects to identify the occurrence of the items in specified time intervals. The two time intervals contained in the schedule were for one year and two years prior to the football season under study. A life change score was derived for each time interval by assigning the scale magnitude to the item reported by the subject and summing the numbers.

After about three months, at the completion of the playing season, the injury record for each of the players was obtained. For the purpose of analysis, the injured group was defined as those players who missed three or more practices and/or one or more games due to a specific injury. Those football players who did not meet these criteria composed the noninjured group. These criteria were accepted because they identified a major time-loss injury. Injuries that did not result in a game or part of a game missed, or three or more practices missed, reflected minor though nagging injuries commonly suffered by contact sport participants. These are incurred by almost all participants at one time or another and are not of interest in this study.

Results

The injured group contained 36 players. The mean one-year life change units (LCU) for this group was 632 (range, 142–2,260) and the mean two-year LCU was 1,008 (range, 299–3,900).

The noninjured group included 46 players. The mean one-year LCU for this group was 494 (range, 150–1,552) and the mean LCU for the two-year interval was 797 (range, 296–1,972). Comparison of scores is summarized in Table 19.5.

Statistical analysis was applied to the differences in mean scores for each group in each time interval. Both time interval mean differences were found to be significant at the 0.05 level.

Not all accumulations of life events are associated with football injuries. For use in prediction of injuries, players were divided into low-risk, moderate-risk, and high-risk groups on the basis of low, moderate, and high LCU (Table 19.6). In the low-risk group (0–400 for one year; 0–700 for two years), 30 percent of the players suffered injuries. In the moderate-risk group (400–800 for one year; 700–1,200 for two years), 50 percent of the players suffered injuries. In the high-risk group (more than 800 for 1 year; more than 1,200 for two years), 73 percent of the players suffered major time-loss injuries.

Discussion

The relationship of the perception of life events accumulation to football injuries shows a significant association. The data indicate that the risk of an injury to a football player increases in direct relationship to the accumulation of

Table 19.5
Mean LCU of Injured and Noninjured Groups

	1 Year Score	2 Year Score
Injured	632	1,008
(N = 36)	(range 142–2,260)	(range 299–3,900)
Noninjured	494	797
(N = 46)	(range 150–1,552)	(range 296–1,972)
Mean Difference	138	211
	(p ≤ 0.05)*	(p ≤ 0.05)*

* Student's t-test

the challenging life events under study. This appears to be true regardless of whether a one- or two-year time interval prior to participation is examined. These results are similar to those summarized by Holmes and Masuda [10] for health changes in general.

This correlational investigation represents only a starting place in the possible role of life events in sports injuries. Certainly the genesis of injury is a complex, multifactor process. A dangerous set of conditions involving high energy exchange has to be dealt with by individuals who are prepared in varying degrees physically and psychologically. Each individual then must react to the conditions in accordance with his or her perception of the situation and his or her ability to respond based on that perception. The role played in this complex interaction by the accumulation of the life change events is unclear at this time. The effect of life change may be to hinder concentration on environmental cues that are crucial

Table 19.6
Rate of Occurrence of Injuries in Low-, Moderate-, and High-Risk Groups Established by Magnitude of Life Change

LOW RISK		MODERATE RISK		HIGH RISK	
One Year*	Two Year**	One Year	Two Year	One Year	Two Year
(N = 32)	(N = 34)	(N = 39)	(N = 33)	(N = 11)	(N = 15)
(0–400 LCU)	(0–700 LCU)	(400–800 LCU)	(700–1,200 LCU)	(>800 LCU)	(>1,200 LCU)
35%	29%	44%	48%	72%	73%

* Life change units (LCU) for one year prior to athletic season
** LCU for two years prior to athletic season

(for example, sensing the blind side block) and/or to block previously learned adaptive responses when difficult and potentially damaging situations are recognized (for example, "freezing up").

It is with some hesitation that these data are published. This is not because of doubts about the relationship of the perception of life events to football injuries, but rather because of the possible misuses of this experimental approach to the study of injury. Individuals associated with an activity as important as major college and/or professional football have enormous concern with the subject of injuries. Often the course of a team's progress rests on the health of key personnel. The perception of life events may be seen by some as a predictive test to be used as a screening instrument so as to know what confidence may be placed in an individual's potential for injury-free competition.

To protect the athlete and to cope with the serious ethical issue involved in such screening, the practice of informed consent could be made routine. There is also the important issue of group versus individual prediction. We are dealing here with group scores and group prediction. Individual athletes with low magnitudes of life change were injured during the season. Other individual athletes with high life-change scores had no injuries. The importance of understanding the complex multifactor nature of sports injuries and the incompleteness of our understanding cannot be emphasized too strongly.

SUMMARY

As a part of this investigation of the perception of life change events in athletic injuries, two studies were done. First, modifications were made in the Social Readjustment Rating Scale (SRRS) developed by Holmes and Rahe, in order to measure more precisely the experiences encountered by athletes and to increase the credibility of the instrument with that population. Second, a correlation study was done with regards to life event accumulations over one- and two-year intervals and to injuries defined in college football.

Modifications of the SRRS to make the Social and Athletic Readjustment Rating Scale (SARRS) were discussed. Results of comparison of the rank ordering showed a high consensus in the rank ordering of social events between football players and a general U.S. male population sample under 30 years of age. The black subgroup of players also showed a consensus in the magnitude of ordering events, though not as great as the white players. In addition, significant differences were found between white and black players pertaining to areas of marriage, discrimination, and errors in game performance. It is felt that the evaluation of the role of life events in athletic injuries must be sensitive to both social and unique athletic events faced by the athlete and to the degree of significance that the athlete gives them.

The Athlete Schedule of Recent Experience (ASRE) was given to 82 college football players. All life-event score accumulations were obtained for each, using the SARRS. The scores of players suffering major time-loss injuries were compared with scores of players not having time-loss injuries. Statistical differences in mean scores over one- and two-year intervals were found between the injured and noninjured groups. Football players with low, moderate, and high life-change scores could be predicted to be at proportionate risk for sustaining injuries.

ACKNOWLEDGMENTS

We acknowledge with thanks the assistance of the University of Washington Department of Sports Programs and the Division of Sports Medicine of the Department of Orthopaedics.

REFERENCES

1. Hinkle, L. E., Jr., and H. G. Wolff. "Ecologic Investigations of the Relationship between Illness, Life Experiences and the Social Environment." *Annals of Internal Medicine* 49 (1958):1373–89.

2. Rahe, R. H., M. Meyer, M. Smith, G. Kjaer, and T. H. Holmes. "Social Stress and Illness Onset." *Journal of Psychosomatic Research* 8 (1964):35–44. Reprinted in this volume, Chapter 12.

3. Holmes, T. H., and R. H. Rahe. "The Social Readjustment Rating Scale." *Journal of Psychosomatic Research* 11 (1967):213–18. Reprinted in this volume, Chapter 2.

4. Masuda, M., and T. H. Holmes. "Magnitude Estimations of Social Readjustments." *Journal of Psychosomatic Research* 11 (1967):219–25. Reprinted in this volume, Chapter 3.

5. Komaroff, A. L., M. Masuda, and T. H. Holmes. "The Social Readjustment Rating Scale: A Comparative Study of Negro, Mexican, and White Americans." *Journal of Psychosomatic Research* 12 (1968):121–28. Reprinted in this volume, Chapter 6.

6. Bramwell, S. T., J. A. Oakland, and N. N. Wagner. "Personality Variables of College Football Players." Unpublished manuscript, 1971.

7. Wagner, N. N., R. McQuellon, and S. T. Bramwell. "The Black Athlete: Achievement or Frustration." *The Seattle Post-Intelligencer*, 14 December 1970, Northwest Today section.

8. Clark, K. B. *Dark Ghetto*. New York: Harper and Row, 1965.

9. Wagner, N. N. *Perspectives on Human Sexuality*. New York: Behavioral Publications, 1974.

10. Holmes, T. H., and M. Masuda. "Life Change and Illness Susceptibility." In *Separation and Depression: Clinical and Research Aspects*, edited by J. P. Scott and E. C. Senay, pp. 161–86. AAAS Publication no. 94. Washington, D.C.: American Association for the Advancement of Science, 1973.

20

Life Events and Prisoners

Minoru Masuda, David L. Cutler,
Lee Hein, and Thomas H. Holmes

Over the past several years an increasing amount of information has been generated that indicates that the accumulation of life events is associated with the onset of illness [1]. The data indicate that the magnitude of accumulated life change is significantly related to the time of disease onset. In addition, when illness is experienced, the greater the magnitude of life change present at time of onset, the more serious is the chronic illness experienced [2]. The illness experience covered a wide spectrum of disease states [1].

The ability to make a magnitude estimation of psychosocial readjustments to various life events led to the development of the Social Readjustment Rating Scale (SRRS) [3]. The incorporation of the SRRS items into the Schedule of Recent Experience (SRE) allowed for the periodic quantification of accumulated life changes as they might relate to illnesses [4;5].

The concept of the psychosocial readjustment required in the responses to life events has expanded out of the area of conventional illness onset into other behavioral areas, including the academic performance of both teacher [6] and student [7], and job performance [8]. In addition, studies have shown a positive relationship between the magnitude of life change and injuries in collegiate football players [9] and traffic accidents [10]. Recent studies have shown that suicide attempters accumulate significantly greater numbers of life events in the year prior to the attempt than do controls [11;12].

To our knowledge, there are no published reports of the relationship of life events and onset of incarceration in prison. The maladaptive responses to environmental challenges that lead to greater disease risks may also manifest them-

This chapter is reprinted with permission from *Archives of General Psychiatry* 35 (February 1978):197–203. Copyright 1978. American Medical Association.

selves in those susceptible to deviant social behavior. This study explores retrospectively the relationship of the accumulation of life events as it relates to prison incarceration and extends further the concept that coping with increasing environmental change results in a variety of overt behaviors. The evolving behavior, whether illness, incarceration in prison, poor job performance, or the like, appears to be an epiphenomenon of the individual's psychobiological adaptive or coping style.

SUBJECTS AND METHODS

Sample Populations

McNeil Island Inmates

McNeil Island is a federal penitentiary located in the southern portion of Puget Sound in the state of Washington. At the time of the study (summer 1971), the prison population was 1,027, all men. The volunteer subjects were randomly selected from inmates who had been in prison five years or less. Of a group of 120, the responses of 98 subjects were satisfactory. The men were informed of the voluntary nature of the exercise and filled out the forms in groups of 1–10. One of the investigators was present at all times to read the directions and answer questions.

Walla Walla Inmates

Walla Walla prison is a state corrections institution in the southeastern rural part of Washington State. It is the oldest of the state institutions and receives the most serious offenders. At the time of this study (summer 1973), there were 1,300 inmates, all men. The sample was selected from inmate volunteers with initial solicitation from organizations such as black, American Indian, lifer, and white inmate clubs. This produced insufficient numbers and, with prison approval, eight inmate volunteers canvassed the entire population one evening. Two hundred names were selected from a total of 350 volunteers. Of these, 121 men filled out questionnaires, of which 78 were usable.

Significant numbers of questionnaires were discarded, in spite of the fact that experimenters were present to administer the questionnaires to small groups of up to 20 in order to explain and answer questions. Many forms were incomplete, and many contained gross responses that indicated confusion as to directions or to event chronology, as well as possibly deliberate distortions.

Schedule of Recent Experience

The Schedule of Recent Experience is a self-reporting questionnaire [5] that asks subjects to indicate the yearly occurrence and frequency of 40 life events over a period of ten years. This yielded life change data for five years (–1 to –5) prior to imprisonment and up to five years after imprisonment (+1 to +5). Each life event has a numerical score derived from the SRRS. For example, marriage has a score of 50, while death of spouse is 100; divorce, 73; business readjustment, 39; change in living conditions, 25; vacation, 13; and so forth. The number of yearly occurrences of an item is multiplied by its score, and the sum of products of all items yields the annual life change units (LCU).

RESULTS

Comparison of Groups

McNeil Island Total Population versus Study Sample

A comparison of the total population of the McNeil Island prisoners and the study sample of 98 showed that the two groups were similar except that the study sample had a greater representation of ages 21–30 than the prison population (45 percent versus 34 percent) and a lesser representation of those over 31 years of age. Data for a similar comparison of the Walla Walla inmates with the study sample were not available.

Characteristics of McNeil Island and Walla Walla Samples

A comparison of the demographic characteristics of McNeil Island and Walla Walla samples indicated relative homogeneity in the two study populations. The only significant differences in distribution between the two samples were the following:

1. Race. There were more blacks at McNeil Island (26 percent versus 11 percent).
2. Occupation. At McNeil Island there were more people in skilled, clerical, and managerial positions, while at Walla Walla there were more students and salespeople.
3. Criminal offenses. In the McNeil Island sample, there were no murders and more armed robbery, grand larceny, forgery, and drug violations; in the Walla Walla sample, there were murders, more burglaries, assaults, and sexual offenses.
4. Number of siblings. The McNeil Island sample had a larger percentage of prisoners with three or more brothers.

Since 18 of 22 demographic variables investigated showed no significant differences in distribution, the data of the two prison surveys were combined. This homogeneous population (Table 20.1) exhibited the following characteristics: 73 percent were white, and 19 percent were black; 90 percent were between the ages of 21 and 45. Only 25 percent were married; the rest were divorced, separated, widowed, or never married. Fifteen percent had only an elementary school education; 50 percent had attended high school; and 23 percent had a college education. More than half had been born and spent most of their lives in larger cities. About 97 percent were at least second-generation Americans. Al-

Table 20.1
Characteristics of Combined Sample

		% of Prisoners ($N = 176$)
Race		
	White	73
	Black	19
	American Indian	3
	Other	5
Age, yr		
	< 21	1
	21–30	43
	31–45	47
	46–65	9
Religion		
	Protestant	40
	Catholic	18
	Jewish	3
	Other	12
	None	27
Marital status		
	Married	25
	Divorced	33
	Separated	12
	Widowed	2
	Never married	28
No. of marriages		
	None	29
	1	40
	2	17
	3	10
	4	4
No. of divorces		
	None	49
	1	34
	2	11
	3	5
	4	2
No. of spouses who died		
	None	95
	1	4
	≥ 4	1

Table 20.1, continued

	% of Prisoners ($N = 176$)
Education	
Elementary	15
High school	50
Technical	12
College	22
Graduate	1
Time at present residence, yr	
1	34
2	41
5	15
10	2
> 10	8
No. of moves in last 5 yr	
1	18
2	25
3	22
4	9
5	8
6	3
7	1
9	15
Place of birth	
Canada	2
Central America	1
Don't know	1
United States	97
Europe	1
Where most of life spent	
Pacific Coast	50
Other	4
East	9
South	8
Southwest	9
Midwest	12
Rocky Mountains	6
Alaska	2

cont'd

Table 20.1, continued

	% of Prisoners ($N = 176$)
Population of birthplace	
Rural	20
< 5,000	8
5,000–50,000	17
50,000–500,000	22
> 500,000	32
Place of father's birth	
Canada	2
South America	1
Central America	1
Don't know	3
United States	86
Western Europe	4
Eastern Europe	2
Place of mother's birth	
Canada	5
South America	1
Central America	2
Don't know	3
United States	84
Western Europe	3
Eastern Europe	1
No. of brothers	
None	28
1	26
2	22
3	12
≥ 4	13
No. of sisters	
None	27
1	33
2	17
3	12
≥ 4	12
Birth order	
Only	12
Oldest	33
Youngest	26
Middle	30

	% of Prisoners ($N = 176$)
Age at mother's death, yr	
Mother alive	78
0–5	6
6–10	3
10–15	1
15–20	1
> 20	10
Age at father's death, yr	
Father alive	56
0–5	6
6–10	4
10–15	3
15–20	7
> 20	25
Occupation	
Service	2.9
Skilled	42.1
Student	4.7
Unskilled	8.8
Armed Forces	2.9
Clerical	4.1
Managerial	5.3
None	10.5
Professional	6.4
Sales	6.4
Other	5.8
Crime	
Murder (first degree)	2.4
Murder (second degree)	1.8
Armed robbery	28.7
Grand larceny	13.4
Robbery	16.5
Assault	6.1
Fraud	0.6
Forgery	10.4
Escape	0.6
Sexual	6.7
Drugs	12.2
Probation violation	0.6

though many of the prisoners' parents were still living (78 percent of the mothers, and 56 percent of the fathers), the data indicate that during the formative years (age 0–20) 11 percent of the mothers and 20 percent of the fathers had died. Of the crimes, 70 percent were against property, and 17 percent were against persons.

Black and White Prisoners

The racial distribution according to age, educational levels, and criminal offense is not significantly different, although there was a trend ($p < 0.10$) for blacks to be involved in more armed robberies and drug offenses.

Significant differences were seen in marital status. A greater percentage of blacks than whites were married and separated from their wives, but fewer were divorced or never married. More blacks had spent most of their lives on the Pacific Coast, the East Coast, in the Rocky Mountains, and in Alaska. The most striking difference was that 70 percent of the blacks came from cities of greater than 500,000 as compared to 30 percent of the whites.

The blacks had higher percentages of students and unskilled workers while the whites had higher percentages of all the other categories, except in the skilled category, where percentages were similar.

Life Change Magnitude

The mean annual life change scores for the combined prison samples for years prior to and years after imprisonment are shown in Figure 20.1. The life change magnitude escalates from a mean of 170 (year –5 and year –4) to a peak at year –1 of 361 LCU and then decreases in prison to 156 LCU in years +4 and +5. The life change score for year –1, the year prior to incarceration, is significantly higher ($p < 0.0005$) than the scores of the other years. In addition, the scores for years –4 and –5 were significantly lower than years –3, –2, –1, +1, and +2. No significant differences were seen in the annual life change scores while in prison. The McNeil Island and Walla Walla samples showed similar annual life change patterns.

Analysis of the pattern of mean annual life change scores is not significantly influenced by religion, marital status, location where most of life was spent, birth order, occupation, or type of offense. However, race, age, and level of education are associated with different life change profiles (Figure 20.2).

Black prisoners ($N = 33$) experienced lower LCU in all years compared to white prisoners ($N = 126$), and a muted peak is seen in the pattern. The life change scores of the blacks are significantly ($p < 0.002$) lower than those of the white prisoners for the year prior to incarceration (–1) and the first year of incarceration (+1) (Figure 20.2, top).

In the years prior to incarceration, the younger prisoners accumulate the most LCU; then, the middle-aged; and finally, the older age group (Figure 20.2, center). The mean scores of the young group are significantly higher than those of the other two age groups in years –4, –3, and –2. They are also higher than those of the middle-age group in years +1, +2, and +3. There were no differences in any of the annual life change scores between the 31–45-year group and the 46–65-year group. While the LCU of the first two age groups decrease with incarceration time, the LCU of the older age group peak at years +1 and +2 and remain high.

The life change scores of the grade school group are significantly different from those of the other educational groups (Figure 20.2, bottom). These scores are significantly lower than those of the high school group in years –5, –4, and –1, and lower than those of the college group in years –4, –3, and –2. There was no statistical difference between the other two educational groups. Neither was there any significant difference between pairs of groups in any of the years while in prison. However, there was an interesting trend. In all years there is a gradation of LCU—the college-educated with the highest scores; the high school–educated, the middle; and the elementary school–educated, the lowest scores.

Frequency of Occurrence of Life Events

The frequency of occurrence of the life change events in prisoners provides a qualitative and quantitative description of the life-style of the prisoners. Table

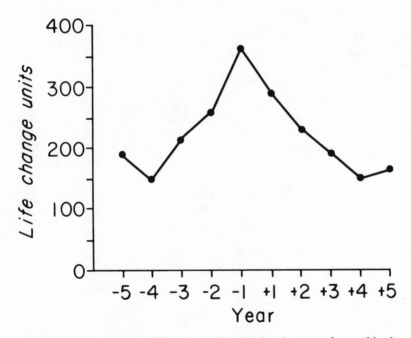

Figure 20.1   Annual LCU before and during imprisonment for combined sample.

20.2 compares the annual frequency of occurrence of life event items in the five preprison years as recorded by prisoners, with the occurrence of life events in a white, middle-class group. This is unpublished data from a combined group of television program responders ($N = 364$) and health cooperative members ($N = 605$). The frequency of events is not similar in these socially disparate groups, and the rank order correlation coefficient (r_s) of the item frequencies is a relatively low 0.336 ($p < 0.02$). In addition, the total annual frequency is lower for the prisoners. However, the frequencies of jail term and minor violations of the law are 0.62 and 0.57, respectively, ranking second and third. For the normative group the frequencies are 0.01 and 0.15, respectively, ranking 40 and 25.5. Change in residence ranks first in the prisoners, but is 23 for the normatives; the prisoners move about four times more frequently. In work-related items, prisoners change more often to a different line of work and have a much greater

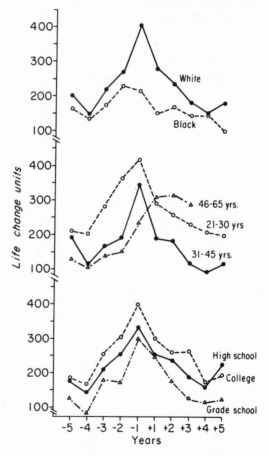

Figure 20.2   Annual LCU according to race (top), age (center), and education (bottom) for combined sample.

Table 20.2
Annual Frequency of Occurrence* of Life Events

Life Event	White Middle-Class Group (N = 969)		Prisoners (N = 176)	
	Frequency	Rank†	Frequency	Rank†
Vacation	1.06	1	.35	5.5
Mortgage or loan less than $10,000	.53	2	.34	7
Change in health of family member	.51	3	.15	18.5
Change in work hours or conditions	.40	4	.37	4
Change in financial state	.36	5	.21	11
Outstanding personal achievement	.35	6	.25	10
Personal injury or illness	.34	7.5	.15	18.5
Change in living conditions	.34	7.5	.27	9
Sex difficulties	.32	9	.13	24.5
Change in sleeping habits	.30	10	.13	24.5
Change in social activities	.29	11.5	.18	13
Change in responsibilities at work	.29	11.5	.30	8
Change in recreation	.28	13.5	.16	15.5
Change in number of arguments with spouse	.28	13.5	.12	27.5
Change in eating habits	.27	15.5	.13	24.5
Death of close family member	.27	15.5	.10	32
Change in number of family get-togethers	.26	17.5	.14	21.5
Son or daughter leaving home	.26	17.5	.02	39
Change in church activities	.23	20	.09	34
Death of close friend	.23	20	.14	21.5
Gain of new family member	.23	20	.18	13
Revision of personal habits	.22	22	.18	13
Change in residence	.21	23	.79	1
Wife beginning or stopping work	.18	24	.15	18.5
Trouble with in-laws	.15	25.5	.11	29.5
Minor violations of the law	.15	25.5	.57	3
Change to different line of work	.14	27	.35	5.5
Trouble with boss	.13	28	.11	29.5
Business readjustment	.11	29.5	.13	24.5
Mortgage over $10,000	.11	29.5	.05	36.5
Beginning or ending school	.10	31	.10	32
Marital separation	.06	32.5	.16	15.5
Change in schools	.06	32.5	.12	27.5
Marriage	.05	34.5	.10	32
Retirement	.05	34.5	.03	38
Death of spouse	.04	36.5	.01	40
Foreclosure of mortgage or loan	.04	36.5	.05	36.5
Divorce	.02	38.5	.06	35
Fired at work	.02	38.5	.15	18.5
Jail term	.01	40	.62	2
Total	9.55		7.75	

* Frequency of occurrence is item incidence/individual/year
† Frequency rank order correlation: $r_s = 0.336$; $p < 0.02$

propensity for being fired at work. In spouse-related categories, the prisoners experience more marriages, divorces, and marital separations.

The frequency of occurrence of individual life events generally parallels the magnitude of total life change and peaks in the year prior to imprisonment. The data on white and black prisoners also show the same phenomena, as did the data separated according to levels of education.

In Figure 20.3, examples of life events of graded frequency magnitude are compared. The clear separation of item occurrences prior to imprisonment disappears in prison, as prison life forces a stabilization. However, life in prison does not always mean stabilization for all. Figure 20.4 illustrates the influence of age on a single item: frequency of change in residence. Preincarceration, the young moved most often; then, the middle-aged; and the elderly moved the least. But in prison, the elderly prisoner reported more moves in the first two years of prison than did the other two age groups. Even in prison, residence changes for the younger and the older are considerable.

COMMENT

The following profile of persons incarcerated in the state and federal prisons under study can be deduced from the data. The prisoner is a white, Protestant man between the ages of 21 and 45 who has been incarcerated for a crime involving property or money. He is the eldest or only son of native-born American parents and had as equal a probability of being born in a rural area as in a city. His early

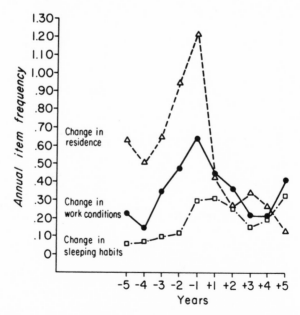

Figure 20.3   Selected SRE item frequencies for combined sample.

life was seriously disrupted by the death of a parent. After achieving a high school education, he spent most of his life in an urban area occupied as a skilled worker. He has had at least three residential moves and frequent job changes in the last five years. He is currently unmarried. He has had a recent previous prison record and at least one citation for a minor violation of the law.

More life events have been experienced by the young than the old prisoners: They are more mobile, have more problems at work, and more financial difficulties. This finding is similar to that of Holmes [13], who used the SRE to construct a ten-year profile of events for general hospital patients.

The life-style of prisoners with a college education is characterized by the occurrence of more life events than that of prisoners with other educational experience. Half of the items occur more frequently in those subjects with a college education, while only two occur less frequently. The increase occurs in: (1) social items, such as change in recreation and residence; (2) occupation and finance, such as change in working conditions and responsibilities, financial state, and securing loans of less than $10,000; (3) family relationships, such as separation or change in health of family member; (4) personal items, such as sex

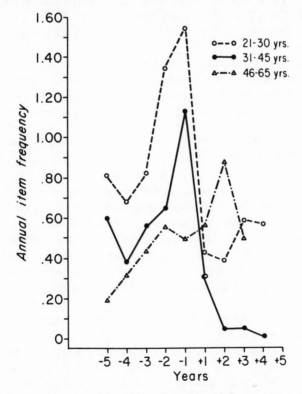

Figure 20.4   Item frequency (change in residence) for age groups of combined sample.

difficulties, personal injury, or illness; and (5) education, such as change in schools and beginning or ending school. These data suggest that the drive to attend college also impels these people to seek new experiences and a wider horizon. College graduates who are criminals are at a greater risk for larger amounts of life change.

The life change magnitude for the elderly incarcerated is significantly higher while in prison than for the young. This is despite the fact that 32 of the 40 items occur equally or less frequently in the old than in the young age groups. Among the items that occur more frequently for the old are death of close family member, death of close friend, change in health of family member, mortgage or loan less than $10,000, and foreclosure of mortgage or loan. These events are of higher magnitudes, clearly occur outside the prison, and are congruent with the age of the subjects. Although the fact of incarceration may, in part, evoke these events, these are not occurrences associated with the life-style in prison.

The older prisoners move more often within the prison confines. Movement within prison indicates placements into greater or lesser security, usually dictated by prisoner behavior and status, subject to prison authorities. Inasmuch as the great majority of within-prison life events occurs less frequently in prison among the elderly, it would lead to the speculation that their behavior is more stable and exemplary. This might lead to changes in prison residence toward lesser security and greater trust.

Both black and white prisoners show a rising accumulation of life change units prior to incarceration in prison, but with the blacks showing lower magnitudes. This is a reflection of the fact that blacks experienced consistently lower numbers of life events. There may be two alternative explanations for this. One might be a speculated difference in "psychological threshold" between blacks and whites that triggers behavior leading to imprisonment. The second alternative is that the low LCU of the blacks is an artifact deriving from the use of SRRS scores obtained from a sample of white, middle-class subjects that was assumed to reflect the U.S. average. However, a study by Komaroff and colleagues [14] on black ghetto residents showed that, for them, life events required significantly greater psychosocial readjustments, that is, their SRRS scores were decidedly higher. These higher scores encompassed the range of life events related to work, finances, housing, and life-style. If the black SRRS scores obtained by Komaroff et al. had been used, the LCU for blacks would have been similar to those for white prisoners. The SRRS scores obtained from many different subcultural and cross-cultural studies [15] show significant differences from the original SRRS. This places a caveat on using inappropriate life event magnitude estimations to estimate life change scores.

Although there are many similarities between the prisoners and the normative group, there are distinct qualitative and quantitative differences in life event occurrences. Prisoners are less stable, more mobile, and at times even transient. They have greater frequencies of change in residence, change to a different line of work, and being fired; they have more financial problems. Instability is also indicated by more divorces and separations, more marriages, and more trouble with in-laws. Prior jail terms and minor violations of the law are clearly the province of the prisoner's life-style. The prisoners in our study experienced one of these two events at least once every two years.

The life history of convicted felons reveals that social and economic forces have played an important part in influencing their careers [16]. There is a common history of severely disordered family and social backgrounds—there are poverty and broken homes, and there may be parental criminality and alcoholism. Poor social and familial backgrounds leading to restricted opportunities and unhappy internal adjustments provide fertile ground for criminal activities.

But it is also clear that social, economic, and racial forces are not the only answer, for only a small fraction of those so exposed become criminals, and there are criminals who have not known poverty, racism, and social limitations. Other factors must enter into the equation; and, of these, a salient factor must be the individual's unique development and personal characteristics.

The criminal and his or her peers live in a U.S. subculture with value orientations at variance with the majority society. Peer group values, loyalty demands, codes of conduct, and denial of society's values are a differentiating part of the criminal subculture. Thus, the criminal's life-style reflects antisocial behavior (as society perceives it) that is a part of the subcultural norm.

This life-style is reflected in the quantitative differences in life event frequencies, displaying a profile of life events that is almost identical to problem areas in the life histories of convicted felons as delineated by Guze [16]. This is further indication of cultural transmission of values from earlier into adult years.

The criminal's world and the life-style that he or she embraces are represented by the total life-event behaviors of which criminal activity is but one inseparable part. The same values and orientations by which the criminal lives are reflected in the total spectrum of living activities, whether relating to marital, work, financial, or living concerns. Separation into criminal behavior and other behaviors, as to primary causation, is seen as inappropriate in viewing the escalation of life events associated with prison incarceration.

This study has shown a mounting accumulation of life change events and an increase in life change magnitude that achieves crisis proportions in the year prior to incarceration in prison. This pattern of life change frequency and magnitude is similar to that observed at the time of onset of a wide variety of health changes [1;17]. It has been suggested elsewhere [18] that these events, by evoking maladaptive behavior, increase susceptibility to biological and psychological disease. These life change data suggest that the commission of, apprehension for, and incarceration for crime parallel the signs and symptoms of an illness. Marital problems or being fired from work may well trigger or accompany a series of events that could lead to illness and hospitalization or to criminal activity and imprisonment.

The data cannot address the issue of criminal behavior that goes unchecked. It addresses itself only to unsuccessful criminal behavior that leads to incarceration. It may be that escalating life changes lead to a malfunctioning of previously successful criminal activities such as to bring about apprehension and imprisonment.

A time gap may occur between the time of the criminal act and apprehension and between apprehension and incarceration in prison. If such time gaps of at least a year do occur in sufficient numbers of cases, then year –2 should also show some elevation of life change. There is such a tendency as exemplified for black and younger prisoners in Figure 20.2 (top and center), for change in residence and change in work conditions in Figure 20.3 (top and center), and for change in residence in Figure 20.4.

Prison life obviously changes the lives of prisoners; this is reflected in the gradual reduction of life changes experienced. This reduction to preprison levels, however, is not abrupt, indicating that prison imposes a set of new living conditions to which adjustment must be made. Stabilization occurs with time as adaptation follows the restrained and regimented life that is led within prison walls, away from spouse, family, work, and so on.

In all retrospective studies there is the issue of accuracy in the recall of life events. Studies [19;20] have shown that there is a decrement in the reporting of life events. That is, events of lesser saliency tend to be lost to recollection with time. But Casey et al. [19] have shown that there is a significant correlation between events remembered one year later (0.74), three years later (0.64), and six years later (0.67). Therefore, there is a considerable degree of reliability in recalling of salient life events.

In the case of this study's prisoner sample, 100 percent were in the second year of prison and 52 percent were in the third year, tapering off to 28 percent, 19 percent, and 14 percent in their fourth, fifth, and sixth years, respectively. All subjects gave SRE responses to years –5 through year +1, but there were reduced numbers of responses in years +2 through +5. Thus, the most immediate years of recollection (and ostensibly the most accurate) varied from years +1 to year +5. This spread would tend to negate the possibility that the most recent year of recollection was an important factor in the shape of the escalating curve of life events prior to imprisonment. The possibility that the year of incarceration was the most vividly remembered is also negated by the above consideration and the fact that the average prisoner experiences 0.62 jail terms a year. It seems unlikely, in view of this history, that imprisonment is that vivid a psychological landmark of reference.

A recent study by Guze [16] of male felons in Missouri correction centers indicated that 78 percent were classified as antisocial personalities, with added percentages due to alcoholism, drug dependence, and frank psychotic illnesses. Guze's demographic data are congruent with the felons' data in this study. This suggests that a similar distribution of disorders also prevails in the prisoners in the present report.

Dudley et al. [21] used the SRE to study populations of alcoholics and heroin addicts. Alcoholism and addiction were common in the felons studied by Guze; recent jail term was also a common life event in the two groups of addicts. It appears that crime and alcohol and heroin addiction commonly coexist in the same populations and have similar natural histories.

REFERENCES

1. Holmes, T. H., and M. Masuda. "Life Change and Illness Susceptibility." In *Separation and Depression: Clinical and Research Aspects*, edited by J. P. Scott and E. C. Senay, pp. 161–86. AAAS Publication no. 94. Washington, D.C.: American Association for the Advancement of Science, 1973.

2. Wyler, A. R., M. Masuda, and T. H. Holmes. "Magnitude of Life Events and Seriousness of Illness." *Psychosomatic Medicine* 33 (1971):115–22. Reprinted in this volume, Chapter 16.

3. Holmes, T. H., and R. H. Rahe. "The Social Readjustment Rating Scale." *Journal of Psychosomatic Research* 11 (1967):213–18. Reprinted in this volume, Chapter 2.

4. Rahe, R. H., M. Meyer, M. Smith, G. Kjaer, and T. H. Holmes. "Social Stress and Illness Onset." *Journal of Psychosomatic Research* 8 (1964):35–44. Reprinted in this volume, Chapter 12.

5. Holmes, T. H., and R. H. Rahe. *Booklet for Schedule of Recent Experience (SRE)*. Seattle: University of Washington, 1967.

6. Carranza, E. "A Study of the Impact of Life Changes on High School Teacher Performance in the Lansing School District as Measured by the Holmes and Rahe Schedule of Recent Experience." Ph.D. dissertation, Michigan State University, 1972.

7. Harris, P. W. "The Relationship of Life Change to Academic Performance among Selected College Freshmen at Varying Levels of College Readiness." Ph.D. dissertation, East Texas State University, 1972.

8. Clinard, J. W. "Life Change Events as Related to Self-reported Academic and Job Performance." *Psychological Reports* 33 (1973):391–94.

9. Bramwell, S. T., M. Masuda, N. N. Wagner, and T. H. Holmes. "Psychosocial Factors in Athletic Injuries: Development and Application of the Social and Athletic Readjustment Rating Scale (SARRS)." *Journal of Human Stress* 1, no. 2. (1975):6–20. Reprinted in this volume, Chapter 19.

10. Selzer, M. L., and A. Vinokur. "Life Events, Subjective Stress, and Traffic Accidents." *American Journal of Psychiatry* 131 (1974):903–6.

11. Paykel, E. S., B. A. Prusoff, and J. K. Myers. "Suicide Attempts and Recent Life Events: A Controlled Comparison." *Archives of General Psychiatry* 32 (1975):327–33.

12. Cochrane, R., and A. Robertson. "Stress in the Lives of Parasuicides." *Social Psychiatry* 10 (1975):161–71.

13. Holmes, T. S. "Adaptive Behavior and Health Change." Medical thesis, University of Washington, 1970.

14. Komaroff, A. L., M. Masuda, and T. H. Holmes. "The Social Readjustment Rating Scale: A Comparative Study of Negro, Mexican and White Americans." *Journal of Psychosomatic Research* 12 (1968):121–28. Reprinted in this volume, Chapter 6.

15. Masuda, M., and T. H. Holmes. "Life Events, Life Event Perceptions, and Life Style." Abstract. *Psychosomatic Medicine* 38 (1976):66.

16. Guze, S. B. *Criminality and Psychiatric Disorders.* New York: Oxford University Press, 1976.

17. Rahe, R. H. "Life Crisis and Health Change." In *Psychotropic Drug Response: Advances in Prediction,* edited by P. R. A. May and J. R. Wittenborn, pp. 92–125. Springfield, Ill.: Charles C Thomas, 1969. Pts. 2 and 3 reprinted in this volume, Chapters 13 and 14.

18. Wolff, H. G. "Life Stress and Bodily Disease—A Formulation." In *Life Stress and Bodily Disease,* edited by H. G. Wolff, S. Wolf, and C. C. Hare, pp. 1059–94. Research Publications of the Association for Research in Nervous and Mental Disease, vol. 29. Baltimore: Williams and Wilkins, 1950.

19. Casey, R. L., M. Masuda, and T. H. Holmes. "Quantitative Study of Recall of Life Events." *Journal of Psychosomatic Research* 11 (1967):239–47. Reprinted in this volume, Chapter 10.

20. Rahe, R. H. "The Pathway between Subjects' Recent Life Changes and Their Near-future Illness Reports: Representative Results and Methodological Issues." In *Stressful Life Events: Their Nature and Effects,* edited by B. S. Dohrenwend and B. P. Dohrenwend, pp. 73–86. New York: John Wiley and Sons, 1974.

21. Dudley, D. L., D. K. Roszell, J. E. Mules, and W. H. Hague. "Heroin vs. Alcohol Addiction—Quantifiable Psychosocial Similarities and Differences." *Journal of Psychosomatic Research* 18 (1974):327–35.

21

Life Events:
Perceptions and Frequencies

Minoru Masuda and Thomas H. Holmes

INTRODUCTION

Holmes and Rahe [1] devised the Social Readjustment Rating Scale (SRRS) in order to quantify the amount of psychosocial readjustment required to cope with 43 life events. The life events were selected on the basis of clinical experience involving more than 5,000 patients whose case histories indicated significant events that preceded onset of illness. The development of the scale was based on the method of psychophysics [2], but in which the stimulus does not have a physical metric but is derived from an internal subjective metric.

The perceived magnitude estimations derived produced a ratio scale, which was a tool in quantifying the amount of life change experienced. The instrument that took advantage of the SRRS was the Schedule of Recent Experience (SRE) [3;4], which recorded the occurrence of the SRRS life events on a periodic basis. Life change units (LCU), then, are the sum of the products of the numbers of occurrences of life events multiplied by assigned SRRS values.

There is considerable evidence [5] that links the accumulation of life change to the onset of illness: The greater the magnitude of life change, the greater the risk of illness and, furthermore, the greater the seriousness of the chronic illness [6].

Since the introduction of the SRRS and the SRE, a great number of studies have been generated supporting the concept and the methods, as well as studies that are critical of some of the methodologic concepts and methodologies [7–9]. The SRRS has thus seen additions, deletions, and modifications of the life event items [10–15], selecting out of "desirable" and "undesirable" items [13;14;16], changes in questionnaire administration (paired judgment [17], card sort [18], and verbal [19]), changes in anchoring modulus item [12] and setting of upper limits [20] or nonanchor [13], category scaling instead of ratio scaling [13], and so forth.

Methodologic issues that relate to the life-change-and-illness concept are retrospective recall of life events [21;22], variations in individual coping abilities [23], psychologic aspects of illness behavior [24], weights and meaning of "negative" and "positive" life events [13], time relations of events to illness [13;25], and so forth. In spite of questions raised, the fundamental concept of the relationship of accumulating life change to illness remains intact.

The concept of life events impacting on individuals to produce a variety of illnesses has been extended to their association with other behaviors such as academic performance of students [26] and teachers [27], as well as job performance [28]. Life change has been associated with traffic accidents [29], incarceration of criminals [30], children's psychobiological adjustments [1;11;31], and injuries to football players [12].

It is the intent of this chapter to focus on the two parameters that are critical to the estimation of life change: the magnitude estimations or perceptions of life events, and the frequency of occurrence of life events. The data from 19 studies emanating from this laboratory have been collated to focus on the extent of variation and on the factors that produce variability in these two parameters. Peoples of differing characteristics and cultures not only perceive differently the significance of life events, but also report a difference in the quality and quantity of life event occurrences. These data point up the advisability of taking these factors into consideration in assessing the relationship of life events to illness. It is also suggested that the SRRS and the SRE may be helpful in the assessment of psychological, sociological, and cultural determinants of life change; life events that happen to people, as well as how events are perceived, are a reflection of their life-style and culture.

METHODOLOGY

The questionnaires used in common in all of these studies were the Social Readjustment Rating Questionnaire (SRRQ) [1] and the Schedule of Recent Experience (SRE) [3;4].

The SRRQ asks the respondent to assign a numerical estimation of the amount of psychosocial readjustment required to cope with the impact of 42 life events. Marriage was the anchoring modulus item with a given value of 500. The subject's perception of the significance of a life event is measured in relation to the given anchor score. All mean scores of life event items are reported here as the geometric mean [32].

The SRE asks the respondent to recall whether a life event occurred or the number of times it occurred on a periodic basis. The retrospective and self-reported data of the studies analyzed here have been standardized to yield a mean annual life event frequency per individual. The periodic data collected ranged from one to five years.

RESULTS

Studies on the Life Event Magnitude Estimation Using the SRRS

Middle-Class Americans

The original study of Holmes and Rahe [1] that developed the SRRS was based on a sample of 394 individuals, generally classified as a white middle-class group. The roles of age, sex, marital status, and education as they affect perceptions of life events were deduced. Demographic comparisons of this group indicated that, while these variables did not affect the highly significant positive rank-order correlation coefficients between groups, they did affect the magnitude estimations assigned to life events.

The Variable of Age

Individuals were separated into three age groups: those under 30 years of age, those 30–60 years of age, and those over 60 years of age. Comparing the young and middle-aged, middle-aged and old, and the young and old, the correlation coefficients on the rank ordering of life event items (r_s) among these three groups were 0.96, 0.96, and 0.92, respectively. However, comparison of the individual life event scores among the three groups revealed many significant differences.

As Table 21.1 indicates, the number of life event items scored differently between the young and the middle-aged was small and almost equally distributed in terms of the direction of these differences. However, 23 items were scored significantly lower by the elderly group (none higher) when compared to both the young and middle-age groups.

The Variable of Sex

Table 21.1 gives similar data on comparison of males and females. The rank order correlation coefficient (r_s) of SRRS items between these two groups was 0.96, but there were 16 items scored differently, all showing females with higher scores.

The Variable of Education

The sample was separated into groups according to education: those having less than college degrees, and those having college degrees and greater. Table 21.1 indicates that those with less than college degrees gave significantly higher scores to 24 life event items and a lower score to only one (death of spouse).

Table 21.1

Variables Affecting SRRS Item Scores: White, Middle-Class Americans (N = 394)

Variable	Group comparisons	Items scored differently[a]	Direction of higher scores
Age	Young (N = 206) vs. middle-aged (N = 137)	8	5, young; 3, middle-aged
	Middle-aged vs. old (N = 51)	23	23, middle-aged
	Young vs. old	23	23, young
Sex	Male (N = 179) vs. female (N = 215)	16	16, female
Education	< College (N = 182) vs. ≥ college degree (N = 212)	25	24, < college; 1, ≥ college degree
Marital status	Ever-married (N = 223) vs. single (N = 171)	15	15, single

[a] Mann-Whitney U-test < 0.05 probability

The Variable of Marital Status

The sample was divided into two groups: those ever married (including widowed, separated, and divorced), and those who were single. Of the 15 items scored significantly differently by the two groups, all were scored higher by the singles (Table 21.1).

A graph that is representative of the differences in individual life-event magnitudes among age groups is shown in Figure 21.1. All mean scores of the 42 life events are displayed in descending order of magnitude as assigned by the three different age groups. It is clearly evident that the general level of life event scoring is lower for the elderly. A similar graph could have been constructed based on the other three variables. Item differences occurred throughout all categories of life events, that is, spouse related, work related, family related, lifestyle related, and so on. The general conclusion to be derived from the data is that, in this white, middle-class group, individuals who were female, less than elderly, single, and with less than a college degree perceived life events as requiring more psychosocial readjustments.

Comparison of Three U.S. Subcultural Groups

This section collates the magnitude estimations derived on the SRRS from three different U.S. subcultural groups: the original white middle-class group [1]

Table 21.2
Subcultural and Cross-national Comparisons on the SRRS

Group	Number	Sum or mean item scores	Range of scores	Scoring spread
Middle-class Americans[a]	394	11,340	54–771	717
Black Americans[b]	64	13,520	150–652	502
Mexican Americans[b]	78	10,597	108–500	392
Western Europeans[c]	139	11,389	63–660	597
Spanish[d]	212	12,727	44–1,524	1,480
Salvadorans[e]	197	10,221	116–500	384
Japanese[f]	112	10,768	40–1,079	1,039
Malaysians[g]	266	15,707	123–814	691

Sources: [a] [1]; [b] [33]; [c] [34]; [d] [35]; [e] [37]; [f] [36]; [g] [38].

and the black American and Mexican American groups from a study conducted in Los Angeles [33]. The rank order correlation coefficients comparing the white middle-class group to the blacks and Mexican Americans were 0.80 and 0.74, respectively (significant at $p \leq 0.001$).

The salient data are shown in Figure 21.2 where the mean magnitude estimates of the ranked items are plotted in descending order. This family of curves indicates the difference in general scoring levels where the black Americans (except for the first and second ranked items) assigned higher scores consistently at the same rank compared to the middle-class Americans. The Mexican Americans assigned intermediate scores and, compared to the middle-class Americans, scored lower in the upper ranked items, and higher in the lower ranked items.

Table 21.2 shows the sum total of each group's mean magnitude estimation as well as the range and scoring spread. The table bears out the scoring level seen in Figure 21.2 and also shows the differences in the range as well as the spread in scores of the life event items. The middle-class Americans showed the widest spread of the three U.S. subcultural groups. The Mexican Americans showed the narrowest spread, and the blacks were in between. The narrowness of the scoring we shall call *constriction*, and these differences imply some mechanism of subjective psychological constraint. Some constriction was seen in the elderly (Figure 21.2) and this will be noted later in cross-national studies.

Cross-national Comparisons on the SRRS

In this section, SRRS data from five cross-national studies were collated, comparing data from the middle-class Americans with Western Europeans [34],

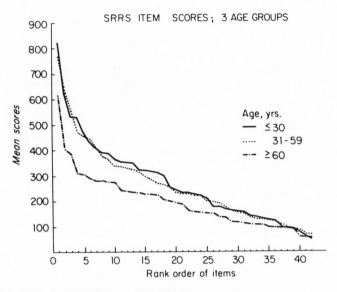

Figure 21.1   SRRS item scores in three age groups.

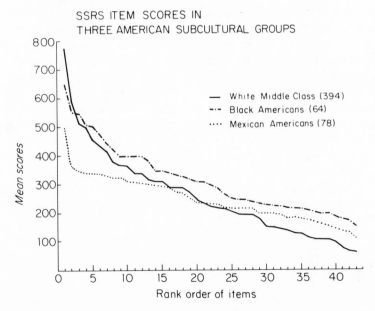

Figure 21.2   SRRS item scores in three subcultural groups.

Spanish [35], Japanese [36], Salvadorans [37], and Malaysians [38]. The rank order correlation coefficients were all highly significant, but there were varying degrees of strengths of correlations (r_s = 0.65–0.91), where the Salvadorans showed the lowest degree of intercorrelation with the other groups.

SRRS rank item scores from three selected cultures are shown in Figure 21.3, to illustrate how differing cultures produce differences in magnitude estimations of life events. The Malaysians perceived life events to have greater impact than did the Americans, while the Salvadorans assigned lower scores as well as exhibiting score constriction (described in the previous section).

The studies from which these data were taken described individual life-event perceptions in these countries, compared them with the Americans' magnitude estimations, and discussed the cultural aspects of these many differences. Here we have pointed up the differences in the general levels of scoring.

Table 21.2 also shows the total mean item scores for each of these national groups as well as the scoring spread of the range of scores. There may or may not be a relationship between the total scores and the scoring spread. The Salvadorans have the lowest scoring spread, but the total scores are not too different from the Japanese, who show the second-highest scoring spread. The Malay-

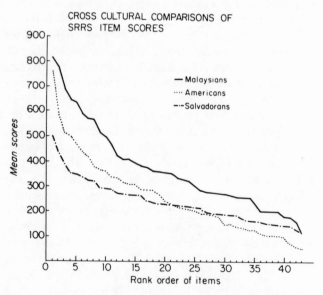

Figure 21.3   Cross-national comparisons of SRRS item scores.

sians, with clearly higher life event perceptions, are intermediate in scoring spread—not dissimilar to Americans and Western Europeans.

Studies on Life Event Frequencies Using the SRE: Studies on 12 Different Groups

The data from 12 studies on disparate groups using the SRE, recording the reported annual frequency of occurrence of individual life-event items, are shown in Table 21.3. The subjects and the numbers in each sample are indicated. The total frequency is the sum of the individual mean item frequencies. The variations among groups in the frequencies of occurrence of individual life events as well as the total frequencies are readily apparent. The greatest numbers of events happened to the study group of heroin addicts with a frequency of more than 26, while medical students had the lowest frequency of about 5, a fivefold difference.

The variations in frequencies shown in Table 21.3 reflect the characteristics of the groups studied. They were disparate in sex distribution (for example, 100 percent of prisoners, football players, alcoholics, and heroin addicts, and the majority of medical students and medical residents were male—only the pregnant patients were all female). Educational attainments were variable, but with relatively good distribution between high school and college educated, except for the subjects attending the university. The groups were predominantly white except that there were about 20 percent blacks among the prisoners, pregnant mothers, and heroin addicts. Except for the university students, the prisoners, and the heroin addicts, most groups were predominantly married. Younger people were seen in the university attendees, pregnant women, and heroin addicts. The other groups were mostly middle-aged, and the only group that had a sizable elderly group (over 60 years of age) was the hospital patient group (27 percent). All groups were mostly from urban areas. It would seem that the factors of age, sex, education, race, and urban/rural living are not the whole answer to the great disparity between groups in terms of life event happenings.

On the other hand, there was a highly significant concordance in the rank order of life event frequencies among the 12 groups (Kendall's $W = 0.648$; $p \le 0.001$). In spite of the differences in the magnitude of frequency of occurrences, life events happen among groups in similar distribution. The items that happened most frequently were change in residence, vacation, change in work conditions, personal injury or illness, change in sleeping habits, and outstanding personal achievement. Life events that happened least frequently were death of spouse, divorce, mortgage foreclosure, retirement, and mortgage greater than $10,000.

Life events were categorized according to item relatedness to work (items 1, 28, 29, 30, 31, and 39); finance (items 9, 22, 34, 35, and 36); personal nature (items 13, 16, and 26); spouse (items 11, 12, 15, 23, 24, 25, and 33); law (items 20 and 21); family (items 8, 10, 14, 17, 18, and 27); life-style (items 2, 3, 4, 5, 6, 7, 19, 32, and 37); and school (items 38 and 40). The item numbers correspond to those shown in Table 21.3. This was done in order to scrutinize more closely the differences between groups, but yet not get lost in individual item differences.

Table 21.4 compares the magnitude of the sums of the item frequencies in each of the above eight categories between two pairs of different groups as examples of how samples that are not markedly dissimilar in demographic characteristics nevertheless incur large differences in life events.

In the first instance, two groups of hospitalized patients are compared, the first group hospitalized for treatment of bone fractures (Table 21.3), and the second group for medical and surgical treatment (Table 21.3). These groups did not differ in education or race, but the fracture groups had a higher percentage of males, those of single status, and those in the younger age group. The large differences between these two groups of patients were remarkable. In most categories of items the fracture patients recorded far greater numbers of occurrences. The calculated ratios of category frequency differences indicated that the disproportion is uneven. Fracture patients incurred more than double the number of life events in work- and money-related life events and the two items of conflict with the law. People who sustain fractures apparently have a style of living, behavior, and orientation that allows for a greater occurrence of life events.

Table 21.4 also compares two groups of university students: college students (Table 21.3) with medical students (Table 21.3). Here the medical students were slightly older; they were mostly males, and greater numbers were married. The college students showed strikingly greater numbers of life event occurrences in all categories, but most strikingly in the items related to finances, family, and life-style. In addition, while lesser numbers of the college students were married, they managed to accumulate 2.5 times more spouse-related life events. The medical students would appear to lead more orderly, stable, uneventful, and regimented lives, presumably based on medical school selection criteria and institutional molding, as well as possibly age.

Item Frequencies in a Normative Group

Of the 12 groups shown in Table 21.3, most were narrowly selected groups of individuals: hospital patients, university students, prisoners, addicts, and so forth. However, there were two larger samples drawn from wider segments of the population. These two were the TV study group [47] and the Group Health sample [48]. The TV study group was comprised of 364 respondents who showed interest in participating in a project after a nationwide life-change-and-illness telecast. The Group Health sample was obtained randomly from the roster of a large health maintenance organization. The demographic characteristics of these two groups did not differ in any marked way in age, sex, race, marital status, education, religion, or urban/rural distributions. Therefore, they were combined to produce a "normative" group of 969 from which we may derive data that may have greater relevance to the general population. The characteristics of this combined sample are shown in Table 21.5.

Table 21.3
Mean Annual Frequency of Individual Life Event Items

Life event items	Prisoners[a] (N = 176)	Pregnant mothers[b] (N = 50)	Fracture patients[c] (N = 37)	Football players[d] (N = 97)	College students[e] (N = 98)
1. Trouble with boss	0.11	0.06	0.28	0.03	0.37
2. Change in sleeping habits	0.13	0.23	0.28	0.17	1.05
3. Change in eating habits	0.13	0.24	0.32	0.16	1.09
4. Revision of personal habits	0.18	0.26	0.31	0.22	0.79
5. Change in recreation	0.16	0.14	0.41	0.15	0.68
6. Change in social activities	0.18	0.24	0.28	0.22	0.61
7. Change in church activities	0.09	0.10	0.11	0.12	0.26
8. Change in number of family get-togethers	0.14	0.16	0.20	0.18	0.50
9. Change in financial state	0.21	0.24	0.45	0.18	0.62
10. Trouble with in-laws	0.11	0.19	0.11	0.04	0.16
11. Change in number of arguments with spouse	0.12	0.14	0.19	0.02	0.14
12. Sex difficulties	0.13	0.04	0.16	0.13	0.34
13. Personal injury or illness	0.15	0.17	0.50	0.17	0.27
14. Death of close family member	0.10	0.12	0.21	0.11	0.17
15. Death of spouse	0.01	0.02	0	0	0
16. Death of close friend	0.14	0.05	0.21	0.10	0.09
17. Gain of new family member	0.18	0.18	0.35	0.11	0.17
18. Change in health of family member	0.15	0.25	0.40	0.13	0.47
19. Change in residence	0.79	0.53	0.77	0.38	1.09
20. Jail term	0.63	0.08	0.11	0.04	0
21. Minor violations of the law	0.57	0.04	0.48	0.23	0.28
22. Business readjustment	0.13	0.03	0.24	0	0
23. Marriage	0.10	0.14	0.06	0.02	0.01
24. Divorce	0.06	0.02	0.02	0	0.01
25. Marital separation	0.16	0.11	0.17	0	0.04
26. Outstanding personal achievement	0.25	0.04	0.58	0.44	0.60
27. Son or daughter leaving home	0.02	0.04	0.17	0.02	0
28. Retirement	0.03	0.12	0.09	0	0
29. Change in work hours or conditions	0.37	0.13	0.73	0.16	0.57
30. Change in responsibilities at work	0.30	0.07	0.42	0.08	0.26
31. Fired at work	0.15	0.02	0.32	0.01	0.06
32. Change in living conditions	0.27	0.17	0.04	0.12	0
33. Wife begin or stop work	0.15	0.15	0.12	0.21	0.01
34. Mortgage over $10,000	0.05	0.05	0.13	0	0
35. Mortgage or loan less than $10,000	0.34	0.14	0.68	0.02	0.18
36. Foreclosure of mortgage or loan	0.05	0.02	0.11	0	0
37. Vacation	0.35	0.21	0.88	0.47	1.16
38. Change in schools	0.12	0.07	0.09	0.22	0.37
39. Change to different line of work	0.35	0.09	0.30	0.19	0.55
40. Begin or end school	0.10	0.13	0.06	0.20	0.46
Total mean annual frequencies	7.76	5.23	11.34	5.04	13.43

Sources: [a] [30]; [b] [39]; [c] [40]; [d] [12]; [e] [41]; [f] [42]; [g] [43]; [h] [44]; [i] [45]; [j] [46]; [k] [47]; [l] [48].

Hospital patients[f] ($N = 460$)	Medical students[g] ($N = 229$)	Medical residents[h] ($N = 89$)	Alcoholics[i] ($N = 66$)	Heroin addicts[j] ($N = 50$)	TV study[k] ($N = 364$)	Group Health[l] ($N = 605$)	Mean item frequency	Rank
0.08	0.05	0.05	0.37	0.38	0.21	0.09	0.17	26.5
0.24	0.16	0.15	0.68	1.24	0.44	0.22	0.42	5.5
0.24	0.17	0.12	0.72	0.98	0.39	0.20	0.40	9.5
0.20	0.17	0.15	0.50	0.86	0.33	0.15	0.34	13.5
0.25	0.17	0.21	0.51	0.72	0.38	0.22	0.34	13.5
0.23	0.18	0.16	0.68	0.82	0.42	0.22	0.35	12.0
0.14	0.12	0.11	0.41	0.34	0.32	0.17	0.19	23.0
0.16	0.11	0.14	0.51	0.52	0.34	0.20	0.26	18.0
0.27	0.13	0.16	0.74	1.10	0.48	0.28	0.41	7.5
0.06	0.02	0.03	0.40	0.38	0.26	0.09	0.15	30.0
0.13	0.02	0.04	0.69	0.60	0.37	0.23	0.22	21.0
0.18	0.10	0.05	0.68	0.58	0.44	0.25	0.26	18.0
0.68	0.10	0.08	1.56	1.38	0.50	0.25	0.48	4.0
0.15	0.07	0.05	0.32	0.24	0.30	0.25	0.17	26.5
0	0	0	0.12	0.06	0.08	0.01	0.03	39.5
0.18	0.05	0.02	0.31	0.88	0.23	0.23	0.21	22.0
0.12	0.05	0.14	0.15	0.28	0.26	0.21	0.18	24.5
0.26	0.13	0.07	0.97	0.84	0.71	0.39	0.40	9.5
0.57	0.54	0.63	1.40	2.32	0.23	0.20	0.79	1.0
0.08	0.01	0	0.75	1.34	0.01	0.01	0.26	18.0
0.17	0.21	0.18	0.76	1.52	0.15	0.15	0.41	7.5
0.11	0.01	0.06	0.23	0.42	0.15	0.08	0.12	32.0
0.04	0.05	0.08	0.15	0.08	0.05	0.06	0.07	35.0
0.04	0	0	0.16	0.06	0.02	0.02	0.03	39.5
0.11	0	0.03	0.48	0.40	0.09	0.05	0.14	31.0
0.22	0.44	0.27	0.47	1.06	0.40	0.32	0.42	5.5
0.06	0.01	0	0.25	0.18	0.21	0.29	0.10	33.0
0.04	0	0	0.18	0.08	0.07	0.04	0.05	37.0
0.33	0.34	0.30	0.94	1.12	0.57	0.30	0.49	3.0
0.25	0.12	0.35	0.46	0.06	0.32	0.28	0.25	20.0
0.04	0.01	0.01	0.26	0.16	0.03	0.02	0.09	34.0
0.20	0.18	0.14	0.65	1.20	0.46	0.27	0.31	15.0
0.11	0.05	0.21	0.25	0.32	0.21	0.16	0.16	28.5
0.05	0.01	0.03	0.12	0.02	0.10	0.12	0.06	36.0
0.24	0.05	0.18	0.51	1.10	0.52	0.54	0.38	11.0
0.02	0	0	0.13	0.04	0.05	0.03	0.04	38.0
0.50	0.53	0.62	0.53	1.16	0.96	1.12	0.71	2.0
0.06	0.25	0.17	0.13	0.30	0.08	0.05	0.16	28.5
0.21	0.25	0.13	0.53	0.72	0.18	0.12	0.30	16.0
0.10	0.16	0.12	0.15	0.42	0.13	0.09	0.18	24.5
7.11	4.98	5.24	19.70	26.28	11.45	7.94	10.46	

299

Table 21.4
Life Event Item Frequencies: Two Pair Comparisons

	Hospital			University		
Categories	Fracture patients[a]	Medical and surgical patients[b]	Ratio F/MS	College students[c]	Medical students[d]	Ratio C/M
1. Work related	2.14	0.95	2.25	1.81	0.77	2.35
2. Finance related	1.61	0.69	2.33	0.80	0.20	4.00
3. Personal	1.29	1.08	1.19	0.96	0.59	1.63
4. Spouse related	0.72	0.61	1.18	0.55	0.22	2.50
5. Conflict with the law	0.59	0.25	2.36	0.28	0.22	1.27
6. Family related	1.44	0.81	1.78	1.47	0.39	3.77
7. Life-style	3.40	2.57	1.32	6.73	2.22	3.03
8. School related	0.15	0.16	0.94	0.83	0.41	2.02
Total	11.34	7.12	1.59	13.43	5.02	2.68

Sources: [a] [40]; [b] [42]; [c] [41]; [d] [43].

Comparison of the Alcoholics to the Normative Group

Table 21.6 compares categories of life event frequencies for the alcoholics and the normative group [45;47;48]. These samples differed in many respects: All the alcoholic subjects were male, more of them were nonwhites, fewer of them were married, and they were somewhat less educated than the normative group.

The alcoholics incurred many more life events in all categories but one; the most striking difference was in the category related to conflicts with the law, where they showed 9.5 times more of these events than did the normatives. Also, more than twice as many events were experienced in work-related, personal, and spouse-related items. The data are clear that the social deviance of alcoholics encompasses a life-style that includes many facets of differences in living experiences.

These differences were further delineated by looking at the ten life events that occurred the most frequently in the lives of alcoholics as compared to the normative group. There were six items that were common to both groups and ranked similarly, although the alcoholics sustained roughly twice the number of life events. In the case of the alcoholics, the number-one–ranked item—personal injury or illness—was experienced five times more frequently than by the normatives. The alcoholics also had six items that were not found in the normatives' top ten; these were change in residence, minor violations of the law, jail term, change in eating habits, change in number of arguments with spouse, and change in social activities. The alcoholics moved 1.4 times a year and experienced inordi-

Table 21.5
Sample Characteristics of Normative Group:
TV Study[a] and Group Health[b] ($N = 969$)

Variable	Categories	Number	Percent
Age	≤ 30 years	145	15.0
	31–45	409	42.2
	46–65	383	39.5
	≥ 66 years	31	3.2
Sex	Male	412	42.5
	Female	557	57.5
Race	White	922	95.1
	Nonwhite	47	4.9
Marital status	Married	886	89.4
	Divorced/separated/widowed	61	6.3
	Single	22	2.3
Education	Grade school	66	6.8
	High school	441	45.5
	Technical	109	11.2
	College	275	28.4
	Graduate degree	72	7.4
Religion	Protestant	593	61.2
	Catholic	235	24.3
	Other/none	138	14.2
Country of birth	United States	886	91.4
	Other	81	8.4

Sources: [a] [47]; [b] [48].

nate conflicts with the law. They also had twice as many changes in eating habits and three times more arguments with their spouses than did the normatives.

The rank order correlation (r_s) between the frequency of occurrence of life events in the normative group and the magnitude estimations of the same life events according to the SRRS [1] was –0.344 ($p ≤ 0.05$). While the inverse correlation is of low-order significance, it does say in general that, the higher the magnitude estimation of life events, the less its likelihood of happening. Holmes and Holmes [49] found a much higher degree of inverse relationship of SRRS magnitudes to frequency of occurrence in their study of daily life changes, where r_s was –0.706 ($p ≤ 0.001$).

Table 21.6

Comparison of Life Event Frequencies of Alcoholics and Normative Group

Categories	Alcoholics[a]	Normative[b]	Ratio A/N
1. Work related	2.74	1.04	2.63
2. Finance related	1.73	1.14	1.52
3. Personal	2.34	0.92	2.54
4. Spouse related	2.53	0.95	2.66
5. Conflict with the law	1.51	0.16	9.44
6. Family related	2.60	1.67	1.56
7. Life-style	6.08	3.21	1.89
8. School related	0.28	0.16	1.75
Total	19.81	9.26	2.14

Sources: [a] [45]; [b] [47;48].

Variables Affecting Normative Frequencies

The data of the combined normative groups were analyzed in terms of 21 demographic characteristics that might affect life event frequencies of occurrence. Variables such as race, sex, religion, urban/rural living, and educational levels did not significantly affect the sum total of event frequencies. But it was also true that many individual life events occurred differentially in some of the variables probed. For example, the women experienced greater amounts of changes in sleeping habits, major injury or illness, and loss of spouse than did the men, while the men experienced more changes in working conditions, minor law violations, and troubles with the boss. In the same way, Catholics experienced more changes in personal habits, recreational pursuits, and social activities, while Protestants reported more outstanding personal achievements. Comparing those with grade school education to those with college degrees, the former experienced more deaths of close friends and marriages while the latter had more outstanding personal achievements and changes in work responsibilities.

However, the variables listed in Table 21.7 were shown to have varying degrees of influence in total item frequencies. Age had the most significant effect, with the young adult incurring greater amounts of life events. Birth order also showed a significant effect, with the middle child or only child experiencing more life events. Native-born Americans incurred more life events than did foreign born. There was also a tendency for women, Catholics, and single individuals to incur more life events. The data indicate that, if one is young, native born, a middle or only child, single, female, and Catholic, then one is at higher risk of incurring greater amounts of life events.

Table 21.7
Some Variables and Total Item Frequencies: Normative Group

Variable	Categories	Number	Total of item frequencies	p[a]
Sex	Male	412	8.95	
	Female	557	9.49	< 0.20
Age	≤ 30 years	145	11.84	
	31–45 years	409	9.18	
	46–65 years	383	8.36	< 0.0001
	≥ 66 years	31	8.87	
Religion	Protestant	593	9.11	
	Catholic	235	9.91	< 0.20
	Other/none	138	8.90	
Marital status	Married	886	9.18	
	Divorced/separated/widowed	61	9.65	< 0.11
	Single	21	11.89	
Country of birth	United States	886	9.42	
	Other	81	7.54	< 0.01
Birth order	Oldest	308	8.68	
	Youngest	229	8.52	
	Middle child	328	10.17	< 0.002
	Only child	104	9.74	

[a] Mann-Whitney U-test; Kruskal-Wallis analysis of variance

Sources: [47;48].

Factor Analysis of Item Frequencies

The relationship of the occurrence of life events one to another or by delineating sets of items that occur with any degree of regularity was analyzed in the data from the normative group. The results of such a factor analysis [50] are shown in Table 21.8. This was a principal-components analysis with unit diagonals and varimax rotation. Only those factors with eigenvalues greater than 2.0, each accounting for at least 5 percent of the variance, are shown. The three factors shown account for 28.4 percent of the total variance.

Factor 1, labeled "life-style," is clearly the one dominant factor that emerges as a cluster of items that occur in concert with each other. Perusal of the items within the cluster indicates the general nature of the factor—items related to everyday

Table 21.8

Factor Analysis of Life Event Frequencies (Normative Group)

Factor 1 (eigenvalue = 6.11)	Factor 2 (eigenvalue = 2.93)	Factor 3 (eigenvalue = 2.32)
Life-style	**Death**	**Spouse**
Change in sleeping habits (0.65)[a]	Death of close family member (0.80)	Marriage (0.69)
Change in eating habits (0.70)	Death of spouse (0.84)	Divorce (0.78)
Change in personal habits (0.65)		Marital separation (0.58)
Change in recreation (0.75)		
Change in social activities (0.77)		
Change in church activities (0.50)		
Change in family get-togethers (0.56)		
Change in financial state (0.53)		

[a] Figures in parentheses = factor loadings

living activities of a personal and social nature. Of these items, change in financial state appears to be different and constitutes a more definitive and distinct event. Perhaps this is a precipitant event, which may trigger the ensuing changes in living.

Factors 2 and 3, "death" and "spouse," have eigenvalues of a lower order, but the clustering of death of spouse and death of family member implies catastrophic death or contiguous death. The item group of marriage, marital separation, and divorce implies significant instances of short-term marital joinings. On the whole, however, the factor analysis would seem to indicate that, except for Factor 1, the actual occurrences of life events do not relate to each other in a significant way. Essentially, most of life events occur independently of each other.

Life change units (LCU) are derived as the sum of the products of the occurrence of life events and their magnitude estimations. It would follow, then, that the likelihood of occurrence of significant impact of any life event will be the actual frequency of that item occurring multiplied by its SRRS score. Such a conception might be called *risk impact*. To be meaningful, however, the frequency of occurrence of life events must be determined on a normative group, as must the SRRS scores. Granted these assumptions on the data presented, a list was constructed of the life events that would be the most likely to be of significant impact (frequency x weight). Table 21.9 is a ranked list of ten life events that impose the greatest risk impact on people.

These high risk-impact life events are spread throughout the different categories of items that relate to family, work, money concerns, spouse, personal matters, and life-style. Most of the events are of more intermediate SRRS value

Table 21.9
Ten Highest Impact Risk Life Events (Normative Group)

Rank	Life event	Annual frequency	SRRS score	Impact risk
1	Change in health of family member	0.509	335	171
2	Personal injury or illness	0.345	416	144
3	Death of close family member	0.272	469	128
4	Change in financial state	0.357	308	110
5	Sexual difficulties	0.321	316	101
6	Change in arguments with spouse	0.283	286	81
7	Vacation	1.060	74	78
8	Gain of new family member	0.229	337	77
9	Change in work responsibilities	0.292	243	71
10	Outstanding personal achievement	0.347	192	67

but of higher frequency. The mean rank of the ten high risk-impact items as to frequency of occurrence was 9.2, while the mean rank of these items on the SRRS magnitudes was 15.6. The table indicates the life events that have the greatest probabilities of impacting on people's lives. It also indicates that, in terms of the impact, events that occur more frequently are of greater importance, generally, than the life events that carry the most weight.

DISCUSSION

Perception of Life Events

The individual's perceptions of the significance and impact of life events are clearly tempered by the uniqueness of his or her nature and environmental experiences. This individuality in expression of the psychological meanings that attach to life events is expressed within any group by the distribution of scores. In spite of large variations seen in the SRRS scores, there is a highly significant concordance in the manner in which individuals and groups rank-order life events. This we have seen in cross-national comparisons of a U.S. sample with Japanese [36], Salvadorans [37], Western Europeans [34], Spanish [35], Malaysians [38], Peruvians [51], and Danes and Swedes [52], as well as in comparisons within U.S. subcultures: black, white, and Mexican Americans [33], Mexican Americans [18], alcoholics and heroin addicts [45], prisoners [30], and rural populations [19]. In these cross-national and cross-cultural studies, conclusions drawn here are necessarily restricted, since the samples were chosen in a manner that possibly may not be a representative expression of all peoples in that country or group.

Significant correlations obtain in spite of the fact that investigators have made a variety of methodologic and content changes to the original SRRS. For example, items were changed, modified, added, or deleted [10–15]. The orientation of impact of life events has been altered into "desirable/undesirable" or "upsetting" [13;14;16]. Investigators have used different methods of scaling techniques: categories versus ratio scaling [13], paired comparisons [17], nonuse of anchoring stimulus [13], histogram scaling [19], slip sort administration [18], and so on. In spite of these modifications, significant rank-order correlations exist among group comparisons to indicate that life events have a universally high degree of correlation in the manner by which psychological impacts are perceived and ordered. However, even as using group means of individuals' perceptions buries the individual's uniqueness, so does ranking correlations of groups bury the group's uniqueness in their magnitude estimation of life events.

The Effect of Age

The present study indicated that older people (over 60 years of age), scored life events significantly lower than did the young and the middle-aged. Horowitz et al. [25] found that younger people (under 30 years of age) rated life events higher than did those over 30 years of age. Jewell [53] also found that older people consistently scored SRRS life events lower when asked to rate them on the basis of "amount of emotion generated." Wyler et al. [54] used a similar psychometric instrument, the Seriousness of Illness Rating Questionnaire, which asked respondents to assign a score to 126 illnesses. Here again the effect of age was consistent—the older group (35–65 years) rated illnesses lower in magnitude, compared to the younger group.

Why should the elderly regard life events as having less impact on their lives; or conversely, why should the young perceive life events as having greater meaning? Is it that the young have experienced less events over their lifetime as compared to the old and thus perceive the unknown experience with greater anxiety or trepidation? Have the old perceived life events often enough over their lifetime to have acquired a greater equanimity concerning life challenges? Are the experiences of the young novel enough for them to assign greater weights than do the old? Or is there some psychobiological component in the aged that affects their perceptions of life events, other than the factor of experiencing?

The Effect of Sex

The present data also indicated that women assigned higher scores to life event items. This was also indicated in the studies of Horowitz et al. [25]. Paykel et al. [13] did not find sex differences in the scaling of life events, and neither did Rosenberg and Dohrenwend [55], who used a miniseries of ten items. Cross-cultural studies have also shown conflicting data on this issue. Japanese samples [36] and young Western Europeans [34] did not show any consistent sex effects in magnitude estimations of life events. On the other hand, female Malaysian medical students [38] exhibited consistently higher scores, as did Spanish females in the general population [35]. Lundberg and Theorell [56], studying patients with myocardial infarction, neuroses, and low back pain, as well as their matched control subjects, found that females allotted higher scores of perceived required readjustment to life events. In two unpublished studies from our laboratory, Hart and Holmes [41] found that female college undergraduates scored life events significantly higher than did the males. Jewell [53] found that women consistently attached greater emotional significance to life events, as compared to men.

On the whole, the data would indicate that women perceive and attach greater numerical weights to life events. Horowitz et al. [25] ascribed this tendency to women's higher alleged emotionality. Whatever "emotionality" may mean, the Jewell study [53] indicated that this was, indeed, so. Woon et al. [38] explained their sex-difference results on the basis of the different but complementary social roles that Malaysian society imposes wherein the male is the logical, realistic, and intellectual one, while the female is the more sensitive, affective, and emotional one. Carey [57] attributed the U.S. sex differences found in attitudes toward problem solving to a similar theme: culture—ours as well as others— ascribes an inferior role to females in the whole of their development as to their reasoning performance capacity, but allowing for a separate role as a person acting more from "heart" than from "mind." If it is accepted that society has imposed a negative stereotypic role on women, and that they, in general, have accepted it, then women are perceived to be freer to be more feeling than thinking. Such a psychological set might allow life events to be perceived by women as having greater emotional impact, whereas in men this might be inhibited as being less congruent with the masculine stereotype. Such a role may also be the reason that more women report more physical distress symptoms and psychological problems, as well as seek more psychiatric help [58]. Uhlenhuth et al.'s studies [59;60] also reported that women reported symptom intensities higher than did men.

The Effect of Educational Level

The educational level was seen here to influence perception of life events, with those having college degrees or greater tending to give higher scores. Miller at al.'s study [19] on a North Carolina rural population is not in agreement, for in their sample those with lower education gave higher scores on the SRRS. The comparabilities of these two samples—one urban and one rural, of differing socioeconomic status and educational levels— are suspect.

The Effect of Race (U.S. Groups)

Black Americans living in poverty areas consistently scored higher than the original white middle-class American group, while Mexican Americans showed constricted scaling [33]. Inasmuch as both ethnic minority groups were from the same low socioeconomic strata and educational levels, the data clearly imply that differing ethnic subcultures carry different perceptions of the meaning of life events. A study on white and Mexican American students in El Paso, Texas [18], showed that the latter gave consistently higher scores to life event items. However, in New York City, Asian, black, and Latin Americans as a group rated four of the ten life event items that they used significantly lower than did the whites [55]. While the data are conflicting as to the direction of the effect of race and ethnicity in life event perceptions (probably due to sample and methodologic differences) it would appear to be a significant factor.

The Effect of Experiencing an Event

Does the experiencing of a life event alter the magnitude estimation of that life event? A study of Masuda et al. [61] attempted to answer that question by asking three groups of hospital patients to assign a score to their illness. The names of the illnesses that they were experiencing were imbedded in a list of 22 other illnesses of varying seriousness derived from the Seriousness of Illness Rating Scale [54]. It was hypothesized that the illness experience would raise the seriousness of illness rank as well as the magnitude. The hypothesis was confirmed: Those currently experiencing the illness assigned higher scale scores as well as higher rankings among the patient groups.

However, Horowitz et al.'s study [25] indicated that subjects who had experienced an event three years earlier did not score differently from those who had not experienced the event. For most recent time periods, however, event experiencing varied in its effect depending on the item categories. Paykel et al. [13] also observed that recently experienced events tended to be scored higher. On the other hand, Lundberg and Theorell [56] found differential results depending on the sample tested. Patients who had experienced a myocardial infarction assigned lower scores to recently experienced events, while a normal control group showed no differences in assigning scores, whether experienced or not. Schless et al. [62] found that depressed patients did not assign different scores to life events on the basis of whether or not an event had been experienced. Rosenberg and Dohrenwend [55], using a miniseries of ten life events on college undergraduates, found that the experiencing of an event was not a factor in the magnitude estimation of the event. The data on the effect of experiencing an event are mixed and inconclusive. It would seem that the role of this variable in the perception of a life event might be dependent on the degree of recency of the experiencing (current or a year before), or to the kind of life event (for example, divorce or being fired from work) or to the kind of subject samples (psychiatric, myocardial infarction, or tuberculosis patients or "normal").

Constriction in Scoring

A phenomenon noted in our studies was termed *psychometric constriction.* Constriction refers to the narrowness of the scoring range of magnitude estimations. This was seen in the SRRS scoring of older people, those with lesser education (in our normative sample as well as in the rural population [19]), in certain cultures [37], and in a U.S. subculture [33]. Furthermore, it was pointed out that the constriction was not related to the general magnitude of the scoring. Constriction was noted previously in the use of another instrument, the Seriousness of Illness Rating Questionnaire (SIRQ) [54], which was administered to physicians and nonphysicians. The scores of nonphysicians (patients and nonpatients) were constricted in comparison to the physicians' scores. The latter rated less serious illnesses lower and more serious illnesses higher. This implied that greater knowledgeability of the illnesses as well as experience with them had allowed larger scope to the scoring. In a subsequent study on the Irish [63], using the SIRQ, the country people in villages showed a similar constriction compared to the people in metropolitan Dublin.

What might be in the common denominator to the phenomenon of constriction in psychometrics? Lesser education, special or otherwise, might apply to some (for example, village Irish [63], rural North Carolinians [19], and nonphysicians [54]) but not to others. Greater general sophistication with life experiences might apply to some (for example, older people, Dubliners [63], and alcoholics [45]) but not to others. Cross-cultural differences of unknown specifics might apply to some (for example, Salvadorans [37] and Mexican Americans [33]). A greater scoring range indicates a greater ability to discriminate numerically the separability of item scoring; or conversely, constriction means the operation of some psychological mechanism that restrains individuals from conceptualizing a wider and more discriminating range of scores.

From all of the above considerations, it is clear that people will perceive the impact of life events and assign magnitude estimations according to a host of known and unknown factors. These may be age, sex, education, socioeconomic status, urban/rural living, race, kinds of illness, severity of illness, life-style, experiencing of events, recency of events, and cultural differences. Investigators are thus reminded that caution should be exercised in applying any general SRRS to a particular sample of subjects on the assumption of appropriateness. This would seem to be true especially with regard to the use of the scale in prediction of risks of illness. It is further pointed out that such predictions of risk in any group may be enhanced by use of that group's own SRRS. Bramwell et al. [12] devised and used the modified Social and Athletic Readjustment Rating Scale on SREs of football players and were able to achieve a higher rate of predictability concerning risk of injuries. Lundberg et al. [64], going further, found that using individual perceptions of life events enhanced the ability to differentiate life changes between myocardial infarction patients and controls. Any individual's risk for illness onset might well be based on the individual's own perceptions of the impact of life events.

The SRRS has been shown to be of special value in cross-cultural studies as a sociological, anthropological, and psychological instrument. Studies in U.S. interracial groups, in special subcultures, and in different illness groups indicate that variable perceptions of life events reflect the psychosocial factors within the group that influence the weightings assigned. Regardless of the methodologic variations and content modifications of the original SRRS, the instrument serves as a valuable tool in studies of group psychosocial and cultural characteristics.

Life Event Frequencies

The studies presented have demonstrated great variability in the frequency of occurrence of life events. This was delineated in terms of total mean frequencies, frequencies based on categories, and individual life events. Furthermore, it is apparent from the analyses that the differences are not distributed evenly across items, but disparities are reflective of group characteristics. Differences in demographic characteristics can lead to differences in the accumulation of the quality and quantity of life events.

Group variations reflect group commonalities that bespeak a particular style of living, group behavior, or orientation. Life events thus are not simply externally imposed on individuals. Much of what occurs is a product of a life-style or culture, which incurs greater or lesser amounts of life events whether one is an alcoholic, prisoner, medical student, or fracture patient. We also noted that, in the case of the alcoholics and heroin addicts, the large amount of life event occurrences was accompanied by highly significant lower scores on the SRRS, but which nevertheless led to high life-change scores. The question, then, that arises is, "Does the underperception of life events allow for greater numbers of life event occurrences, or does the large number of event happenings lead to an underperception?" Bell et al.'s studies [65] comparing alcoholic detoxification patients with community respondents found that the former experienced 3.5 times as many upsetting life events than did the latter. They suggested that the higher life event items incurred by the alcoholics were "the consequences of maladaptive interpersonal and social behavior."

Paykel's studies [66] on the frequency of life events in individuals with psychiatric disorders showed that those with depressive disorders reported greater frequencies in all categories of life events over general population controls. Furthermore, within the depressives, the suicide attempters accumulated even greater numbers of events, which peaked dramatically prior to the attempt. This was confirmed by Cochrane and Robertson [20] in Edinburgh where their sample of "parasuicides" incurred 2.5 times more life events than matched controls. The increased number of events were weighted toward the unpleasant, and such events would or could not have been influenced by the subjects. Uhlenhuth and Paykel [59] found that psychiatric day-patients and inpatients also incurred more life events as compared to outpatients and relative controls. Dekker and Webb [67] also found that psychiatric patients accumulated greater amounts of life changes as compared to controls.

In the analyses of the normative group, while the variables of race, sex, religion, urban/rural living, and education did not affect the sum total of life event occurrences, it was also true that there were differential scorings in many individual items and, therefore, these variables are factors to contend with in total life changes because of differential perceptions concerning the impact of life events.

The Effect of Age

Age was seen as a factor, with young people accumulating more life events and the elderly accumulating less. Uhlenhuth et al. [60] found similar results in their mean stress scores, with younger people scoring almost three times greater than those over 30 years of age. Dekker and Webb [67] also found a significant negative correlation between age and life change scores. Ander et al.'s study [68] on middle-age and elderly men in Sweden (52–65 years of age) found a fall in the mean number of life events with advancing age, even in this narrow range of ages. Markush and Favero [15] found that younger people in Kansas City, Missouri, and Washington County, Maryland, showed higher life change scores than did other ages. Differences were found in the numbers of occurrences of life events in the lives of different groups of patients at a Veterans Administration Hospital [69]. Younger Vietnam War patients (27 years old) incurred almost twice as many events compared to male extended-care (56 years old) and residential (55 years old) patients.

Thus, there is a consistency that age significantly influences the frequency of life event occurrences, the young incurring greater amounts than the old. Uhlenhuth et al. [6] have suggested a curvilinear fall with age. These findings suggest that youth is the time for the greatest amount of increased behaviors, of learning new experiences, of expansion of horizons, and of engaging in activities that lead to exposure to greater life events. In the middle-aged, stability and maturation intervene, with a settling of careers, family, and routinized life. In the elderly, the aging process and associated psychobiological changes lead to a life of lesser stimulation and lesser participation to the extent of less self-generated and/or externally generated life events.

The Effect of Sex

Our studies indicated that sexual status did not affect the occurrence of total life events, but there were differential life-event occurrences between men and women. On the other hand, Uhlenhuth and Paykel's studies [59] on psychiatric patients indicated that women showed lower mean stress scores, reflecting less item occurrences. Their Oakland, California, study, however, on community respondents [60] showed that sex was not a factor in mean stress scores. Dohrenwend [70] found in her Manhattan, New York, study of household respondents that women accumulated greater life change scores than did men. Dekker and Webb [67] found no difference in their studies on patient groups and normals as regards sex and life change scores, as did Markush and Favero [15] in their community studies in Kansas City. Therefore, it would seem that the role of sex as a factor in frequency of life events is ambiguous.

The Effect of Marital Status

Our normative group data indicated that singles accumulated larger numbers of life events than did the married and those who were widowed, separated, and divorced. This is somewhat discrepant from the results of Uhlenhuth et al. [60], who found in their community respondents study that, while married people did show the lowest scores, singles were intermediate to the widowed, separated, and divorced.

The Effect of Education

While educational status was not seen in the normative group as exerting an overall effect on event frequency, the study on prisoners [30] had indicated that higher educational levels were associated with increased amounts of life changes prior to prison incarceration. Markush and Favero [15] found that community people with higher education also had higher life change scores and that this was due to reporting greater numbers of life events but having generally lower scale scores.

The Effect of Social Class

The variable of social class as affecting life change and frequency of life events is cloudy. Dohrenwend's study [71] based on income showed that the poorer (less than $4,000 annually) in Washington Heights, New York, experienced more life events than did those with higher incomes. In Dohrenwend's 1973 study [70] in the same area, educational status was chosen as an indicator of social class. Here again, social class was inversely related to life change scores. However, Myers et al. [14], studying New Haven, Connecticut, households and using Hollingshead and Redlich's [72] social class system (occupation and education), found no relationship between social class and numbers of life events. They did, however, find that lower class individuals experienced greater numbers of high-impact, "undesirable" events than did the other social classes, and thereby might be at greater risk for higher life change. Uhlenhuth and Paykel [59] and Dekker and Webb [67], however, did not find social class to be a factor in their studies on life changes among psychiatric patients, relatives, and normals.

The Effect of Race

The normative group data showed no black-white differences in total numbers of life events. But in our study on prisoners [30], blacks had significantly lower numbers of life events. Dohrenwend's study [70] in Washington Heights showed that blacks exhibited lower life change scores. This was also the finding of Uhlenhuth et al. [60] among Oakland household respondents. But Markush and Favero [15] found no such difference in Missouri and Maryland. While ethnicity is a possible factor in life event frequencies, the significance and direction of this effect are unclear.

Of the variables investigated in the above studies, as they might affect life event frequencies, most results have been conflicting. It is probable that these ambiguities can be attributed to sample characteristics, methodologies, and statistical evaluations. There were, however, two variables that were consistent. One was the factor of age, where young people accumulate more life events and the elderly accumulate less. The second consistent factor was marital status, where married people show lesser amount of life events and life changes.

Factor and Cluster Analyses

The factor analytic study of the normative group on event frequencies showed three factors involving 12 items. These were labeled "life-style" (the strongest association by far, containing seven items); "death" (containing two items); and "spouse" (with three items). Cluster analyses of an event's occurrences have been done on large groups of naval personnel (Rahe et al. [73] and Pugh et al. [74]). As might be expected—not only from the method used, but also from the disparity of the two groups' characteristics—there were differences in clustering, but there were also striking similarities. Their Cluster 1, "personal and social," is very similar to our Factor 1. Theirs includes nine items of which seven were the items in Factor 1. Cluster 2, "work" (four items), and Cluster 4, "disciplinary" (three items), are not represented in our analyses. Cluster 3, "marital," included eight items, two of which were the same as in our "spouse" factor. Rahe et al.'s analyses included 22 of our 42 items in significant interrelationships while we found only 12 of 40 items to be thus, and of these 12 only 7 could be said to be of some strength. Thus, our conclusion would bespeak a relative lack of interrelationship of life events while Rahe et al.'s conclusions would consider these interrelationships to be stronger. It is also possible that the differences in methodology between our factor analysis and Rahe et. al.'s cluster analysis could account for these differences.

Both conclusions could be correct, for the differences could relate to sample differences between our normative community groups and their naval service personnel. These differences are considerable in terms of sex, age, socioeconomic status, education, and—most of all—the kind of regimented and regulated lives that navy personnel lead. These analyses lend further support to the concept that the expression of different groups in terms of frequency of occurrence of life events can also be exhibited in different clusterings of life event relationships.

Since life change units are based on the sum of the products of SRRS scores and item frequency, the directions in which variables affect these are of clear importance. The data from studies mentioned here (by no means complete) that address these issues are conflicting in either or both parameters. Only with age is there reasonable data congruence—not only do young people perceive life events as having greater impact, but also they incur greater numbers of life events. In other words, to be young is to be at double jeopardy in life changes because of similar directions in both parameters. The reverse is true for the elderly. One other variable might also cast the individual in double risk—the status of being single. Conversely, the status of being married confers a double protection.

The delineation of possible variables as affecting the SRRS and the SRE does not negate the central concept of life changes as they affect onset of illness. These studies only point up the factors whose recognition may well increase the predictive risk of illness and the increased knowledge of differing illness thresholds among individuals and groups [75].

SUMMARY AND CONCLUSIONS

1. Data from this laboratory and from other investigators have shown that there is significant variability among groups, not only in their perceptions of the impact of life events, but also in the frequency of occurrence of these events.

2. Variables that were indicated to be of significance in either or both parameters are age, marital status, sex, socioeconomic status, ethnicity, education, culture, and experiencing of event.

3. These variabilities impose cautions on investigations that relate life changes to illness. Predictions concerning the risk of illness for differing groups might be enhanced by using their own Social Readjustment Rating Scale (SRRS).

4. Cross-national and U.S. subcultural studies have shown that group life-style is reflected in group perceptions and event frequencies. The SRRS and the Schedule of Recent Experience (SRE) are, thus, useful instruments to probe psychological, social, and cultural differences among groups.

REFERENCES

1. Holmes, T. H., and R. H. Rahe. "The Social Readjustment Rating Scale." *Journal of Psychosomatic Research* 11 (1967):213–18. Reprinted in this volume, Chapter 2.

2. Stevens, S. S. *Psychophysics: Introduction to Its Perceptual, Neural, and Social Prospects.* Edited by G. Stevens. New York: John Wiley and Sons, 1975.

3. Hawkins, N. G., R. Davies, and T. H. Holmes. "Evidence of Psychosocial Factors in the Development of Pulmonary Tuberculosis." *American Review of Tuberculosis and Pulmonary Diseases* 75 (1957):768–80. Reprinted in this volume, Chapter 11.

4. Rahe, R. H., M. Meyer, M. Smith, G. Kjaer, and T. H. Holmes. "Social Stress and Illness Onset." *Journal of Psychosomatic Research* 8 (1964):35–44. Reprinted in this volume, Chapter 12.

5. Holmes, T. H., and M. Masuda. "Life Change and Illness Susceptibility." In *Separation and Depression: Clinical and Research Aspects,* edited by J. P. Scott and E. C. Senay, pp. 161–86. AAAS Publication no. 94. Washington, D.C.: American Association for the Advancement of Science, 1973.

6. Wyler, A. R., M. Masuda, and T. H. Holmes. "Magnitude of Life Events and Seriousness of Illness." *Psychosomatic Medicine* 33 (1971):115–22. Reprinted in this volume, Chapter 16.

7. Dohrenwend, B. S., and B. P. Dohrenwend, eds. *Stressful Life Events: Their Nature and Effects.* New York: John Wiley and Sons, 1974.

8. Gunderson, E. K. E., and R. H. Rahe, eds. *Life Stress and Illness.* Springfield, Ill.: Charles C Thomas, 1974.

9. Rabkin, J. G., and E. L. Struening. "Life Events, Stress, and Illness." *Science* 194 (1976):1013–30.

10. Coddington, R. D. "The Significance of Life Events as Etiologic Factors in the Diseases of Children. I. A Survey of Professional Workers." *Journal of Psychosomatic Research* 16 (1972):7–18.

11. Coddington, R. D. "The Significance of Life Events as Etiologic Factors in the Diseases of Children. II. A Study of a Normal Population." *Journal of Psychosomatic Research* 16 (1972):205–13.

12. Bramwell, S. T., M. Masuda, N. N. Wagner, and T. H. Holmes. "Psychosocial Factors in Athletic Injuries: Development and Application of the Social and Athletic Readjustment Rating Scale (SARRS)." *Journal of Human Stress* 1, no. 2 (1975):6–20. Reprinted in this volume, Chapter 19.

13. Paykel, E. S., B. A. Prusoff, and E. H. Uhlenhuth. "Scaling of Life Events." *Archives of General Psychiatry* 25 (1971):340–47.

14. Myers, J. K., J. J. Lindenthal, and M. P. Pepper. "Social Class, Life Events, and Psychiatric Symptoms: A Longitudinal Study." In *Stressful Life Events: Their Nature and Effects*, edited by B. S. Dohrenwend and B. P. Dohrenwend, pp. 191–205. New York: John Wiley and Sons, 1974.

15. Markush, R. E., and Favero, R. V. "Epidemiologic Assessment of Stressful Life Events, Depressed Mood, and Psychophysiological Symptoms—A Preliminary Report." In *Stressful Life Events: Their Nature and Effects*, edited by B. S. Dohrenwend and B. P. Dohrenwend, pp. 171–90. New York: John Wiley and Sons, 1974.

16. Brown, G. W. "Meaning, Measurement and Stress of Life Events." In *Stressful Life Events: Their Nature and Effects*, edited by B. S. Dohrenwend and B. P. Dohrenwend, pp. 217–43. New York: John Wiley and Sons, 1974.

17. Ruch, L. O., and T. H. Holmes. "Scaling of Life Change: Comparison of Direct and Indirect Methods." *Journal of Psychosomatic Research* 15 (1971):221–27. Reprinted in this volume, Chapter 4.

18. Hough, R. L., D. T. Fairbanks, and A. M. García. "Problems in the Ratio Measurement of Life Stress." *Journal of Health and Social Behavior* 17 (1976):70–82.

19. Miller, F. T., W. K. Benty, J. F. Aponte, and D. R. Brogan. "Perception of Life Crisis Events: A Comparative Study of Rural and Urban Samples." In *Stressful Life Events: Their Nature and Effects*, edited by B. S. Dohrenwend and B. P. Dohrenwend, pp. 259–73. New York: John Wiley and Sons, 1974.

20. Cochrane, R., and A. Robertson. "Stress in the Lives of Parasuicides." *Social Psychiatry* 10 (1975):161–71.

21. Casey, R. L., M. Masuda, and T. H. Holmes. "Quantitative Study of Recall of Life Events." *Journal of Psychosomatic Research* 11 (1967):239–47. Reprinted in this volume, Chapter 10.

22. Rahe, R. H. "The Pathway between Subjects' Recent Life Changes and Their Near-future Illness Reports: Representative Results and Methodological Issues." In *Stressful Life Events: Their Nature and Effects*, edited by B. S. Dohrenwend and B. P. Dohrenwend, pp. 73–86. New York: John Wiley and Sons, 1974.

23. Antonovsky, A. "Conceptual and Methodological Problems in the Study of Resistance Resources and Stressful Life Events." In *Stressful Life Events: Their Nature and Effects*, edited by B. S. Dohrenwend and B. P. Dohrenwend, pp. 245–58. New York: John Wiley and Sons, 1974.

24. Mechanic, D. "Discussion of Research Programs on Relations between Stressful

Life Events and Episodes of Physical Illness." In *Stressful Life Events: Their Nature and Effects*, edited by B. S. Dohrenwend and B. P. Dohrenwend, pp. 87–97. New York: John Wiley and Sons, 1974.

25. Horowitz, M. J., C. Schaefer, and P. Cooney. "Life Event Scaling for Recency of Experience." In *Life Stress and Illness*, edited by E. K. E. Gunderson and R. H. Rahe, pp. 125–33. Springfield, Ill.: Charles C Thomas, 1974.

26. Harris, P. W. "The Relationship of Life Change to Academic Performance among Selected College Freshmen at Varying Levels of College Readiness." Ph.D. dissertation, East Texas State University, 1972.

27. Carranza, E. "A Study of the Impact of Life Changes on High School Teacher Performance in the Lansing School District as Measured by the Holmes and Rahe Schedule of Recent Experience." Ph.D. dissertation, Michigan State University, 1972.

28. Clinard, J. W. "Life Change Events as Related to Self-Reported Academic and Job Performance." *Psychological Reports* 33 (1973):391–94.

29. Selzer, M. L., and A. Vinokur. "Life Events, Subjective Stress, and Traffic Accidents." *American Journal of Psychiatry* 131 (1974):903–6.

30. Masuda, M., D. L. Cutler, L. Hein, and T. H. Holmes. "Life Events and Prisoners." *Archives of General Psychiatry* 35 (1978):197–203. Reprinted in this volume, Chapter 20.

31. Padilla, E. R., D. J. Rohsenow, and A. B. Bergman. "Predicting Accident Frequency in Children." *Pediatrics* 58 (1976):223–26.

32. Masuda, M., and T. H. Holmes. "Magnitude Estimations of Social Readjustments." *Journal of Psychosomatic Research* 11 (1967):219–25. Reprinted in this volume, Chapter 3.

33. Komaroff, A. L., M. Masuda, and T. H. Holmes. "The Social Readjustment Rating Scale: A Comparative Study of Negro, Mexican and White Americans." *Journal of Psychosomatic Research* 12 (1968):121–28. Reprinted in this volume, Chapter 6.

34. Harmon, D. K., M. Masuda, and T. H. Holmes. "The Social Readjustment Rating Scale: A Cross-cultural Study of Western Europeans and Americans." *Journal of Psychosomatic Research* 14 (1970):391–400.

35. Celdrán, H. H. "The Cross-cultural Consistency of Two Social Consensus Scales: The Seriousness of Illness Rating Scale and the Social Readjustment Rating Scale in Spain." Medical thesis, University of Washington, 1970.

36. Masuda, M., and T. H. Holmes. "The Social Readjustment Rating Scale: A Cross-cultural Study of Japanese and Americans." *Journal of Psychosomatic Research* 11 (1967):227–37. Reprinted in this volume, Chapter 5.

37. Seppa, M. T. "The Social Readjustment Rating Scale and the Seriousness of Illness Rating Scale: A Comparison of Salvadorans, Spanish and Americans." Medical thesis, University of Washington, 1972.

38. Woon, T., M. Masuda, N. N. Wagner, and T. H. Holmes. "The Social Readjustment Rating Scale: A Cross-cultural Study of Malaysians and Americans." *Journal of Cross-cultural Psychology* 2 (1971):373–86.

39. Schwartz, J. L. "A Study of the Relationship between Maternal Life Change Events and Premature Delivery." Master's thesis, University of Washington, 1973.

40. Tollefson, D. J. "The Relationship between the Occurrence of Fractures and Life Crisis Events." Master's thesis, University of Washington, 1972.

41. Hart, C., and T. H. Holmes. Unpublished data.

42. Holmes, T. H., and A. R. Wyler. Unpublished data.

43. Holmes, T. S. Unpublished data.

44. Rahe, R. H., and T. H. Holmes. Unpublished data.

45. Dudley, D. L., D. K. Roszell, J. E. Mules, and W. H. Hague. "Heroin vs. Alcohol Addiction—Quantifiable Psychosocial Similarities and Differences." *Journal of Psychosomatic Research* 18 (1974):327–35.

46. Roszell, D. K., J. E. Mules, G. Glickfeld, and D. L. Dudley. "Life Change, Disease, Perception and Heroin Addiction." *Drug and Alcohol Dependence* 1 (1975/76):57–69.

47. Holmes, T. H. Unpublished data.

48. Celdrán, H. H. Unpublished data.

49. Holmes, T. S., and T. H. Holmes. "Short-term Intrusions into the Life Style Routine." *Journal of Psychosomatic Research* 14 (1970):121–32. Reprinted in this volume, Chapter 15.

50. Nie, N. H., C. H. Hull, J. G. Jenkins, K. Steinbrenner, and D. H. Bent. *SPSS: Statistical Package for the Social Sciences.* 2nd ed. New York: McGraw-Hill, 1975, pp. 468–85.

51. Janney, J. G., M. Masuda, and T. H. Holmes. "Impact of a Natural Catastrophe on Life Events." *Journal of Human Stress* 3, no. 2 (1977):22–34. Reprinted in this volume, Chapter 7.

52. Rahe, R. H. "Multi-cultural Correlations of Life Change Scaling: America, Japan, Denmark and Sweden." *Journal of Psychosomatic Research* 13 (1969):191–95.

53. Jewell, R. W. "A Quantitative Study of Emotion: The Magnitude of Emotion Rating Scale." Medical thesis, University of Washington, 1977.

54. Wyler, A. R., M. Masuda, and T. H. Holmes. "Seriousness of Illness Rating Scale." *Journal of Psychosomatic Research* 11 (1968):363–74. Reprinted in this volume, Chapter 8.

55. Rosenberg, E. J., and B. D. Dohrenwend. "Effects of Experience and Ethnicity on Ratings of Life Events as Stressors." *Journal of Health and Social Behavior* 16 (1975): 127–29.

56. Lundberg, U., and T. Theorell. "Scaling of Life Changes: Differences between Three Diagnostic Groups and between Recently Experienced and Non-experienced Events." *Journal of Human Stress* 2, no. 2 (1976):7–17.

57. Carey, G. L. "Sex Differences in Problem-solving Performance as a Function of Attitude Differences." *Journal of Abnormal and Social Psychology* 56 (1958):256–60.

58. Chesler, P. "Patient and Patriarch: Women in the Psychotherapeutic Relationship." In *Women in Sexist Society*, edited by V. Gornick and B. K. Moran, pp. 251–75. New York: Basic Books, 1971.

59. Uhlenhuth, E. H., and E. S. Paykel. "Symptom Intensity and Life Events." *Archives of General Psychiatry* 28 (1973):473–77.

60. Uhlenhuth, E. H., R. S. Lipman, M. B. Balter, and J. Stern. "Symptom Intensity and Life Stress in the City." *Archives of General Psychiatry* 31 (1974):759–64.

61. Masuda, M., N. Wong, A. Felicetta, and T. H. Holmes. "Magnitude Estimation of Current Illness." Abstract. *Psychosomatic Medicine* 37 (1957):92–93.

62. Schless, A. P., L. Schwartz, C. Goetz, and J. Mendels. "How Depressives View the Significance of Life Events." *British Journal of Psychiatry* 125 (1974):406–10.

63. McMahon, B. J. "Seriousness of Illness Rating Scale: A Comparative Study of Irish and Americans." Medical thesis, University of Washington, 1971.

64. Lundberg, U., T. Theorell, and E. Lind. "Life Changes and Myocardial Infarction: Individual Differences in Life Change Scaling." *Journal of Psychosomatic Research* 19 (1975):27–32.

65. Bell, R. A., K. A. Kelley, R. D. Clements, G. J. Warheit, and C. E. Holzer. "Alcoholism, Life Events, and Psychiatric Impairment." In *Work in Progress on Alcoholism*, vol. 273, edited by F. A. Seixas and S. Eggleston, pp. 467–79. New York: New York Academy of Sciences, 1976.

66. Paykel, E. S. "Life Stress and Psychiatric Disorder: Applications of the Clinical Approach." In *Stressful Life Events: Their Nature and Effects*, edited by B. S. Dohrenwend and B. P. Dohrenwend, pp. 135–50. New York: John Wiley and Sons, 1974.

67. Dekker, D. J., and J. T. Webb. "Relationships of the Social Readjustment Rating Scale to Psychiatric Patient Status, Anxiety and Social Desirability." *Journal of Psychosomatic Research* 18 (1974):125–30.

68. Ander, S., B. Lindstrom, and G. Tibblin. "Life Changes in Random Samples of Middle-aged Men." In *Life Stress and Illness*, edited by E. K. E. Gunderson and R. H. Rahe, pp. 121–24. Springfield, Ill.: Charles C Thomas, 1974.

69. Nelson, P., I. N. Mensh, E. Hecht, and A. N. Schwartz. "Variables in the Reporting of Recent Life Changes." *Journal of Psychosomatic Research* 16 (1972):465–71.

70. Dohrenwend, B. S. "Social Status and Stressful Life Events." *Journal of Personality and Social Psychology* 28 (1973):225–35.

71. Dohrenwend, B. S. "Social Class and Stressful Events." In *Psychiatric Epidemiology: Proceedings of the International Symposium at Aberdeen University, July 1969*, pp. 313–19. London: Oxford University Press, 1970.

72. Hollingshead, A. B., and F. C. Redlich. *Social Class and Mental Illness: A Community Study*. New York: John Wiley and Sons, 1958.

73. Rahe, R. H., W. M. Pugh, J. Erickson, E. K. E. Gunderson, and R. T. Rubin. "Cluster Analyses of Life Changes: I. Consistency of Clusters across Large Navy Samples." *Archives of General Psychiatry* 25 (1971):330–32.

74. Pugh, W. M., J. Erickson, R. T. Rubin, E. K. E. Gunderson, and R. H. Rahe. "Cluster Analyses of Life Changes: II. Method and Replication in Navy Subpopulations." *Archives of General Psychiatry* 25 (1971):333–39.

75. Hinkle, L. E., Jr. "The Effect of Exposure to Culture Change, Social Change, and Changes in Interpersonal Relationships on Health." In *Stressful Life Events: Their Nature and Effects*, edited by B. S. Dohrenwend and B. P. Dohrenwend, pp. 9–44. New York: John Wiley and Sons, 1974.

22

Death and Dying

Thomas H. Holmes

The boast of heraldry, the pomp of pow'r,
And all that beauty, all that wealth e'er gave,
Await alike the inevitable hour:
The paths of glory lead but to the grave.

From Gray's "Elegy in a Country Churchyard"

Death is omnipresent. It permeates our culture and influences and molds fashions in attitudes, values, and behavior in explicit and implicit ways. Death is the subject of some of the world's great paintings, music, architecture, and literature. It is a major concern of medicine and the law. Myriad economic facets are implicated in its thrust. Death is a central theme of religion. It predicts the future. By the process of *differential mortality*, it determines the genetic composition of succeeding generations. That is, death of the young throughout human history has exerted a major influence on natural selection and the evolution of mankind. Thus, death has a dual role in determining both the biology and the sociocultural environment of human beings.

Despite its universality, as well as man's continuous experience with it, death still embodies much of the unknown. Biologically, death tends to occur prematurely. Most bodily systems are still reasonably intact and capable of functioning at the time of death, despite the age of the individual.

Another biological dimension that is poorly understood is the mechanism by

This chapter is reprinted with permission from *Aging: The Process and the People*, edited by Gene Usdin and Charles Hofling (New York: Brunner/Mazel, 1978), pp. 166–83. Copyright 1978 by the American College of Psychiatrists.

which death is achieved. Certainly the cardiovascular system is the system of sudden death; and the lethal effect of trauma, poisons, and lack of oxygen on bodily mechanisms is reasonably well understood. However, this leaves the mechanisms of death in most instances unexplained. This is especially true of most chronic diseases, a notable exception being disorders of the heart.

This leads to an examination of dimensions of two questions: (1) What accounts for the time of onset of death? and (2) What are some of the psychophysiologic mechanisms by which death is achieved?

CULTURAL EXPECTATIONS OF DEATH

As part of the process of acculturation, intuitive knowledge about death is acquired by members of the society. At least five categories can be identified where the cultural expectation of death is high: (1) individuals during time of crisis; (2) those with disease; (3) those who live dangerously; (4) the very old or very young; and (5) those who are considered sinful.

These cultural expectations of death appear to have broad relevance. They provide a universe of discourse for formulating "voodoo death" in primitive societies, as written about by Cannon [1], and death in contemporary Western society. Like the medicine man with his bone pointing, the modern physician has techniques for communicating to the patient and the family that the time has come to die. Compliance by the involved person is not unusual.

Crisis

The cultural expectation of death is high during time of crisis. Data generated by the systematic use of the Schedule of Recent Experience (SRE) [2;3] indicate that most, if not all, illnesses have their onset or exacerbation in a setting of high life change. Of relevance to time of death are the studies of heart disease, athletic injuries, fractures, accidents in children, burns, other injuries, and serious suicide attempts [4]. Reasoning from these morbidity studies of the time of onset of diseases involved frequently as cause of death, one can infer that life changes also account, in part, for the time of occurrence of death from these diseases.

Two studies have been done that support this inference. Rahe and Romo [5] did a retrospective study of time of coronary heart disease deaths using the SRE. Townes et al. [6], using the SRE, followed a small number of families prospectively from the time of diagnosis of leukemia in a child to the child's death. Both studies indicate that death occurs in a setting of increasing life change or a life crisis.

Mortality experience of prisoners of the Japanese during World War II documents not only the immediate impact of the crisis on the death rate, but also that the effect may be long lasting. During the first year of imprisonment, the death rate was three times that ordinarily expected. By the second year, the death rate was eight times the expected rate [7]. Liberation after the war and rehabilitation to health did not alter the mortality experience. Six years later the same high death rate in these people persisted [8].

Clinical experience also supports the inference that death occurs in unique life situations composed of salient events and emotional states. Engel [9;10], using an intuitive approach, documents the occurrence of sudden death in settings of anniversaries, loss, danger, threat, or triumph, coupled with strong emotional reactions such as hopelessness, helplessness, relief, or pleasure.

Hackett and Weisman [11;12;13] report a series of patients with "predilection to death." These patients predicted their own death in the near future as appropriate and reasonable—and were free, for the most part, from conflict, tension, anxiety, or depression.

"Blind alley behavior" is another reaction to a life crisis that culminates slowly in death. Here the individual's perception is that for a variety of reasons he or she has gone as far in life as possible. There is no way left to go, and it is too late to retrace the steps to another route, or to start over. The individual retires to a state of relative hibernation and either chronic invalidism or death. Stewart Wolf [14] has called this state, which is similar to Hackett's predilection to death category, "the end of the rope" syndrome.

Disease

The cultural expectation of death is high for people who are sick or who have disease. When the correlation of morbidity rates to death rates per unit of time is observed, the relationship is very small, but positive. The total number of illnesses experienced per day by the more than 215 million Americans generates only a very small number of deaths. Most sick people on any given day do not die!

It is only when the relationship of selected diseases to death is examined that the correlation is salient. In the United States, the total number of deaths from cancer, diabetes, anemia, and diseases of the gastrointestinal tract, the heart, the nervous system, and the genitourinary system account for about 85 percent of the deaths experienced by males 45–65 years of age [15;16]. These diagnoses have many of the aspects of "hex words" [11], since death so often closely follows the assignment of the patient to the category.

This cultural expectation of death is well based in other clinical facts. Bruce and his co-workers [17] studied prospectively 5,459 males of whom 2,532 were without heart disease, 592 had hypertension, and 1,586 had coronary artery disease with histories of angina pectoris, coronary occlusion with myocardial infarction, or cardiac arrhythmia with arrest and resuscitation. It is not surprising that of the 140 deaths, 118 of them occurred in males previously diagnosed as having coronary artery disease. Nor is it surprising that, the more serious the disease, the higher the death rate. In serious disease the annual rate was 97.9 per 1,000 men; in moderately serious disease the rate was 25.3 per 1,000 men; and for mild disease, 6.6 deaths per 1,000 men. The mortality rate was four times as great in the serious disease category as in the mild disease category.

In historical perspective, types of diseases that result in almost certain death change over time [18]. Ushered in by the industrial revolution, tuberculosis, along with other infectious diseases, ravaged and decimated the Western world. The death rate was estimated as high as 500 per 100,000 population in urban areas. As a consequence of social evolution and natural selection by differential mortality resulting from infectious diseases, resistance to the "selecting" diseases emerged. Between 1800 and 1900, the death rate was reduced by half, and it has been steadily declining until recently. This helps account for the fact that tuberculosis is a cohort disease. That cohort of the population born between 1880 and 1920 has produced most of the tuberculosis morbidity and mortality experienced in the United States since 1880. As this cohort has aged, the ages of onset and of death have paralleled the progression. The death rate from infectious disease in the older population is still of epidemic proportions and accounts for the fact that pneumonia is still one of the ten leading causes of death.

An urban-industrial life-style has become the modern mode, replacing the old rural-agrarian way of life. As this has transpired, the social and biological evolution that has emerged has largely eliminated the infectious diseases as a cause of death. Now attempts at coping with the problems of the urban-industrial life-style have generated a new set of causes of death. Cancer, cardiovascular-renal disease, and diabetes constitute the new fashion in death.

Living Dangerously

The cultural expectation of death is high for people who live dangerously. Accidents and injuries account for a high proportion of deaths, despite safety engineering, accident prevention, education, and antibiotics. Death from accidents and injuries is an epiphenomenon of living dangerously. The settings in which the activities commonly associated with injury or death occur include: the home; the streets and highways; the light airplane; the sports arena for participants in racing, football, baseball, mountain climbing, and hunting; and the field of combat for both civilians and armed service personnel.

The available evidence suggests that accidents and injuries occur when, in the midst of many life changes, the individual is preoccupied with things other than the immediate activity and acts impulsively. This behavior, occurring in an environment where lethal, high-energy sources abound, enhances the occurrence of an accident with injury and the probability of death.

Aging

The cultural expectation of death is high for the very young and the very old. Aging is a biological process by which man approaches the life expectancy of species homo sapiens of 100 ± 15 years. The physiological age of an individual

[15;16] can be defined as the current distance from that age of 100. When life expectancy is short, the physiologic age is advanced. There is a close correlation between advancing age and death rate for adults. The rate is relatively high for infants and children, and low during midadolescence. There are more deaths in the first year of infancy than are seen to accumulate in the same population followed until it is age 30. The age-specific death rate for adults, that is, the rate for cohorts in the population, doubles every 8.5 years beginning in early adulthood and continuing through senescence. For example, as a cohort in the general population age 40 progresses to age 48.5, the death rate of that cohort doubles. This biologic constant of the increase in risk of death has been called by Hardin Jones "the force of mortality" [15;16].

The biology of aging involves genetically regulated metabolic and enzyme functions and the integrity of the cardiovascular system. These phenomena are strongly influenced by a variety of environmental and demographic factors, which in turn influence the rate of aging [15;16]. The following are associated with a reduced rate of aging and time of death (their converse, with accelerated aging and time of death): (1) rural habitat, (2) habitat in Sweden, Norway, or the Netherlands, (3) married, and (4) female gender. Constitutional factors associated with a longer life span (younger physiologic age) include: (1) normal weight and serum lipoprotein level, and (2) longevity of forebears, (that is, parents and grandparents lived to be 80 or older).

As the aging process advances, the progressive deterioration of integrity of the bodily systems generates a state called "disease" by modern medicine. These diseases, defined by their signs and symptoms, are correlated with physiologic age, and, in general, are correlated in adults with chronological age as well [15;16].

The gradual disappearance of the major and minor infectious diseases [15;16] has contributed to reduction in rate of aging and increase in longevity. The tendency to survive accidental injury, as well as tuberculosis, pneumonia, influenza, and bronchitis, is *increasing* at the same logarithmic doubling of the death rate as the general tendency to die.

People in 1950 were aging less rapidly than people in 1900 [15;16]. A person in 1950 at age 71 had the same physiological age as a person in 1900 at age 56. That is, the person has aged less rapidly, and a total of 15 years has been added to his or her useful life. This is calculated to be a gain in human efficiency of about 10 percent.

Sin

The cultural expectation of death is high for sinners. "For the wages of sin is death" certainly expresses the powerful Christian sentiment about the relationship of morality and death. The converse, "the good die young," is a cultural apology for the conviction that infants, though "conceived in sin," have not had enough experience in their short lives to be personally sinful. The great American morality plays—the cowboy stories of a past generation; the police stories of the current generation—have a consistent theme: The good guys always win; crime and sin do not pay.

The Judeo-Christian mandate, "thou shalt not kill," is translated by the law into rubrics regulating man's aggressive and destructive behavior. These often reflect society's requirement of "an eye for an eye and a tooth for a tooth"; or as Gilbert and Sullivan's Mikado decrees, "Let the punishment fit the crime." Although there currently exists controversy over whether or not the death sentence is cruel and inhumane punishment, a powerful and vocal segment of society insists that execution of criminals who have committed specified homicidal acts is the requisite of justice. A few prisoners who have admitted their crime of murder insist that punishment by execution is appropriate and should be consummated.

A prominent moral value placed on illness in the Western world holds that illness is tantamount to sinfulness, or even weakness. Since it is "sinful" to smoke cigarettes, death from lung cancer is sinful; since it is sinful to overeat (gluttony), it is sinful to be obese and die of the consequences; since it is sinful to abuse alcoholic beverages, it is sinful to die of cirrhosis of the liver or bleeding esophageal varices. In caricature, even the upwardly mobile, ambitious business-man, who is often unethical if not immoral, and aggressively insensitive to the rights of the other person, must pay the ultimate price of reaping the bitter gall of empty success: loneliness, dissatisfaction, disease, and death.

THE PSYCHOPHYSIOLOGIC MECHANISMS OF DYING

The previous section defines five categories in which the cultural expectation of death is high: crisis, disease, danger, age, and sin. The dynamic interaction of these forces helps determine the time of death. This section examines some of the psychophysiologic mechanisms by which death comes about. The cultural set provides the stimuli; the psychophysiologic mechanisms provide the response, which culminates in death. The logic of this section is inferential by method, and the inferences are often intuitive.

Suicide

Suicide is the problem-solving behavior for hopelessness. Hopelessness is defined as that state in which the individual's perception is that there is no answer to the situation. There is nothing that the individual can do, and nothing anyone else can do. The present is intolerable, and the future seems bleak, dark, empty, and meaningless. Living is purposeless.

There seems to be general agreement that four dynamic factors contribute to the emergence of hopelessness: (1) a sense of importance; (2) a sense of guilt, that is, of having done those things that should not have been done and/or having left undone those things that should have been done; (3) a sense of anger, that is, the conscious, willful intent to attack, injure, destroy; and (4) a sense of deprivation or of loss.

The epidemiology of suicide indicates that old age, male gender, chronic disease, recent alcohol intake, plans for the act, selection of a lethal method, and writing a note account for much of the variance. On the other hand, gesture suicide occurs in young females who, after recent alcohol intake, impulsively apply a nonlethal method, often in the presence of others. Here the probability of death is low.

Reasoning from clinical observations of patients with serious suicide intent, the following sequence seems evident. When the high intensity of the intolerable affect of hopelessness is established, it occurs to the patient that committing suicide is the only possible solution. This conscious decision is often followed by temporary relief of the hopelessness, and may be followed by plans for the successful execution of the act. The completion of the self-destruction does, indeed, alleviate the problem.

Fainting

Fainting is a common cause of sudden death, even in the absence of structural heart disease. Graham et al. [19] have determined that fainting is the consequence of diphasic or go–stop behavior. Their clinical studies define a hyperdynamic cardiovascular response followed immediately by a hypodynamic cardiovascular phase during which the faint occurs. Anxiety, apprehension, tension, and other intense action-oriented behaviors, such as the excitement of those who only watch sports activities from the sidelines, are characteristic coping behaviors, occurring simultaneously with the hyperdynamic cardiac response. This behavior is mobilized to adapt to some critical event in the immediate present. Venapuncture in the blood bank caricatures the stimulus. Once the critical event is passed and survival no longer depends on active coping, the hypodynamic cardiovascular phase promptly ensues. As vagal activity replaces sympathetic, there is a drop in pulse rate and systolic and diastolic blood pressure. Loss of consciousness occurs with the reduced blood flow to the brain. Lethal epiphenomena of the faint are asystole, arrhythmia, apnea, and convulsions.

Death by Coronary Occlusion and Myocardial Infarction

Here the point of departure is an older individual with disease, atherosclerosis of the coronary vessel, whose life-style is to approach problems with a go–stop behavior. As described by Friedman and Rosenman [20], this behavior includes tension and an intense drive under pressure toward a goal. Once the deadline is achieved, there is a letdown, at which time the death occurs— from thrombosis of the coronary vessel and myocardial infarction.

Physiologically, during the action-oriented go behavior, a hyperdynamic state of the cardiovascular system occurs: Pulse rate, cardiac output, and diastolic and systolic blood pressure increase [21]. Simultaneously, blood viscosity and hematocrit increase, and bleeding time and clotting time decrease [22]. Circulating adrenal hormones and free fatty acid increase. Once the deadline is achieved, a hypodynamic cardiac state accompanies the letdown or relief or stop behavior, and there is a decrease in pulse rate, cardiac output, diastolic and systolic blood pressure, and circulating hormones. Under these circumstances there is a dramatic decrease in coronary circulation of blood ready to clot when it encounters the atherosclerotic plaque and narrow arterial lumen. This state seems ideal for the propagation of a blood clot and its lethal consequences.

Arrhythmias

Although a variety of cardiac arrhythmias are compatible with life, they often are the mechanism that so disrupts the function of the heart that death is the outcome. A number of investigators [23–27] have established the participation of these rhythmic dimensions of cardiac dysfunction that may accompany adaptive behavior: paroxysmal auricular fibrillation, nodal rhythm, ventricular tachycardia, and ventricular fibrillation. These phenomena have been observed to occur during action-oriented behavior, during the letdown or stop phase following action, and during prolonged periods of nonaction-oriented behavior such as withdrawal, helplessness, and depression. These psychophysiological reactions, especially in association with progressive structural disease of the heart, are probably commonly involved in the mechanism of death.

Irving and Bruce [28] have made direct observations of the occurrence of ventricular fibrillation with resuscitation immediately following exercise. Patients with serious coronary heart disease were observed during and after maximal exercise testing on a treadmill. Exertional hypotension or a decrease in or limited increase in systolic blood pressure was observed *during* or shortly after the exercise (go phase of the behavior). The reduced perfusion pressure further limited blood supply to the already overburdened cardiac muscle. This alteration in the environment of the neural and muscular components of the heart appears to set the stage for arrhythmia at the termination of exercise, which culminates in death.

Kidney Function: Water and Electrolyte Balance

Life situations, emotions, behavior patterns, and the renal excretion of fluid and electrolytes may set the stage for the occurrence of death [29]. Action-oriented behaviors were associated with excretion of water, sodium, and potassium. The range of behaviors included preparation for violent action such as anger, tempestuous and aggressive behavior, and feelings of excitement, apprehension, tension, and anxiety. Such changes, along with hormonal changes associated with action behavior, may contribute to altered neural and cardiac muscle states that may lower the threshold to arrhythmias and heart failure.

Nonaction-oriented behaviors were associated with fluid and electrolyte retention. The range of behaviors included listlessness, inactivity, and feelings of despair, hopelessness, and depression. Many of these behaviors fit into the attitude of being overburdened, having too much to do, carrying a heavy load, having too much responsibility, and wanting others to help [30]. In the presence of certain types of heart disease, this reaction may contribute to progressive, intractable heart failure and ultimately death.

Death Associated with Infectious Disease

In a prospective study of 109 patients hospitalized for tuberculosis, the relationship of emotional state, behavior, course of pulmonary tuberculosis, and the urinary excretion of 17-ketosteroids (17-KS), as an index of resistance to infections and inflammation, was investigated [31]. In general, minimal tuberculosis occurred in younger, anxious, action-oriented females who had moderately elevated 17-KS excretion. Acute, exudative, bilateral, far-advanced tuberculosis occurred in older males who were withdrawn, nonaction-oriented, overwhelmed, and depressed, and who had reduced resistance as exhibited by low 17-KS excretion.

Those patients whose disease improved either rapidly or moderately exhibited mood and behavior and 17-KS excretion that rapidly approached normal. Those whose disease progressed and those who died continued to show withdrawn, depressed, overwhelmed behavior associated with widely fluctuating or decreasing urinary steroid levels.

Comment

Action-oriented behavior, nonaction-oriented behavior, and the sequential occurrence of action–nonaction, or go–stop behavior appear to be the critical coping or adaptive techniques, the epiphenomenon or by-product of which is sudden death.

Respiratory System Function and Death and Dying

During a 15-year period in my laboratory, the interrelationships of respiratory function, feeling state, behavior, and social status in many patients with advanced diffuse obstructive pulmonary disease were studied and compared and contrasted with subjects with normal pulmonary systems [32]. The high mortality rate of the subjects with advanced pulmonary disease provided prospective data [33] of death and dying behavior in these patients. In a sample of 40 such subjects followed for four years, 29 died (72 percent). Ten of the remaining 11 subjects, however, were able to live outside the hospital. Characteristics of the sample under observation relating to the cultural expectation of death include age and constitutional factors, disease, and life crisis. Dying behavior and death in these patients were evaluated and formulated within a universe of discourse provided by acute experiments and natural history observations in a large number of patients and normal subjects. Two distinct patterns of adaptive or coping behavior were documented: (1) action-oriented behavior, and (2) nonaction-oriented behavior. Both patterns occurred in response to crisis situations requiring adaptation.

The action-oriented behavior was characterized physiologically by respiratory hyperventilation: increased minute ventilation and alveolar ventilation, and decreased alveolar carbon dioxide. Metabolically, increased oxygen consumption and carbon dioxide production occur. Psychologically, the action orientation includes attitudes of "something must be done," anger, anxiety, and tension. This integrated behavior is often associated with dyspnea or shortness of breath.

The nonaction behavior was characterized physiologically by respiratory hypoventilation: decreased minute volume and alveolar ventilation, and increased alveolar carbon dioxide. Metabolically, decreased oxygen consumption and carbon dioxide production occur. Psychologically, this nonaction-oriented behavior includes withdrawal, non-participation, sleep, depression, and a hibernationlike state. This psychophysiologic state is also often associated with dyspnea or shortness of breath. In subjects with a normally functioning respiratory system, this coping behavior falls well within the physiological range of the organism and is well tolerated.

In subjects with advanced obstructive pulmonary disease, either of these coping styles can have ominous consequences. The hyperventilation is inadequate to keep up with the increased carbon dioxide production and oxygen consumption. Also, during hypoventilation, and despite the lowered level of metabolism, the embarrassed respiratory system is unable to keep up with the reduced carbon dioxide production. The result of either the hyperventilation-action pattern or the hypoventilation-nonaction pattern of adaptation in the presence of advanced obstructive pulmonary disease is acidosis. As the chronic disease progresses, decreased appetite and relative starvation contribute metabolic acidosis to the clinical picture. When the body's reserves of buffer ultimately are depleted, the uncontrolled acidosis establishes an internal environment incompatible with life.

The occurrence of dyspnea is not only highly uncomfortable but is often so disturbing as to enhance the anxiety or depression and set up a vicious circle that perpetuates the disability and discomfort.

These patients learn to adapt by frequent use of a variety of mental mechanisms, prominent among which are denial, repression, withdrawal, and nonparticipation. They learn to avoid situations that provoke emotions because they know that increasing discomfort and disability will ensue. Techniques of management such as group therapy or dynamic interviews are not only poorly tolerated, but usually avoided after initial exposure. Power struggles or interpersonal conflicts with staff are particularly devastating.

As the disease progresses with age, activity is curtailed, interpersonal and social relationships are restricted, and the quality of life is diluted as sources of satisfaction disappear. When they approach the end of the road or the blind alley of chronic invalidism, these patients use a variety of adaptive techniques. Depression with feelings of hopelessness is prevalent, although suicidal preoccupation is seldom identified. Preoccupation with dying, however, is common, and the achievement of death is often considered by the patient as a goal that is both relevant and appropriate to the situation.

Although fear is expressed by some of these patients as the time of death approaches, many find the process comfortable. The main source of distress, however, is not the prospect of death, but continues to involve power struggles and conflicts with staff and family. The maintenance of vigilance and control by the patient in these interpersonal and social relationships assumes critical importance for the patient. This is especially salient when the staff and family and friends protest the patient's decision to die and seek to interfere with or modify the dying behavior. In such situations the patient may withdraw into increased depression or become aroused, hostile, angry, and even abusive. The source of discomfort is seldom the prospect of death, but the interpersonal situation. The psychological distress, combined with the physiological distress, places the patient's survival in serious jeopardy by engendering respiratory decompensation. When free from such conflicts, many of these patients describe the dying process as a normal event in every human's history and are quite comfortable with the situation and the prospects.

It was not always possible to establish the mechanisms by which death occurred in these patients. In some cases, however, where it was possible to monitor respiratory and metabolic processes during dying behavior, one pattern did emerge. Despite the occurrence of occasional action-oriented behavior and hyperventilation, the predominant trend was that of respiratory hypofunction with decreased ventilation, oxygen consumption, and carbon dioxide production. Respiratory quotient fell, indicating the prominent role of fat metabolism and its contribution to the acidosis already engendered by the progressive respiratory failure. The terminal event seemed to correlate with a precipitous fall in the already reduced blood pH.

Psychologically, these patients were inactive, nonparticipating, sometimes withdrawn, sometimes with an undercurrent of depression and hopelessness. However, some of these patients described themselves during the experience as relaxed, calm, and comfortable. There was little spontaneous complaint of shortness of breath.

This pattern of quiet, calm, insulated behavior, with a physiological pattern of respiratory hypofunction and preeminence of fat metabolism, we have labeled *hibernation behavior*. Death, when it does appear, occurs as an epiphenomenon or by-product of this style of adaptation.

During this study of patients with diffuse obstructive pulmonary disease, data that predicted outcome were examined. The Berle Index [34], a predictive index of psychosocial assets, was used to compare the deceased with the living at 18 months and at four years from beginning of observations. The following respiratory variables were used to compare the two groups: percent vital capacity, percent maximum breathing capacity, pH of the blood, and partial pressure in arterial blood of oxygen and carbon dioxide.

Comparison of the physiologic variables revealed that both the living and the dead had had significant impairment, and the biologic state of the two groups was not significantly different. The exceptions were an elevated partial pressure of arterial carbon dioxide among the 16 patients who died compared to the 24 living at 18 months, and a higher percent vital capacity among the 11 living patients compared to the 29 patients who were dead by the end of four years of observation.

In contrast, the psychosocial assets as measured by the Berle Index clearly distinguished the two groups at both 18 months and four years. The survivors at both times of comparison had significantly more assets than the ones who had died.

Another comparison was made between the two groups by combining the quantity of psychosocial assets with a physiologic variable. The percent maximum breathing capacity was chosen as the variable most representative of functional respiratory capacity. When this number was combined with the score of the Berle Index, the total obtained discriminated even more significantly between the living and the deceased. The greater the biological and psychosocial assets, the greater the probability of survival.

SUMMARY

The evidence suggests that death is a by-product or epiphenomenon of man's goals and the techniques used in their achievement. The mechanisms are of learned behaviors that often have adaptive value.

The time of occurrence is determined by man's expectation of death for himself or the culture's expectation of death for him—or both in concert!

> To every thing there is a season, and a time
> to every purpose under the heaven:
> A time to be born, and a time to die.

> Ecclesiastes, III, 2

REFERENCES

1. Cannon, W. B. " 'Voodoo' Death." *Psychosomatic Medicine* 19 (1957):182–90.
2. Holmes, T. H., and R. H. Rahe. "The Social Readjustment Rating Scale." *Journal of Psychosomatic Research* 11 (1967):213–18. Reprinted in this volume, Chapter 2.

3. Holmes, T. H., and M. Masuda. "Life Change and Illness Susceptibility." In *Separation and Depression: Clinical and Research Aspects,* edited by J. P. Scott and E. C. Senay, pp. 161–86. AAAS Publication no. 94. Washington, D.C.: American Association for the Advancement of Science, 1973.

4. Petrich, J., and T. H. Holmes. "Life Change and Onset of Illness." In *The Medical Clinics of North America,* vol. 61, no. 4, *Symposium on Psychiatry in Internal Medicine,* edited by A. Reading and T. N. Wise, pp. 825–38. Philadelphia: W. B. Saunders, 1977.

5. Rahe, R., and M. Romo. "Recent Life Changes and the Onset of Myocardial Infarction and Sudden Death in Helsinki." In *Life Stress and Illness,* edited by E. K. E. Gunderson and R. H. Rahe, pp. 105–20. Springfield, Ill.: Charles C Thomas, 1974.

6. Townes, B.D., D. A. Wold, and T. H. Holmes. "Parental Adjustment to Childhood Leukemia." *Journal of Psychosomatic Research* 18 (1974):9–14.

7. Bergman, R. A. M. "Who is Old? Death Rate in a Japanese Concentration Camp as a Criterion for Age." *Journal of Gerontology* 3 (1948):14–17.

8. Cohen, B. M., and M. Z. Cooper. *A Follow-up Study of World War II Prisoners of War.* Veterans Administration Medical Monograph. Washington, D.C.: Government Printing Office, 1954.

9. Engel, G. L. "A Life Setting Conducive to Illness: The Giving-up–Given-up Complex." *Annals of Internal Medicine* 69 (1968):293–300.

10. Engel, G. L. "Sudden and Rapid Death during Psychological Stress." *Annals of Internal Medicine* 74 (1971):771–82.

11. Hackett, T. P., and A. D. Weisman. " 'Hexing' in Modern Medicine." In *Proceedings of the Third World Congress of Psychiatry* 2 (1961):1249–52.

12. Hackett, T. P., and A. D. Weisman. "The Treatment of the Dying." In *Current Psychiatric Therapies,* vol. 2, edited by J. Masserman, pp. 121–26. New York: Grune and Stratton, 1962.

13. Weisman, A. D., and T. P. Hackett. "Predilection to Death: Death and Dying as a Psychiatric Problem." *Psychosomatic Medicine* 23 (1961):232–57.

14. Wolf, S. "The End of the Rope: The Role of the Brain in Cardiac Death." *Canadian Medical Association Journal* 97 (1967):1022–25.

15. Jones, H. B. "A Special Consideration of the Aging Process, Disease, and Life Expectancy." *Advances in Biology and Medical Physics* 4 (1956):281–336.

16. Jones, H. B. "The Relation of Human Health to Age, Place, and Time." In *Handbook of Aging and the Individual,* edited by J. E. Birren, pp. 336–63. Chicago: University of Chicago Press, 1959.

17. Irving, J. B., R. A. Bruce, and T. A. DeRouen. "Variations in and Significance of Systolic Pressure during Maximal Exercise (Treadmill) Testing." *American Journal of Cardiology* 39 (1977):841–48.

18. Holmes, T. H. "Infectious Diseases and Human Ecology." *Journal of the Indian Medical Profession* 10 (1964):4825–29.

19. Graham, D. T., J. D. Kabler, and L. Lunsford. "Vasovagal Fainting: A Diphasic Response." *Psychosomatic Medicine* 23 (1961):493–507.

20. Friedman, M., and R. H. Rosenman. *Type A Behavior and Your Heart.* New York: Alfred A. Knopf, 1974.

21. Stevenson, I., and C. H. Duncan. "Alterations in Cardiac Function and Circulatory Efficiency during Periods of Life Stress as Shown by Changes in the Rate, Rhythm, Electrocardiographic Pattern and Output of the Heart in Those with Cardiovascular Disease." In *Life Stress and Bodily Disease,* edited by H. G. Wolff, S. Wolf, and C. C.

Hare, pp. 799–817. Research Publications of the Association for Research in Nervous and Mental Disease, vol. 29. Baltimore: Williams and Wilkins, 1950.

22. Schneider, R. A. "The Relation of Stress to Clotting Time, Relative Viscosity and Certain Other Biophysical Alterations of the Blood in the Normotensive and Hypertensive Subject." In *Life Stress and Bodily Disease*, edited by H. G. Wolff, S. Wolf, and C. C. Hare, pp. 818–31. Research Publications of the Association for Research in Nervous and Mental Disease, vol. 29. Baltimore: Williams and Wilkins, 1950.

23. Stevenson, I. P., C. H. Duncan, S. Wolf, H. S. Ripley, and H. G. Wolff. "Life Situations, Emotions, and Extrasystoles." *Psychosomatic Medicine* 11 (1949):257–72.

24. Stevenson, I. P., C. H. Duncan, and H. G. Wolff. "Circulatory Dynamics before and after Exercise in Subjects with and without Structural Heart Disease during Anxiety and Relaxation." *Journal of Clinical Investigation* 28 (1949):1534–43.

25. Duncan, C. H., I. P. Stevenson, and H. S. Ripley. "Life Situations, Emotions, and Paroxysmal Auricular Arrhythmias." *Psychosomatic Medicine* 12 (1950):23–37.

26. Stevenson, I., C. H. Duncan, and H. S. Ripley. "Variations in the Electrocardiogram during Changes in Emotional State." *Geriatrics* 6 (1951):164–78.

27. Rahe, R. H., and A. E. Christ. "An Unusual Cardiac (Ventricular) Arrhythmia in a Child: Psychiatric and Psychophysiologic Aspects." *Psychosomatic Medicine* 28 (1966): 181–88.

28. Irving, J. B., and R. A. Bruce. "Exertional Hypotension and Postexertional Ventricular Fibrillation in Stress Testing." *American Journal of Cardiology* 39 (1977): 849–51.

29. Schottstaedt, W. W., W. J. Grace, and H. G. Wolff. "Life Situations, Behavior Patterns, and Renal Excretion of Fluid and Electrolytes." *Journal of the American Medical Association* 157 (1955):1485–88.

30. Grace, W. J., and D. T. Graham. "Relationship of Specific Attitudes and Emotions to Certain Bodily Diseases." *Psychosomatic Medicine* 14 (1952):243–51.

31. Clarke, E. R., Jr., D. W. Zahn, and T. H. Holmes. "The Relationship of Stress, Adrenocortical Function, and Tuberculosis." *American Review of Tuberculosis* 69 (1954): 351–69.

32. Dudley, D. L., in collaboration with C. J. Martin, M. Masuda, H. S. Ripley, and T. H. Holmes. *The Psychophysiology of Respiration in Health and Disease.* New York: Appleton-Century-Croft, 1969.

33. Dudley, D. L., J. W. Verhey, M. Masuda, C. J. Martin, and T. H. Holmes. "Long-term Adjustment, Prognosis, and Death in Irreversible Diffuse Obstructive Pulmonary Syndromes." *Psychosomatic Medicine* 31 (1969):310–25.

34. Berle, B. B., R. H. Pinsky, S. Wolf, and H. G. Wolff. "A Clinical Guide to Prognosis in Stress Diseases." *Journal of the American Medical Association* 149 (1952):1624–28.

Bibliography of T. H. Holmes's Published Writings

1946

1. With H. G. Wolff, H. Goodell, and S. Wolf. "Life Situations, Emotions and Nasal Disease; Changes in the Nasal Function Associated with Varying Emotional States and Life Situations." *Transactions Association American Physicians* 59 (1946):88–93.
2. With S. Wolf, H. G. Wolff, and H. Goodell. "Alterocoes nas funcoes nasais relacionadas com as emocoes cotidianas." *Revista Brasileira de Medicina* 3 (1946):872–75.

1947

1. With H. Goodell, S. Wolf, and H. G. Wolff. "Changes in the Nasal Function Associated with Variations in Emotional State and Life Situations." *Transactions American Academy Ophthalmology* 51 (1947):449–60.

1948

1. With H. G. Wolff, S. Wolf, W. J. Grace, I. Stevenson, L. Straub, H. Goodell, and P. Seton. "Changes in Form and Function of Mucous Membranes Occurring as Part of Protective Reaction Patterns in Man during Periods of Life Stress and Emotional Conflict." *Transactions Association American Physicians* 61 (1948):313–34.

1949

1. With S. Wolf, H. Goodell, and H. G. Wolff. "Physiologic Mechanisms of Psychosomatic Phenomena." *Pennsylvania Medical Journal* 52 (1949):681–88.
2. With H. Goodell, H. G. Wolff, and S. Wolf. "Evidence on the Genesis of Certain Common Nasal Disorders." *American Journal of Medical Science* 218 (1949):16–27.

1950

1. With H. Goodell, S. Wolf, and H. G. Wolff. *The Nose: An Experimental Study of Reactions within the Nose in Human Subjects during Varying Life Experiences.* Springfield, Ill.: Charles C Thomas, 1950.
2. With S. Wolf, T. Treuting, H. Goodell, and H. G. Wolff. "An Experimental Approach to Psychosomatic Phenomena in Rhinitis and Asthma." *Journal of Allergy* 21 (1950): 1–11.
3. With H. G. Wolff. "Life Situations, Emotions and Backache." In *Life Stress and Bodily Disease*, edited by H. G. Wolff, S. Wolf, and C. C. Hare, pp. 750–72. Research Publications of the Association for Research in Nervous and Mental Disease, vol. 29. Baltimore: Williams and Wilkins, 1950. (Also published in *Psychosomatic Medicine* 14 [1952]:18–33.)
4. With T. Treuting, and H. G. Wolff. "Life Situations, Emotions and Nasal Disease: Evidence on Summative Effects Exhibited in Patients with 'Hay Fever.' " In *Life Stress and Bodily Disease*, edited by H. G. Wolff, S. Wolf, and C. C. Hare, pp. 545–65. Research Publications of the Association for Research in Nervous and Mental Disease, vol. 29. Baltimore: Williams and Wilkins, 1950. (Also published in *Psychosomatic Medicine* 13 [1951]:71–82.)

1951

1. "Muscle Spasms, Professional Cramp and Backache." In *A Textbook of Medicine*, 8th ed., edited by R. L. Cecil and R. F. Loeb, pp. 1443–47. Philadelphia: W. B. Saunders, 1951. (Revised for 9th ed., pp. 1568–72, 1955; 10th ed., pp. 1521–24, 1959; and 11th ed., pp. 1546–48, 1963.)

1953

1. With L. D. Carlson, H. L. Burns, and P. P. Webb. "Adaptive Changes during Exposure to Cold." *Journal of Applied Physiology* 5 (1953):672–76.
2. With E. R. Clarke and D. W. Zahn. "The Relationship of Stress, Adrenocortical Function and Tuberculosis." *Transactions 49th Annual Meeting National Tuberculosis Association* 49 (1953):144–47.

1954

1. With T. L. Dorpat. "Tic, Torticollis, Coccydynia and Muscle Spasms." In *Manual de Terapéutica Clínica,* edited by A. R. Ros. Havana, Cuba: Cultural S.A., 1954.
2. With E. R. Clarke, Jr., and D. W. Zahn. "The Relationship of Stress, Adrenocortical Function and Tuberculosis." *American Review of Tuberculosis* 69 (1954):351–69.
3. With N. G. Hawkins. "Environmental Considerations in Tuberculosis: Ecologic Factors in Tuberculosis Morbidity." *Transactions 50th Anniversary Meeting National Tuberculosis Association* 50 (1954):233–38.
4. With A. H. Stewart, I. H. Weiland, A. R. Leider, C. A. Mangham, and H. S. Ripley. "Excessive Infant Crying (Colic) in Relation to Parent Behavior." *American Journal of Psychiatry* 110 (1954):687–94.

1955

1. With H. S. Ripley. "Experimental Studies on Anxiety Reactions." *American Journal of Psychiatry* 111 (1955):921–29.
2. "Stress in Disease: Participation of the Airways in Man's Response to Threat." *Transactions American Academy Ophthalmology and Otolaryngology* 59 (1955):439–43.
3. With T. L. Dorpat. "Mechanisms of Skeletal Muscle Pain and Fatigue." *Archives of Neurology and Psychiatry* 74 (1955):628–40.
4. With A. H. Stewart, C. A. Mangham, H. S. Ripley, and R. W. Deisher. "Case Study of Joan." In *Mental Health and Infant Development*, vol. 2, *Case Histories*, edited by K. Soddy, pp. 97–127. Proceedings International Seminar World Federation for Mental Health, Chichester, England. London: Routledge and Kegan Paul, 1955.

1956

1. "Multidiscipline Studies of Tuberculosis." In *Personality, Stress and Tuberculosis*, edited by P. J. Sparer, pp. 65–152. New York: International Universities Press, 1956.
2. "Adjustment and Prognosis in the Tuberculous." In *Personality, Stress and Tuberculosis*, edited by P. J. Sparer, pp. 266–74. New York: International Universities Press, 1956.
3. With J. J. Lane and E. R. Clarke. "The Relationship of Tuberculin Sensitivity and Adrenocortical Function in Humans." *American Review of Tuberculosis and Pulmonary Diseases* 73 (1956):795–804.

1957

1. With N. G. Hawkins, C. E. Bowerman, E. R. Clarke, Jr., and J. R. Joffe. "Psychosocial and Psychophysiologic Studies of Tuberculosis." *Psychosomatic Medicine* 19 (1957):134–43.
2. With N. G. Hawkins and R. Davies. "Evidence of Psychosocial Factors in the Development of Pulmonary Tuberculosis." *American Review of Tuberculosis and Pulmonary Diseases* 75 (1957):768–80.
3. "Comprehensive Medicine: A Definition." Proceedings of the Third Annual Institute of Professors of Psychiatry West of the Mississippi, pp. 16–20. State University of Iowa, September 1957. Mimeographed.
4. With H. S. Ripley. "Interdisciplinary Teaching in the Basic Behavioral Sciences of Man." Proceedings of the Third Annual Institute of Professors of Psychiatry West of the Mississippi, pp. 11–15. State University of Iowa, September 1957. Mimeographed.
5. With M. Masuda. "Studies on Ketosteroids in Urine of Normal Children Using Alumino Chromatographic Fractionation." *Pediatrics* 19 (1957):424–30.

1958

1. "Panel on Back Injuries." In *Proceedings of the International Association of Industrial Accidents Boards and Commissions*, pp. 138–44. Washington, D.C.: Government Printing Office, 1958.

2. With J. K. Jackson. "Alcoholism and Tuberculosis." *Human Organization* 16 (1958): 41–43.
3. With T. L. Dorpat. "Backache of Muscle Tension Origin." *Northwest Medicine* 57 (1958):602–7.

1959

1. With J. K. Jackson. "Alcoholism and Tuberculosis." In *Sociological Studies of Health and Sickness*, edited by D. Apple, pp. 179–85. New York: McGraw-Hill, 1959.
2. "The Scholar and the Devil's Advocate: Patient Care as a Social Process." *Journal of Medical Education* 34 (1959):85–91.
3. With T. D. Tjossem, A. R. Leider, R. W. Deisher, and H. S. Ripley. "Emotional Reactions and Skin Temperature Responses in Children Aged Two to Four Years." *Journal of Psychosomatic Research* 4 (1959):32–43.

1961

1. "Comprehensive Medicine: Generalizations about the Natural History of Disease; Factors That Influence the Course of Disease." *Medical-Surgical Clinical Symposia: Psychiatry*. Kansas City: University of Kansas School of Medicine, 1961.
2. "The Individual as a Biological Organism." In *Family-centered Social Work in Illness and Disability: A Preventive Approach*, pp. 86–92. Social Work Practice in Medical Care and Rehabilitation Settings Series, Monograph no. 4. New York: National Association of Social Workers, 1961.
3. With J. R. Joffe, J. W. Ketcham, and T. F. Sheehy. "Experimental Study of Prognosis." *Journal of Psychosomatic Research* 5 (1961):235–52.

1963

1. "Infectious Disease and Stress with Special Reference to Tuberculosis." In *The Psychological Basis of Medical Practice*, edited by H. I. Lief, V. F. Lief, and N. R. Lief, pp. 155–62. New York: Harper and Row, 1963.
2. With R. G. Wright. "Psychological Aspects of Hospitalization." In *The Psychological Basis of Medical Practice*, edited by H. I. Lief, V. F. Lief, and N. R. Lief, pp. 219–31. New York: Harper and Row, 1963.
3. With N. E. Ely and J. W. Verhey. "Experimental Studies of Skin Inflammation." *Psychosomatic Medicine* 25 (1963):264–84.
4. "Nasal Function and Headache." *Transactions American Academy Ophthalmology and Otolaryngology* 67 (1963):770–74.

1964

1. With D. L. Dudley, C. J. Martin, and H. S. Ripley. "Changes in Respiration Associated with Hypnotically Induced Emotion, Pain, and Exercise." *Psychosomatic Medicine* 26 (1964):46–57.

2. "Infectious Diseases and Human Ecology." *Journal of the Indian Medical Profession* 10 (1964):4825–29.
3. With D. L. Dudley and C. J. Martin. "Psychophysiologic Studies of Pulmonary Ventilation." *Psychosomatic Medicine* 26 (1964):645–60.
4. With R. H. Rahe, M. Meyer, M. Smith, and G. Kjaer. "Social Stress and Illness Onset." *Journal of Psychosomatic Research* 8 (1964):35–44.

1965

1. With W. S. Kogan and T. L. Dorpat. "Semantic Problems in Evaluating a Specificity Hypothesis in Psychophysiologic Relations." *Psychosomatic Medicine* 27 (1965):1–8.
2. With R. H. Rahe. "Social, Psychologic and Psychophysiologic Aspects of Inguinal Hernia." *Journal of Psychosomatic Research* 8 (1965):487–91.
3. With D. L. Dudley, M. Masuda, and C. J. Martin. "Psychophysiological Studies of Experimentally Induced Action Oriented Behavior." *Journal of Psychosomatic Research* 9 (1965):209–21.

1966

1. With G. N. Nelson and M. Masuda. "Correlation of Behavior and Catecholamine Metabolite Excretion." *Psychosomatic Medicine* 28 (1966):216–26.
2. With D. L. Dudley, C. J. Martin, and H. S. Ripley. "Hypnotically Induced Facsimile of Pain." *Archives of General Psychiatry* 15 (1966):198–204.
3. With M. Masuda and R. N. Notske. "Catecholamine Excretion and Asthmatic Behavior." *Journal of Psychosomatic Research* 10 (1966):255–62.

1967

1. With R. H. Rahe. "The Social Readjustment Rating Scale." *Journal of Psychosomatic Research* 11 (1967):213–18.
2. With M. Masuda. "Magnitude Estimations of Social Readjustments." *Journal of Psychosomatic Research* 11 (1967):219–25.
3. With M. Masuda. "The Social Readjustment Rating Scale: A Cross-cultural Study of Japanese and Americans." *Journal of Psychosomatic Research* 11 (1967):227–37.
4. With R. L. Casey and M. Masuda. "Quantitative Study of Recall of Life Events." *Journal of Psychosomatic Research* 11 (1967):239–47.
5. With R. H. Rahe. *Booklet for Schedule of Recent Experience (SRE)*. Four-page questionnaire. Seattle: University of Washington, 1967.
6. With D. L. Dudley and H. S. Ripley. "Hypnotically Induced and Suggested Facsimile of Head Pain." *Journal of Nervous and Mental Disease* 144 (1967):258–65.
7. With E. Dambacher, W. Kirby, M. Masuda, and K. Hoffman. "Critique of the Study: Nurse Specialist Effect on Tuberculosis." *Nursing Research* 16 (1967):327–32.

1968

1. With D. L. Dudley and C. J. Martin. "Dyspnea: Psychologic and Physiologic Observations." *Journal of Psychosomatic Research* 11 (1968): 325–39.

2. With A. R. Wyler and M. Masuda. "Seriousness of Illness Rating Scale." *Journal of Psychosomatic Research* 11 (1968):363–74.
3. With A. L. Komaroff and M. Masuda. "The Social Readjustment Rating Scale: A Comparative Study of Negro, Mexican, and White Americans." *Journal of Psychosomatic Research* 12 (1968):121–28.
4. "Life Style, Life Events and Disease." In *Highlights of the Thirteenth Annual Conference, Veterans Administration Cooperative Studies in Psychiatry*, pp. 91–99. Washington, D.C.: Veterans Administration, 1968.

1969

1. In collaboration with D. L. Dudley, C. J. Martin, M. Masuda, and H. S. Ripley. *The Psychophysiology of Respiration in Health and Disease.* New York: Appleton-Century-Croft, 1969.
2. "Presidential Address: Some Observations on Medical Education." *Psychosomatic Medicine* 31 (1969):269–73.
3. With D. L. Dudley, C. J. Martin, and J. W. Verhey. "Response to Noxious Stimulation as an Indication of Successful Psychologic Defense Mechanisms in the Diffuse Obstructive Pulmonary Syndrome." *American Review of Respiratory Disease* 100 (1969):572–74.
4. With D. L. Dudley, J. W. Verhey, M. Masuda, and C. J. Martin. "Long-term Adjustment, Prognosis, and Death in Irreversible Diffuse Obstructive Pulmonary Syndromes." *Psychosomatic Medicine* 31 (1969):310–25.

1970

1. With A. R. Wyler and M. Masuda. "The Seriousness of Illness Rating Scale: Reproducibility." *Journal of Psychosomatic Research* 14 (1970):59–64.
2. With T. S. Holmes. "Short-term Intrusions into the Life Style Routine." *Journal of Psychosomatic Research* 14 (1970):121–32.
3. "Psychologic Screening." In *Football Injuries: Papers Presented at a Workshop*, pp. 211–14. Sponsored by Subcommittee on Athletic Injuries, Committee on the Skeletal System, Division of Medical Sciences, National Research Council, February 7–8, 1969. Washington, D.C.: National Academy of Sciences, 1970.
4. With D. K. Harmon and M. Masuda. "The Social Readjustment Rating Scale: A Cross-cultural Study of Western Europeans and Americans." *Journal of Psychosomatic Research* 14 (1970):391–400.
5. With M. E. Amundson, eds. "Classical Readings in the Natural History of Disease." Seattle: Department of Psychiatry and Behavioral Sciences, University of Washington, 1970. Mimeographed. (Revised 1978.)

1971

1. With L. O. Ruch. "Scaling of Life Change: Comparison of Direct and Indirect Methods." *Journal of Psychosomatic Research* 15 (1971):221–27.
2. With A. R. Wyler and M. Masuda. "Magnitude of Life Events and Seriousness of Illness." *Psychosomatic Medicine* 33 (1971):115–22.

3. With T. Woon, M. Masuda, and N. N. Wagner. "The Social Readjustment Rating Scale: A Cross-cultural Study of Malaysians and Americans." *Journal of Cross-Cultural Psychology* 2, no. 4 (December 1971):373–86.

1972

1. With M. Masuda. "Psychosomatic Syndrome: When Mothers-in-law or Other Disasters Visit, a Person Can Develop a Bad, Bad Cold. Or Worse." *Psychology Today* 5 (April 1972):71–72, 106.

1973

1. With S. V. Gunning. "Dance Therapy with Psychotic Children: Definition and Quantitative Evaluation." *Archives of General Psychiatry* 28 (1973):707–13.
2. With G. de Araujo, P. P. Van Arsdel, Jr., and D. L. Dudley. "Life Change, Coping Ability and Chronic Intrinsic Asthma." *Journal of Psychosomatic Research* 17 (1973):359–63.
3. With K. M. Hong. "A Case Study of Transient Diabetes Mellitus Associated with Culture Change." *Archives of General Psychiatry* 49 (1973):683–87.
4. With M. Masuda. "Life Change and Illness Susceptibility." In *Separation and Depression: Clinical and Research Aspects*, edited by J. P. Scott and E. C. Senay, pp. 161–86. AAAS Publication no. 94. Washington, D.C.: American Association for the Advancement of Science, 1973. (First published in *Personality and Socialization*, edited by D. R. Heise, pp. 434–49. Chicago: Rand McNally, 1972. Also published in *Stressful Life Events: Their Nature and Effects*, edited by B. S. Dohrenwend and B. P. Dohrenwend, pp. 45–72. New York: Wiley-Interscience, 1974.)

1974

1. With B. D. Townes and D. A. Wold. "Parental Adjustment to Childhood Leukemia." *Journal of Psychosomatic Research* 18 (1974):9–14.
2. With D. L. Dudley, P. P. Van Arsdel, Jr., and G. de Araujo. "Quantification of Psychosocial Variables in Intrinsic Asthma: Relationship to Physiologic Variability." *Psychotherapy and Psychosomatics* 24 (1974):129–31.
3. With D. L. Dudley. "Comfort-Productivity Scale." Department of Psychiatry and Behavioral Sciences, University of Washington, 1974. Mimeographed.

1975

1. With C. C. Williams, R. A. Williams, and M. J. Griswold. "Pregnancy and Life Change." *Journal of Psychosomatic Research* 19 (1975):123–29.
2. With T. S. Holmes. "Risk of Illness." *Continuing Education for the Family Physician* 3 (1975):48–51.
3. With S. T. Bramwell, M. Masuda, and N. N. Wagner. "Psychosocial Factors in Athletic Injuries: Development and Application of the Social and Athletic Readjustment Rating Scale (SARRS)." *Journal of Human Stress* 1, no. 2 (1975):6–20.

1976

1. With E. H. Bruce, M. K. Edwards, and R. A. Bruce. "Is Coping with Life Stresses Enhanced by Cardiac Rehabilitation Programs?" In *Physiological Approach to the Rehabilitation of Coronary Patients*, edited by U. Stocksmeier, pp. 75–83. New York: Springer-Verlag, 1976.

1977

1. With J. G. Janney and M. Masuda. "Impact of a Natural Catastrophe on Life Events." *Journal of Human Stress* 3, no. 2 (1977):22–34.
2. With J. Petrich. "Life Change and Onset of Illness." In *The Medical Clinics of North America*, vol. 61, no. 4, *Symposium on Psychiatry in Internal Medicine*, edited by A. Reading and T. N. Wise, pp. 825–38. Philadelphia: W. B. Saunders, July 1977.

1978

1. With C. C. Williams. "Life Change, Human Adaptation and Onset of Illness." In *Clinical Practice in Psychosocial Nursing: Assessment and Intervention*, edited by C. Longo and R. A. Williams, pp. 69–85. New York: Appleton-Century-Croft, 1978.
2. With M. Masuda, D. L. Cutler, and L. Hein. "Life Events and Prisoners." *Archives of General Psychiatry* 35 (1978):197–203.
3. With M. Masuda. "Life Events: Perceptions and Frequencies." *Psychosomatic Medicine* 40 (1978):236–61.
4. With C. K. Smith, S. W. Cullison, and E. Polis. "Life Change and Illness Onset: Importance of Concepts for Family Physicians." *Journal of Family Practice* 7 (1978): 975–81.
5. "Death and Dying." In *Aging: The Process and the People*, edited by G. Usdin and C. K. Hofling, pp. 166–83. New York: Brunner/Mazel, 1978.
6. "Life Situations, Emotions, and Disease." *Psychosomatics* 19 (1978):747–54.

1979

1. "Development and Application of a Quantitative Measure of Life Change Magnitude." In *Stress and Mental Disorder*, edited by J. E. Barrett, R. M. Rose, and G. L. Klerman, pp. 37–53. American Psychopathological Association Series. New York: Raven Press, 1979.
2. With D. K. Stevenson, D. C. Nabseth, and M. Masuda. "Life Change and the Postoperative Course of Duodenal Ulcer Patients." *Journal of Human Stress*, 5, no. 1 (March 1979):19–28.

1980

1. With C. A. Walters, B. B. Galluci, D. M. Molbo, and B. L. Pesznecker. "The Association of Numerous Life Changes with Cervical Dysplasia and Metaplasia." *Cancer Nursing* 3 (1980):445–50.

2. "Stress: The New Etiology." In *Health for the Whole Person*, edited by A. C. Hastings, J. Fadiman, and J. S. Gordon, pp. 345–62. Boulder: Westview Press, 1980.
3. With J. Petrich. "Psychiatric Presentation of Pulmonary Disorders." In *Psychiatric Presentation of Medical Illness: Somatopsychic Disorders*, edited by R. C. W. Hall, pp. 177–89. New York: Spectrum Publications, 1980.

1981

1. With S. R. Burchfield and R. L. Harrington. "Personality Differences between Sick and Rarely Sick Individuals." *Social Science and Medicine* 15-E (1981):145–48.
2. With J. M. Petrich. "Recent Life Events and Psychiatric Illness." *Psychiatric Annals* 11, no. 6 (1981):14–31.
3. With M. E. Amundson and C. A. Hart. "About the Schedule of Recent Experience." *Psychiatric Annals* 11, no. 6 (1981):19.
4. With M. Masuda. "Variations in Life Events in Different Groups: Clinical Significance." *Psychiatric Annals* 11, no. 6 (1981):48–65.
5. "In Memoriam: Minoru Masuda, Ph.D., 1915–1980." *Psychosomatic Medicine* 43 (1981):301–3.
6. With M. E. Amundson and C. A. Hart. *Manual for the Schedule of Recent Experience (SRE)*. Rev. ed. Distributed by University of Washington Press, Seattle. Copyright 1981 by Thomas H. Holmes.

1982

1. With J. Petrich and C. A. Hart. "Recent Life Events and Illness Onset." In *Life Stress*, edited by S. T. Day, pp. 109–20. New York: Van Nostrand Reinhold, 1982.
2. "This Week's Citation Classic: 'The Social Readjustment Rating Scale.'" *Current Contents* 14, no. 41 (1982):22.
3. With C. A. Hart and J. Petrich. "Life Change: Its Perception and Application." In *Critical Problems in Psychiatry*, edited by J. O. Cavenar and H. K. Brodie, pp. 308–31. Philadelphia: J. B. Lippincott, 1982.

1984

1. With E. M. David, eds. *Life Change Events Research, 1966–1978: An Annotated Bibliography of the Periodical Literature*. New York: Praeger, 1984.

1985

1. "Psychoneurosis." In *Conn's Current Therapy*, 37th ed., edited by R. E. Rakel. Philadelphia: W. B. Saunders, 1985.

Index

About the Contributors

MINORU MASUDA, Ph.D., was professor of psychiatry and behavioral sciences, University of Washington School of Medicine, until his death in 1980. His prominent place in the Holmes laboratory is signaled by his coauthorship of almost half the papers collected in this volume. During the many years of our collaboration, he distinguished himself as a generous colleague, a gracious critic, and a gentle man.

MARION E. AMUNDSON, B.A., worked in the Holmes laboratory as secretary and colleague beginning in 1949. She served in the Department of Psychiatry and Behavioral Sciences, University of Washington School of Medicine for 36 years.

GILBERTO DE ARAUJO, M.D. (U.W. Residency program, 1971), is currently affiliated with the Universidade Federal do Parana, Curitiba, Parana, Brasil.

STEVEN T. BRAMWELL, M.D. (U.W., 1971), is an orthopedic surgeon and was formerly clinical assistant professor in the University of Washington School of Medicine.

ROBERT L. CASEY, M.D. (U.W. Residency program, 1967), was formerly clinical associate professor of psychiatry and behavioral sciences, University of Washington School of Medicine.

DAVID L. CUTLER, M.D. (U.W. Residency program, 1970), is associate professor of psychiatry, Oregon Health Sciences University School of Medicine in Portland.

ROBERTS DAVIES, M.D., was clinical associate professor of psychiatry and behavioral sciences, University of Washington School of Medicine, until his retirement in 1984.

DONALD L. DUDLEY, M.D. (U.W., 1964), is medical director of the Washington Institute of Neurosciences, Seattle, Washington, and clinical professor of neurological surgery, University of Washington School of Medicine.

CHERYL A. HART, B.S., was research assistant in the Department of Psychiatry and Behavioral Sciences, University of Washington School of Medicine from 1975–79.

NORMAN G. HAWKINS, Ph.D. (U.W., 1956), is now retired from the Department of Sociology and Anthropology, Slippery Rock State College (Pennsylvania), where he served on the faculty until 1974.

LEE HEIN, M.D. (U.W., 1973) and Diplomat American Board of Family Practice, is in private practice in Bellingham, Washington.

T. STEPHENSON HOLMES, M.D. (U.W., 1970), is clinical assistant professor of psychiatry and behavioral sciences, University of Washington School of Medicine.

KANG-E MICHAEL HONG, M.D. (U.W. Residency program, 1973), is director and associate professor, Division of Child and Adolescent Psychiatry, Seoul National University Hospital in Seoul, Korea.

JAMES G. JANNEY III, M.D. (U.W., 1973) and Diplomat American Board of Family Practice, is in private practice at the Mid-Columbia Family Health Center in White Salmon, Washington.

GEORGE KJAER, M.D. (U.W., 1959) and F.A.P.A., is in private practice at Sacred Heart General Hospital in Eugene, Oregon.

ANTHONY L. KOMAROFF, M.D. (U.W., 1967), is vice-president and chief of general medicine, Brigham and Women's Hospital, and associate professor of medicine, Harvard Medical School in Boston, Massachusetts.

MERLE MEYER, Ph.D. (U.W., 1963), is professor and chair, Department of Psychology, University of Florida in Gainesville.

RICHARD H. RAHE, M.D. (U.W., 1961), is professor of psychiatry, University of Nevada School of Medicine in Reno, Nevada.

LIBBY O. RUCH, Ph.D., is associate professor, Department of Sociology, University of Hawaii at Manoa in Honolulu.

MICHAEL SMITH, M.D. (U.W., 1962), is clinical professor of obstetrics and gynecology, University of Washington School of Medicine, and is in private practice at the First Hill Women's Clinic in Seattle.

PAUL P. VAN ARSDEL, Jr., M.D., is professor of medicine and head of the section on allergy at the University of Washington School of Medicine.

NATHANIEL N. WAGNER, Ph.D., was professor of psychology and obstetrics/gynecology, and director of clinical training, Department of Psychology, at the University of Washington until his death in 1978.

ALLEN R. WYLER, M.D. (U.W., 1969), was formerly associate professor of neurological surgery, University of Washington School of Medicine.

ABOUT THE EDITORS

THOMAS H. HOLMES was emeritus professor of psychiatry and behavioral sciences, University of Washington School of Medicine, from his retirement in 1984 until his death in December 1988. He joined the faculty of the School of Medicine in 1949. The Thomas H. Holmes Endowment Fund was established in the Department of Psychiatry and Behavioral Sciences to honor Dr. Holmes's pioneering work and to encourage promising research by young investigators. Dr. Holmes held an A.B. from the University of North Carolina and an M.D. from Cornell University Medical College.

ELLA M. DAVID is an editor and writer in Seattle, Washington. She was formerly research publications editor at the University of Washington, where she worked with Dr. Holmes from 1978 to 1984. They collaborated on an earlier volume, *Life Change Events Research, 1966–1978: An Annotated Bibliography of the Periodical Literature*. Ms. David holds a B.A. from Scripps College and an M.A. in English from the University of Washington.